821408

The Multinational Company

The Multinational Company

Behavioral and Managerial Analyses

E.J. Kolde
University of Washington

Lexington Books
D.C. Heath and Company
Lexington, Massachusetts
Toronto   London

Library of Congress Cataloging in Publication Data

Kolde, Endel Jakob, 1917-
    The multinational company.

    Bibliography: p.
    1. International business enterprises. I. Title.
HD69.I7K65   658.1'8   74-2136
ISBN 0-669-93351-1

To Helga and Del

Contents

List of Figures

List of Tables

Preface

The multinational company has become a global phenomenon in both scope and significance. Despite some superficial similarities to certain forerunners, it is essentially a new and still evolving mode of economic enterprise. Transcending national economies and the analytical frameworks of existing theories, it has posed baffling problems and great new expectations to the contemporary world.

The rise to dominance of the multinational company has been swift and startling. While businessmen, politicians, labor leaders, and many other segments of the society have focused more intensely upon its nature and potentialities, the multinational firm itself has continued to forge a global expansion of trans-boundary links among economic enterprises in all spheres of life.

The most striking new institution on the international scene in the past decade is the multinational enterprise . . . The rate of growth of international production (largely controlled by multinational enterprises) is conservatively estimated at twice that of the wholly-domestic production of the free world. If one projects this trend over the next decade or so, the influence of multinational enterprises can be seen to rise significantly relative to GNP.[1]

Much of the technology, capital resources, and managerial talent that are needed to solve the contemporary world's economic problems are the possession of the multinational corporation.

If a corporation's sales were to be equated with a nation's output of goods and services, then 51 of the world's 100 biggest money powers would be international corporations and only 49 would be countries.

Large international companies currently do about $500 billion of annual business in each others' territories, or about one-sixth of the world's gross product. That's more than the entire gross national product of Japan. . . .

The conclusion to be derived from these facts, analysts say, is inescapable: The era of the multinational corporation, the so-called super-company, is upon us—to the point that a few hundred concerns have in recent years grown beyond the size of all but the wealthiest nations and currently dominate much of the world's production, resources and financial affairs. . . .

And they are still growing—growing, in fact, at a rate double that of purely domestic companies—and consequently are creating an economic and social movement that some observers compare in significance to the Industrial Revolution.[2]

Despite exhortations of alarm, especially but not only by ultra-nationalists and antiwelfare leftists, the tempo and techniques of multinationalization of business firms have been gaining momentum. No longer is the acquisition of foreign-based operating affiliates an exclusive domain of corporate giants; the vast majority of medium-sized U.S. industrial companies are now multinationals, and thousands of small firms—including those under first-generation owner-managers—are now producing and marketing beyond American borders. From a global perspective the process of multinationalization has just begun. While during the 1955-65 decade transnational business expansion seemed like an American specialty, it now has become a highest priority objective in most other countries, notably in Western Europe and Japan.

And as in the U.S., the multinationalization process cuts deeper into a country's industrial structure as it builds up speed.

"Judging by what is being said in annual shareholders' meetings, about one out of three second-echelon companies is thinking of investing abroad," says Dr. Helmut Giesecke, chief of the foreign economic section of the Association of German Chambers of Commerce.[3]

Communist countries, too, are scurrying to establish transboundary industrial connections. From a few initial efforts limited to long-term infrastructural projects, they have moved to joint-venture formation with capitalist corporations in manufacturing and marketing both of producer and consumer goods sectors. Progress has so far been impeded by mutual fears and uncertainties of how best to link a capitalist and communist enterprise. But as the present lack of executives who are knowledgeable, not to mention experienced, in the other party's economic system is overcome, a greater frequency and volume of capitalist-communist multinational business compacts is very likely to be formed.

In sum, the pervasiveness of multinational enterprises is increasing and their impact on both domestic economics and international economic relations will be increasingly significant. They are the institutions that will be making more and more of the decisions as to the allocation of the world's resources, determining the degree and structure of international economic integration.[4]

Knowledge Gap

Its pervasive impact has made the multinational company a most perplexing force in the contemporary world. It has provided not only a new focus for international economic relations, but also an issue of intense importance in domestic affairs.

The multinational corporation is rapidly becoming one of the most popular topics of debate among American leaders, and journalists. Opinions range from enthusiastic support for the multinational company to complete opposition to the whole concept.[5]

Neither the positive nor the negative potentialities of the multinational company have so far been adequately identified, let alone explained. The realities of this new mode of economic enterprise and international integration have outpaced scholarly literature on its nature and meaning. The result is a critical gap in knowledge that this book is designed to bridge. The book is primarily directed to university audiences, international managers, and public officials. But educated classes in many other walks of life should find it an important source of useful knowledge.

As the first comprehensive analysis of the multinational company this book has no existing rival. Although the word "multinational" has been used in the titles of some recent texts (Hays, Korth and Roudiani; Roebuck and Simmons; Richard Robinson), these are essentially general introductions to international business that must cover a great many other subjects besides the multinational firm. Thus none of them can approach the in-depth, interdisciplinary treatment of the multinational firm which is presented in this work.

A more specialized text is *Strategy of Multinational Enterprise Organization and Finance* by two European authors: M.A. Brooke and H.L. Rimmns (London: Longman, 1970). This is largely a normative volume with a very limited topical coverage. Despite the word "strategy" in its title, much of its content is rather elementary, taken from introductory texts and case descriptions.

In the nontext category several books have been published on the multinational company. Their primary concern has been to describe the development of the multinational companies. Probably the best among them is *The Multinationals* by Christopher Tugenhat (London: Palican Books, 1973). The author is a feature writer for the *Financial Times* and an ex-member of British Parliament. His lucid style and oratorical skills produce a lucid essay that gets the maximum value from his spotty and often anecdotal information. Though a very interesting and readable little book, it is neither intended as nor suitable for a college text.

The main strength of Raymond Vernon's *Sovereignty at Bay* (New York: Basic Books, 1971) is a massive statistical base (compiled mostly by students at Harvard Business School); but its qualitative superstructure is narrow and shaky. Professor Vernon's preoccupation seems to be to validate the product life cycle hypothesis as the main explanation why American manufacturers have gone multinational. That this is at best only one among several factors that have contributed to the multinationalism of business will be discussed in the main text of the present work. In other respects Vernon's work remains true to orthodox notions of economic and political theory and casts almost no light on the inner rationality of the multinational company and on the behavioral incentives that flow from it. The book fails to differentiate the contemporary multinational company from either the uninational company as such or the colonial company as its ancestral forerunner. Lacking these differentiations,

Vernon's book is best classified as an economic historic treatise rather than an analysis of the modern multinational company.

As to journal articles, theses, and other specialized studies, of which scores have appeared recently, the only identifiable common denominators are disagreement and contradiction; mutually reinforced findings are not commonplace. Neither singly nor jointly, therefore, can they substitute for this book.

Interdisciplinary Analysis

The most difficult barriers to the understanding of the multinational company stem from its scope and complexity. From an academic perspective, it is simply too large and multiferous a subject to fit the conceptual framework or analytic techniques of any one discipline. Therefore, it cannot be adequately researched in the context of ordinary business or economic studies. Though this fact seems to be quite widely accepted, publications on the multinational company have remained narrowly based. Direct investments, product life cycle and strategy-leads-structure hypotheses, business policy, and the traditional functional fields define the foci and problem formulations for most of these publications. By starting with the assumption that the multinational company is but a geographic extension of the domestic firm, many of these studies are stillborn from preconception. The motivities and inner logic which are unique to the multinational company, and thus, its most important aspects, receive no notice in such publications.

In this book an interdisciplinary approach has been adopted to avoid the pitfalls of the specialist's narrow perspective and to rid the scene of any sacred cows. Theoretical formulations, analytic techniques, and factual learning from all social sciences including law have been used along with those of business administration itself. The result is a more realistic and intellectually defensible synthesis of the contemporary multinational company than is possible by any unidisciplinary method.

The Perils of Ethnocentrism

A fundamental difficulty common to all international research is ethnocentrism—the tendency to regard one's own culture superior to others'. It arises from the fact that people internalize many beliefs and values of their native country, which sets them at odds with other value systems. A researcher, therefore, tends to view the conditions and problems in the value context of his own culture. This tendency bears a reverse relationship to the researcher's personal experience with the other cultures: the less cross-cultural exposure he has had the greater his dependence on his native values.

Ethnocentric distortions are significantly reduced by intensive studies of languages, literature, history, and politics of the relevant countries. In the older international disciplines this type of preparation has been required as necessary background for scholarly pursuits. The same cannot be said about international business scholarship; much of it is still conducted with the same academic preparation as domestic business research. As a result, the distinction between ethnocentric rationalizations and objective findings is not always recognized.

Geocentric objectivity has been a basic criterion for this book. All qualitative considerations have been subjected to a critical cross-national scrutiny, and unresolved differences stated in their specific partisan context to eliminate any nationalistic preconceptions. The author's multicultural experience served as a safeguard for geocentric objectivity. Having lived and worked in nine different countries for extended periods and in thirty-two others for shorter terms, he possesses both the sensitivity and skill to objectify and externalize cross-national information. The insistence on geocentric objectivity had its constraining effects on the book, in that the work of some prominent authors had to be screened out as doubtful sources. The specialist in the field of international business should have no difficulty in noticing that the conceptualizations, interpretations, and normative implications of this book do not support the claims of some earlier writers on the subject. Rather than identifying and arguing their fallacies, these works were simply excluded from this book.

Scope and Organization

The topical coverage of this book follows the outline for a graduate seminar that the author has taught for several years. To keep the book within its present size, several subtopics had to be excluded and others deemphasized. The discussions of inclusion and exclusion were based on the perceived importance of a topic and/or the availability of relevant information, including theoretical formulations.

The factual base for the book rests on research. The results of a number of primary research projects conducted either by the author himself or under his direction have provided the most critical inputs. Studies of other researchers were scrutinized for additional information. The author's participation in strategic planning, executive development, and major negotiations of multinational companies in many parts of the world helped to focus the analysis on strategic realities and to provide the adhesive for bonding theory with policy and practice.

1 The Multinational Firm

The multinational firm has come to occupy an increasingly important position in the economic, social and political affairs of the contemporary world. The phrases *nationwide operation, national company*, and *national market*, which once projected the ultimate in corporate success, no longer denote such eminence in the economic world; nor do they describe the ultimate goal, the apex of accomplishment, to the leaders of business. The horizons for business growth have receded, the scope of activities expanded, and the dimensions of the firm multiplied. *International, transnational,* and *multinational* are the new magic words, the modern slogans for stature, importance, and achievement. But there is no certainty that even they will do in the long run. Forces are at work which are eroding national boundaries from the economic landscape not only in free industrial countries, but also in the developing areas and even in the communist realm. The how and where of this process are better left to the future. It is a long-range process which runs a very uneven course, often oscillating and sometimes reversing itself. But its basic direction is unmistakable: more transboundary ties and greater intermeshing of entrepreneurial activities of different countries. And thus, the global firm—a worldwide enterprise in the fullest sense of the phrase—is looming just beyond the horizon.

As business transcends the national boundaries it changes in form and grows in substance. The spectra of managerial choice and actions are widened, the incentives and impediments to success multiplied, and the norms of corporate behavior varied. By changing itself, business causes its environment to change also. "With the growth of multinational enterprises, it has become readily apparent that their activities, and indeed their very existence, have major consequences not only for the way business is conducted, but also for many political, economic, and social organizations linked with the industrial system."[1] The institutional structure that well served the domestic uninational firm can hardly cope with the transnational demands of a multinational company; the export-import intermediaries that specialized in transboundary trade are ill equipped to perform the nontrade international processes required by the multinational firm; the formal education, intellectual orientation, and professional norms that qualified people for positions of leadership in the uninational firm leave wide gaps in the range of capabilities required in the multinational company; and the uninational social setting becomes but a factional part of the pluralistic whole within which the multinational firm must function.

The rise of the multinational firm is exerting increasing and inescapable

1

influences on nearly all aspects of economic relations, both domestic and international. Much of what was normal is becoming abnormal, what was modern and effective is reduced to obsolescence and antiquity. Even the principles of international politics and economics which long have formed the bedrock of education for international responsibility are becoming controversial and contradictory to observable realities.

Central to the modern developments is the multinational firm. It reflects a very significant new reality. As even a casual observer must have noticed, it represents a decisive break with the past and is building the format for the future.[2] It is an integrative force that interlocks different countries' systems in ways never postulated in the past. But it is also a dynamic force and thus, ipso facto, a source for change and competition that affects us all. Yet neither economic nor political theory as currently formulated can explain or even recognize its existence.

What are the nature and characteristics of this theoretical impossibility? Where are its historic roots? From whence are derived its superior powers, growth, and dynamism? How do its organization and behavior differ from other types of enterprise? Who can man it? Where are its controls and communication center? What impact does it have on business, the nation, the society, and international relations?

These are some key questions which this book seeks to answer. It is a report on research that has taken the author to many parts of the globe. More significantly, it is a study that is uninhibited by theoretical bias or dogmatic prejudice; it does not try to fit the multinational firm into this or that preexisting conception or theory. Instead it focuses on the subject in all its aspects and dimensions utilizing the analytical equipment of different disciplines to achieve balance and depth.

The firm has always been resistant to purely formal definition and structural definity. A multinational firm is a long and complex creation. Its parts bear a relation to the whole which today may be very different than yesterday.

It should not be too distressing to note, therefore, that the concept of the multinational firm has been badly confused to date.[3] In literature and journalistic commentary several notions have gained currency that are quite incomplete or inadequate.[4] Terms and phrases that strike a semantic vacuum show a high incident to stick. It is important to expose and discard these misleading notions before attempting a satisfactory definition of the multinational firm.

Inadequate Criteria

Managerial Orientation

To start with the least satisfactory of all definitions, we have the notion that a company is a multinational firm if its management has an international orientation or outlook. Although this is a normal and desirable characteristic of a multinational firm, it is hardly sufficient as a criterion for distinguishing between multinational and uninational companies. Pushed to its logical conclusion, this concept leads to the absurd proposition that a company is anything its management thinks it to be; and that the nature of the firm changes any time its management changes its mental images or reshuffles its ranks.

While managerial attitudes can affect the activities of a company, they can never *be* the company. As the attitude of an athlete can affect his performance, the attitude can never take the place of the physiological systems that are required for any performance; a legless amputee can never be a distance runner nor a blindman a mountain climber no matter how great their enthusiasm for the sports. Similarly, any company as a functioning organization, a going concern, must possess the material organs for a real capacity. Plant facilities, work force, management, financial assets, ongoing interactions with sources of input, be they human, material, or intangible, and with the absorbers of outputs (consumers, marketers, or accumulators); these are the anatomic minima without which no industrial enterprise can exist irrespective of how people think about business or its place in the world. Its actual organs define the absolute magnitudes of corporate capabilities. In addition every industrial enterprise is endowed with certain relative capacities and incapacities that determine to what extent, if at all, the absolute capacities can be utilized. The relative capacities include the firm's positions vis-à-vis its competitors regarding natural resources, markets, technology, manpower, capital, and especially its efficiency and cost, which strongly affect society's propensity for its product. All these capacities are functions of scale and location. While microeconomic analysis continues to be frustrated by inconclusiveness in factual verifications of the theoretical models of the economies of scale, there remains no room for doubt that location, both in theory and in practice, is a basic determinant of the absolute as well as the relative capacities of a firm, that is, its real capability.

Management orientation is not synonymous with corporate assets, organizational hierarchy, or the productive capacity that makes a firm a firm. It is not even synonymous with executive action that brings about change. All it can be is a prelude to action and, as such, has no effect upon the nature of the firm until implemented through action programs that change the organizational and economic realities of the firm.

Ownership Distribution

A second criterion for distinguishing multinational firms from nonmultinational companies is the distribution of its stock ownership. The advocates of this criterion insist that to be multinational the ownership of the firm must be distributed in a more or less balanced fashion among the residents of several different countries. In this formalistic view, ownership is the all-inclusive, overriding aspect of the firm that determines everything else. In a small, closely held enterprise such as a family corporation, such a emphasis on ownership may well be justified. But for a company with defused stock ownership, and its corollary, the separation of effective control from ownership, any notion that ownership defines the scope and character of the enterprise is no closer to modern business realities than a glider is to a space rocket.

Geographic Scope of Markets

A third notion of the multinational firm focuses on the markets that are served. If a company's products are marketed in a number of different countries, it is classified as a multinational company; if not, it is something else. By this definition all a firm needs to do to become multinational is to start exporting. It would not be required to have an export organization of its own, but could utilize international intermediaries such as export trading companies, commission houses, or combination export manager firms, and thus have no direct contact with foreign areas, not to mention operating bases abroad. To call this type of a company *multinational* is to confuse it with the tradition-honored terms of *foreign trade* and *international marketing*, which much more amply and accurately describe the idea here involved.

Foreign Investments

In economic theory there is no explicit reference to multinational enterprise. Implicitly, however, all problems of international business are assumed to be covered in the study of foreign investments and trade. In the days of the classical economist this assumption was acceptable, as it reflected quite accurately the actual conditions; the movements of goods and investments did, in fact, represent nearly all that could be considered international or multinational business. In the light of today's reality any such assumption is inadequate, if not completely fallacious.

Direct foreign investment denotes the acquisition by an enterprise of specific productive capabilities abroad such as warehouses, mining properties, assembly plants, or power stations. As such direct investments are the vehicles for the birth and growth of multinational enterprise. But the two can never be considered synonymous. The essence of any business enterprise is production, distribution, and other operational activities that generate outputs and profits; the essence of investment is to produce the facilities and other productive capabilities that the enterprise needs to function. Thus, foreign investments play a role in the complex activities of a multinational firm, but only a supporting role. Furthermore, the typical multinational company tends to minimize its international capital transfers by drawing upon indigenous resources for both equity and loanable funds where feasible, and by plowing back profits to its affiliates in different countries.

Definition of Multinational Enterprise

The basic notion in any definition of multinational enterprise is a number of affiliated business establishments that function as productive enterprises in different countries simultaneously. To have such capacity the firm must possess host-country-based production units such as factories, mines, retail stores, insurance offices, banking houses, or whatever operating facility is characteristic to its business. In their absence, any claim on multinationality becomes nebulous.

As used in this book, the term *multinational firm* covers the entire continuum of internationalization, from the acquisition of transnational operating capability to a complete global integration of the firm.

The emphasis on structure to this point should not be interpreted to imply that the multinational enterprise is only a mechanical concept. This would be erroneous indeed. At its center lie the dynamic ideas of growth and management.[5] Adaptation, assimilation, and reconciliation of conflicting forces of its pluralistic environment are as organic to the life processes of the multinational enterprise as are the national subunits to its organizational structure. And the structure itself is seldom static. Both the form and functions of its parts—the foreign-based affiliates—respond to new incentives and disincentives, to the growth of another affiliate and the decline of a third, to legal and economic changes, and to the strategies and policies promulgated on the multinational level of the firm itself.

In sum, the multinational firm represents the totality of organizing and operating business establishments in an international context. It embraces not only all the popular notions discussed above—managerial orientation, ownership distribution, political composition of markets, and the flow of funds and management talent across boundaries—but also such functions, processes, and relationships as forms of organization, physical location and design of facilities, and the entire functional spectrum from allocation corporate resources to distribution of output, and from engineering to relations with foreign governments and people—all in an environment segmented by political boundaries, varying levels of economic development, and cultural plurality.

What holds this multinational firm together? Not ownership, not markets, not the orientation of its executives—although all these can help—but its management. It is not possible, therefore, to understand or to explain the multinational firm in terms of any stated factor or condition, since the dynamic processes, systems, and interdependencies that modern management entails are not reducible to any single denominator.

To understand the multinational firm one must understand first, its management, which is the integrative force focusing on growth and efficiency; second, its variegated, pluralistic environment, which represents a disintegrative counterforce from which the problems and possibilities peculiar to multinational business arise.

Contrasts Between Uninational and Multinational Business Environment

Legal Aspects

The environmental forces that determine the opportunities, constraints, and incentives for a multinational firm are significantly different from those that circumscribe the uninational company. The latter enjoys a relative homogeneity and consistency in external factors in that the legal precepts—laws, ordinances, and public policies—of any particular country establish a rather explicit standard of executive conduct and business behavior that is acceptable to the society at large. These standards are normally applicable to all firms, on either a nationwide or industry-wide basis. This protects the firm against "illegal methods" of competition and guarantees that the rules of the business game are the same for all rivals in the market. It also guarantees a high degree of consistency in the standards, as they are subject to the same legislative authority and constitutional principles. Third, these standards are enforceable through the system of courts, police, and other law-enforcement agencies of the nation. Thus, evasion and violation of the standards can occur only at the peril of prosecution and punishment.

The legal framework of a multinational firm is quite different. None of the above mentioned factors apply to it. It faces as many different systems of laws, ordinances, and public policies as there are sovereign countries in its operation area. No two countries have identical laws or policies, not to mention specific regulations or governmental directives. Thus, there can be no uniform legal standards that govern its entire organizational scope; each of its various national subentities is subject to different legal requirements. And what really complicates the matter is the absence of any central authority to at least referee the application of the incongruous national standards and to protect the firm against multiple jeopardy, and jurisdictional transgressions by jealous national authorities. The greater the conflicts among the different national laws and policies, the more radically must the multinational firm differ from its uninational counterpart in both its organizational and behavioral features.

We may speculate that a continued presence of the multinational firm will sooner or later lead to a widespread demand for international or supranational harmonization of business law and economic policy. To date, there is no basis for any early optimism that this will happen.

Cultural Aspects

Important as it is, the legal framework is but one aspect of a firm's environment. Usually it is a researchable, definable, and ascertainable aspect: the statutes, court decisions, and policy statements of the nation are available to the interested firm for scrutiny. The same cannot be said about the cultural aspects of the environment. Social customs, ethical norms, and other cultural values vary in countless ways from country to country. So do language, world view, and the aspirations of individuals. No book, no discipline, no specific source of information can provide concrete information on what these cultural environmental forces are and how exactly they operate. More often implicit than explicit, frequently taking their expressions in the symbolic and indicative rather than verbal canons or definable edicts, their effect upon business enterprise has proven to be even more unyieldingly pervasive and constant than that of the statutory constraints. It is perhaps more in this area than in any other where the successes and failures of international executives are determined in the long run. Cross-cultural sensitivity and comprehension are intricate, perplexing subjects, to which we shall return later. Suffice it to say at this point that there are no easy solutions to problems of cross-cultural adaptation. To be sure one's alertness and awareness can be increased, but this is hardly enough for executive effectiveness. Upon awareness he must build the ability to diagnose, to interpret, and to make predictions about the forces at play. This requires personal exposure to foreign cultures and experience with international processes, but there is no guarantee that experience will suffice. For many the task of multicultural problem-solving is beyond their aptitudinal horizons; for others, it imposes abnormal or extra-professional demands as something that has not been part of the folklore of managerial preparedness to date.

Economic Aspects

Standards of life, patterns of consumption, purchasing power, market structure, institutional arrangements, and business practices all have their local roots and peculiarities. They all have a more or less direct bearing on business opportunities, organization, and methods of operation. To ignore them is seldom possible; to suppress them has become suicidal, with the end of the colonial control.

Economic factors are more researchable and ascertainable than cultural elements. But concrete information in this area is generally scarce and often inaccessible, due to the inadequacy of public information agencies, and to the high cost of collecting and keeping abreast of such information. Individual companies, especially with modest potential in a particular country, often find the environmental research function prohibitively expensive. The development of international standards and studies by international public bodies such as the United Nations, European Economic Community, Latin American Free Trade Association, etc., is creating new sources of knowledge and helps to alleviate the problem at least in certain aspects and regions of the world. However, at the same time the tempo of development is increasing, and with it the rate of obsolescence of existing data.

Heterocultural Environment

Thus, there is much that differentiates and little that integrates the environmental structures of a multinational company. Its environment is pluralistic and heterocultural in the most inclusive sense of these terms. Perhaps we should not even talk about an environment but environments, yet it is the sum of the various national systems plus their interactions that constitute the total environmental setting for the multinational firm. There is, therefore, no way of avoiding or circumventing the contrasts and conflicts in standards of performance and norms of behavior that societies in different countries impose upon the firm. The choice for the modern multinational firm is not between accepting or rejecting the environmental heterogeneities, but between adaptive adjustment and retreat from the multinational arena.

Comparison with the Uninational
Multiunit Firm

The multinational firm is by definition a multiunit company. As such it should be juxtaposed with the domestic multiunit firm. Are the two different in any significant respect?

A multiunit structure gives rise to several categories of problems that are in many ways different from those encountered in a single unit company—intracompany trade, interunit conflicts and rivalries, administrative autonomy, and top management control, just to mention broad areas. Obviously, all these are present in a multinational company. But this apparent similarity quickly disappears when we delve below the generalized headings. Take, for example, intracompany trade. In the domestic setting the different units can always trade in their own currency. They are all subject to more or less the same competition, their transactions can be consummated unhampered by customs duties and other trade barriers; their credit conditions are for all practical purposes identical and their price and cost figures quite easily comparable. None of this is typically true for trade among the units of a multinational firm.

As to interunit nontrade relations, the domestic company is able to communicate in its national language, depend on standard customs, the same legal principles, and more or less congruent expectations of individuals in comparable positions. The multinational firm may find that these and many other nonproblem areas for the uninational company constitute complex problems for the multinational firm, whose units are staffed by different nationalities whose cultural norms and value scales seldom coincide.

That the same is true about administrative authority, delegation of power, control, and coordination will become evident in subsequent chapters where these matters are discussed. The methods and techniques of solving the problems of the domestic multiunit firms can be helpful for the multinational company, but only as a takeoff point, not as a final solution. The greater number of factors, the built-in incongruities imposed upon by the contrasting environmental forces, and the generally higher degree of complexity in the multinational company are problems that require correspondingly more intricate models, formulas, and concepts than are necessary in domestic management.

Contrast with the Colonial Company

The modern multinational firm has often been confused with colonial companies that used to dominate business activities which transcended the mother country's boundaries during the colonial era. The history of the colonial firms is as old as that of colonial empires and the imperialistic ideologies that inspired their acquisition.

The prototypic format of the colonial company can be described by five essentials:

1. It was engaged in extractive industry—mining, plantation, usually topical agriculture, petroleum production, or the exploitation of some other natural resource of the colonized area; it did not emphasize manufacturing and marketing activities, as does the modern multinational company.

2. It was subservient to the mother country's home market. The colonial company was in India not to serve the needs of Indian economy or population but to supply the British industry and commerce with raw materials; it was in Java not because the Indonesians wanted rubber, but because the Dutch did. In other words, the colonial company owed both its origin and allegiance to its metropolitan (mother country) headquarters; it did not cater to the needs and development of the indigenous economy as does the modern multinational company.

3. It existed in an isolated enclave from both economic and social points of view—an unintegrated foreign body often at odds with the society within which

it functioned. In contrast, the modern multinational company is an integral part of the economies of all countries in which it has operational facilities.

4. There was little transfer of technology, capital, or cultural values between the colonial company and the indigenous society. The investment multiplier was rendered inoperative by the enclave strategy and the alien, exploitative goals of the firm. It therefore produced but minimal economic growth and direct benefit to the native population.

5. It was endowed with political powers, often reinforced by military forces to coerce compliance with its decisions. In many ways the large colonial companies such as the British East India Company, the Lavent Company, the Dutch East India Company, the Hudson Bay Company, etc., acted as highly autonomous satellite states within the colonial empires. Dominated by the mercantilist doctrine, the rulers of the empires utilized the colonial companies both to maintain control over the subject peoples and to increase the inflow of treasure to the empire, i.e., to supply the mother country with cheap raw materials from the colonies that could be converted to exports or substituted for imports, so that a surplus in the balance of trade would result.

Unlike the modern multinational firm, therefore, the colonial company did not have to adapt itself to the indigenous conditions of the society where it operated. Its privileged status and political powers enabled it to impose its own will and motives upon the indigenous peoples. Industrial and agricultural developments in the colonies were limited to products wanted by the mother country for consumption or trade; development of products or industries that might have competed with the latter's industries was suppressed, regardless of local needs.

The colonial companies also possessed a near perfect monopoly on trade, which was centered on the mother country through strict navigation laws and punitively discriminatory tariff systems which harshly penalized any direct trading by the subject people in the colony with any country outside the colonial empire. In brief, the colonies were regarded as subservient economic appendixes to the European home country, and the colonial companies charted as instruments for the exploitations of this ideology.

Any modern multinational company misguided enough to attempt such behavior finds itself promptly facing expropriation or complete nationalization proceedings, and can consider itself lucky if permitted to leave the host country with a one-way ticket without the loss of its investments. Most such corporate efforts are stillborn in the contemporary world—an expatriate enterprise that fails to justify its genuine contribution to the host country's best interest as conceived by its government and people is disqualified before it ever comes into being. Power now lies with the countries, not with the company.

The Lingering Halo of the Colonial Company

This is not to say that the colonial company has not left a mark on contemporary business. On the contrary, its lingering halo continues to confuse both the public and the businessman. (The notorious recent publicity surrounding some old American multinationals serves to illustrate the point. Notice that they have been associated exclusively with the extractive and utility industries.) A number of today's multinational firms have their roots in the colonial era. Some, particularly British, Dutch, Belgian, and French headquarter firms, are only recent converts from colonial activities to competitive international business. Others, such as the early international ventures of the United States, Swiss, and Swedish companies—though not legally chartered as colonial companies—often behaved as if they were. For the arch model for international business behavior of that period was the colonial company.

In the institutional structure of the colonial empires the colonial company held a very dominant position. As the main vehicle for extracting wealth from the subjugated lands it was indispensible to government and invincible to competitors. Its privileges and power aroused adoration and its methods and attitudes were copied and imitated by business everywhere. The mode of the colonial company, thus, became the *role model* to all overseas business operations of that era. How the colonial companies acted set the norms for international business behavior. That these norms may seem atrocious to the contemporary reader make them no less valid or dominant in the colonial setting. Historic facts, especially those involving mores and values, must be interpreted in the context of their own time.

To what extent the early multinational firms were patterned after the colonial companies was a joint function of geography and product specialization. In Europe international business ventures were based on arm's-length dealings, and were not significantly different from their contemporary counterparts. In the other continents that was seldom true. The companies in extractive industries (mining, petroleum, and topical agriculture) were the most influenced by the colonial model, and its inertia in managerial attitudes, organizational structures, and operating policies is still haunting those industries. A number of recent corporate catastrophes in the form of expropriations and nationalizations of affiliates are attributable, at least in part, to this unholy inheritance. The manufacturing firms were generally less directly committed to the colonial company model, since their motive for overseas expansion was not the control and exploitation of natural resources, but the utilization of technical advantages and market potentialities. The early multinational manufacturing ventures, except subsidiaries of colonial companies, received their initial impetus from some technical advantage. Singer, Western Union, Bell, Edison, Westinghouse, Kodak, and National Cash Register were prominent pioneers in multinational manufacturing in the late 1900s. Though their later paths have differed, their early histories were very similar: each was based on a new invention or major technical improvement, and obtained patents and established manufacturing affiliates abroad, primarily in Europe, to exploit the then largest industrialized market of the world.[6]

Since the international success of the manufacturing companies derived from their technical superiority rather than from the control of host country natural resources—a sharp contrast with the mining, oil, and plantation companies—they had from the start much less in common with the colonial company. Yet many of the attitudes, tactics, and policies, especially in reference to host country people and governments, were borrowed from the colonial repertoire.

The collapse of the colonial empires after World War II exposed the older multinational firms as remnants of the dreaded system. This stigma, though often undeserved, still taints the public image of the multinational firm in many circles. A long process of agonizing reappraisal and reorganization has transformed most of those companies into more responsive and socially viable enterprises. However, the process is by no means complete. Especially in the extractive industries, the agony of adaptation has often proven unbearable for the firm. A number have gone under and many others appear to have adopted the strategy of benign neglect—accommodate direct demands of the host society but do no more. That this strategy will accomplish anything besides buying time is less than certain. Hopes for the survival of these firms must rest on the experience of a much larger number of companies whose modernization took a decisive leap forward once the old cadres had been displaced from strategic decision-making positions. The time has just about run its course for most of the xenophobic old hands to retire. It is a fairly safe bet that their replacements, indoctrinated as they may be, will serve a positive integration of the companies into their host societies rather than expect those societies to change in the image of the firm. The newer multinational companies, free from any colonial heritage, provide scores of examples on how this can be done.

2 Transboundary Linkages

The purpose of this chapter is to provide the general perspective from which both the internal and external implications of the multinational firm can be portrayed within a conceptually consistent and factually accurate frame of reference. First, the discussion will focus on conventional conceptualization of internation economic relations: the theory of trade and its underpinnings, the transboundary transaction. Second, the discussion will shift to the description of contemporary multinational organizations and activities, to show how transboundary economic linkages have been changed by them. By contrasting the old conceptions with the new realities, we can reveal not only the characterization of the two systems, but also the nature and the magnitude of change in the fundamental underpinnings of international relations that are attributable to the emergence to dominance of the modern multinational firm.

Some of the more basic questions posed in this analysis are: Can the existing transboundary linkages be accommodated by accepted theories of economics and political science? Are these theories still relevant, or are they obsolete? What factors and relationships emerge from our study of the multinational firm which require new and different conceptualizations? What is the scope and character of the contemporary system of internation economic ties? Do these ties have noneconomic implications? How does the multinational firm relate to the uninational state or country?

The Conventional View—International
Trade Linkage

In the conventional conceptionalization of internation economic relations, each independent country is viewed as a separate national economy, that is, a self-contained and essentially self-sufficient system for producing and distributing the particular society's output. As a nation state, the society maintains its political self-determination by regulating external interferences within its internal affairs. In pure theory at least, the nation state represents absolute sovereignty: the nation is the sole, exclusive source of political power, economic welfare, and social control all wrapped in one. National boundaries define the territorial scope of a nation's sovereignty as well as the nonsovereignty of all other nations. The original and fundamental purpose of national boundaries is to tell the outside world to stay out.

13

But demarcation lines are not enough. If the sovereignty of a society is to remain unadulterated by outside influences, it must surround itself with peripheral barriers that will guarantee that no transboundary linkages could exist that would be outside the discretionary tolerance of the organs endowed by the society to exercise its sovereignty.

National economy is the name for the subsystem that is responsible for producing and distributing goods and services needed for the economic welfare of the nation. Regardless of its design—whether centralized or decentralized, individually or collectively owned—the national economy, too, connotes a closed system in pure theory. Being in its origin nothing more than an elaboration of the economic aspects of perfect national sovereignty, it could hardly connote anything else without being a self-contradiction.

Thus, the concept of national economy connotes a system in which all normal activities, transactions, and institutions are conceived to be intranational in scope: to take place or to exist wholly within the territorial boundaries of the country. Any transboundary extension constitutes a deviation from the normal— a leakage from the national economy or economic system of one sovereignty to that of another. Literature in economic and political theories has concerned itself to date exclusively with these leakages in all their myriad aspects.

The starting point for both economic and political theories is the premise that international economic activities are subordinated to intranational activities. They represent factors that may come into play only if the result is to make the national economy a more productive or otherwise desirable system, as perceived by the polity of the particular sovereignty. International economic activities can take but one form: foreign trade, which consists of exporting and importing of goods. The nation state trades only if it can profit in real terms; that is, when the production of an export surplus of one good takes less resources than the production of another good which can be imported in exchange of the export surplus. The gain from trade is a saving of resources. By *not* producing an importable good the nation can release more of its own natural resources than are required for producing an exportable surplus of another good by which to pay for the import. Thus, the nation is conceptualized to be a self-centered system, which will never trade with other nations unless it can profit by doing so. The measure of the profit is the increment of its total collective welfare. So goes the theory. From it we have derived the conceptual limits for international economic relations.

The Transboundary Transaction

The decisive factor in any international trade activity is the transboundary transaction, i.e., the export sale of one national economy and the import purchase of another. This is true for the simple reason that in the absence of the transboundary transaction no international trade is conceivable. The transboundary transaction, thus, represents the original act upon which depend all the other aspects of international trade relations.

Since in modern times all national economies are monetized, the theoretical system does not require that an export be directly offset by an import, but allows both to take place separately so long as there are monetary exchange reserves available to pay for the transboundary shipment. Thus, from every trade transaction arises an international payments obligation, but only because export and import transactions of the country are not bilaterally consummated. This is to say, the payments transactions are the inescapable corollaries of the trade transactions. From this comes the proverbial "trade and payments" idiom.

In the presence of the transboundary trade transaction other aspects of international trade relations can emerge and take on a multitude of manifestations; in its absence the entire edifice will collapse. If there is no export, there can be no import, no international payment, no foreign trade effect on employment, on interest rates, on prices, on economic growth, or any other business. Neither can there be any foreign economic policy, balance of payments, or foreign exchange market. None of the subjects which now constitute the diverse fields of international economic relations would have either factual base or rational relevance to the society.

The absolute primacy of the transboundary trade transaction in the conceptual system which has structured our view of internation economic interactions must clearly be grasped before the impact of the modern multinational firm on international relations can be appreciated.

Foreign trade literature distinguishes four channels or institutional variants through which the transboundary trade transaction may link different national economics. They are shown in Figure 2-1.

Variants 1 and 2 represent what has been called the *indirect trade channel:* indirect in the sense that the producer in the country of origin does not have direct contact with the foreign market. For the opposite reasons, variants 3 and 4 have been labeled *direct channels.* Taking into account the organizational and legal characteristics of the channel members, especially the export and import intermediaries, these four trade channels can be further divided into a number of subvariables, as is usually done in managerial analysis of the subject. All that such differentiation can do is to show who does it: how many and what type of firms and institutions participate in the process. But there can never be any question about what is to be accomplished. The fundamental purpose remains always the same: selling goods produced in one national economy to be consumed in another. Regardless which teams of participants or channel members carry it out, the actual economic linkage between the two countries is never anything else than the particular transboundary transactions: no transboundary transactions equals no trade, no internation economic linkage; many transactions equals much trade, tight linking of the domestic economy with the outside world.

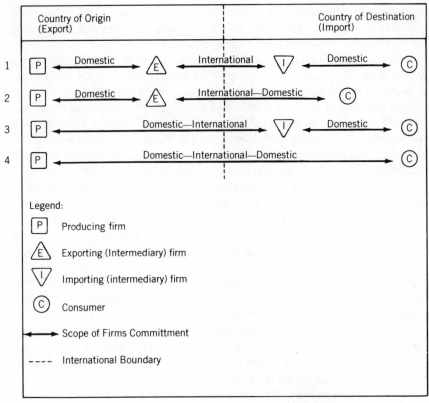

Figure 2-1. Channels of International Trade

To keep score of the transboundary transactions the balance of international payments accounting was devised. Despite its misleading name, this system of social accounting is not limited to payments, but includes all transfers of value in or out of a country, that is, all transboundary transactions. In economic theory, the balance of payments represents the totality of a nation's international economic activities. Something that is not recordable in the balance of payments is, according to the theory, *external* to the internation economic interactions. Profits earned by a foreign-based subsidiary, for example, is a nonactivity for international purposes viewed from this perspective. Again, the decisive element in internation economic relations is the transboundary transaction and nothing else can qualify as such. The transaction itself consists of a three-step cycle: offer, acceptance, and payment. The financial stakes involved in any transaction are measured by the sum to be paid. While there may be derived losses or benefits, the direct commitment is always the size of the transaction. This is important to bear in mind when assessing the potential strength and durability of any given trade relationship. The risk of loss from interrupting the trade relationship between any two nations is the sum of transactions in process of being negotiated on that day. This sum is only a fraction of the "flow" statistics—the aggregate of transactions consummated over a given period—that is customarily used. There may be delayed losses arising from not having the trade transactions of future days. But they will occur only if alternate trading partners are unable to offer benefits comparable to the terminated relationship. Very rarely does any nation hold either monopoly or monopsony position in world trade. The interruption of a particular trade relationship need not change the volume but only the direction of trade. Consequently, trade as a transboundary linkage is inherently tenuous; it can be cut and redirected by either governmental authority or changing competitive conditions at any time.

Transboundary Linkages of
Multinational Companies

When a firm expands its productive capabilities across international boundaries, and establishes foreign-based subsidiaries or other affiliated plants, it also crosses the boundaries of our conventional notion of international economic relations and proceeds in a manner quite different from the theory of trade. Instead of first exporting goods from its home country and subsequently importing payments, it will start with exporting payments to be invested in the prospective foreign-based facility. Here the international payment becomes the original, autonomous factor rather than a consequence of an export or import of goods, as in the trade transactions.

The capital transfer transaction, while at odds with the theory of comparative advantage and moving for the "wrong" reason, is however still within the scope and capabilities of international economics, since it will show up in the balance of payments along with all other international transactions. But so far as international economics is concerned, this is the end of the matter; the capital has been transferred, the transaction recorded, and so long as the capital stays in the country of destination (the host country of the prospective affiliate), it is of no further relevance to international relations, or so our conventional doctrine has it.

For the enterprise the capital transfer is only the initial move, the beginning of international activities. To fully expose the conceptual conflict, suppose that for a number of years there are no other transboundary transfers of money or goods; the affiliate is established and operated exclusively for the purpose of serving the host's country market. Factories are built, production lines designed, people hired, trained, and paid, goods produced and sold, revenues generated and collected, and a myriad of other activities carried out in the host country under the direction and for the benefit of the investing enterprise. In the balance-of-payments framework none of this is recordable and so is of no relevance to international relations. In the contexts of the company and the two societies involved these happenings are realities that cannot be rendered nonexistent by any set of assumptions or classifications.

The traditionalist counterargument to this point is to insist that sooner or later the initial direct investment must produce a return to the investors; that to yield any dividends to the owners of the parent company the foreign venture must remit, or as it is usually said "repatriate," its profits to the headquarters country. These dividend remittances, regardless of how long delayed, will ultimately take the place of the payment in the trade transaction and cumulatively over the life of the venture measure also the scope of the foreign-based activity.

This argument does not stand the test of reality. First, the owners of the parent company need not all be resident nationals of the headquarters country; and even if they were, the return on the investment in the foreign-based facility can accrue to them through capital gains, higher stock prices, or even direct distributions from the affiliate in local currency, which are banked or reinvested in the host country.

The fact that a foreign-based activity may remain territorially limited to the host country, as it sometimes does, by no means implies any financial limitation; in fact, it can far outgrow the initial amount invested by the parent company. More often than not, the initial direct investment provides only the seed money to commence operations that are later enlarged from year to year through earnings of the affiliate itself.

Although the affiliate is established in a different country than the parent firm, and even though as a legal entity it is normally a creature of that foreign nation, its coming into being creates transboundary relationships that are not necessarily reflected in either its legal charter or financial record. The general nature of these relationships is shown in Figure 2-2. They form the currently emerging system of transboundary linkages and, as we shall argue below, defy most of the rules promulgated for internation economic interaction by our orthodox theories.

Turning to the rationale of these new linkages, each has to be considered individually. *Financial flows*, shown in the chart next to the initial investment, should be a rather self-evident intertie between the headquarters and the affiliate once the latter is a going concern; any further elaboration of this would seem superfluous.

Property holdings are probably the most offensive to the trade theory advocate, since the permanency and immobility of most industrial property aborts any and all attempts to reduce it down to the trade transaction level. Factories and machines are embodiments of productive capacity and earning potential. To realize either, they must be used. The return from these assets accrues as a gradual stream over their life, and not in one transaction. Even though individual machines or structures may have relatively short or terminable lives, a corporate enterprise as a composite seldom has a foreseeable life

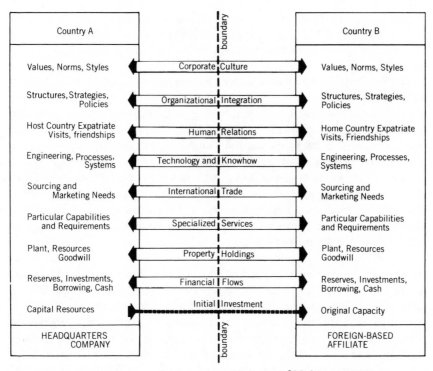

Figure 2-2. Typical Transboundary Linkages of Multinational Firm

expectancy, but can be looked upon as an open-ended, long-range proposition continuing into perpetuity. There is, therefore, the tendency for the foreign-based affiliates to gain both in significance and in permanency as their property holdings grow and diversify.

Another linkage of utmost importance is the *technology and know-how* channel. Like all the others in the chart, this channel really represents a whole subsystem of transboundary linkages. But for our present purposes, no great violence is done by not discriminating among the many different types of intelligence and knowledge which, ranging from abstract science to routinized procedures, take on separate manifestations in the modern business firm. The crucial new truth is the categorical imperative for both the headquarters company and the affiliate to utilize to the fullest each other's technological resources, regardless of whether the know-how has been acquired through internal activities such as research, development, production, and marketing experience, or through environmental endowments of the respective country, including universities, other firms, and public projects. Again we have a simultaneous two-directional source-use relationship across international lines. It is an organic aspect of any multinational firm, regardless of whether it utilizes complex or simple technologies. That the implications of this linkage may be far greater in a high technology industry than in the low technology one in no way alters the fact that the linkage is there whenever a firm transcends international boundaries.

Organizational integration between the headquarters firm and the foreign-based affiliates constitutes another new transboundary tie. It, too, is very different from the trade transaction, by being a permanent structural extension of the company into different countries and providing the means for the exercise of multinational direction, coordination, and control to the firm. As discussed in the chapters of organization, this complex and little understood subject has a crucial bearing on the operational capabilities and behavioral characteristics of the multinational firm. Much remains to be learned about this intriguing matter. But like the transmission of technology, the organizational integration is an absolute imperative; its opposite disintegration is clearly an irrationality of suicidal potential for any multinational firm.

The *human relations* linkage consists of personal interactions and involvements between the employees of the headquarters company and those of the affiliates. It involves nationals of different countries and adds a strictly human dimension to the transboundary connectedness of various national affiliations in a multinational enterprise. Discussion in subsequent chapters will elaborate on several important aspects of this relationship, including the use of expatriate managers and technicians, the recruiting and development of multinational cadres, and the rotation and promotion of people in an international context. The basic points to be emphasized at this stage are the coming into existence of direct personal contacts among nationals of different countries, and their sharing of common objectives and participating in the same experiences as members of the multinational organization. Under the traditional trade linkage any international contacts were reserved to either the very exclusive fraternity of import-export intermediaries or the few foreign trade sales people of the direct trading firm. The vast majority of employees never had any reason or opportunity to come occupationally in contact with nationals of other countries.

From the shared experiences emerge sooner or later the beginnings of what in Chapter 6 is termed *cosmopolitan corporate culture*. They help to bridge the gaps and conflicts among the systems of values, norms, and styles of behavior of different nationalities. To a small degree goods also can be said to disseminate culture and to facilitate international empathy. But this is limited to the material sphere, and is strictly impersonal. When organizational structures, common work experiences, and direct personal interactions are added, the whole complexion of the transboundary relations changes. The implications of the emerging cosmopolitan corporate cultures to world relations in all their aspects are most profound.

International trade is perhaps the most bizarre linkage in the new system. The empirical tendency of the firm to continue exporting and importing goods after it has acquired multinational productive capacity is in direct contravention of textbook economics. The latter insists that the choices for a firm to reach foreign markets are two: to export or to make a direct foreign investment. If it exports, the goods are made at home and consumed abroad; if it invests in foreign production capacity, the goods are assumed to be both manufactured and consumed abroad, and thus there can be no international trade.

To certain industries this doctrine is still applicable. Brick manufacturers, cement mills, and a few other completely standardized staple products could serve as examples. But to the vast bulk of business activity, especially to manufacturing and service-industries, the old export-or-invest doctrine represents a parodic distortion of reality. Two case studies will illustrate why.

A United States refrigerator manufacturer decided to establish a manufacturing subsidiary in a Latin country to which it had been exporting for many years. After all the market researches, cost calculations, and operations optimalization equations had been completed, it was clear that one key component, the cooling machine, was best mass produced on an export basis, while all the other parts and the assembly work should be done by the affiliate itself. The new refrigerator, tailored to the local consumer requirements and priced accordingly, enjoyed a much greater sales than U.S. refrigerators previously exported to that country. The result was that exports from the parent company grew to a volume four times greater than the exports of finished refrigerators had ever been. *Export trade of the firm did not stop after the direct investment—it quadrupled.* Only now the exports consisted of semi-manufactures instead of finished refrigerators.

The second case involves an automobile manufacturer. This company increased its exports to a Near Eastern country threefold after completing a local assembly plant. The reasons: lower freight and transportation insurance on parts than on finished cars, lower import duties, and significant saving in some assembly operations due to local labor rates and other costs. These savings enabled the company to cut its finished car prices and to increase its sales. Again, the acquisition of foreign production capacity did not displace international trade, but increased it. The composition of the goods changed—the finished cars disappeared and parts were substituted—but the dollar value of trade increased.

Numerous other case studies reveal the same story: the firm's exports continue and grow after foreign-based production plants have been established. On the import side the same is true. Although no comprehensive data exists to measure accurately the trade effect of multinational firms, a large number of observations has led this author to the conviction that in the vast majority of business firms (excluding the extractive industry), the establishment of multinational production facilities tends to be accompanied by an increase in international trade and not the reverse, as postulated in the orthodox theory. It also appears that as the firm becomes more fully established internationally, there is an increased tendency for multilateral trade between the different national entities of the company.

The trade linkage of the multinational firm differs in one respect from the classic notion of foreign trade—it is not trade among independents or unrelated residents of different countries. Rather, it is trade among units of a multinationalist enterprise. All these trading units are harnessed to the same ultimate objective: to serve the corporate interest, whatever its definition in any particular firm. Thus, it remains intracompany despite being internation, i.e., internal from the viewpoint of the firm as a totality but external for all the nations whose boundaries are traversed by the trade. It goes beyond the scope of any individual nation. Such intracompany international trade opens many new possibilities.

One more linkage remains on the chart, namely *specialized services*. Suffice to say that the reference here is to various specialized capabilities that are more or less normal outgrowths from the division of labor among the different units in the multinational structure. Because of their existence, the interdependence among the affiliates and headquarters is increased, and so is the utilization of the other transboundary linkages.

Only the initial investment in the chart is a one-way and one-time transfer comparable to other payment transactions. All the others are more than transactions; they are permanent interties between the headquarters company and the affiliate. Unlike the international trade transaction, these new linkages are not discontinuous sequences of the offer-acceptance-payment cycles, but represent channels for continuous interactions where both units may be simultaneously contributors and beneficiaries to each other. They are two-way relationships.

As indicated earlier, this list of linkages is not an exhaustive one. Many others could be added, and all of these discussed can be split up into several component relationships. The point here has been not to catalogue, but to outline, not to perfect the elaboration of the multinational business system, but to define its general scope. Clearly, the shift from foreign trade to multinational business is restructuring of the entire system of transboundary relationships among nations and affecting not only the economic sphere life, but inevitably many other aspects. Particularly decisive is the impact of the new relations upon business firms themselves. If a company in itself becomes multinational, its entire scope and complexion take on new dimensions. If it remains uninational, it finds the channels for export-import interactions radically altered and its opportunities to trade in the traditional manner reduced. The new system of transboundary linkages means the emergence of a new set of international institutions, and a decline and possible disappearance of some old ones such as export and import houses, foreign trade specialist firms, and various governmental agencies devoted to the international trade activities as such.

With institutional change come changes in international cadres, in foreign affairs expertise, and in the methods of social control of these new institutions. In government the old instruments of international economics policy can hardly suffice in this new context. Even the objectives of national policy and its international implementation may require revision and new formulations. Thus, the role of government and the interest of the public are both at stake.

In business the stakes seem even higher. Here the shaping of the new international institutions is spearheaded by the multinationalization movement, and with it goes an imperative not only to understand and accept the changes imposed by the shift from national to multinational systems in all aspects of the firm, but also to participate in and profit by this change-producing shift.

The specifics of these implications are spelled out in subsequent chapters. Our task here has been to provide the background against which more detailed discussions can be projected, and especially to help the reader understand that the theory of trade is clearly inadequate to provide a realistic explanation of contemporary international economic relations. Resting on a single transboundary link, the foreign trade transaction, it lacks the conceptual scope and analytical methodologies to come to grips with the wide spectrum of nontrade linkages which modern multinational companies have created. More enduring in constitution, costlier in termination, and less vulnerable to international trade barriers, these new linkages represent a broader and deeper fusion of national economic systems with one another than is conceivable with the trade linkage alone. The possibilities for a continuous integration of different national economies are vastly greater with the new linkages than with the trade linkage only which, as said before, has been the basis for the conventional explanation of international economic relations.

3 Operational Motivities of the Multinational Firm

Multinational business figures in a variety of recent writings, much of it in a negative light and much out of context. Fragmentary observations and piecemeal analyses by observers with narrowly restrictive perspectives, not to mention preexisting antibusiness biases, have prompted premature conclusions which often have done little to enlighten us about the real nature of the multinational firm.

Understanding its innate operational capabilities is fundamental to any objective comprehension of this new world institution. Our objective in the present chapter is to spell out the origins and manifestations of operational power and economic efficiency of the multinational firm. They are referred to as *motivities*, the available energies or real power which signify the scope of operational capacities of the firm. This is not to say that all or even any given percentage of multinational firms fully exploit these motivities; rather, the attempt here is to describe the sources, characteristics, and limits of the powers which, arising from its concurrent existence in a number of different countries, are inherent in the phenomenon of the multinational firm.

To sharpen the focus, the subject is exposed in a comparative setting, juxtaposing the multinational with a uninational firm. Instead of trying to elaborate the totality of the operational capabilities, which by necessity would have to overlap vast areas of familiar ground, we shall concentrate on the differences in operational motivities between the uninational and multinational firms. This will achieve two objectives: to describe the operational makeup of the multinational firm and to yield comparative ratings of the different kinds of motivities for both firms. In brief, it will enable us to assess which, if either, is inherently superior or inferior to the other as a system of producing tangible economic results.

While the discussion is intended to be primarily analytical, it rests on studies of over five hundred multinational companies. This enables us to add a historic dimension reflective of the patterns and stages that have characterized the international expansion and multinationalization processes in different industries.

From the developmental perspective, the motivities peculiarly important to the operational capabilities of multinational firms fall into three basic stages: functional expansion, international consolidation, and postinternational or balanced-multinational operations. These are not sequential but overlapping stages. The international consolidation stages do not exclude the motivities of

25

the functional expansion phase, which often precedes it, but utilizes them more completely by bringing to bear other motivities on the company's activity. Similarly, the balanced-multinational operational stage will be inclusive of all the motivities of both the previous stages.

Functional Expansion

What might be termed the primal growth motivities of multinational enterprises relate to two basic functions: marketing and sourcing. In market-oriented industries and in others with a history of export marketing as a significant element in the volume of output or profits, the marketing motivities have energized the international expansion of originally uninational companies. In the extractive industries and natural resource dependent manufacturing, the propulsion for foreign expansion has come primarily from the procurement and production side, conveniently lumped together as the *sourcing function.*

It would be, therefore, quite incorrect to claim greater importance or historic primacy to either marketing or sourcing as such. The evidence available to date seems to attribute similar roles to both. They have been co-contributors to the process of internationalization, one having been the change agent in the market-oriented sectors and the other in the resource-oriented sectors. It must be added also that in most specific instances the motives which have impelled American companies to establish permanent facilities abroad have often been complex; several different factors, including some purely coincidental, may have been responsible for a particular action. The patterns, however, are fairly clear.

Marketing Motivities

Access to new markets is a necessary precondition for the growth of any market-dependent firm. In the domestic realm, this access can be presumed to be limited only by the constraints imposed by competition of other firms and by governmental regulations that apply equally to all like businesses. Thus, the determinant of growth is the company's ability to outperform competition in gaining consumer patronage. This depends ultimately on the relative degree of correspondence between the qualities of the company product and the requirements of the market. By having control over the product qualities and marketing methods, the firm can view its growth as essentially an internal matter. This is why product development, distribution channels, pricing, and sales promotion preoccupy the management of the market-oriented domestic companies.

In the multinational realm, the problem is different. Access to markets is not only a question of surpassing competition in terms of product and marketing performance, but also requires the ability to negotiate international borders before the domestic managerial factors of any target market can be brought into play at all. The only exception in this sequence is the initial demand analysis to establish which countries are to be counted as potential markets and how they rank.[1] But this knowledge is of no managerial use until additional information has been obtained that shows the ways, means, and costs of reaching the potential markets.

For commercial cargo, an international border presents a multiwall barrier. First, there are what might be called the *visa requirements*, which include the whole complex of officially instituted border controls: tariffs, border taxes, export and import quotas, licenses, customs controls, and currency restrictions, plus health, safety, and various other legal requirements applicable to importation of goods. Only through compliance with all these can sellers of foreign-made goods gain any access rights to the particular national market.

Second, the border represents discontinuities and breakoff points for various technical, economic, and cultural factors, causing a break in the market. Thus, the underlying rationale for both the utility and price of a product undergoes a certain shift on the border. What is a usable product on one side may be unusable or less usable on the other because of technical conditions; what is considered a necessity in one country may be a luxury in another due to income differences; and what is adorable or exciting in one may be abominable and dull in another, depending upon cultural values influencing consumer taste.

To actually enter a country the firm must be able to compensate for these international discontinuities by adapting both its product specifications and marketing practices to the indigenous milieu. This can be done only by first acquiring the necessary level of understanding of this new milieu, including not only its "business and economic" indicators but more important the "nonbusiness" cross-cultural discontinuities, so that their effect upon both the utility and pricing attributes of the product can be assessed. The capabilities for such analysis have been considered so far something outside the required competence region of professional management, not to mention its functional subfields.

To sum this up, the access rights that a firm acquires through fulfilling the visa requirements can by no means guarantee the actual access capability of the firm. Contrary to the usual economic-theoretical assumption, no group of nation states ever forms a homogeneous market, but a heterogeneous mosaic of countless variances. In addition to penetrating the formal barriers between them, the firm must be able to bridge the discontinuities that every international border represents in varying degrees and combinations. Before the firm possesses this capability it has no actual access capabilities to a particular nation's markets, and all its technical and managerial potentials as conceived in a domestic framework are of no use. Only after the problem complexes, access rights, and access capabilities have been solved does the domestic managerial calculus enter into play. Whether or not the firm will be able to grow from this point on depends again on its ability to outperform its competition in terms of consumer satisfaction. Although even here transplantation of practices and systems from one country to another seldom obtain optimal results, still the same basic variables and problem-solving techniques normally apply in most countries.

The access rights and market discontinuities associated with international borders impede the uninational firm in expanding its export sales and import purchases. Growth derived from foreign revenues and supplies is, therefore restricted. No amount of experimentation with different methods and practices, including institutional specialization, has ever been able to neutralize these impediments for the uninational firm. Since the inception of the modern nation state system of world organization, which is to say throughout its entire history, international trade has remained heavily encumbered by the impediments of the border. Domestic (nationally inner-directed) operations have therefore always been the mainstay of the uninational business enterprise. International markets, if cultivated at all, have been conceived as something extra, a sort of lucky bonus which need not be subjected to the same costing or profitability standards as the main body of the firm's business. The record of dumping, subsidization, and other perverted pricing practices bear sorry witness to the prevalence of this view.

On the theory that any export price which exceeds a firm's variable cost contributes to its profitability, a differential between domestic and export prices signifies neither bad economics or bad management. True enough. Even though it is using sound economics, the uninational company finds itself compelled to regard the entire world outside its home country as nothing more than a vast array of potential marginal additives to the domestic market but as not synonymous with it. More important, export pricing is rarely based on marginal analysis, but on managerial assessment of both economic and noneconomic factors. The prevalence of export discounts, therefore, underscores the uninational firm's inability to serve different world markets as a geocentrically functioning enterprise.

The uninational firm is perpetually constrained by the dual core of trade barriers; it lacks the capacity to deal conclusively with either the access rights to a country or the market discontinuities at the border. At best, it can hope to lessen their constricting hold, but never to escape from it. Even if perfectly free trade—the abolition of all and every formal entry restriction—should by some yet unknown miracle be realized one day, the market discontinuities would still remain. Therefore, the textbook utopia of an undifferentiated world market will remain unobtainable. The market discontinuities at the boundaries are very different from any heterogeneity based on some socioeconomic aspects which may be found within a uninational market, including even such relatively pluralistic ones as the United States or the Soviet Union. First, there is the difference in magnitude for almost any relevant variable. Second, there is the difference in the number and relationship of factors which show variations in inter- as compared to intranation markets. And third, there are also new kinds of variables such as languages, social structures, opinion markets, life styles, etc. Each national society is not only a political but also a cultural sovereignty: the origin and manifestation of the normative systems which govern motivation and behavior of that society. International boundaries demarcate where one sovereignty ends and another starts. Unless one postulates a perfectly integrated, nationless, borderless, uniracial, and unilingual world society—something in the remotest reaches of fantasy—the global market will always present a mosaic of dissimilar component markets rather than a uniform whole. Consequently, the marketing capabilities of the uninational firm are insufficient to fully exhaust the business possibilities abroad. The market discontinuities at international boundaries severely curtail the uninational firm's ability for transnational growth. The changes in terms of social, economic, and even physical ingredients of both production and distribution spheres of the firm which each new country requires pose successive cost barriers that at best can be met only partially and selectively if no resident operating affiliates are formed.

In sum, the capabilities of the uninational firm are inherently unequal to the business and profit potentialities of a multinational market.

From this nonequality of capabilities and potentialities has sprung the initiative that is now transforming the market-oriented uninational firm into its multinational counterpart. In the market-oriented sector, the acquisition of foreign-based affiliates unlocks new spaces for growth and the very inception of the multinational firm becomes synonymous with the extension of the opportunities to grow beyond the limits of the uninational company.

A 1959 study of the reasons for international expansion showed that the need to obtain access rights and marketing capabilities accounted for 53 percent of the foreign-based affiliates of American companies. The sample consisted of 533 affiliates representing all major sectors of manufacturing. Taking from this sample only the affiliates which fell into the market-oriented classification, the result was that 93 percent owed their birth to the headquarters company's desire to acquire unimpaired operating capabilities in particular foreign markets.[2] Thirty-one percent of the affiliates had been established primarily to assure access rights to the host country's market, that is, to overcome legal trade restrictions, and foreign exchange regulations. Sixty-two percent had been created to give the firm access capabilities to overcome the market discontinuities at the national border. Thus, contrary to the oft-repeated presumption, legal trade restrictions, though significant, have been relatively much less important reasons for the mushrooming of foreign-based affiliates than have the inherent characteristics and requirements of the different countries as markets.

At the time of that study, the concept of the market discontinuities was yet to be recognized. International trade barriers were more or less looked upon as a two-dimensional array in which the space was mostly occupied by the legal trade restrictions. Therefore, the questions were structured not in terms of our present frame of reference but in terms of the views of the management personnel involved in analyzing the situation for their respective firms. Their views were strongly influenced by the traditional textbook notions of foreign trade and marketing. Inefficiency of indigenous marketing institutions, dissatisfaction with the performance of international middlemen, long-run expansion goals, and local consumer resistance represented the main groups of their concerns. All these are aspects of the access capability in our present conception of the subject. They are problems for no other reasons than the discontinuities in the market which are caused by international boundaries.

To probe the full spectrum of marketing motivities, followup studies were conducted in 1965 and 1970. Unlike the 1959 survey, these later studies focused on the actual achievements and operating experiences of the multinationalized firms rather than the initial reasons for their international expansion. Thus, the results should reflect the marketing superiorities actually attained of the multinational structure over a uninational one.

The 1965 study yielded, in summary, the following comparative marketing superiorities for the multinational firm:

Avoidance of tariff and nontariff trade barriers

Protection against import competition

Easier product adaptation to local consumption requirements

Lower transportation cost

More efficient warehousing (lower inventory requirements and shorter economic distances)

More reliable and up-to-date market information

Easier adjustment to changes in demand

More effective advertising and promotion

Less sales resistance

The most comprehensive picture emerged from the 1970 study. In addition to the factors indicated in the 1965 study, several other motivities were identified. Among these, intracompany international trade and strategic flexibility have emerged as the most decisive long-range marketing advantages of an established multinational firm. Greater and clearer product differentiation was stressed as another important operating motivity.

Strategic Flexibility

Having a resident affiliate in each country provides the multinational firm with the ability to adjust its marketing strategies within wide ranges whenever conditions demand. Unlike the uninational firm, it depends neither on international trade controls nor on domestic sourcing limitations. This is not to say that it is immune to changes in trade controls or in sourcing possibilities; only that the multinational firm possesses means for compensating for these changes which its uninational competitor lacks. If and when conditions warrant, the multinational firm markets across international boundaries and consolidates several national markets; but under different conditions, it can move in the opposite direction and segment its marketing operations into sharply separated national markets, for example when either trade barriers or other factors make this optimal. Between these two extremities lies a wide range of possible strategies. They may be varied in reference to degrees of national market segmentation as well as to different regions of the world.

Such a broad range of options for realizable strategies provides the multinational firm with a high degree of immunity against environmental adversities, be they internal business conditions of a country, restrictive governmental policies, or disturbances in international affairs.

Marketing Dynamics

This flexibility is not limited to marketing of already established products, but extends also to new product introductions as well as to other marketing innovations. Thus, it encompasses all the developmental aspects that constitute marketing dynamics. For example, a multinational firm can choose from among a wide variety of different countries the market in which to test a new product. For a typical consumer product, the initial testing might be done in a small country such as Belgium, Denmark, or Finland, where regional variances in demand characteristics are small and where the preexistence of highly refined statistical information provides an environment for completing the tests at relatively low cost. In contrast, the uninational company has hardly any alternative to its own home market to do the testing regardless of how well or ill suited it may be. The lack of own marketing capacity precludes other countries from serving as operationally acceptable test markets.

Equipped with the low-variance results of its test country, the multinational company has several options. It can, like a uninational exporting firm, follow the principle of similitude—always selecting the country that is most like the last tested market in respect to the conditions that govern the consumption of the product—and sequence the introduction of the new product to the rest of the world gradually. This would enable it to limit the need for adapting the process in any point of time (and/or the expansion curve) to the differences in consumption requirements between two countries only: the last-established market and the next most similar country to it. In other words, by introducing the product in one country at a time and always picking the country which offers the least amount of resistance for the next market, the company can concentrate its capacities to adapt on a small and more readily dependable set of revealed demand differences, and at the same time minimize the aggregate cost of the introduction. Although the uninational firm can follow the same procedure, it lacks the ability to choose a starting point by being always tied to the home country for the original test marketing.[a] This limits it to sequencing the introduction either backward or forward from the home market, and does not allow it to preselect the optimal sequencing of the countries. The multinational firm has no such inhibition. Its test market can be what best serves the particular purpose: a large, medium-sized, or small country; developed or underdeveloped; multiracial or uniracial; whichever serves as the best laboratory for the test and yields the lowest cost path to the attainment of a global market coverage.

While in a gradual introduction of new products the uninational firm still retains a fighting chance against its multinational competitor, it becomes badly outclassed when a simultaneous introduction in several countries is necessary. The best it can do is to buy nontest market information such as economic projection and statistical computations. But none of this can normally replace market-testing the product itself. An untested plunge of the product into the various national markets is the only way the uninational firm could implement a big-bang introduction strategy.

The multinational company, on the other hand, possesses the operational capability to conduct simultaneous market tests in many countries, and if deemed essential, to proceed both with adaptation and promotion on a global front. Although requiring large initial investment, such a big-bang strategy can in certain cases be ultimately more profitable than a gradual introduction. This is particularly true for product categories that are subject to rapid technological change, where obsolescence severely curtails the life cycle and thus demands an open-throttle sales program from the very start; it is also true in product lines where imitation is easy and patent protection is not obtainable. A further incentive for the global big-bang introduction strategy derives from the emergence of integrated supranational markets such as the EEC, EFTA, LAFTA, etc. In such mass markets, the immediate sales potential is often of such a magnitude that the delays involved in a gradual introduction are clearly counterproductive for the firm. Finally, the multinational firm can resort to a simultaneous multicountry introduction simply to outdistance its uninational exporting competitors, who, as explained earlier, lack the operational capacity to challenge the multinational company in any other way than a gradual introduction.

In product adaptation, too, the multinational firm is in an advantageous position. If the product modifications are relatively minor, such as the transla-

---

[a]To the extent that there is internal pluralism in the home market, the uninational firm can choose the segment best for initial testing and later broaden its scope to other segments. But the internal plurality may be very different from the plurality of the external, multinational markets. The two have never been found to be the same.

tion of the label, operating instructions, and the like into local language or conversion of voltage in an electrical appliance to the local standard, there may be no significant advantage in having it done by the local affiliates over a centralized operation. But when the modification involves the actual product design, composition, or performance configuration to meet local demand, the multinational firm obviously gains superiority. Its options range from using one standardized model worldwide to custom-tailoring the product to each national market; between these extremes lie various degrees of adaptation such as having an American model, a European model, a semideveloped-country model, etc. Technically, the uninational company can also design and manufacture customized products for any number of countries which its export operations embrace. But to market them, the customized models must be entered to their respective countries as imports. Thus, they are subject to all the trade barriers associated with customs controls and other export-import regulations. The exporting company must also overcome the relatively greater difficulties of serving the market from a distant, foreign supply base instead of the indigenous affiliate that for the multinational firm may act both as a producing and distributing organization.

Sourcing Motivities

Potentially the greatest operation superiority of the multinational firm over its uninational rival lies in its ability to combine marketing and production arrangements throughout the world in an optimal fashion. That is, it need not limit its choice to completely customized and globally standardized models, but can choose modular designs in which certain modules or subassemblies are standardized globally, others continentally, and still others to specific countries or even sections of a country. This enables it to achieve any desired degree of customization to individual country consumption requirements, without sacrificing the economies of mass production and international specialization. The multinational company achieves economies of scale from mass-producing the global and continental modules at the same time that it benefits from international specialization by having each module produced in the country possessing the most advantageous conditions for it.

For complex-component industries (automobiles, appliances, aircraft, computers, electronic systems, etc.) commonality is typically achievable in a significant share of components or subcomponents if production planning is focused on multinational maximization of their use. *Business Week* reports that through the policies of emerging multinational firms in Europe

British, French, and Spanish companies are gradually being harmonized. Rootes announced that it will move toward a greater interchange of components, such as transmissions and engines, with Simca and Barreiros. This could lead to total commonality, which Ford has achieved with its Capri and Escort models produced in Britain and Germany.

Commonality, which American companies . . . are building into their European operations, permits them to shift production from one country to another as easily as production is juggled from one plant to another in the U.S. Ford already has been threatened with a slowdown by 150 British draftsmen who are protesting a transfer of some of their technical work to the Ford plant in Cologne.[3]

Only recently have multinational companies begun to understand the existence of this flexibility and to purposefully use the marketing superiorities flowing from this flexibility. In this new type of rivalry the uninational firm has found itself badly outmatched and outperformed. By combining sourcing and marketing motivities, the multinational firm can attain operational superiority over the traditional one-country-plus-export market type of enterprise.

Resource Endowments

The uninational company is wholly dependent in its production possibilities on the domestic resource endowments. In contrast, the multinational firm has access to all the resource endowments of all the countries in which it has operating facilities; its resource base, thus, is very much greater and richer than that which any one country enterprise can ever possess. While this may seem a self-evident truth for resource-based industries, it is often obscured in our modern industry by the great number and intricate diffusion of further refinements and constant recombinations of the original resource inputs. Each participating firm in this process tends to focus on its own immediate supplier industries, which may be already several layers removed from the extractive industries providing the initial raw materials for the process. Thus, the role of natural resources is often ignored or misunderstood.

The problem is further complicated by the fact that the intermediate products acquire a greater mobility as they ascend through the different layers of manufacturing industries to higher levels of refinement. The higher elevation means greater distance from the original natural resource; it also means that the product becomes more tradeable and less tied to the primary inputs or original resource base. That is to say, the immediate input sources of the product become more and more disengaged from the natural endowment constraints, and instead depend more and more upon trade and marketing arrangements.

Theoretical Misconceptions

Perhaps even more fundamental than the natural resource endowments to the productive powers of the contemporary business enterprise is the technology base. A serious blind spot in international economic theory has obscured the importance of the technology base by making the implicit assumption that knowledge is perfectly mobile and equally accessible to business firms in all countries. Therefore, production functions should be the same in all countries and international cost of production differences accountable by resource endowments only. Accepting this proposition, the theorist can show that, through international trade, all international differences in the prices of productive factors can be eliminated and complete cost parity of inputs achieved for producers in all countries.[4] Despite the actual disparity in input prices "the factor price equalization model has tended to become the cornerstone of international trade theory. And, since the same world production possibilities are attainable in this model with commodity trade alone as with commodity plus factor trade, the tradition of ignoring factor movements has been further justified."[5]

While these assumptions greatly simplify the problem of theoretical model building, they mutilate to the point of perversion the realities of contemporary international life. Not only are available technologies and the consequent production functions in actual fact very different in different countries today, but the differences have been increasing as certain peoples specialize and as some countries progress at faster rates than others in different fields. Even in a national context technology is neither uniform nor universal. Much of the newest and especially the economically tested and applicable technology—what we call know-how—belongs to particular companies and patent owners. It is not a public good, but private property. In the long run this proprietary technology tends to become generally known and widely applied throughout the country, due to expiration of patents, leakages from confidential files, competitive intelligence, or deliberate disclosures by the proprietor company as its new advances render old technology relatively harmless competitively. Thus, there is a continuous transformation of proprietary technology into national technology, but the two are never synonymous wherever private property rights exist.

The nonproprietory technology is a composite of technical literature (text-books, research findings, journals, and academic gatherings) and the issue of technical know-how from companies that operate within the country. The latter's contribution may take any or all of these forms:

1. Sales of hardware or services, such as new machinery and equipment, test devices, computer software, and related consulting services.
2. Technical-service activities backing up these sales or introducing new products.
3. Demonstrations of modern management technologies at seminars, conferences, exhibitions, etc.
4. Technical assistance to suppliers and customers on special problems.
5. Observation and imitation of nonproprietary technologies.[6]

Since the business firms are the major producers, adaptors, and users of technology, they create collectively what might be called a national infrastructure of knowledge and give the proprietory sphere, and through the spillover from it also to the nonproprietary sphere of technology, a particular national character. While individual pieces of technical knowledge may be globally available, the composite technology that is necessary to support and sustain a modern industry tends to be localized in specific countries, due to the fact that much of its supply originates with the on-going business activities. Although there is a continuous transformation of national technologies into world technology similar to the transformation of proprietary to nonproprietary technology, the two can never be the same.

To view technology as an internationally free good is to ignore the real nature of both proprietary and nonproprietary technology. Therefore, the notion of a globally homogeneous knowledge and technology horizon is absurd under existing world conditions.

Similarly, to assume away the numerous political divisions, notably the East-West and North-South struggles, is to divorce the explanations from the context of the contemporary world within which they exist. As Baldwin put it,

Today we frequently observe the phenomenon of an international firm weighing the alternatives of producing a particular commodity in one country and then shipping it to the market of another country or transferring technology and production factors to this latter country and manufacturing the product there. The possibility of various patterns of trade in intermediate inputs makes the set of feasible alternatives facing the international firm even more complex. . . . Recent events, especially in connection with the operation of international firms, have, however, made it increasingly inappropriate to ignore the interrelations between output and input flows. Trade theorists could in the past partly justify their position on the grounds that different decision-making units were usually involved in commodity and factor flows and that in the nineteenth century a large share of factor flows were directed at the production of noninternationally traded services, e.g., canal and railway services, or commodities effectively unavailable in the developed countries.[7]

This concession succinctly summarizes the basic flaw in economic theory which has long crippled analytical study at international gatherings of the economic-theoretical elites. It might mark the beginning of a more realistic and sophisticated theoretical treatment of transboundary economic relations than has been offered by the neoclassical formulation. If so, it would signify the start of a new era in economic thought.

Transfer of Natural Inputs and Technology

Professor Baldwin offers some valuable suggestions how the theory should be reconstructed to accommodate the multinational firm:

A useful starting point for a model of trade theory in outputs and inputs is the simple notion that a country's demand for a particular commodity can usually be met in any one of three ways: by producing the commodity entirely within the country from existing primary inputs; by importing the final product . . . ; or by importing some of the primary and intermediate inputs needed to produce them. The specific manner chosen to meet the demand depends not only on the relative costs among countries of producing commodities . . . , but upon the costs of transferring outputs and inputs (including knowledge) from one country to another. Trade theorists have traditionally stressed the transportation component of transfer costs. However, another very important part of transfer costs that economists recently have begun to emphasize are information costs. . . . Since technological knowledge is not usually freely transferable among countries, production functions are not assumed to be necessarily identical among countries in the model suggested here.[8]

Professor Baldwin goes on to point out that the market mechanism is usually rather inefficient. Patent leasing and other similar international arrangements have proven especially ineffective when the knowledge level in the recipient country is considerably lower, which prevents it from appreciating the full value of such transfers.

Thus, the more complex the technology to be transferred in relation to the level of technical skills in the recipient firm and the more rapid the flow of new products and productive methods from the more advanced country, *the more efficient it becomes for firms in the technically advanced country to transfer their knowledge by establishing foreign subsidiaries* [italics added]. The fact that much of the knowledge is specific to particular individuals, who acquire the value only as members of an integrated technical team, also reinforces the advantages of transferring knowledge through the international firm mechanism.[9]

To this should be added that far more important than specific individuals are the integrated groups, i.e., the companies as organizations that possess, generate, and utilize productive know-how, be it technical or managerial.

The multinational firm gains further comparative strength from two additional sources as countries advance economically. First, there is a tendency of branded and otherwise differentiated products to displace standardized commodities when incomes rise and demand diversifies. Second, there is a growing need for capital goods, which often have to be fitted to specific technical and economic requirements of the market where they are to be used. These tendencies favor the production of goods in the country of use; they also permit the multinational firm to capitalize on the particular experiences of any one of its affiliates by transferring whatever either is of universal applicability or meets a similar set of conditions to other production facilities. Hence, potential mass-production application is seldom excluded, even though the original product, process, or facility may have been designed to serve a limited one-nation market.

Transport Efficiency

Rapid advances in transportation and communication tend to reinforce the superior productive powers of the multinational firm. They are constantly reducing

the opportunity costs of sending highly paid technicians and managers abroad for short periods and thereby enabling the international firm to become *economically feasible with smaller productive units* [italics added]. . . . In recent years advances in production and managerial technology together with technological improvements in transportation and communications have greatly increased the potential technical labor.[10]

From the viewpoint of an individual firm there are two additional facts: (1) no country can ever possess a monopoly on technological know-how; (2) it is inconceivable that technology could become completely nonperishable. If not put to use within a certain time the economic value of any particular piece of know-how will evaporate as new superior knowledge and techniques displace it. While the generation of new knowledge has no geographic balance, it is nevertheless a global process. A firm that has access to a large number of the various national knowledge systems has gained an advantage over the one-country firm by the simple fact of being multinational. If such a firm in addition is an active participant in the search and generation of new know-how, as is typical for any modern multinational firm, its comparative production power is further magnified.

Product Innovation

Combined with the stimuli from its diverse and multifaceted demand, the resource and technological diversities embue the multinational company with a wide spectrum of new product opportunities. While the uninational firm is faced with a smaller number of stimuli for new product ideas and a finite number of potential competitors, whose actions it may, in some manner, be able to predict, the multinational firm is faced with a much larger potential array of new product opportunities, a larger array of potential markets into which to introduce new products, and a greater number and variety of competitors.

Product innovation usually takes place in the largest accessible market for that product. The largest accessible market does not have to be the most developed country. It depends on the incident of invention and on the characteristics of the product. Furthermore, product introductions do not always have to proceed from the direction of the more developed to the less developed countries. Witness, for example, the small automobile and the lightweight motorcycle, all developed first in countries somewhat less economically advanced than the United States. By knowing the characteristics of various national markets, we ought to be able to predict what kinds of new products ought to be coming forth from various countries. It has been hypothesized that because the United States is a large high-income market, and one in which labor costs are comparatively very high, it should be the prime innovator of high-income or labor-saving goods. Conversely, we should find that innovations dependent on other factors should come first from markets with other characteristics.

Head-start Companies

The head-start phenomenon helps to further elucidate the multinational production motivities of a firm. For a number of companies international expansion has been imposed by the fact that they invented a new product line for which there was no competitive substitute for a considerable period. Classic illustrations of such basic product inventions include German optics, Swiss watches, Swedish bearings, and Paris fashions. During the head-start period the initiators—be it a firm or an industry association such as a guild or cartel—can influence both cost and market factors so as to give it a superiority over any potential competitor. The cost advantage results mainly from the accumulation of proprietary technology during the lead period. As the pioneering enterprise makes improvements in production techniques and develops new machine tools to increase productivity, its cost curve keeps shifting downward, creating an increasing gap between the cost constraints of potential competitors and the firm itself. The market superiority for the head-start firm derives from its unique position as the inventor and sole supplier of the new product.

During the lead period the firm can decisively influence consumer concepts of the value and the utility of the product and create "in its own image" the qualities, preferences and loyalties that will form the pattern of the emerging market. It can in other words capture the new market not only as a supplier in the physical sense, but also as the architect of the value system that will govern and direct its growth.[11]

The more successful the head-start firm is in shaping the consumer values in the formative stages, the greater market superiority it will gain over any competitive challenger.

The head-start advantages, once achieved, compel the company to multinationalize its production capacity. "To preempt foreign markets before indigenous competition has emerged is an almost self-evident strategy."[12] Because of international trade barriers and market discontinuities, the firm can rarely do this through exporting, but needs local affiliates. By investing in the local operating affiliates, the head-start firm secures not only the optimal location for the control of the market and marketing channels, but also the indigenous resources strategic for successful manufacturing within the host economy. To put it in the negative, if the head-start firm did not capitalize on the foreign production opportunities before local competition emerged, it would have to concede to others the growth and earning potentials of these markets. In time, the resultant foreign competition could challenge the firm not only on the world market, but also on its home ground.[b] Consequently, the investment in multicountry production capacity becomes imperative for the head-start firm simply as a defensive strategy: to protect its production and marketing superiorities against foreign usurption. But this is to understate the point. No growth-oriented company would restrict its actions to self-preservation, but would actively use the head-start advantages for international expansion. "The dominance gained by the head start firms has a built-in tendency to flow across international boundaries either because of the centrifugal force that the very dominance itself generates or because of the pull of the vacuum abroad."[13] Once the multinational production structure is in existence, the inherent superiorities of this structure over a uninational one as discussed above will compound and ultimately supercede the head-start advantages.

Product Life Cycle

A slightly different explanation of the reasons for the rise of multinational production plants is offered by the product life-cycle theory. It hypothesizes that new products are born in high-technology, high-income countries, which are the only ones capable of either conceiving or initially consuming them. Therefore, the initial operation must be strictly domestic. As a product matures, its production techniques are perfected, production costs lowered, and its utilities become appreciated by consumers abroad, leading to profitable export operations. The deeper the exports penetrate another country's market, the more ripe it becomes for local productions as constraints for plant size are relaxed and import restrictions keep the outside supplier at a disadvantage. To prevent the local competition from taking over the export market, the initiator firm in the United States will have to build its own production plants in that country. Therefore, as the product moves along its life cycle, it will ultimately reach a point where multinationalization of its production will become inevitable. If the original producer fails to provide for this necessity, other firms will find it profitable to undertake the task. The process of multinationalization will proceed from the more-advanced to less-advanced countries until at an "old age" the bulk of production could originate in relatively backward countries.[14]

---

[b]An infamous example of such a failure was the Westinghouse Company's handling of its air-brake business. Enjoying enormous head-start advantages in the early years, the company was later seeking shelter behind U.S. tariffs as its failure to acquire multinational production facilities of its own left the field for European imitators.

Like the head-start phenomenon from which it has been deduced, the product life-cycle theory is totally inapplicable to nonmanufacturing sectors of multinational business. Thus, it supplies no explanation why either the raw material producers (mining, oil, forest products, and tropical plantation agriculture) or the service industries (transportation, banking, insurance, retailing, engineering, etc.) have been multinationalized. Can anything with such vast omissions be accredited as an acceptable general theory?

Even if limited to manufacturing industries, the product life-cycle concept serves better as an ex post facto rationalization of the initial multinationalization of some early runners than an explanation of the contemporary world enterprise. First, the theory is organization blind: it recognizes no differences as to capabilities and behavioral rationality between uninational and multinational corporate structures. It overlooks the greater capabilities of the multinational firm to integrate worldwide production and marketing operations and to plan its strategies in terms of worldwide demand patterns and factor availabilities; its multinational structure both presupposes and promotes geocentric perspective which seems unattainable for the multinational firm.

Second, the product life-cycle model denies innovative powers to the vast majority of nations; this is badly at odds with empirical evidence. One must also question the relevance of export phase not only to the thousands of firms which already are multinational, but also to the unaccountable new products that are born in a multinational structure and never in their commercial life enter either the uninational or the export stages of the product life-cycle theory.

While helpful in some respects, such hypothetical extrapolations can be misleading. A safer and more complete explanation can be found in factual studies.

Company Experience

Surveys of the multinational firms reveal that the existence of production affiliates in different countries has offered these companies a number of advantages which in their management's opinion they would not possess in the absence of the affiliates. They are:

1. Lower plant construction cost. By having choices of sites in several countries a given amount of capacity can often be acquired with less investment than in a one-country situation.
2. Lower wages and fringe benefits. Both these at cost elements vary from country to country.
3. Better quality control of adapted or customized products and those requiring in-person inspection and testing. The advantages here come partly from the separation of the customized product from its other versions and partly from the salary differential of high-caliber inspectors.

4. Availability of specialized skills such as designers, artisans, scientists, and other unusual and exceptional talents.
5. Easier-to-meet technical standards.
6. Easier adaption to local consumption requirements (taste, preferences, technical norms, safety, and other legal requirements).
7. Procurement economies: lower cost of primary and intermediary inputs.
8. Availability of special raw materials or other inputs.
9. Transportation economies: lower freight rates for raw material than finished goods, shorter haul, etc.
10. Multinational production smoothing. In the engineering and design of plant facilities there is a built-in tendency to stick to established systems and design parameters, i.e., to use in new branch factories what has been used in other facilities of the company before. This is to say, there is a resistance to designing unique plants or facilities. This counteracts the need for customizing processes and products to individual countries requirements.

But unlike multiunit domestic companies, the multinational companies' experience seems to indicate that this resistance is weakened considerably by the fact that the plants will be in different countries. The existence of a distinctly different operating environment apparently helps to break the engineers' apathy to risk new and different designs. More important, the existence of dissimilar production facilities is claimed to increase the company's ability to effectively meet fluctuating national conditions, enabling it to offset cutbacks in or with increases in another country more readily than is possible with standard designs. Thus, reallocation of both markets and plant facilities can become a normal part of long-range strategy of the firm.

Corporate Learning

The interactions of sourcing and marketing motivities generate a self-sustained transformation of corporate norms, attitudes, and practices after a firm has acquired a multinational scope in its plant and other operating organizations. The president of a firm that has been undergoing this transformation for the last several years said:

Originally it was quite simply because our major automotive customers rather strongly "suggested" that we establish manufacturing facilities in the various countries where they proposed to build trucks and cars in order to supply them with the same components that they are accustomed to obtaining from us in Detroit—but made by local labor from local materials.

Very soon, however, "these fledgling international plants acquired a life of their own." Due to the "economic facts of life" of a variety of markets, these plants had to develop new engineering, manufacturing and marketing capabilities with domestic know-how. "Today, our overseas operations are no longer 'carbon copies' of what we do in Cleveland or Detroit. We make components for Volkswagen and Ford, Fiat, Remington Rand and AEG in Europe, Australia and South America, that differ substantially from our U.S. products." No longer are the company's forty-seven international operations the "ugly stepsisters" who used to be a constant source of irritation at the domestic plants, with their never-ending requests for drawings, specifications and technical assistance. Now there is a constant exchange between our domestic and international plants, and many new ideas, techniques and products are finding their way back to the U.S. operations."[15]

4 Financial Motivities: Concepts and Causes

International differences in the field of finance are many. Interest rates, availability and cost of capital, taxes, and profits all vary from country to country; so do also rates of inflation and price structures, exchange rates, and monetary risks, including the freedom of transfer and use of funds. How the various financial variables motivate the multinational company is the purpose of this chapter.

Theory of Foreign Investments

The recent burgeoning of multinational enterprises has confounded the economic theory of investment. It used to be thought that international investments were nothing more than exports and imports of capital, not really distinguishable from international commodity flows. The reason for the capital flows was believed to be differences in rates of return in capital-importing and capital-exporting countries. Since currencies as such can rarely be shipped in any significant quantities from one country to another, the "normal" method for transboundary capital transfers was considered to be portfolio investments: capital exports representing payments made for the import of securities from a foreign country and, conversely, capital imports representing the payment received for domestic securities exported to a foreign country. Direct foreign investments were regarded as a special case where both the investor and investee companies belonged to the same ultimate owners. Otherwise they were believed to justify no differentiation from portfolio investments.

The validity of this theory was seriously challenged by the occurrence of cross-investments: Agfa investing in the U.S. at the same time as Kodak was investing in Germany, or British chemical industry establishing plants in Switzerland while Swiss chemical facilities were being built in Britain.

If it was the differences in rates of return that caused international capital flows, such simultaneous investments in opposite directions should not have occurred; yet they not only did occur, but have become commonplace in today's business. No longer can we shrug off such cross-investments as corporate excentricities, as we did in the 1930s and 1940s. There clearly is much more involved in international direct investments than the traditional theory postulates.

While the body politic of the economic orthodoxy is not yet ready to

45

concede this fact, the search for an entirely new theoretical framework has been already initiated. In one relatively recent view direct investment is the last stage in the product life cycle, which is applicable only to manufacturing companies, and probably not even to the entire manufacturing sector. We will return to it later when analyzing the empirical studies.

In another new version of the theory, the foreign investment is a form of gambling. The fact that multinational firms have shown a tendency to use a large share of their affiliate profits for expanding the affiliate's own capacity has been interpreted to mean that they start small foreign ventures with the hope of pyramiding them into large stakes, "much as a gambler leaves his winnings on the table."[1] Any firms that pursue the objective of growth, whether at home or abroad, would qualify for gambling classification in this overstretched meaning of the term.

Portfolio theory offers a third new hypothesis. It postulates that the ultimate source of direct investments is the saver whose welfare is increased "when more real investors compete for his funds with the attractive asset package to do so" than the domestic capital market alone can offer.[2] His welfare gain may result from either higher yields or lower perceived risks abroad than at home. Several recent papers support this hypothesis. In one, Grubel constructed a two-country model to demonstrate that international diversification of portfolios reduces risk measured as the variance of the whole diversified portfolio; the model assumed for both countries independent public policies and saver's preferences, which were defined as a function of expected yield and perceived standard deviation.[3] In another paper Levy and Sarnat present data to show that saver's gains, in terms of higher mean rates of return and/or lower standard deviations of optimal portfolios, can be achieved by internationalizing a purely domestically diversified portfolio.[4] This model assumes that the variance of yields is greater among countries than it is within any one country. Whether or not any factual correlation exists between the postulated saver's gains from international portfolio diversification and the actual supply of direct foreign investment remains to be demonstrated.

However, two potentially significant implications arise if the findings of these studies are to be applied to the multinational firm. One is that to the extent the firm can experience a reduction of risk through wider international diversification of its operations it can offset anticipated lower rates of return on specific projects. In this sense, the multinational firm could benefit from investments which, for the uninational firm, are clearly uneconomic.[5] Second, the securities of the multinational firm should be more attractive to the saver than those of a like domestic company. Thus, indirectly at least, the supply of capital available to the multinational companies appears to be stimulated by the saver's surplus derived from portfolio diversification.

Still another thesis to explain the multinationalization of business has been advanced by Stephen Hymer and subsequently endorsed by some other recent writers on the subject. They hold that the primary determinant for direct investment is *monopoly power*, and that therefore it is not investment theory but the theory of monopolistic competition that explains the growth of multinational business. This argument rests on the so-called domestic advantage doctrine: the dubious assumption that it is inherently less costly and more efficient to operate domestic operating units of a firm than foreign-based ones. Therefore, a firm is postulated to invest abroad only if it can extract from the host country a monopolistic profit—defined as an excess over the factor returns of a competitive firm—which exceeds the extra cost of foreign operations. Thus, the multinational firm is portrayed as being ipso facto a perpetrator of monopolistic exploitation—a detestable antisocial abnormality. By implication, uninational firms are profitless, earning only competitive factor returns.

Put in a factual context this argument boomerangs. First, evidence against the assertion that foreign units are less efficient and costlier to operate is too massive to make it even plausible. The weight of the evidence is on the other side. Any financial reports, management case studies, and industry surveys show the foreign affiliates to be lower-cost operations far more often than not.

Second, neither evidence nor logic lends credence to the proposition that uninational companies could be regarded as less inclined to cultivate monopolistic advantages than multinational companies. Any firm that invests in any operating facility does so with the sure conviction that it has gained or will gain an advantage over other firms, i.e., that it will make a profit. That sometimes the anticipated profits may later turn out to be only quasi-rents for the head-start period (excess over a perfectly competitive firm's factor returns until other firms enter the field) is beside the point. At the time of the investment decision, the managerial conviction of a competitive (monopolistic) advantage is a necessary precondition without which no investment will be made. Hence, all plant investments in a free society presuppose the perception by management of a competitive advantage. If one chooses to call this monopoly power, then all investments depend upon it, be they domestic or foreign. To say that direct foreign investments depend on the perception of a competitive advantage by the investor, but leave it unsaid that the same is true about domestic direct investments, is to imply that such an advantage is something clandestine and peculiar to international investments only.

Neither experience nor reason support the proposition that international direct investors are or have to be more irresponsible or less guided by generally accepted decision criteria than domestic investors. A study of the actual record suggests that, due to a relatively greater ignorance about foreign opportunities, companies have generally been less aggressive in seeking out and utilizing foreign investment opportunities than domestic ones. To compensate for the greater possibility of error due to the ignorance, they have typically required a greater or more clearcut competitive advantage from any proposed foreign investment project than for its domestic alternatives, that is, greater return to offset greater perceived risk. Apparently, this difference in the degree of competitive superiority has been mistaken by some economists as a difference in kind.[a] Based on this misconception, the native advantage doctrine fades into unreality and ends up with conclusions completely antithetical to the factual record.

In the contemporary world the direct investing firm is not the old colonial company who was endowed by the colonizing country's government with political powers that were often used to exploit the subjugated people. Though misguided attempts to emulate the colonial tycoons still occur they are now an exception rather than the rule, and should not be confused with the inherent characteristics of the modern multinational firms. The direct foreign investors today are mostly the modern multinational companies or the uninational firms first embarking upon international expansion and using international investments as means of conversion to a multinational structure. Both of the latter are dependent on the host country government for legal sanction to any investment project they contemplate, and neither possesses the power to pursue its interests through political, not to mention military, means. Failure to realize the distinction between the old-time colonial company and the modern multinational company imbues the issue of direct foreign investments with righteous overtones of political morality which are wholly misplaced.

The record of recent business history has been pointing with a growing clarity to the fact that the most significant and lasting advantages of the contemporary direct investing firms is the achievement of a multinational operating system, more than any preexisting advantage such as a patent, trademark, or the like. Preferred treatment promised by the host government (tariff protection, tax holiday, industrial development assistance, etc.) can be decisive for certain specific decisions, especially from a short-run perspective. But in the longer run, the decisive advantage of the multinational direct investing firm arises from what we have termed the operational motivities in this study, namely the simultaneous operational capability in many different national environments: drawing its sourcing inputs from the multiple resource endowments of many countries, all as part of one coordinated enterprise; selling in a multitude of different markets, and utilizing the economic and social changes of different countries to minimize external hazards to the welfare of the firm. To put it differently, the multinational capability structure creates an internal economics—which harbors the superior powers of the contemporary direct foreign investor over its uninational counterparts. This superiority is not something accidental or clandestine as the advocates of the national advantage doctrine would seem to believe, but an intrinsic property of the multinational firm as such.[b]

---

[a]Some study of financial decision-making processes and criteria would help to further elucidate this point for readers who are unfamiliar with them.

[b]Being a natural rather than artificial or contrived superiority, it cannot be eliminated without eliminating its source: the multinational structure. Whether or not any nationalistic or other ideological values are worth the price of deliberate denial to the world society of the greater productivity of the multinational enterprise will be the subject for later discussion.

The notion of a "native advantage" which the monopoly theorists propagate makes no distinction between the multinational and uninational structure, but visualizes business firms as organizationally sterile and institutionally indifferent machines processing internationally homogenized factor inputs into undifferentiated goods that are globally consumable. All of this is totally unreal, and simplistic to the point of parody.

Empirical Findings

Two major studies have been conducted of why United States firms have invested overseas, the first in 1966 by the Conference Board[6] and a government study published in 1972.[7] In the Conference Board study, 100 companies filed questionnaires, representing one-sixth of total U.S. foreign direct investment. One of the main findings was that overseas production is the normal response to demand growth, given the obstacles to product movement across national boundaries. Strong support was found for the "barriers to trade" theory of foreign direct investment, and for the importance of government incentives. In addition, the "defensive" nature of foreign investment was stressed by many companies, with stemming the domestic loss from foreign imports, or from foreign investment in the domestic company's home country, being the main reason why the investment was undertaken. In this case, lower overhead and labor costs were frequently cited for the move overseas, and the alternative of increasing exports was ruled out because the foreign competitor is likely to have the advantage in his home market. Companies repeatedly stressed that competitive pressures in the relevant market were resulting in declining exports at the time direct investment was undertaken.

Most executives interviewed in the study stressed the basic complementariness of domestic and foreign investment. Exporting was not in general seen as a substitute for overseas production, and the ability to make such a substitution was seen as becoming increasingly more difficult. (The impossibility of exporting what is now manufactured overseas should be very apparent when one considers that for the United States, overseas production is greater than export volume in all general categories except nonelectrical machinery.) Furthermore, the desire to export (including third-country exporting) was itself a major determinant in the decision to undertake foreign investment for 35 percent of the companies interviewed. The fact that there are no acceptable substitutes produced in the United States for much U.S. production abroad (service industries, utilities, and extractive industries are examples) makes the substitutability premise even more untenable.

A distinction must be made between the reasons why a company invests overseas in the first place and the motivation for subsequent investment. In making initial investments, the main determinant was the level of potential demand in the prospective countries. The faster-growing markets characterized by higher levels of domestic investment and income were also those which attracted most U.S. investment. Despite the fact that higher rates of return were often available in many of the less-developed countries, the growth of foreign investment was much higher in the developed countries.

With regard to investments made subsequent to the initial investment, the Conference Board study showed that businessmen view further investment in terms of contribution to the entire earning position in the foreign market, and not in marginal terms. Most executives expressed the view that new investment capital is "not readily distinguishable" from improvement or modernization capital, and that capital is free to move to high-rate areas only within the constraints of maintaining the company's existing position. The overriding concern for most companies is development and maintenance of market share, with many executives expressing the view that if sales are increased, increased profits will follow as a matter of course. The overall emphasis on staying competitive in the relevant foreign markets was extremely strong for almost all of the companies interviewed. The orientation of investment toward this end was termed the "organic" approach by the authors of the study, and its adoption by most multinational companies is in clear contrast to the "incremental" view of foreign direct investment theorized by many writers on the subject.

The findings of the Commerce Department studies back up the conclusions of the Conference Board study in many ways. That investment in the United States is not a substitute for U.S. foreign investment is clearly seen in both reports, for instance. Similarly, the predominant marketing orientation of multinational corporations is borne out in the Commerce Department studies, although some differences are apparent in the conclusion of each individual study. In the second study, the authors state that "most U.S. foreign direct investments are defensive in the sense that the investor is trying to maintain his place in the world market." Tariffs and cost differentials are the main "apparent causes" of multinationals going overseas. The conclusions of the third study are somewhat different: its authors believe that the fundamental force impelling corporations to invest abroad is the quest for profit. However, no real evidence is given to support this statement, and the study seems to equate profitability with competitive position in the market. The general truth of the "organic" theory of investment is acknowledged in the discussion, but a more aggressive attitude is attributed to investors than in the Conference Board study. Explicit support is also given in the second study to Vernon's product life-cycle theory, and in fact the study goes somewhat further in developing an "industry life-cycle" concept. Foreign investment is thereby seen as extending the useful life of technologies beyond the time when exports, due to cost considerations, would no longer be competitive. The industry life-cycle concept is illustrated in Figure 4-1.

Case studies of individual companies and two industries are offered in support of this thesis. The evidence is too sketchy and strained to be fully convincing. Hopefully, further studies will help to clarify this matter.

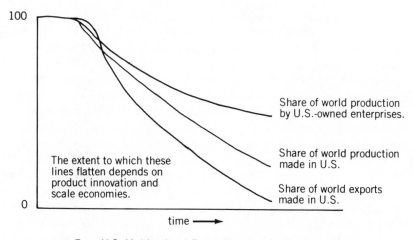

100

The extent to which these
lines flatten depends on
product innovation and
scale economies.

0

time ——▶

Share of world production
by U.S.-owned enterprises.

Share of world production
made in U.S.

Share of world exports
made in U.S.

From U.S. Multinational Enterprises and the U.S.
Economy, (U.S. Department of Commerce, 1972)

Figure 4-1. Industry Life Cycle

Marketing Focus. It is becoming increasingly important, from a competitive point of view, for corporations to establish a strong initial foothold in foreign markets if they wish to maintain or build their market positions, and this requires direct investment as early as possible once the market potential has become apparent. Indeed, the Conference Board study pointed out that foreign investment is often made prior to any immediate economic justification for it, because the companies concerned wanted to get into the market first and foremost, and progressively build up their investments later on if the potential materialized. The most important realization that should emerge from the two studies is that multinational corporations operate overseas to satisfy market demand, and they can only do this satisfactorily by producing overseas: to rely on exports would be to sentence the corporation to a minute share of the market. It is this aspect of the multinational corporation—that its market opportunities are matched by its operating capabilities—that enables it to succeed on a global basis. When one realizes that even the U.S. oil companies market over 90 percent of their overseas production abroad, the failure to realize the distinction between the old-time colonial company and the modern multinational company seems an unfortunate error.

The overriding marketing focus of U.S. foreign investors seems to deemphasize rate of return as a criterion for investment, a conclusion that is also evidenced by the apparent flow of investment capital into areas that do not yield the greatest return. The aggregate figures that are generally used in pointing up this fact can be misleading, however. For instance, average yields on investment in less-developed countires were "roughly twice those in developed countries," by the Commerce Department estimates.[8] The difference was due primarily to the oil industry: its average yield was 33.1 percent in 1970 for less-developed countries and 4.8 percent in developed countries. The high yield in the less-developed countries has been a result primarily of pricing agreements between the oil companies and the host governments, and the desire of oil companies to take most of their profits at the wellhead. When oil companies are excluded from the analysis the differential is much smaller. Average manufacturing yields were 12.3 percent in less-developed countries and 12 percent in developed countries. It is likely, therefore, although not conclusive, that rate of return does play an important role in channeling overseas investment funds. Nevertheless, wide variations exist in individual investment returns for companies, and it is possible that many corporations have overestimated the potential return on their foreign investments. The cutbacks and liquidations effected by some multinational corporations overseas in the past few years seem to bear this point out. In theoretical terms, any investment made to preserve an existing market position may involve an assessment of incremental return by estimating the amount of profits that would be lost if the particular investment was not undertaken, but there is little evidence that most multinational corporations do this at present. Finally, it may be noted that many large multinational corporations are just not interested in making small investments overseas, and concentrate instead on the big markets, so that profit levels as well as rates are an important factor.

5

Financial Motivities: Managerial Environment

All economic-theoretical attempts to explain the phenomenon of the multinational firm conceive it as an exclusive creature of direct international investment: the firm internationalizes its assets by transferring capital from the headquarter's country to the various host countries. Thus the internationalization process requires, or is supposed to be preceded by, international capital flows that are equivalent to the subsequent capitalization of the foreign-based affiliates. While the various theories differ as to what causes the firm to set in motion these international capital flows, they all hold such flows fundamental for the emergence and growth of the multinational firm. To what extent is this premise fulfilled by corporate experience? Is the multinational firm a creature of international capital transfers? Do its affiliates depend on their growth on the headquarters company's outbound direct investments? What incentives and impediments circumscribe rational decisions in multinational financial management? To what extent? When and why do the managerial behavior differ from economic-theoretical precepts? These and similar questions are at the core of the present chapter.

Funding of Investments in Foreign-Based Affiliates

A multinational firm can develop at least three different financial paths. First, a company could transfer all the funds to be invested from outside to the host country to establish an affiliate; this, however, has happened seldom. Second, it may transfer only a part, often just a small fraction, of the intended investment, while the rest will come from local borrowing and/or from the profits of the affiliate itself. This has been by far the predominant method. Third, the direct investing firm may completely avoid international capital transfer, instead utilizing the capital resources of the host country exclusively. Business firms have shown an increasing propensity to follow this last course, accomplishing their direct investment without any international capital movements whatsoever. The local sourcing of the investment capital has come less frequently from stock sales than from borrowing, reinvesting of affiliate profits, and more recently from the earnings of licensing operations set up specifically for the purpose of generating capital with which to start an affiliate in the country involved.

An illustrative pattern of financing an affiliate's growth is illustrated by Table 5-1, which is based on data of an actual case.

Table 5-1
Sourcing Pattern of Investment Capital for Foreign-based Affiliate

Stage	Existing Investment	Capital In	Transfers Out	Profits	Local Borrowing	New Investments	Operational Capabilities
1	0	100	0	0	0	100	None
2	100	0	0	20	30	50	Sales
3	150	0	0	30	50	80	Sales & Warehousing
4	230	0	0	50	70	120	Sales Warehousing Service Shops
5	350	0	20	70	70	120	Sales Warehousing Service Shops Assembly
6	470	0	40	90	70	120	Sales Warehousing Service Shops Assembly Partial Mfg.
7	590	0	80	120	80	120	Sales Warehousing Service Shops Assembly Partial Mfg.

At the end of stage seven this company possessed an investment that was 590 percent of its original transfer of capital. In addition, the affiliate had engendered return transfers equal to 120 percent of the original in transfer. And if the market is large enough, the affiliate could continue growing with no additional in-transfer of funds. This pattern hardly suggests any identity between international capital flows and the growth of direct foreign-based business affiliates. Had this company raised the original 100 through licensing or simply banking its export proceeds in the host country, there would have been no out-transfer of capital whatsoever connected with the birth and expansion of the affiliate. While still uncommon, such cases are no longer rare.

Aggregate Analysis

Aggregate statistics show (on a log scale) an approximately parallel trend line between the book value of U.S. overseas affiliates and gross outflows of new capital, as can be seen in Figure 5-1. However, except in 1957, there was a net financial inflow (inflows from earnings less outflows) in every year during the 1950-70 period, while book value increased at the same time in every year. Thus,

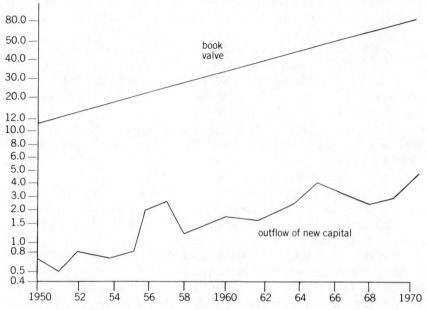

Figure 5-1. Capital Outflow and Book Value of Foreign Affiliates

in net aggregate terms, the increase in the book value of U.S. foreign direct investment has been financed completely through earnings. Furthermore, book value underestimates the increase in gross assets of affiliates financed by other than U.S. capital outflows, since it measures only the increase in equity.

The Conference Board Study shows that most U.S. companies do not think in terms of "company-owned funds" and funds borrowed on the "outside," but rather in terms of U.S. capital against locally generated capital (earnings plus local loans). Highly liquid companies were as exacting as others in judging the essentiality of sending U.S. funds abroad. The need to borrow abroad was not a deterrent to investment, although more reluctance was shown to borrow long-term than short-term (probably because long-term borrowing abroad has generally required parent guarantees). Most companies desired some local financing, and unavailability in certain countries was a deterrent to investments considered marginal. The company's position in the U.S. market had a substantial influence on the resources it employed in serving foreign markets: most small firms had capital constraints which necessitated the use of "seed money" or licensing operations as their initial investment, with the profits used for subsequent expansion. New international companies were found to prefer parent loans to equity contributions, in the belief that interest and principal would be easier to repatriate than dividends, and that a fixed repayment schedule would offer more incentive to the subsidiary to produce. Undercapitalization was a common problem among such companies, and among other things, led to an impaired ability to borrow locally. Government pressures often prevented companies from relying too heavily on local loan capital.

An arbitrary influence on the funding of U.S. direct investment overseas has been the capital controls programs of the United States government. U.S. companies first became active in the Eurobond market in 1965, with the imposition of the Voluntary Foreign Direct Investment Program. When the controls became mandatory in 1968, the amount raised in the market by U.S. companies rose to $2.1 billion in that year, compared with $1.2 billion for the previous three years (1965-67) combined. The slight easing of controls in April 1969, and again in 1970, was a factor in the somewhat reduced U.S. borrowing in the market after 1968.

Some distinction is apparent between investments in developed countries and investments in less-developed countries in the financing methods used by multinationals. Companies surveyed in the Conference Board study generally required more local capital for investments in politically or economically unstable areas. However, the ratio of capital transfers to total equity funds (capital transfers plus reinvested earnings) used in investment is slightly higher for the less-developed countries, dispelling the often-held notion that multinationals rely mainly on reinvested profits in their investments in less-developed countries.

In summary, it is clear that direct investment overseas is not always accompanied by a capital outflow from the parent company equivalent to the amount of the investment: some proportion of the investment is invariably financed by local capital. The amount of local capital obtained depends upon several factors, including its availability in the host country, the size of the investing corporation, government regulations and pressures, and corporate attitudes. In addition, financial structure norms regarding appropriate debt-equity ratios vary considerably between countries. Considerable ingenuity has been shown by U.S. firms in overcoming the controls program on foreign direct investment in the United States, and in some cases investments have been financed with no capital outflow whatsoever. Most large multinational corporations, however, have adopted "balanced" financial structures for their overseas affiliates, in the belief that this will best serve their long-run interests, by minimizing conflict with the governments and other organizations with which they must deal.

Specific Financial Advantages of
The Multinational Firm

"Many European industrialists feel that affiliates of the multinational enterprise have an 'unfair' advantage in financing. The advantage comes from the financial power of the parent, the high earnings of the affiliates, the ability to transfer funds among affiliates of the enterprise, and the greater ability to sap the internal and external financial resources."[1] The quote provides a succinct assessment of not only the European subsidiaries of American firms, but the affiliates of multinational firms anywhere. In what ensues, the purpose is to provide systematic elaboration and analytical validation of the inherent financial specifics which the multinational company enjoys.

Even more basic than cost of capital is the availability of it. Be it investments in new capacity or satisfying the needs for working capital, availability constitutes the absolute parameters for managerial choice. The cost of capital can act only within the limits of these parameters in motivating managerial action.

Host Country Capital Markets. The importance of international capital markets for multinational firms has grown significantly over the past few years, as is indicated in Table 5-2.

As one author states: "Multinational corporate borrowers in the Eurobond market have a distinct advantage over other types of borrowers, because they have more flexibility in tailoring the terms of their new issues to current investor needs. The relative freedom of choice of currency or artificial currency constructs in which securities can be denominated is particularly important."[2] Eurocurrency financing allows the multinational company to spread risks across

Table 5-2
Corporate Issues in the Eurobond Market (Figures are in Millions of Dollar Equivalents)

| Year | All Total Eurobond Issues | Corporate Issues | | | | |
| | | U.S. | | Non-U.S. | | |
		Amount	% of Total	Amount	% of Corporate	Amount	% of Corporate
1963	150	10	7				
1964	650	130	20				
1965	1,050	790	75	360	46	430	54
1966	1,150	940	82	450	48	490	52
1967	2,000	1,580	79	560	35	1,020	65
1968	3,700	3,160	85	2,170	69	990	31
1969[a]	3,000	2,360	79	1,050	44	1,310	56

[a]Preliminary figures.

Source: Adapted from tables appearing in Robert Stobaugh, "Financing Foreign Subsidiaries of U.S.-Controled Multinational Enterprises," *Journal of International Business Studies*, Summer 1970, pp. 78-81.

several currencies, banks, and countries, and results in a better protection of capital: in addition it provides a ready alternative when restrictions are placed on borrowing in local capital markets.

More recently, some companies have begun to issue equities in the Eurocapital market, a trend that some observers believe will grow significantly in the future since, as one author states, "Development of an equity market will widen the number of issuers to include either smaller or under-capitalized companies . . . where a debt instrument would not be sufficiently satisfactory to investors but where an equity opportunity would be attractive."[3] In view of current developments, Saltzman also expects significant growth in short- and medium-term private placements in the market; increased sophistication in the various instruments used, and a growing use of offshore equity issues for overseas holding companies of U.S. multinationals. A number of multinational corporations already have their stock listed on several exchanges, among which are Exxon, ITT, ATT, Ford, General Motors, Royal Dutch Petroleum, Du Pont, Eastman Kodak, IBM, Philips, General Electric, Goodyear, and many others. As the next stage several companies have announced their intention to float new issues of stock in their European host countries, with the apparent double objective of raising capital and multinationalizing ownership of the firm.

Host Country Money Markets. In addition to the overseas capital markets, multinational corporations can take advantage of foreign money markets. The tremendous growth of international banking over the past decade has been in part a response to the parallel growth of multinational corporate activities. Since the overseas branches of United States banks have been the main repositories of Eurodollar holdings (which are now estimated at over $70 billion), and as the main function of these branches has been to serve United States overseas affiliates, these affiliates have had first access to sizable funds. Moreover, other credit instruments have become available to these affiliates. The recent use of "finance bills" in the London discount market has enabled some corporations to finance working capital in this manner, as well as to obtain additional needed credit in periods of monetary restraint, when bank overdrafts are limited. Large multinational companies have an advantage in the market because credit extension is closely matched to the overall credit standing of the company. The introduction of Euro-commercial paper has created another dimension in the financing capabilities of multinationals:[4] again the nature of the market gives the large multinational corporations a distinct advantage. The great extent to which U.S. multinational corporations have utilized the diversity of funds sources available to them is shown in Table 5-3.

In a study of United States multinational corporations, Stobaugh found that corporate size and other variables influenced financing patterns employed. Small multinationals (with "typical" foreign sales of about $50 million, representing approximately 18 percent of total sales, and manufacturing affiliates in eight

Table 5-3
Sources of Funds for U.S.-owned Foreign Manufacturing Affiliates

Percent of Total Sources			
Retained earnings	20.5	14.9	19.8
Depreciation and depletion	28.7	28.6	38.9
Funds from U.S.	11.8	22.2	4.4
Funds obtained abroad:			
from foreign affiliates	1.6	3.1	1.4
from financial institutions	9.4	15.3	6.5
other foreign liabilities	21.1	10.3	23.5
Issue of equity securities	5.2	.0	2.8
Other sources and adjustments	1.7	5.6	2.7
TOTAL	100.0	100.0	100.0

Source: *Survey of Current Business*, November 1971, and the 1966 Department of Commerce Census (*U.S. Direct Investments Abroad 1966*).

foreign countries) tended to view each subsidiary as an independent operation and made little attempt to take the overall system into account into its financing decisions.[5] In comparison with "large" and "medium" multinationals, the small companies were more likely to rely on retained earnings and local borrowings, and were less likely to use decision rules (as in determining the amount of parent equity contribution). With respect to raising funds, the small multinationals generally used relatively few sources, relying mainly on banks, even though the use of nonbank sources by some of these firms suggests that these sources are potentially available.

The central characteristic of medium multinationals (which typically had foreign sales of $200 million, representing 29 percent of total sales, and manufacturing affiliates in fourteen countries) was the "system optimization viewpoint of its central staff." Compared with small and large multinationals, the medium-sized firm was more willing to use parent funds when local long-term funds were not available, or when local borrowing was restricted by credit squeezes. The desire to maintain close control over the system, however, made the medium-sized firms less likely than the others to use intercompany accounts to transfer funds, even though this would seem to be suboptimal for system performance.

The large multinationals (typically with $1 billion in foreign sales, representing 30 percent of total sales, and manufacturing affiliates in twenty-one countries) were too complex to implement rigid system optimization rules, and generally relied on detailed "guidelines" with actual decisions within the guidelines left to local management; so that the strategy of the company was somewhere in between that of the total decentralization of small companies and the high centralization of medium-sized companies. A general guideline used by most large multinationals was to provide equity equal to fixed assets, giving subsidiaries a strong independent borrowing base, and allowing flexibility in meeting various future financing needs. Large multinationals were further observed to use a wide variety of financial sources, and were much more likely than the other multinationals to obtain funds from local nonbanking sources, and by issuing bonds in the local capital markets and in the Eurocapital markets.

Other variables which were found by Stobaugh to influence the financial behavior of multinationals were the percentage of subsidiaries wholly owned by the firm, and the technology level (as measured by expenditures on research and development as a percentage of sales revenue). Firms with mostly wholly owned subsidiaries were more willing than those which operated mainly through joint ventures (other things equal) to use parent funds or guarantees on local debt, and to use intercompany accounts for funds transfers. High-technology firms, compared with low-technology firms of the same size and affiliate structure, were more likely to borrow locally regardless of interest rates, and to use nonbank sources of financing. Lesser use of intercompany accounts was also a feature of such firms.

Financial Sourcing Superiority of
the Multinational Firm

Perceiving the financing capabilities of multinational corporations in their vital role as reinforcing the firm's operating abilities enables us to appreciate the real advantage of a multinational corporation over its uninational competitors—the ability to transfer funds internally between affiliates. Both short-term and long-term funds can be readily mobilized by multinationals and sent to where they are most needed. Just as the multinational firm can maintain a high level of overall capacity utilization by diverting production to a plant affected by a temporary falling off in its domestic market (which a uninational firm cannot do), so it can maintain a high level of funds utilization by generating funds in one country and deploying them in another.

Access to many external capital markets is an obvious advantage of a multinational company. Each country offers another reservoir. What is less obvious is the internal financial capacities of the multinational firm. First, as a multiunit and multienvironment system, it can not only source its capital needs simultaneously from all countries, but can also raise more capital than any collection of separate national companies of equal size. This is possible because as an internationally integrated organization the multinational company can outbargain the nationally segregated financial institutions of the different capital markets. That is to say, the multinational firm's credit worthiness in any particular country is not limited to its holdings of assets in that particular country, but is magnified, often multifold, by its ownership of assets in other countries: in addition to its holdings in the host country, the multinational firm can influence the lender, and if required, can pledge as collateral of its assets elsewhere. From this each affiliate of the multinational firm derives the capacity to qualify for a larger loan or other capital contribution than is possible for an uninational competitor, whose total assets may be identical to those of the local affiliates.

"Foreign affiliates are thought to have a competitive advantage in being able to tap local banks more readily and at lower costs than domestic borrowers. . . . Affiliates have obtained substantial lines of credit at commercial banks, and large American companies have been able to borrow in Eurodollar market more readily and cheaply than competing European companies."[6]

Would this not limit the latter's borrowing power in other countries? Only if formal instruments of collateral security have been executed and if laws of all countries regulating financial transactions involved have more or less identical provisions. Neither is often the case. Lenders to major corporate ventures are typically more concerned with the total asset portfolio, cash flows, and competitive status of the company than with pairing specific assets of the company with specific credits. Also, the regulatory stipulations vary widely from country to country, leaving ample opportunities to shrewd financial planners to use their residency in the country and their overall corporate size as a simultaneous leverage in many countries. Therefore, the multinational firm can normally outborrow its uninational rivals in most, if not all, the countries where it has affiliates.

Cost and Profitability of Capital

The conventional cost of capital analysis deals with two factors: the rate required by the source, and the cost of raising the capital. The sum of these two is equal to the cost of capital. If there are several alternative sources, the least sum will indicate the best source. This analysis rests on the assumption that the sourcing and using of capital are wholly independent from each other. Capital from any source is considered equally suitable for whatever business venture is contemplated. Therefore, only the two types of capital acquisition costs (rate and raising) are considered.

For international investment analysis the conventional cost of capital concept needs to be broadened. While the sourcing and using of capital in some international projects may be unrelated, for many they are interdependent or even inseparable: either the source is country specific, excluding transfers to other areas and thus limiting use in the source country only; or it is both country and project specific use, requiring the capital to be invested in a specified manner in the source country.

National Investment Incentive Policies. Nearly all countries of the world have governmental policies to officially guide and influence investment trends. For inward foreign investments, which many countries seek as sources of economic growth but at the same time fear as subversive to local control, the governmental involvement is particularly decisive. Most countries have highly structured programs with concrete incentive scales and directives which may govern both the types and regional distribution of new investments in addition to their total volume.

Typically, the investment incentive programs take the form of governmentally guaranteed low-interest loans, direct contributions to equity capital, accelerated depreciation and write-off privileges, contributions and/or allowances for research and development, preferential tax treatment including tax holidays for a given number of years, guarantees for foreign exchange allocations, exemptions from capital transfer restrictions including profit repatriation, and long-term governmental purchase agreements to assure a market for the new investment.

Such policies and programs affect the profitability of all multinational investments. First there is a geographic or horizontal effect. The national investment programs tend to change the comparative advantage pattern by erecting a superstructure of international differences upon the normal economic factors. In addition to relative profitabilities they also affect the ease of entrance for new inward investments. The redistributive effect of this superstructure upon multinational investments becomes particularly pronounced when it reinforces the underlying comparative advantages of the countries involved.

Second, there is a sectoral or vertical effect. Within each host nation the existence of investment policies tends to increase the anticipated returns in the officially preferred industries. The increase varies according to the priority scale of that nation; if the scale has multiple gradients, the profitability expectations will tend to reflect a similar pattern. In the nonpreferred sectors, the level of anticipated return from a particular investment may remain unchanged in absolute terms, but will be negatively affected relative to the profitability of investments in the preferred sectors. For example, an 8 percent return which in the absence of governmental investment incentives compares favorably with other investment opportunities in a country will look questionable if, due to the official incentives, the return expectations in certain other investments have risen to something substantially higher, say 12 or 15 percent.

Not all national priority scales are based on vertical sectors of the economy. Quite often they specify a number of features which, if present, may qualify an investment project for preferential classification. Use of locally manufactured inputs, importation of new technologies, development of managerial expertise and industrial labor skills, contribution to foreign exchange earnings, and infrastructural development are among the typical nonsectoral specifications for preference-rated investment projects.

Although the national policies and programs have in the past emphasized primarily inward foreign investment, they are no longer so restricted. Outward investments and other transboundary capital transfers have also been brought under governmental surveillance in a growing number of countries. Increasingly, these controls take the form of taxes, fees, or other requirements involving economic sacrifices that put them in the category of cost and profit factors for international investments. Traditional "go or no go" type of government licensing, without a "price," is no longer the rule.

Pluralism of Multinational
Financial Environment

The investment incentive policies represent but outcroppings of general differences among national financial environments. Each country has its self-contained national monetary systems with its attendant financial apparatus. More than any other aspect of economic life, the monetary system in all countries is endowed with exclusive national authority and direct governmental functions.

The unique significance attached to a country's currency and monetary system is vividly underscored by the fact that among a score of international integration schemes around the globe none has shown readiness to replace the independent national monetary systems with a supranational monetary system. Even in the European Economic Community, where trade, agriculture, and to a substantial degree the labor market have been integrated since 1958, the national monetary systems of the member states have yielded very slowly to supranational coordination, not to mention unification.

The interties among the national financial systems are incomparably weaker and more unstable than the internal financial institutions and processes within any country. Separately each nation's financial environment may offer a high degree of consistency and uniformity. But taken together they reflect international inconsistency and multiversity which render the multinational financial environment for business highly pluralistic or even compartmentalized both in structure and dynamics. Such compartmentalization is never encountered in a one-country context. As a result the considerations of financial policy, cost of money, profitability of investments and divestments, as well as cash management all take new and different aspects in a multinational firm. Conventional assumptions and conceptualizations, therefore, are inadequate and can be actually misleading for analyzing the multinational financial realities.

Interest Rates

Each country has its own structure and level of interest rates, which seldom bears any definite relationship to the interest rates in other countries. Rate-making processes, and even the factors influencing the processes, also vary internationally. Besides differences in their natural and human resources, countries differ vastly as to their political and economic systems. Here, too, the conventional prototypes of capitalism, socialism, and communism have been outdated by actual developments. Though it would still be correct in some sense to delineate the range of existing economic systems by putting capitalism and communism on the opposite polar positions and everything else between them in a linear array, such thinking would conceal and confuse much more than it revealed about the inner workings of any particular national economic system. An increasing number of parallel intermediate models have come into being, such as Japanese, Swedish, French, Yugoslav, and Israeli, which defy any unidimensional categorization. At the same time, the polar position countries— the U.S. as the archetype for capitalism and the U.S.S.R. for communism—have themselves diverged radically from their respective theoretical models.

It is, therefore, a dangerous fallacy to expect that the levels and movements of interest rates can be explained in all countries by traditional supply-and-demand analysis. Even in the so-called market economies, roughly equivalent to noncommunist countries, the determination of interest rates, including the rates of return on investments, has been subject to an increasing number of sociopolitical inputs. In other words, the influence of nonmarket factors on the money and capital markets are everywhere present. What varies is the nature of the noneconomic factors and the degree of socialization of the rate-making processes. Each country has its own.

As a consequence, each contemporary nation has not only its own interest-rate structure but also its own interest-rate dynamics; that is, changes in interest rates over time tend to proceed along separate paths in different countries. Thus, the internal financial environment in almost any country undergoes changes in relative disregard to other countries. From the multinational point of view the separate national systems create a global pattern of constantly shifting surfaces as to the cost of capital and the rates of return. These shifting surfaces underlie all financial operations of the multinational firm, creating both problems and possibilities nonexistent for a uninational company.

The analysis to this point yields an important generalization: namely, that due to differences in national financial environments both the cost of capital (international sense) and the profitability of capital vary internationally. Since the two are often linked it is useful to broaden the cost of capital analysis to include costs not only of acquisition but also of utilization. Both bear directly upon the profitability of the multinational investor. While money may be raised more cheaply in country A than in countries B or C, this advantage may be either reinforced or reversed by the official incentives (like tariff protection or tax holiday) and impediments (like higher taxes, required profit distribution, etc.).

But obviously these national differences can be combined also in a positive way: sourcing the investment in the country where the cost of capital is lowest and using it where the rate of return is greatest. This allows the multinational investor to capitalize simultaneously on the special advantages of both, or for that matter, any number of, countries. This ability gives the multinational firm a range of financial options that the uninational firm lacks. The latent potential for these options is inherent in the pluralism of the multinational financial environment. But the only conceivable medium for actively realizing the potential is the simultaneous operational presence in many countries that only a multinational firm possesses. Consequently, it is the multinational structure of the firm that opens up these latent options for managerial cultivation and endows the multinational firm with financial superiority over its uninational competitors.

International Transferability of Funds

No country ever practices the textbook version of absolute convertability. Control over the national currency is universally claimed by governments of all countries in the contemporary world. Official restrictions on international transfers of capital vary among nations both as to form and severity, but they are nearly always present. Some countries use an elaborate system of exchange licenses with or without quotas, others impose some form of transfer tax (interest equalization tax, for example), and still others depend on multiple exchange rates. Whatever the form of the capital transfer controls, their international economic effect is always to reduce a uninational company's ability to cultivate foreign business ventures. By definition, the domestic uninational company is inescapably subject to all capital transfer constraints of its home country. The narrower the constraints, the greater is their constraining effect upon the international potential of the uninational company.

The multinational company, however, is not similarly constrained. By possessing affiliates with assets and separate juridical personalities in many host countries, it has significant advantages over the uninational firm. First, it is not limited to any country as its operating base, but can launch its projects from whatever affiliate happens to be most advantageously situated to serve that particular purpose. If the capital transfer restrictions of the headquarters country foreclose a certain foreign investment opportunity or make it too costly to pursue, one of its overseas affiliates, its European regional headquarters for example, can assume the parentage for the contemplated venture. The multinational company's choice of juridic parentage for international ventures includes all the separate national and regional entities in its structure. And if none of them singly is suited for a desired investment objective, a consortium consisting of several affiliates may be formed. By possessing a legitimate choice to assign juridical parentage of its various ventures to its affiliates, the multinational company can not only immunize itself to a high degree against national transfer restrictions, but can, in many cases, reap competitive benefits from such restrictions, which tend to curtail and weaken the host countries' indigenous firms relatively much more at times.

The distribution of its capital resources throughout the world endows the juridical apparatus of the multinational firm with real financial power. To this must be added its potentialities to borrow in host country markets. Through forward planning and enlightened financial policies, based on research and careful projection of national foreign exchange policies, the multinational firm can distribute its capital reserves and borrowing so as to maximize its global ability to perform investments, divestments, and international capital transfers without being constrained by the currency and foreign exchange controls of any host country.

Such conscious cultivation of its superior financial flexibility is still in a beginning phase in the typical multinational firm. Too many corporation treasures still limit their policies to what essentially is a uninational frame of reference with some traditional foreign exchange techniques added. The rise of the Eurodollar and Eurobond markets helped to broaden the perspective. The devaluation of the U.S. dollar and its pending aftermath seem to have ushered in a new era which from here on can only accelerate the shift toward a truly multinational financial planning and decision-making in business.

The multinational firm enjoys a superior capacity not only to overcome national transfer restrictions but also to take advantage of national investment incentive policies, discussed earlier. The national support programs for inward investments have become an important source of new business opportunities in many parts of the world. The ability to make the necessary inward investments, though they often are but a fraction of the ultimate capitalization requirements, is the prerequisite for participation in these opportunities. The same applies to growth opportunities unaffected by governmental measures.

Discriminatory Currency Regulations

In much financial literature, the multinational firm is treated as a foreign entrant investor, i.e., a firm that makes its first investment in a particular host country. This grotesquely distorts the real situation.

An established multinational firm is neither foreign nor necessarily a new entrant investor; rather, it holds a dual status being concurrently a resident enterprise and also a member of an international corporate family. Its investments normally have the purpose of expanding locally existing enterprises—its affiliates in the country—and do not cause new firms to enter the country from outside. The only exceptions are the investments made for expanding the territorial scope of the firm to new countries which is the case primarily during the conversion from uninational to multinational structure. After that the push to enter any additional countries weakens rather abruptly and further outward expansion plays only a minor role in the firm's investment expenditures.

This is to say, the discriminatory regulations can retard a multinational company's activities only in its initial entry phase to a particular country. Thereafter, the restrictions act for its advantage by serving as a shield against other entrants and potential competitors. The rhetoric of discriminatory retardation of international investments must, therefore, be dismissed as inappropriate for explaining the financial motivities of the multinational firm.[7]

In the next section this point will be elaborated upon from another perspective.

Currency Controls

A uninational company is wholly dependent upon its home country's constraints in reference to any international capital transfers, be they short- or long-term transactions. If there are no official restrictions this dependence becomes academic. If, however, restrictions do exist, as has been the case with the United States and many other countries, the uninational company's ability to respond to foreign opportunities or to participate in international ventures is accordingly curtailed. The tighter the regulations the greater is this constraining effect.

The multinational company, on the other hand, can develop a high degree of immunity to restrictive currency controls, and need not lose its operational flexibility because of them. First, having separate juridic personalities in many countries—its different national affiliates—it has a wide range of choice as to which of these will act as the principal in any particular venture. If the U.S. exchange restrictions foreclose a particular undertaking, the Swiss or Swedish affiliate of the company may not be similarly constrained; and if no single national entity of the multinational firm can fully achieve the desired international objective, several of them may combine into a consortium to meet the need. Second, this juridic apparatus is reinforced by the multinational distribution of existing capital reserves, as well as the potentialities to borrow. That is, the firm may, by an appropriate distribution of its capital reserves and borrowing, perform a wide variety of international investments, divestitures, and transfers without violating the currency and exchange controls of any particular country, which may be wholly impossible for the uninational firm.

The superior flexibility is not limited to neutralizing the negative consequences of official restrictions. It applies equally in the case of official investment stimulation policies. Such programs as governmental investment guarantees, low-interest investment loans, tax holidays, special aid programs, and other official measures to stimulate economic growth have become commonplace in a multitude of countries. While varying widely in scope and continuity, the governmental support programs for growth have become an important source for corporate opportunities throughout the world. But only the companies that possess the flexibility for the inward transfers of the needed financial resources can capitalize upon them. Needless to add, the same is true for investment and growth opportunities unaffected by governmental measures.

Impact of Nonfinancial Factors

Reliance on local capital sources for investments in affiliate companies is frequently encouraged by various noneconomic requirements. For example, most multinational firms try to cultivate the stance of political neutrality in reference to host country affairs. By doing so the multinational firm avoids offending the local population, who might well view a powerful foreign-controlled firm as a threat to their national sovereignty. However, the firm also finds itself in the position of having little or no say in the political decisions that can seriously effect its affiliates' well-being. If capital is raised in the host country, the indigenous people, as owners and lenders, are assumed to be more likely to protect the affiliates, and if the affiliate were to fail for whatever reason, the financial risk and consequently the loss would be largely borne by the indigenous people, not the parent firm. (Unless, of course, the parent guaranteed the affiliate's debts.)

Other nonfinancial reasons for raising capital overseas include the existence of various forms of pressure or regulatory constraints from the host country governments, which may be seeking assurances that the country will not just benefit from the salaries and increases in technological competence, but also from financial or equity participation. Related to this is sometimes a hoped-for psychological benefit from local participation: if the affiliate is viewed as an integral part of the host country's economy, with reliance on the local population for funds, better employee and community relations can be expected and the dangers of political harassment and expropriations avoided.

Multicurrency Asset and Liability Portfolios

The multinational firm functions in a multicurrency environment. Its expenditures and revenues accrue in as many different monetary units as there are countries in its operating orbit. Its obligations and claims cover the same spectrum of currencies. Even more fundamentally, each national affiliate of the firm has its assets valuation expressed in terms of the respective countries' money. This is to say that both the property holdings as well as cost and revenue flows of the multinational company find their original monetary expression in several different currencies. Traditional financial practices and accounting conventions, designed to serve the needs of the uninational firm, have concealed the monetary plurality by using in corporate financial statements only the headquarters country's currency, with all other currency figures converted to it, which creates the illusion that the multinations monetary environment is no different from a single currency system.

The formula commonly used for conversion of the values is the official exchange rate. While this gives the procedure judicial legitimacy, it does not give accurate expression as the real values embodied in the underlying local currency figures. To avoid distortions in conversion from local currency to the head-quarters currency it would be necessary for the official exchange rates to be based on a strict purchasing power parity. This, in turn, would require an absolutely unrestricted convertibility of currencies, which is possible only if national governments completely refrain from all attempts to influence the rates of exchange or balances of payments one way or another. No government has ever been content to trust the external standing of its currency to the forces of supply and demand on world market.

In the days of the gold standard system the ideal model for governmental foreign-exchange policy was to let the bullion-specie-flow mechanism align the country's currency value-wise with other countries' monetary units. This was accomplished by tying the national money supply (through assignment of a fixed gold cover to the currency unit) to the country's gold reserves, and allowing gold bullion to be freely substituted for paper currency whenever any doubt arose as to the true value—international purchasing power—of the money. Gold exports and imports thus had a direct bearing upon domestic prices and business conditions. In doctrine, at least, the national governments accepted as justifiable external influences upon the national economy, the justification being the convertibility of its currency. In fact the governments were less daring: they never completely trusted the doctrine and, under various disguises, exerted political authority on the foreign-exchange market.

The abolition of the gold standard in the depression hysteria of the 1930s caused the classic free-exchange principle to be replaced with the managed-money doctrine. The latter disallowed any sanctity to international transactions, and prescribed regulatory surveillance over all international activities that might affect the domestic economy. This put governments in the exchange business to stay. National exchange monopolies were formed under a variety of names (foreign-exchange authority, exchange stabilization board, etc.) to adminis-tratively fix the rates of exchange and to license the rights to international payment transactions. Lacking objective measures of purchasing-power parities, and pressured by nationalistic politicians to insert noneconomic factors into the process of exchange-rate determination, these foreign-exchange authorities have been neither obligated nor able to maintain value equivalence between the domestic money and other currencies. Behind simulacrums of economic ration-ality, purchasing-power disparities among official exchange rates have since become a chronic condition, which has prevailed to date.

The charter of the International Monetary Fund sanctioned the managed-money doctrine as the only true and legitimate international monetary system, which was institutionalized by the formation of the Fund itself. Thenceforth, the Fund has served as the officially accepted structure for legitimate monetary relations among nations. Chronic disparities in official exchange rates have been an unavoidable condition of the administratively assigned parities and arbitrarily maintained rates under this system.

There are no signs that either the managed-exchange-rate doctrine or the exchange-rate disparities will disappear in the foreseeable future. Although the recent monetary crisis has forced some major currencies to float to achieve better purchasing power parity in exchange rates, the world's monetary establishments show no inclination to relinquish the monopolistic control they have enjoyed for more than a generation. The monetary environment of the multinational firm, therefore, is likely to remain what can only be described as a multicurrency system, in which official exchange rates deviate in various degrees from purchasing-power parity as well as from the IMF gold parity rates.

This places the multinational companies in a position where reliance on official exchange rates as indicators of true purchasing power of corporate assets is clearly inappropriate; true values are distorted and management misled if all corporate accounting is conducted in a single currency, such as the U.S. dollar, to which all foreign currency assets are converted on the official exchange-rate basis; and substantial profits and losses can be caused by the international monetary differences and disparities, avoidance of the losses and maximization of the profits becoming, therefore, self-evident imperatives for multinational financial management.

A partial but greatly inadequate measure to deal with the difficulty of relying on official exchange rates has been to value different assets at the exchange rates valid at the time of the original accounting entry: fixed assets and securities such as machines and bonds are converted at the rate that was in effect at the end of the accounting period.

Better protection against the negative consequences of exchange-rate disparities can be attained by substituting purchasing-power-parity indexes for the official exchange rates. These enable the firm to ascertain true relationships and comparative asset values of its affiliates in different countries. Nothing less than reliable purchasing-power indexes can be equal to the task. (How such indexes might be constructed and kept current is a subject that cannot be covered here.)

With the aid of the purchasing-power-parity indexes, current values can be realistically compared among affiliates and the distortions in a single currency accounting system avoided. This will enable the headquarters top management to gain a more accurate overview of the company's financial developments, and to make interaffiliate comparisons that show substantive rather than merely official differences.

As to risks of loss and opportunities for profit, the disparities in official exchange rates create various arbitrage possibilities and cross-rate differentials which the multinational firm must learn to utilize in its short term payments and interaffiliate transfers.[a] Through skillful management the firm can derive a special contribution to its profits from the plurality of monetary systems in its operating area; i.e., the firm can avoid currency losses of devaluation of profit from them.

The international monetary differences are not limited to exchange-rate disparities. Besides being an official unit of account, each country's currency represents a complex system that is fundamental to economic and political life of that nation. All trends and developments in the economic-political aspects affect, and in turn are affected by, the monetary situation to some degree. As each country has its own integral developments, its monetary dynamics too follow their own peculiar patterns. They may have no resemblance to those of any other country. This introduces into the monetary environment time-related diversities and contrasts that could be nonexistent in the present, but will project themselves on future time horizons, thereby changing the relative profit potentialities of the different country affiliates of the firm. Among the main time-related financial variables are rates of interest, inflation, shifts in the commodity price structure, devaluations and revaluations of currency, taxes, and leads and lags between factor prices (especially wage rates) and consumer prices.

Each variable adds a new element of uncertainty and opportunity. For example, interest rates are rarely stationary. Forecasts of national interest rates are therefore more important than forecasts of worldwide average levels. The firm's own activities may also have very different effects upon the interest rates in different countries: floating securities of certain amounts can cause interest rates to move up on a country like Denmark or Uruguay, but have no effect in West Germany or the United Kingdom. Thus, the questions of where, how much, and how often issues are to be floated bear very different connotations to multinational firms than they do in the domestic business setting.

Taxes help to further illustrate the point. The acquisitions and divestments of a multinational firm represent accumulated capital gains and losses which produce simultaneous tax consequences at least in the respective host countries and the headquarter's country. Their effect on the total tax burden of the firm may be complex, but never negligible. The total sum of taxes to be paid by the multinational firm depends further on the manner in which the various acquisitions are connected to the official (de jure) organizational structure, i.e., how the parenthood to different acquisitions and divestments has been assigned. If governmental currency restrictions necessitate the creation of intracorporate dividends or other transboundary transfer conduits to maneuver liquid assets according to corporate needs, the best interest of the firm may be served by appropriate trade-offs between minimizing the tax burdens and achieving desired

[a]The reader not familiar with such techniques will benefit from reading E.J. Kolde, *International Business Enterprise*, pp. 117-18, or some other international finance text.

capital maneuverability or accessibility for planned deployment in different countries.

If the management of a multinational firm restricts its view to the perspective of a one-currency system, as most companies do that are relative newcomers to the multinational scene, the different monetary risk factors of its affiliate domiciles may seem nothing else than troublesome complications that must be viewed as added risks of operating outside the headquarters country. Such an ethnocentric headquarters will by its own narrowness of view shut the company off from rational utilization of the existing diversities in its multinational financial environment.

However, sooner or later ethnocentrism must make room for a more geocentric approach, which in the financial field means that each country's currency and its monetary dynamics are studied and evaluated on their indigenous merits, and that in planning corporate goals, strategies, and financial practices the diverse conditions in different countries are given full consideration.

When the ethnocentrism of the single-currency financial thinking is replaced by the more realistic geocentricism, the fear of "foreign currencies" disappears along with other xenophobic managerial attitudes. Instead of being looked upon as something that should be kept to the absolute minimum at all times and converted into headquarters currency at the first possibility, asset accruals in other country currencies acquire particular desirability in that, over and above their inherent purchasing power at any particular moment, they each represent a different complex on both risk and return possibilities, which greatly augments the choices available to management in mapping the company's future. Furthermore, they help to bring out and to put into factual context the corporate opportunities present or emergent in different countries.

Except for purely legalistic accounting such as tax reporting, there is no need to convert all profits, liquid assets, or financial reserves of the firm into headquarters currency. This does not mean that the assets will be restricted to countries where originally earned or acquired. Instead, the company can now construct multicurrency portfolios of its assets so as to optimize the use of its financial resources, both present and future, in the multicountry rather than just the headquarters-country framework. Techniques of constructing the currency portfolios are still in their infancy and the state of the art remains fluid. However, in theory there are no serious unresolved issues. The practical questions are primarily economic-statistical: How many currencies should be included in any particular asset portfolio? What proportion would each particular currency represent? Should some currencies be completely excluded? etc. Before appropriate mathematical equations can be developed in answer to any of such questions, forecasts of the different countries' economic and political trends need to be prepared to provide the information inputs necessary for the statistical calculations.

As the technologies of both forecasting in the different-country environment and constructing multicurrency asset portfolios improve and spread, we can be certain that sooner or later all companies with multinational operating structures will discover the illogic of the single-currency information system, and will place their financial management on the multi-currency basis.

6

Culture Context of Multinational Organizations

Ritual, art, poetry, drama, music, dance, philosophy, science, myth, religion are all as essential to man as his daily bread: man's true life consists not alone in the work activities that directly sustain him, but in the symbolic activities which give significance both to the processes of work and their ultimate products and consummations.

Lewis Mumford
The Myth of The Machine
New York: Harcourt Brace Jovanovich Inc., 1962.

Organization is a creature of culture. The structural and behavioral characteristics of every productive enterprise derive from the attitudes, values, and beliefs of the society in which it exists. Since a multinational company must also be multicultural, its organization, even on its irreducible base, consists of a circuitry of culturally differentiated process systems: some cooperating, some competing, and some neutral, but all co-acting as organs of the corporate entirety. Each subsystem represents a potential force to transmit its internal dynamics to one or more of the others and to send shock waves throughout the entire circuitry, the multinational structure. To explain and clarify this contention is the primary objective of this chapter. How to integrate culturally differentiated and organizational systems, how to prevent interaffiliate conflicts from misconsuming corporate resources, and how to synchronize the entire heterocultural circuitry are the fundamental problems of multinational corporate relations.

Culture-conditioned Behavior

Human behavior is controlled by drives and impulses that demand gratification or that avoid pain. The biological and physiological drives—the animal aspects of human behavior—relate largely to the individual's physical subsistence, i.e., the absolutes of his ability to exist. While the basic biophysiological needs always remain, they are cast into an elaborate psychological edifice as a person is socialized by his elders and compatriots. Instead of foodstuffs (grain, meat, vegetables, etc.), not to mention nutritional absolutes (calories, vitamins, hydrocarbons, proteins, etc.), the culture-conditioned human perceives his nutritional requirements in such culinary terms as sukiyaki, sauerbraten, chow mein, biroski, lutefisk, spaghetti, or boef à la mode, depending upon the culture that defined his taste. Clothes, dwellings, sex, and all other biophysiological underpinnings of life become similarly defined and endowed with emotional investments.[a]

Instinctive behavior mechanisms . . . are the source of love and friendship, of all warmth of feeling, of appreciation of beauty, of the urge to artistic creativeness, or insatiable curiosity striving for scientific enlightenment. These deepest strata of the human personality are, in their dynamics, not essentially different from the instincts of animals, but on that basis human culture has erected all the enormous superstructure of social norms and rites whose function is so closely analogous to that of phylogenetic ritualization. *Both phylogenetically and culturally evolved norms of behavior represent motives and are felt to be values by any normal human being* [italics added]. Both are woven into an immensely complicated system of universal interaction.[1]

Even the human animal characteristically clings to the association with others and struggles for survival in cooperation with them. The association can start fulfilling its functions—the maintenance and reproduction of life—only when its members begin cooperating more than they counteract one another, that is, when individuals in the group agree on priorities as well as methods of joint action. At this point a human society begins. The modern man is inconceivable outside of society. In his behavior the motivations of biopsychological drives are indistinguishable from the motivations that have been acquired through learning from others by inculcation, by example, and by coercion. His beliefs, folkways, mores, taboos, and other rules of conduct flow from the accumulated experience of the society to which he has been socialized.

In the process of socialization each individual invests with emotion most aspects of culture, especially those which he exemplifies. Similarly, the society as a collective invests with sanctity the norms and customs that are believed crucial to societal welfare and safety. Strict mores with accompanying sanctions and judgments prescribe and restrict the activities of individuals in these aspects of life.

No individual personifies the total culture of his society. The rules and beliefs vary among the members as individual habits of thought and action. Some aspects of culture are universal, some others are manifested by certain segments or subcultures of the society, and still others are scattered at random. But any variant behavior is usually restricted by the sanctions and tolerances attached to it by the particular culture.

To paraphrase, culture is the living heritage of a society's accumulated

[a]An Estonian who, due to an injury, lost his sense of taste at a mature age prepared a nutritionally and economically optimal food budget that cost him the equivalent of eleven cents a day. Yet he continued to relish roast pork, pancakes, and sausages—food characteristic of his country—despite the fact that they were ludicrously expensive and dangerously wanting in nutritional content compared to his scientific diet. His physiological inability to actually taste the foods had become secondary to the culturally acquired symbolism or psychological need which only the traditional foods of his culture could satisfy.

experience, both conscious and subconscious. Its most readily observable manifestations include beliefs, laws, customs, knowledge, art, and other common norms and expressions—including material things—of a people as a collective whole. But its deeper structures combine instinctive drives with sociointellectual learning to form behavioral impulses that are yet to be adequately exposed. "We may expect ultimately to identify in human beings an original nature which has very definite form or structure."[2]

National Culture

National culture can be defined as a system of values and habits that are shared by most citizens of a country. Shared values and habits imply shared learning and shared motives.

Physiological urges are modified and transformed into cultural appetites. Every activity has its emotional as well as its functional components. Love and hate, anxiety and security, guilt and shame, self-esteem and self-depreciation . . . the jokes and insults, the proverbs, the causes for quarrels and methods of reconciliation, the most often repeated myths and stories, the varying or rigid composition of work or play groups, the metaphors for technical processes, even habitual physical postures, can all provide clues.[3]

Family traditions, artistic and religious heritage, economic organization, political structures, and power relationships are similar elements in the national culture composite. The shared value orientations and behavioral norms of a national culture include not only what is considered normal but also what is considered abnormal by a particular culture.

Internal Pluralism. In theory, a nation's value system may consist of a single set of standards, or it may contain many sets that vie with one another. In reality no contemporary national culture is known to be completely monolithic. While some are clearly more pluralistic than others, all possess certain features of differentiation as well as integration; i.e., each country is in some respect a multiple system of values, yet the different or even contradicting features have some common roots.

Cultural Relativity

The cumulative aspect of culture can be viewed as the crystallization of a people's social learning at any particular point in its evolutionary path. It is not, however, the same as the totality of the people's history. Rather, culture is a distillation from history: the interpretations a particular people have placed upon the events of its history, successes, failures, discoveries, and relationships in its social and natural environments. From this cumulative fund derives the operational system of culture.

In multinational organizational analysis the operational aspect of culture is of crucial iimportance, for it provides the normative guidelines, methods, and techniques of how things should be appraised, how problems should be solved, how social relations should be conducted, and how individuals should behave. It is the society's master plan for personal behavior and social interaction.

While any people's culture has its inner logic, at least in terms of its own evolutionary past, every culture is a mixture of rational, irrational, and nonrational elements. This seems to be just as true for the most civilized and science-dependent societies as for the primitive cultures of aboriginal tribes. Indeed, as the capacity for capricious behavior is greatly increased by the relatively larger discretionary incomes people enjoy under modern industrial civilization, the irrational and nonrational elements of culture could possibly show a positive correlation to the modernism of society. In any event, there is no evidence that cultural determinants of any society, regardless how rich or industrialized, could be divorced from the psychological assessments and emotional processes of the population. Any schemes to substitute systems of abstract logic to the systems of psychological gratifications inherent in culture are, therefore, beyond informed conception. Through science and technology, objective rationality can gain an enlarged space within a culture, especially in a strongly tradition-based one. But this is more a process of enlargement of its total scope than trading of its mechanism for another.

Ethnocentrism

It is perfectly right and legitimate that we should consider as "good" the manners which our parents have taught us, that we should hold sacred social norms and rites handed down to us by tradition and culture. What we must guard against, with all the power of rational responsibility, is our natural inclination to regard the social rites and norms of other cultures as inferior. The dark side of pseudo-speciation is that it makes us consider the numbers of pseudo-species other than our own as not human, as many primitive tribes are demonstrably doing, in whose language the word for their own particular tribe is synonymous with "Man." ... The moral of the natural history of pseudo-speciation is that we must learn to tolerate other cultures, to shed entirely our own cultural and national arrogance, and to realize that the social norms and rites of other cultures, to which their numbers keep faith as we do to our own, have the same right to be respected and to be regarded as sacred.[4]

A widely propounded fallacy in the advanced industrial countries holds that all nations evolve in a series of evolutionary steps in a unilinear path. The Americans, British, and French are likely to place their own respective countries at the pinnacle of this path, and look upon all other peoples' cultures as backward and inferior to theirs. Cultural maturity, thus, is rationalized to be a correlate of economic progress. The claim for cultural superiority by members of subindustrial societies, who regard the relatively greater reliance on materialistic considerations in industrial societies as evidence of moral and spiritual degeneration, is similarly irrational.

Cultural forms have meaning only in relation to their particular historical context. Societies are relative to one another, not higher or lower on some absolute scale. Even primitive cultures, although technologically backward, have values that are useful to people in highly industrialized countries. And by no means are all of the norms and practices of modern societies more beneficial than those of others. There are elements in what we consider the modernity that have wrought havoc in both rich and poor countries. Nor is modernity free from purely culture-bound behavior. Its taboos are more sophisticated, its votive offerings and sacrifices ritualized on a higher level, than primitive man's, but they are real nonetheless. The modernized countries have translated the tribal idiom into modern behavioral terms, but they have not removed the cultural and psychological bases for human action.

Each society, however primitive or advanced, must always remain a self-generating system of values, institution, and social structures. Cross-cultural differences will therefore be inherent in any intersociety comparisons, including international business.

Interculture Conflict

Since all peoples are creatures of their particular cultures, every country represents a different setting for organizational design and behavior. As long as the organizational scope is limited to the cultural setting of one particular nation, problems arise only to the extent to which there are conflicts between the organizational aspirations and cultural norms or to which there are inner contradictions or inconsistencies in the cultural system. The latter may be caused either by existing social structures or by rapid changes in certain sectors of the culture which, due to structural rigidities, may not become smoothly assimilated into its normative system. As the tempo of change is increasing in all aspects of life, the intracultural maladjustments present similarly increasing problem complexes for organizational resolution. The impact of culture, particularly the dynamics of it, cannot be ignored in organizational thought, even in a one-country context. And when the focus is widened to a multicountry spectrum, the intercultural contrasts greatly overshadow the intracultural factors of a uninational setting. Neither the internal nor the external environment of a multinational organization can be rationally treated in isolation of these cultural variables.

Many of the cross-cultural contrasts and variations are suitable and inextricably bound to complex hierarchies; others are less so. A cross-cultural comparison is never a matter of sorting or juxtaposing isolated facts; it is always something in the nature of complex systems analysis. Routine procedures and reference catalogues can be of little help in this effort. This is not to say, however, that there are no handles by which to get hold of the problem. The component elements of culture have been quite well defined and established by social sciences. These elements are conceptual rather than substantive components; they exist in all cultures as phenomena, but their factual meaning and dimensions may be quite different in different cultures. The component concepts in terms of which cross-culture contrasts can be identified and examined include, at the primary level: class, role, position, rank, worldview, and anomie. For organizational study some others such as social structure, law, national character, personality, prestige, leadership, and problem-solving styles are probably equally basic. Narrower subsystems of culture can be specified to meet the needs of any concrete situation.[5]

Company Culture

As illustrated in Figure 6-1, the indigenous organizational culture of each corporate entity in a multinational structure is subject to a ceaseless intrusion from its environmental system, the national culture of its domicile. Though reciprocating with its own inputs to the national culture, the company remains but a local constituent in the nation as a whole. In this respect the corporate culture is a microcosm in the national macrosystem. Thus the different functional variables of the national culture are reflected in the functional aspects of the corporate culture. Although the transfer from the national macroculture to the corporate microsystem is never complete, it is irresistible; the two systems can seldom sustain irreconcilable contradictions. Their differences are either temporary or limited to the "normal" variance of the national norms.

The corporate deviations from the national norms stem primarily from four sources. First, the company is often not only the recipient of national culture but a contributor to it, by originating and introducing new cultural dimensions, which the national culture can absorb only after a period of maturation and dissemination. The reverse situation, where the company lags rather than leads in cultural progress, produces deviations in the opposite direction.

Second, to the extent to which information flow between the corporate and national cultures is impeded, unintentional norms different from the society's general standards can arise in the company organization. Laws concerning corporate disclosure requirements and executives' social responsibilities have direct bearing on this type of differences.

Third, motivational indifference between management and the society on a

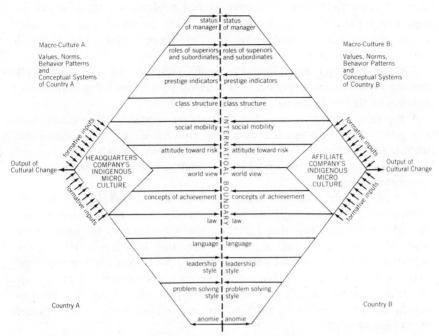

Figure 6-1. Functional Model of International Culture Conflicts in a Binational Organization

whole may allow contradictions to occur between the corporate and national cultural concepts that underlie organizational design and behavior. It is simply a case of nobody being affected by or concerned about the divergent values. (The second and third sources are closely linked, and can be unscrambled only after considerable difficulty in any particular case.)

Fourth, national culture is always much broader in scope and more pluralistic in composition than the corporate culture, as long as the company remains uninational in scope. It can wholly absorb not only an indigenous company's culture in its entirety, but all domestic company cultures in the nation's domain. The reverse—corporate culture absorbing the complete national culture—is impossible. Consequently, the corporate culture can receive inputs from its national environment on a selective basis only, accepting what is deemed necessary or irresistible and screening out the rest. In this screening and selecting the management's philosophy and personal biases significantly affect the outcome. Managerial attitudes affect also the tempo and timing of organizational adaptation to environmental changes. On the lag end of the adaptive procession are companies whose internal power structure responds only after the exchanges in external culture have become manifested in overt new norms, with clearly perceived costs to the organization of deviant behavior. On the lead end are companies practicing anticipatory adaptation. They constantly scan the futuristic horizons to detect environmental focus of change "before they emerge in overt and dynamic form."[6] This involves risk.

The scanning requires a definite allocation of resources but can promise only plausible yields; its cost-benefit ratio is therefore statistically indeterminate and, as such, a matter of managerial judgment.

A company's culture must, therefore, always consist of a combination of norms that in certain ways is unique. The probabilities are infinitessimal that two companies would make identical acquisitions from the national culture and have precisely the same sensitivies to and abilities of internalizing the various environmental impacts.

Thus, it is quite correct to argue that each organization develops its own microculture or "personality," different from all others. But we should never lose sight of the fact that this differentiation is confined to the scope of the national culture, unless the company is operating in a transnational space. Suggestions that cross-cultural research need not go beyond interorganizational studies within the same country fail to recognize this fundamental fact. There are certainly some similarities between interorganizational culture conflict in uninational settings and internation culture conflict, but to equate one with the other would be absurd.

Toward a Cosmopolitan Corporate Culture

If we widen our perspective from one-country setting to the heterocultural base of a multinational firm, the problem of company culture takes on new dimensions. No longer limited to receiving inputs from a cohesive national culture, the organization finds itself not only able to have a choice from all the national cultures harboring its affiliates but, even more important, also compelled to reconcile the idiosyncracies among its various affiliates for which culture contrasts are responsible. Thus, adaptation of company culture to all national cultures in the corporate orbit becomes imperative, and its expansion to incorporate certain elements from each axiomatic.

That kind of cultural bridge-building can succeed only if both the structural materials and traffic patterns avoid incompatibility with the national cultures concerned. No direct, one-to-one correlation between the transnational corporate culture and its various host country cultures is conceivable. Rather than thinking here in terms of achieving culture compatibility in the sense of becoming identified with it, it is more realistic, experience has shown, to limit one's goal to the avoidance of culture incompatibility; to aim toward a neutrality status for the corporate culture vis-à-vis its multinational environmental cultures, than to seek intimate identification with them. The neutrality criterion offers the only viable basis for harmonious relations between a multinational company and its heterocultural environment. International conflicts make impartiability, i.e., equalization of involvement in all its host countries, impossible for the company; commitment to the cultural system of one or a few from among its many host environments will sooner or later expose the firm in a countercultural or even counternational light in the others. This would unstabilize and undermine the company's continued existence, at least in the countries whose cultures are deemphasized.

Constructive Neutrality. But what is neutrality? It is easier to say what it is not. First, true neutralism is never synonymous with negativism. Prejudiced partisans, especially in the political field, have attacked neutrality as being negative. In their conception everybody who is not for their partisan aims is automatically against them. Second, neutralism is not hypocritical: its central strategy is not to play both ends against the middle or to shield partisan machinations. Such negative connotations accrued to the term during the Cold War era, when a number of governments raised the neutralist banner to qualify for maximum foreign aid from both the West and the East or to create a false façade for their own aggressive designs (Nehru, Nkruma, Sucarno, Nasser, etc.). After the Cold War such pseudoneutralism lost much of its strategic luster, and is hardly a factor in contemporary world. Yet the foul aftertaste it left still lingers on, and for many the terms *neutrality* and *neutralism* still bear an insincere, if not sinister, sound. Fortunately, in a purely cultural context there has been less corruptive usage of the neutrality concept, certainly not enough to make us seek a synonym for it.

For the purposes of the multinational corporate culture, neutrality could be defined as a positive system of principles and norms to guide the decision-making processes of all its entities and affiliates so as to avoid or to minimize clashes with its various national environments, and to facilitate optimal involvement and participation of the company in the productive systems of its host countries.

Initiating Cultural Change and
Managerial Modernization

Under colonialism optimization of business operations was attempted through economic and political exploitation and social and cultural subjugation; that is, coercion. Due partly to the colonial heritage and partly to cultural unawareness, efforts still continue, too often, to impose upon all affiliates of a multinational company the value system of the headquarters country—the underlying assumption being that that culture represents the only true values for modern society, and as such, is superior to indigenous cultures. It will be accepted sooner or later; once the peoples of other cultures are fully exposed to it, the inevitable outcome will be their repentance and conversion. While very gratifying to the headquarters' executives' nationalistic egos, there is no justification for any claim of Western cultural superiority.

A tremendous psychological infrastructure is built in a culture. To maintain the integrity of this system, it is necessary to introduce change through the system itself: by enlarging its scope, modernizing its processes, and opening up areas for innovation. Bloc infusions of alien culture, such as is the case when corporate foreign-based affiliates are imbued with American corporate culture under headquarters pressure, is often counterconstructive or even toxic to the indigenous cultural patterns. Mutilating the established structure tends to weaken and unstabilize the social climate, increase anomie, and induce hostility not only against the methods and conduct but also the ultimate objectives of the American culture. This undermines for a very long time any subsequent efforts to achieve cultural empathy and constructive cooperation, even if cultivated by gradual and well-considered ways.

Culture systems are intricate and basically conservative. Yet they are never inherently rigid, but plastic, supplied with built-in laws of dynamics. Change comes slowly, or more precisely, at speeds that its internal dynamics can accommodate. Any effort to change the cultural patterns has a domino effect; breaking one pattern tends to lead to dislocations in others. There is thus what might be called the change-absorptive capacity of each culture: it can accommodate only a given maximum of change at any particular time to remain structurally stable and operationally balanced. It is not only a matter of the methods by which cross-cultural transfers are made, but also the magnitudes of change that the transfer precipitates in the recipient culture. If the absorptive capacity is exceeded, either by too extensive or too sudden external infusion, a dual system of mutually inimical norms results, and if it persists, an internalization of the conflict between the native and imported values will provide the change for eventual violent exceptions which may seek either social or political outlets, but which, in any case, will embroil the multinational company as the agent of anomie and decay in the cultural ecosystem of the host nation.

Ethnocentric and Egalitarian Approaches

American companies expanding internationally have, with a few notable exceptions, dispatched their managers to other countries not to learn more about the host culture and to adapt to it, but to change it or, as it is usually put, to "help introduce modern managerial values." In the history of the shift from domestic to multinational operations, there has been a conflict between the traditional ethnocentric and an emerging egalitarian perception of the peoples outside the United States.

The first follows closely the colonialist dictum: the strong do what they can and the weak do what they must. It overlaps much of the chauvinistic prejudices of American superiority, especially in regards to economically less-developed nations which, because of their material backwardness, are conceived as formless matter waiting to be shaped and developed by expatriate enterprise. The up-and-coming American executive of the 1950s and 1960s regarded much of the world as an appendix to the U.S. business system, and the rest as merely exotic.

This vision of the world was through a narrowly monocultural tunnel. Understanding the social realities of other cultures was not in the field of this view. To most such executives the initial culture shock and subsequent setbacks in their expatriate assignment have brought the sobering realization that the native social fabric of any country, advanced or backward in industrial development, can be as tenacious as that of our own. They have had to learn painfully that what was most on their minds and dearest to their hearts was often only fitful and tangential to the concerns of their host peoples and their leaders, and that any congenial progress of their expatriate firms required an understanding and appreciation of the indigenous socioeconomic order, most of all the human values. Those expatriate managers who failed to learn these lessons have long since repatriated, firmly convinced of the hopeless "backwardness" of the other peoples.

Although progress has been substantial, this problem has still been far from surmounted. All we have achieved is the recognition of the problem; the capability to deal with it is quite a different matter. And there still remain many who fail to even recognize the problem. While established multinational firms typically do prepare their new recruits for overseas assignments, the preparation is typically limited to some rudimentary seminar, with or without some travel. Cultural matter, save some possible allowance for language instruction, is usually not part of the preparation. Management schools of multinational companies seldom have more than few-day segments, if any, on international aspects, of management. Many recent entries to multinational business proceed on the "management is management" dictum, with no regard whatsoever to the potential expatriate's cultural competence. Unless he has had direct foreign experience or comes from the half-dozen business schools that have developed any substantive programs in international business he is not much better off than his predecessors of the 1950s. (Many universities claim to offer international business and some even confer advanced degrees without having any bona fide offerings in the field; the inclusion of some standard course in political science or international economics to the candidate's requirements is naively believed to suffice.) What is worse, some senior executives and university professors whose own frames of reference have been limited to the traditional curricula of American business, law, or engineering schools have rigidly refused to emerge from the intellectual confinement to which the unicultural curricula of their alma maters had committed them. There are also the xenophobes to whom the mounting pressures for greater cultural awareness seems to have signaled the start of a holy war against "foreign subversion of good old American ways."

The Change Agent Syndrome. The notion that an American expatriate abroad is first of all a change agent with a mission to Americanize the host country seems to prevail no less among educators and government personnel than businessmen.

I recall a remark made to me by a colleague at my former university as I set out to be a "change agent" overseas. "Good luck," said this professor cheerfully, "but don't improve things before I get there next year. I have a grant from the Ford Foundation to study the society out there as it is now, warts and all." The warts were intact a year later, and his study was duly made, but the incident illustrated the gap then dividing university men bent on scrutiny from other university men bent on change. For the scrutinizers, "technical assistance" was a clumsy and ignorant attempt to inflict upon Third World countries ill-fitting foreign substitutes for traditional values and institutions. For the change agents, the traditional culture, if conceded to exist at all, was viewed as an obstruction to reform, to be ignored or undermined and eventually swept away.[7]

To achieve empathic integration between the corporate culture and its multicultural environment—a prerequisite for mutually supportive growth—no unilateral transfers, especially imposition from a financial or political power base, will do. The resistance to such imposition may not be immediate or even overt, but in time and often through covert expressions; it never fails to materialize. Management cannot approach this problem with balance-sheet or organization-chart criteria. Cultural empathy can be achieved only through cultural sensitivity based on the living realities of the national societies concerned. Appreciation of all the cultures involved and attitudes sympathetic to their cardinal values are required from those responsible for shaping the company's cultural milieu.

The complexity of the problem depends on the number of countries. As the corporation's territorial scope expands the probabilities of culture conflict multiply, as each new country adds new complications to the mix. Conversely, the opportunities for culturally indifferent corporate values shrink. They remain fewer and fewer alternatives and neutral possibilities, and the pressure for knowledge how to handle the situation intensifies geometrically.

Cosmopolitan Corporate Culture

In a common peril—the pressures for alignment with host societies as evidenced by rising public criticism, official attitudes, and nationalizations of affiliates—the multinational firms have sought aid through cooperation and mutual assistance.

Formal and informal exchanges of experience with one another, trade association activities, conventions and seminars for different executive groups and functional specialists, and various other means of disseminating information about successful experiences of different companies have created the means for collective corporate learning of cross-cultural conflict resolution. There has been developing among international executives, so to speak, a "brotherhood of intense necessity" that has fostered close fraternal relations regardless of the individual's own nationality or the domicile of his parent company. A survey conducted by a graduate seminar under this author's supervision showed that both the search for and the reliance on such collective standards has been increasing in decision areas which involve a host society's sociopolitical sensitivities. Responses from 218 multinational companies could be summarized as follows:

Activity	Percent of respondent companies:	
	1966	1972
Contributing to information collection and dissemination	44	68
Participating in the development of general action modes and/or behavior guides	27	56
Using external precedents (industrywide or some other corporate experience) as primary decision criteria	62	83

Imitation and standardization of decision modes and policy provisions have become quite commonplace. Intercompany differences, while always present, show a distinct tendency to decline, especially in the problem areas that are of general, and therefore common, concern to the majority of multinational companies. From the shared experiences has been emerging an international system of business values—a *cosmopolitan corporate culture*, which might be visualized as a functionally oriented superstructure bridging the national cultures of different countries.

In an idealized concept, this emergent superstructure rests on the different host countries' cultural systems, maintaining neutrality towards each. In practice, pure neutrality has been neither achievable nor sufficient for corporate needs. In many respects the cosmopolitan standards in multinational business have, in fact, progressed beyond the neutrality objective; in others, they are only in a formative stage. Because of its pragmatic base, the development has been far from uniform and lacks internal consistency. No doubt business scholars will find here a fruitful area to dig and to rearrange for many years to come.

Diffusion of Enmity. Despite its theoretical imperative, the emergent cosmopolitan business culture introduces something very original into the relations between the multinational firm and its heterocultural environment. It takes the focus off any particular firm and its national origin, and creates a broad-based corporate culture that carries greater influence as well as stability than any individual company culture could. In a sense, it takes the firm out of isolation in reference to its external cultural relations and places it into the context of this transnational normative system, which maintains relative constancy throughout the world. If clashes between this corporate culture and any particular national culture occur, they do not expose the company as a deviant culprit but as a member of a cosmopolitan elite against whose standards the indigenous norms do not enjoy the popular presumption of moral superiority. Instead of a righteous animosity and unreasonable condemnation of the firm, there is a real basis for a social discourse, an intercultural dialogue, that opens rational approaches for eliminating the conflicts.

Vanguard of Indigenous Change. Operating from a base of superior knowledge and effectiveness, the multinational company, which is outwardly identified with the cosmopolitan corporate elite, can greatly contribute to the adaptation and development of indigenous value systems in favor of free initiative and enterprise, achievement orientation, and productive activity as socially desirable and morally sanctioned fundamentals of a modern society. In this context of the cosmopolitan corporate elite, the company, rather than being an intruder, can become identified with the vanguard of modernity, deserving of glamour and bestowed with institutional charisma to lead. It can, in brief, become a prime mover of indigenous change in its host countries' normative system; a leadership which unlike direct cultural imports would not mutilate and disrupt the intricate social systems of the different host cultures of the company but would, instead, engender growth and development through the indigenous means of those cultures toward the values essential for the effective utilization of their natural and human resources.

Developmental Stages

A basic problem in developing a viable corporate culture for a multinational company arises because the parent company's executive styles, ideologies, and assumptions are typically culture specific and the top echelon executives not interculturally sophisticated. A further difficulty results from the fact that even modern management theory is still culture bound, nearly all research having been done in uninational settings, primarily in the United States. What results is a tendency to view as universal normative systems and patterns of behavior that a more informed scrutiny would show to be artifacts of American culture. In other words, there is a built-in tendency for ethnocentrism in all multinational companies. To counteract it and to consolidate the corporate culture of the parent company with those of other countries is a main mission of the international organs and the international executive corps of the firms. The challenge is to prevail upon the top policy-making bodies (1) that the company need not choose to be the missionary of the parent country's cultural system; (2) that it may be foolish to tie down the thinking and planning of the entire multinational corporate structure in that fashion even if the corporation possesses the power to prevail; (3) that if American norms can be extended and applied abroad over its affiliates, other countries' norms and values can be utilized for advantage in the United States through some mechanisms; and (4) that the company's interest is best served if the corporate culture represents a system of values and executive styles that optimizes the effectiveness of the organization across all cultures. The challenge, in other words, is to create a corporate culture that facilitates communication vertically within the hierarchy as well as horizontally among affiliates, thus creating behavioral flexibility throughout the company structure.

That the process of consolidating cultural differences is a difficult and slow one has already been emphasized. Only over time can the internal cultural system be fully synchronized with its multinational environment and converted to the cosmopolitan corporate culture. At least five stages of this evolutionary process can be distinguished as shown in Figure 6-2. Needless to add, these are not discrete classifications, but points on an uninterrupted path.

The international executive corps in the company must serve as the mediating instrumentality connecting and integrating as best it can the operating affiliates of the firm in different cultures. It also must provide the momentum that will maintain the forward motion of the evolutionary process, lest the company's cultural development stagnate in an early phase and never reach its cosmopolitan goal. In this respect the international executives of U.S.-headquartered multinational companies have been only moderately successful. A large proportion of the companies are still in the early stages of developing a cosmopolitan culture, stage 3 being usually regarded as a remarkable progress. However, conscious efforts are being made in an increasing number of firms, which have been striving to reach the higher stages.

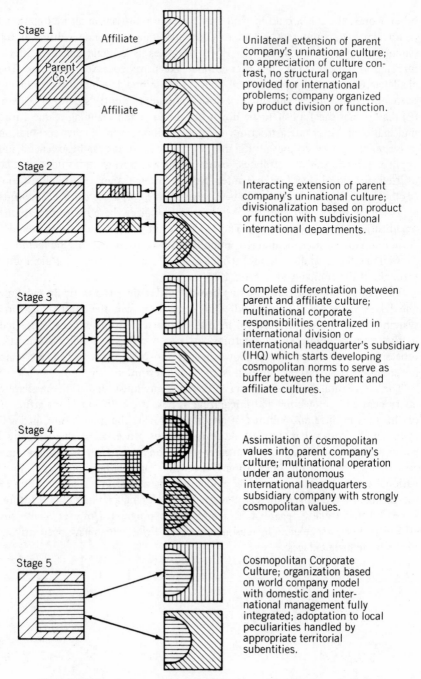

Figure 6-2. Evolutionary Stages of Cosmopolitan Corporate Culture

7 Structural Members and Factors of Multinational Organization

Every organization must have an executive system for decision-making and implementation. To become operative the system needs sources of power and channels of influence to activate the membership and to make the organization go. The power rests with the members who have been endowed with the right to decide for, or on behalf of, other members. They are the executives. But they are not all equal. In a superorganization the executive corps itself needs an executive system. Some executives must be endowed with more power and others with less, to create a chain of superior-subordinate relationships that engages every member to the power drain of the organization and the latter to the organizational objectives, thus integrating the entire membership into a coherent, purposefully functioning enterprise. This explains the familiar pyramid of the power structure of organizations, be they small or large, business or nonbusiness.

But while all organizations must have structure to be distinguishable from unorganized assemblies of individuals, character, development, and behavioral implications can contrast sharply among organizations. In multinational organizations the tendencies for structural contrast is normally rooted in intercultural variations in the relevant patterns and norms.

De Jure or Statutory Structure

To have legal standing organizations must be formed in accordance with the laws of the country where they are to function. These laws are usually the more explicit the more important the potential role an organization can play. Since a business firm can involve the vital interests of the society, all countries have made various statutory rules for its formation and operation. Although there has been some imitation and international coordination, the various national statutes regulating business organization and activity are essentially different in each country. As such they represent invisible internal parameters for all organizations. Furthermore, the law of any sovereign nation can be satisfied only on its own terms. To be able to commence operation a firm must first be granted a charter and license for business by the government of the country in whose jurisdiction it is to function. The charter will define the form, the officers, the purposes, the ownership, and possibly the activities and methods of the organization. Since only charters consistent with the statutory provisions can be issued, any applicant is automatically restricted to the choices provided by the legislation of the particular country.

Consequently, a U.S. company cannot export the juridic structure of its organization to another country where it might wish to establish an affiliate. The affiliate must be structured in terms of the laws of the host country to qualify for its charter and license. Even if the laws of two countries happened to provide for the same form of organization, the choice of the affiliate structure would still have to be based upon the juridic alternatives provided in the host country law rather than the parent company's structure. The relevant comparisons are the alternatives internal to each legal system rather than cross-system similarities. Take, for example, a U.S. firm juridically organized as a corporation going to set up a subsidiary in Germany. If it imitated its own domestic structure and formed the subsidiary as a German corporation (*Aktiengesellschaft*, or A/G) it would deny itself the relatively greater freedoms it could have enjoyed by choosing the limited liability company (*Gesellschaft mit beschränkter Haftung*, or G.m.b.H.). It is characteristic to the laws of many countries to provide for organizational forms other than the corporation with juridic personalities separate from their owners, and with the owners' financial liability limited to their equity investments. The U.S. situation, where the corporation is the only juridic form so endowed, is an exception rather than the rule internationally.

Because of the necessity to comply with the legal norms and because of the different opportunities that these norms offer in each country, the design of a multinational company organization must always start with its juridic structure. The legal profession and the international relations people customarily refer to the juridic aspects as the *formal organization.* Since the organization theorist, however, means something quite different by *formal organization* a confusion is unavoidable if this term is used in multinational organizational analysis. It is therefore preferable to replace the terms *formal organization* with *de jure* or *statutory* structure in the meaning of the legal form, and with *de facto* or *managerial* structure in the meaning of command hierarchy as used by the organization theorist.

A multinational firm is actually a complex of companies or, in strict legal terminology, an international compact among legally autonomous organizational creatures of different national sovereignties. Its overall juridic design cannot be sacrificed for the bricks and mortar work as is so often the case in domestic organizational study. As we will see later, the intrasystem dynamics, both overt and covert, of a multinational company flow to a significant extent from the interactions among the various national subsystems of this multinational complex.

To dismiss the de jure structure as a formalistic shell would be to misunderstand its economic implications. Being the only officially recognized linkage of the company to the different legal systems of its host nations, it remains always an organizational reality, which fundamentally affects multinational corporate behavior. This is particularly true in financial and legislative matters, including such strategic areas as maximizing the managerial freedom of action and corporate security, minimizing taxes and exchange losses, optimizing cash flows among the various entities of the firm, and qualifying for industrial development assistance, tariff protection, or governmental contracts in different countries.

International Boundaries and Organizational Design

In nearly all companies, except very new ones, the organizational space for multinational functions has been provided through a gradual enlargement of what originally had been created to serve the limited objectives of exporting and importing activities. That original unit was the traditional foreign trade department, or the export department, or their functional equivalent under some other name. This progression rests on the underlying assumption that the international and foreign operations of the firm require differentiation from domestic operations, i.e., that either the managerial functions or the operational methods or both acquire different dimensions when the organizational scope transcends national boundaries. As we shall see, not all companies have explicitly accepted this assumption. The view does exist although in a small minority, that international boundaries are wholly irrelevant to organizational design, and that business is business regardless of country or culture. To these internationally indifferent organizations we shall return, after having examined the models that have been developed with the specific objectives of meeting the international requirements of the firm.

The Structural Trilith

A very decisive structural component in a multinational organization is the junction where the *domestic* becomes separated from the *foreign*. Since this can occur only on a level below the highest managerial authority of the company, the domestic-foreign junction forms a trilithic relationship with the hieratical space which is reserved for the higher authority as illustrated in Figure 7-1.

Such a trilithic arrangement is fundamental to all organizational structures that make any distinction whatsoever between its domestic and nondomestic functions or operations. In the absence of the trilith, there can be no structural accommodation of any foreign or multinational activity except the same as is provided for a like domestic function. Thus, the trilith constitutes a fundamentally unique component in the structure of a multinational company. The location and frequency of the trilith in the hierarchy are decisive for both the power distribution and dynamics of the organization. The higher its hierarchical

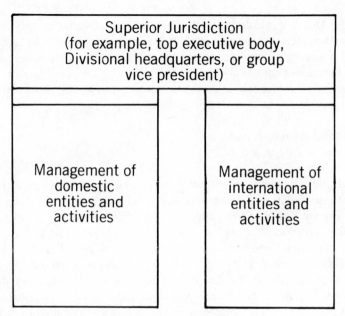

Figure 7-1. Structural Trilith

elevation the greater its influence. If, for example, the trilith were inserted immediately below the chief executive officer, the company would in effect have dualistic structure throughout. If, at the other extreme, it were first employed on the level of an operational subentity, such as a plant or department, most of the organizational structure would remain unaffected.

Structural Members of the Trilith

Superior Jurisdiction

What constitutes the superior jurisdiction depends on the hierarchical elevation of the trilithic joint. In all cases it must include the top management, which for the purposes of this study is defined as embracing all the executives and specialists whose primary duties are part of strategic planning, coordination, and control. Besides the directors and the chief executive officer, two major groups normally participate in the top management responsibility—the general staff executives of the corporation, and, the general operating executives. With the former belong the heads of various functional departments: accounting, finance, marketing, manufacturing, research, personnel, government relations, legal services, economics, taxation, transport, etc. All other staff units directly associated with the board of directors or the president (or their counterparts outside the U.S.) are also part of the general staff. Some of these may carry out work of primarily administrative nature, for example, finance, economics, and government relations; others, such as research and development, personnel, and marketing, are engaged in specialized operational activities, often with continuous participation in operating decisions. However, all the general staff units are primarily responsible for developing information in their specialized fields and supplying the operating management the respective professional expertise when appropriate.

The general operating executives are distinguished from the staff executives in that they are heads of the principal operating units (groups or divisions), rather than service units. In non-American multifunctional companies an arrangement often exists under which more than one headquarters executive is assigned to man a top operating position. This type of multiple management at the top differs from the American committee system in that the executives in the multiple part have a permanent joint management responsibility, while the committees are usually formed as either communication mechanisms or task forces for special purposes. Moreover, the demarcation between the general staff executives and the general operating executives becomes academic when viewed in the context of the policy-making process. Since both groups are a major part of the top echelon and serve as members of the corporate governing body, their identities as either the heads of staff or operating entities become irrelevant in all but strictly divisional decisions.

From Chairman to Chief Executive Officer

As corporations have grown in size, complexity, and sophistication, the classical concepts of both presidency and chairmanship of the board of directors have been changing. The chairman traditionally played the role of the elder statesman of the corporation, his primary job being to preside over the meetings of the board and to oversee the president's execution of the board's decisions. It often was, and in many companies still is, a highly paid position of semiretirement—a position where honor and prestige rather than executive performance were the prime considerations. To become chairman was to move "upstairs," away from the hustle and bustle of the main floor where the action was.

This elder statesman's role is now disappearing. In a large number of companies the chairman has been harnessed for a full-time top executive job. In some companies he shares the top man's duties with the president of the firm, letting the latter handle more the problems where operational decisions dominate and concentrating his own efforts on planning, policy formulation, and external relations of the corporation. This is perhaps still the most typical arrangement in firms having a full-time chairman of the board.

However, a new thrust has been gaining momentum since the late 1960s. This involves increasing the chairman's responsibilities to that of the *chief executive officer*—the commander-in-chief—of the corporation. This implies more than the words may connote. It converts the chairman from an overseer or general spokesman to the bearer of the ultimate responsibility for corporate actions and results. It usurps much that traditionally used to be identified with the presidency. The change in the position of the chairman has meant a concentration of the company-wide executive functions into his personal purview. As a result, the traditional functions of chairmanship have become but an incidental part of the position; as the new title *chief executive officer* implies, the main task now centers on planning, leadership, and control on company-wide and ongoing bases.

Multiple Presidency and
Subcorporate Autonomy

Contrary to the concentration and consolidation processes that have characterized the chairman's position, the concept of the presidency has been recast more and more into something resembling a general in the battlefield. His tasks have increasingly become identified with the actual "battle command"—the operations management. Just as different war theaters require different field generals, so too the different activity theaters of a large corporation require different operating executives. The bigger and the more diversified the company, the greater becomes the parallelism with the military in the command structure of the higher echelons. The point here is not about imitation but about inherent rationality.

Up to recently business leaders resisted this rationality, or at best tried to meet its presciptions through middle- or upper-middle management appointments, but always stopping short of allowing any split in the presidency of the firm. Now the barrier has been broken and the monocracy principle of the president is challenged by a polycratic structure in which the presidency is divided into several parallel positions. A forerunner to such an arrangement was the Nestlé Company, headquartered in Switzerland, which in the 1950s already split its presidency (or managing directorship, in European terminology) into two positions, each empowered to act alone in any critical situation but dependent upon the other's concurrence in major policy decisions. Regarded in horror as a two-headed monster by the orthodox organization people, the dual presidency of Nestlé was widely predicted to end in a corporate disaster. To the amazement of the critics, the disaster not only failed to materialize but, under its dual presidency, the company experienced its greatest growth and expansion on a global scale.

The Nestlé experience cannot be discounted as a freak devoid of any general significance. A decade later many U.S. companies started to introduce similar arrangements. The splitting of the presidency has frequently been camouflaged by retaining the traditional titles of chairman and president, but reallocating responsibilities so as to have in fact a dual presidency. The next step has been the replacement of the president with an *office of presidency.* The office may consist of three or four executives all empowered to commit the company individually as if he were the single president whenever conditions make consultation with other members of the presidency unwise. It is the Nestlé model expanded and refined. The main advantage is to enlarge the presidential capacity from one face-to-face solution at any time and place to several simultaneous solutions. In a far-flung multinational structure this is very important.

The 1969 reorganization of the Westinghouse Electric Corporation serves as an illustration of the third stage, where all pretenses of honoring the conventional format of the unity of the presidency are dropped. In a sweeping reorganization the company promoted its previous president to the vacant position of chairman, whose responsibilities were increased to be commensurate with its new role: the chief executive officer. The presidency was split into four separate positions, each heading a companylike grouping of profit-center divisions. The four new presidents, who held parallel line positions, were given full authority in operating their subcorporate groupings as autonomous enterprises. Coordination among the subcompanies was obtained through an eight-man policy committee, chaired by the chief executive officer of the corporation. Each new president in turn had two or three executive vice presidents in charge of the various operating units of his subcompany. General staff services were placed in the central head office and were divided among three vice-chairmen, who report directly to the chief executive officer. The basic scheme of the new organization is shown in Figure 7-2.

Ford Motor Company initiated a similar reorganization in the summer of 1969, when Henry Ford II created a triple presidency, each man directly responsible to himself, as chairman and executive officer. General Electric, Standard Oil, and several other major corporations have abolished single-man presidencies. But unlike Westinghouse and Ford, they have camouflaged the change by employing titles like vice chairman, executive vice president, or the like. It should not be surprising if the multiple presidency and its attendant subcorporate autonomy would become the rule rather than the exception among major corporations in the 1970s and 1980s.

One observer succinctly summarizes this ongoing change this way:

Many factors make one-man control obsolete, among them: the broadening product base of industry; impact of new technology; the scope of international operation; the separation of management from ownership; the rise of trade unions and general education. The real power of the "chief" has been eroding in most organizations even though both he and the organization cling to the older concept. . . .

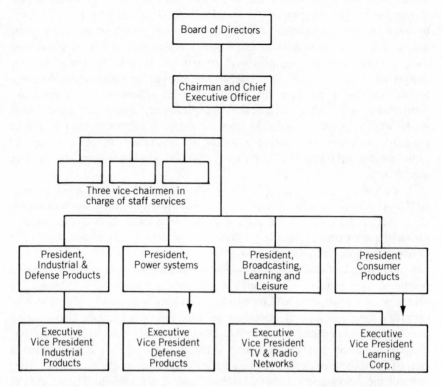

Figure 7-2. Multiple Presidency of the Westinghouse Company (Based on 1969 Reorganization)

This problem is essentially one of power and how power is distributed. It is a complex issue and alive with controversy, partly because of an ethical component and partly because studies of leadership and power distribution can be interpreted in many ways, and almost always in ways which coincide with one's biases (including a cultural leaning toward democracy).

The problem of power has to be seriously reconsidered because of dramatic situational changes which make the possibility of one-man rule not necessarily "bad" but impractical. I refer to changes in top management's role.

Peter Drucker has listed 41 major responsibilities of the chief executive and declared that "90 percent of the trouble we are having with the chief executive's job is rooted in our superstition of the one-man chief.[1]

Put in a multinational perspective, the imperative for adopting multiple presiding gains even greater urgency than is reflected in these observations of professors Bennis and Drucker.

Effect of Staff Units on Structure

Since these four components—the board of directors, president and/or chief executive officer, general staff executives, and general operating executives—are always part of the top management, it cannot be their presence or absence which determines the organizational, or for that matter the numerical size of the top management of a company. Rather, it is (1) the distribution of the staff activities between the headquarters and the various operating divisions, and (2) the distribution of decision-making authority throughout the organizational structure. If both are highly diffused, the personnel as well as the influence of the headquarters is limited. In such a case the trilith, if located immediately beneath the top management, would have a thin cross-block. If, on the other hand, the staff sources are concentrated and decision-making centralized, the headquarters staff groups will swell the ranks and the headquarters constantly overshadows on-the-spot managers. This would create a trilith with a massive cross-block.

But how about the jambs of the trilith? Does the diffusion of staff and decision-making ordinarily lead to massive jambs and the concentration to thin ones? Study of actual organization designs shows that the answer to both parts of this question must be in the negative. In multinational firms where the structural divide between domestic (the headquarters country) and international is positioned right below the top management, the jambs are frequently asymmetrical, with the domestic much larger than the international. This is particularly characteristic to U.S.-headquartered multinational firms.

Why such a lack of balance? The reasons are difficult to find. Most executives either fail to realize that there is a nationalistic or anti-international bias in these organizational structures, or if they do, cannot explain it except to attempt to rationalize its qualifications. The only people with some real insight into the problem are usually the senior people in the international divisions and the president and/or chairman who must bear the final responsibility for the structure. The former, the top men in the international division, are usually the best informed, but they are by the fact of their positions suspect and as such greatly hampered in counteracting the anti-international bias. Furthermore, the cultural benefits, social prestige, and the romantic-cosmopolitan aura which often goes with senior international appointments seems to induce polarization of management attitudes against the international entities and executives.

The bias expresses itself first in denying or deemphasizing the international dimensions of management and claiming jurisdiction over as many international activities as possible to the domestic divisions, whatever their design. The slogan "Good management starts at home, and good management at home is good management abroad," characterizes this position. Second, the international organizations are denied separate staff units which would be at par with their domestic counterparts. With but a few exceptions, companies contacted during this investigation had substantially smaller, usually 3 to 1 or 4 to 1, staff support for the international entities than the domestic ones. The problem is reduced in companies where the headquarters general staff units of the top management are dominant. But even here the influence of the domestic divisions often tilts the scales against the international entities. Even more serious is the narrowness of perspective of the staff specialists. Having been exposed only to the U.S. environment, the majority of staff experts lack the cultural and social perspective to practice their specialty outside the U.S. This seems to apply no less to lawyers and financial consultants than to advertising or labor relations councilors. The result is that the international division can rarely get the most effective staff support or accurate information, and must rely on its own limited devices to protect itself and the firm against the misjudgments and misapplications resulting from the inward-looking orientation of the general staff personnel.

Immigrant Staff

To cope with the problem, the international divisions have increasingly resorted to recruitment of foreign nationals, especially Europeans, to their own staff positions. Two factors have stimulated this policy: American salary scales have enabled the division to attract foreign people of the highest intellectual and personal caliber, yet save in comparison with any similar appointments filled from among U.S. applicants. But the policy has seldom been an unqualified success. With the exception of engineers, lawyers, and economists, the imported staff personnel seem often to have been lacking the professional preparation to be fully effective. This weakness is particularly conspicuous in the fields of specialization which fall in the purview of the American graduate business school. To a lesser extent the same could be said about the other areas of social science.

From company to company the pattern reemerges where the immigrant specialist works well in relatively simple techniques- or statistics-based analysis but starts running into serious problems when called upon to handle more complex problems. Frequently foreign nationals have been picked with their native country as the main target for international expansion. The record is unclear as to the wisdom of this practice. In a number of cases the immigrant seems to have performed effectively as long as the company's interest remained centered on his native land. But often, when the company subsequently broadened its vistas, the effectiveness of the immigrant staff member deteriorated appreciably. Not infrequently the imported expert has proven to be quite uninformed about the business dimensions of his native country, bringing with him more ideals, façades, and folklore about what the people like to imagine their nation and country to be than the factual knowledge and unbiased insight that is imperative in business research. In general, it appears that the immigrant staff expert can best perform in functions where language and mathematics suffice as his main tools.

It is not clear from this study if the policy of recruiting immigrant staff personnel for the international divisions of American companies has been a help or a hindrance to the development of a balanced and bias-free structural design. While the immigrant specialists have helped to underscore the peculiarities of the international managerial functions and the inadequacies of the domestic-oriented general staff activities, they have at the same time created two new organizational restraints impeding international development. First, being placed in the predicament of correcting and criticizing the activities of the main staff units, the immigrant specialist is cast in a negative role which tends to fuel rather than dampen the anti-international fires among the top-management staff. Second, being a social outsider, the immigrant specialist has rarely proven effective in influencing the thinking and orientation of his corporate colleagues or attracting the best American talent to his department. Although several outstanding exceptions to this exist, the generalization still holds true in nearly two-thirds of the companies that were the subject of observation in this study.

In a number of firms staff units follow certain executives who have become identified with specific specialities. Then when the executive is reassigned, say from the headquarters to a divison or from one division to another, the staff unit will follow him. The reasoning is that the senior executives' "proven" experience is more essential for the efficiency of the staff unit than its hierarchical location. It goes with this reasoning also that all the staff sources of the particular type have to be centralized into this one unit.

In companies where this philosophy predominates, the organizational entity for international management seems to have had the most difficulty in getting its own or otherwise competent staff support. Their staff resources have been channeled to the regular staff units which, although growing in size, frequently have failed to recognize the need for new skills, and thus continued doing what it had been set up to do for the domestic structure of the firm. In some firms, the growing need for staff services of the international division have fostered an even greater asymmetry in the staff organization, adding to the central, essentially domestic, staff divisions, and keeping the international management undernourished with vital staff support.

8

Structural Models of Multinational Corporate Organization

The first issue in multinational organization design is the distinction and relationship between domestic and international management. If the distinction is considered all pervasive, structural separation of the two must be provided; if the distinctions are few or insignificant, only minor adjustments in structure are needed to take care of the problem. The importance attributed to the distinction will determine the number and hierarchical elevation of the structural triliths that define the respective areas of domestic and international management in relation to their superior jurisdictions, as well as the nature of the superior jurisdictions.

Subfunctional Trilith

If the international objectives of a firm were limited to export sales, its international management tasks would be few and most of its organization and executive personnel would be unaffected. The activities affected would be selling, credit, shipping, and possibly market-research functions, which are usually all combined under the marketing executive.

Structural models of the subfunctional differentiation have been perfected by the long tradition of scholarship in foreign trade organization and administration.

The Built-in Foreign Trade Department

The most embryonic form of international organization is the so-called built-in export and built-in import departments. In the case of the built-in export department, the company recognizes international managerial functions only to the extent of certain operations, primarily procedural and documentary techniques that differ from or are not encountered in domestic marketing. Among them are drafts, letters of credit, foreign trade controls, customs clearance, international shipping, packing, marine insurance, and related practices. The built-in export department's responsibility is to supply the supervision necessary to enable the regular marketing personnel to perform these foreign trade functions. It is essentially a one-man department, the export manager being the only one fully and solely concerned with international business. Instead of having his separate personnel, the export manager must utilize the regular sales staff. This minimizes the investment in the organizational apparatus of the export operations, but at the same time reduces the export manager to a superclerk whose main contribution is to supervise other clerks in filling out documents and following proper foreign trade procedures. On strategic planning, policy formulation, or even marketing tactics, the export manager has but marginal influence at best.

The built-in department has its natural habitat in companies using the indirect export method, that is, in companies that channel their exports through an international intermediary, such as an export trading company, and thus abdicate to the intermediary most of the policy decision and operational activities concerned with international marketing. To a lesser extent, the built-in department has been successfully used by direct exporting companies with a simple, standardized product line, mostly in the raw material or semimanufacture categories. In consumer goods, except staples, and for diversified industrial lines, this organizational form has never sufficed.

On the import side the same holds true, except that the built-in import department, which is more rare than its export counterpart, is housed in the purchasing department and subject to the control of the purchasing agent of the company.

Separate Foreign Trade Organization

Where the strategy was to have direct trade linkage with foreign countries, the classical prescription called for either a separate export or import department divorced from the domestic marketing and purchasing departments or, in larger firms, a foreign trade division with executive personnel, facilities, and operational autonomy approximating those of other functional departments of the firm. In strategy and policy-making authority, however, it remained subordinate to the marketing or procurement division, depending on whether it was charged with export or import responsibilities.

Separating international trade from the domestic marketing and procurement activities removed the organizational limitations of the built-in arrangement and allowed more adaptive and effective practices to be employed in foreign trade. However, the activity of the organization still was limited to trade: export and import operations and no more. It was a functionalist concept which had its place in a function-based organization structure. But when functionalism started losing ground to territorially and product-based corporate structures, the export departments became square pegs in round holes.

Whatever its legal status or operational size, the foreign trade departments and divisions remained on a low level in the organizational scheme of the firm. Being subfunctional, their effect upon the top echelon of the company was at best in the two functional areas—marketing and procurement—and even here it was only indirect, through the respective domestic department or division. The foreign trade departments formed functionally isolated organizational extremities from which there was seldom any access to a broader corporate responsibility.

Subdivisional Trilith

In product-based divisional organizations the structural accommodations for the international aspects of business have shown a greater flexibility and variety than in the functional scheme. If operating in the framework of the foreign trade philosophy, each product division could conceivably establish its own foreign trade department; it could be either the built-in or self-contained type, depending on the nature, volume, and channels of the trade involved.

Although there have been actual instances of complete divisional foreign trade autonomy, the general tendency in product-based organizations has been to avoid multiple channel and incoherent foreign trade, particularly export operations, by combining all international marketing activity into a company-wide export unit. Foreign-sourced procurement may be similarly consolidated. Such export and procurement units, however, though company-wide in form, remain subdivisional in substance: the unit providing the "technical services" of export and import know-how and interdivisional information but having nothing more than advisory functions concerning decisions on product, price, quantity, priority, and other substantive matters. It has been typical for the subdivisional foreign trade departments to have some product people assigned to them by the different divisions to handle the substantive aspects of the respective divisions of foreign trade.

However, a purely foreign trade activity has rarely characterized the international ambitions of a product-based divisional organization. It appears that since a product division is not dominated by any one functional activity, such as marketing or procurement, but represents a cross-section of all functional fields from production to promotion, its expansive tendencies have rarely any singleness of bias, such as maximizing sales or increasing market share, as is typically the case with marketing departments. A multiprong approach—increasing production, expanding plant capacity, broadening the product line, or generating greater earnings—is natural in the context of the personal qualifications and the priorities of a product division. It looks not only for markets and marketing opportunities but also, and often even more, for sourcing and production possibilities, and it possesses the capability—which the marketing department normally lacks—to enter foreign countries through the transfer of production, technology, investments in plant facilities, and the utilization of indigenous resources in addition to export or import activities.

The establishment of a foreign unit by the division automatically creates international managerial responsibilities of a multifunction type. The foreign unit may be dominated by the divisional head office or it may be granted a high degree of autonomy. But in any event, the operational management of the foreign-based plant requires on-the-spot problem solving and supervision, which means that even at the irreducible minimum the establishment of the foreign-based plant is coupled with the creation of an international operating management organization commensurate with the size and character of the plant.

Limitations of Subdivisional Structures

Each foreign-based facility compounds the international organization; and each new country or cultural region requires adaptations to its peculiarities. The increasing complexities of the sociocultural problems strain the divisional management's capabilities and act as a restraint for further national expansion. The more technology-oriented the divisional decision-maker, the greater is the restraint, as well as the pressure to augment the management capabilities to overcome the restraint. Consequently, an organizational adjustment and enlargement above the plant management level becomes a necessity. How this enlargement will take place depends often on whether one or several product divisions are interested in international expansion. As long as the international ventures are confined to one division, top management will be willing to sanction any reasonable proposals which the division might initiate. When several divisions become involved however, the permissiveness of top management is sharply reduced. First arise the serious problems of capacity utilization, efficiency, and profitability of international ventures. If each product division would have complete autonomy over its own international activities, the entire divisional structure of the corporation would have to be repeated in each of the countries which it enters. At best, such an unintegrated multidivisional structure could be rational only in a small number of the very largest foreign markets, such as the EEC or EFFA. For most of the world, the repetition of a multidivisional structure in every country would involve extensive duplication and prohibitive overhead for practically any corporation. Indeed, the large investment and organizational burden of such a structure would prevent entry into any country or trade bloc except those already having a massive unsatisfied demand for its products—a rare occurrence. Also, if each division were left free to devise its own approaches, facilities, and organizational structures for international activities, each could then conceivably adopt a separatist arrangement different from all others for its foreign-based management. For example, one division employing local nationals, another relying on expatriates, and a third developing a cosmopolitan cadre; or one having only wholly owned subsidiaries, the other joint ventures, and the third minority interests or licensing arrangements.

The International Division Model

Most top managements are allergic to the interdivisional inconsistencies, and especially to the organizational barriers to corporate growth that are posed by the multiple subdivisional arrangements for international management. Also, most product division presidents find it too ulcerous to bear the full burden of international ventures, especially in the early stages of the international growth of the company. The typical result is that the control of investments in foreign-based facilities and the subsequent enlargements of above-plant executive apparatus of international activities are removed from divisional autonomy, and a separate organization—the international division—is set up to handle the international affairs on a company-wide basis. At what point this occurs depends primarily on the characteristics of the product lines and the markets of the firm. From the product standpoint the most important factor is technology: if each product division is endowed with a sophisticated technology that is not possessed by other divisions, the tendency is much greater for the product division to maintain its separate identity, including its own control over international activities, than in product divisions, where the technological differentiation is low. Contrary to the belief of some writers on organization, all product divisions are not significantly different from others in terms of underlying technologies, but owe their existence to marketing, production, or control considerations. In those which are technology-based a real barrier exists, which must be surmounted before the multinational managerial responsibilities can be transferred to the international divisions. This technological barrier remains even after an international division has been set up, and prevents it from becoming anything more than a service auxiliary to the technology-based product division. It also appears that product diversity as such favors product division control over the international activities, and tends to act against an early consolidation of international activities of the company. If the products are technology intensive the diversification usually follows the boundaries of the technologies involved. Hence, the product divisions are in a more fundamental sense technology divisions, and as such pose special skill requirements for the international division, which are not easily met. On the other hand, diversification of low-technology products (products that require simple methods or utilize well-known, mature techniques) seem to present no technical difficulties for shifting the foreign activities into the international division. In other words, product diversification as such does not determine what kind of organizational adjustments a company will experience when its international activities grow. More important than diversity is the underlying technology: if there is a divisionalization in terms of the technologies, and especially if the technologies are unique or subject to rapid change, the shift of multinational management functions from product divisions to the international division is not only complicated, but may either be postponed indefinitely or bypassed completely in favor of a more advanced form of multinational organization.

Market diversity counteracts the technologically based product diversity by inducing structural adjustments of the organization that reduce the market complexities for the decision-maker. That means territorial or areal specialization of executives, which is best achieved in a territorially oriented structure. If the products of the firm are relatively homogenous the territorial imperatives dictate the structural design; if the products are diversified, any shift be it toward territorial or toward product divisionalization, involves a trade-off. Thus the ultimate outcome is decided by whichever factor outweighs the other in the judgment of the managerial cadres of the firm. Naturally the previous experience of the key executives and the past history of the company tip the scales in borderline and near-borderline cases. However, when market complexities clearly outweigh product complexities or vice versa, there is usually no doubt about the direction of the structural dynamics of the organization. Market complexities have often been overemphasized by companies that are in the early stages—roughly the first eight to ten years—of international production and marketing activities. This is due primarily to managerial inexperience and lack of flexibility in decision-making and marketing practices. As a consequence, the international division is attributed great "technical" significance during this stage, that is, it is looked upon as the sole embodiment of the company's capabilities for international action. This places the international division in the category of highly specialized, if not esoteric, departments which may be both admired and envied, but little understood by much of the organizational population. As the familiarity with international problems spreads, confidence among executives increases, and a more matter-of-fact assessment of the international department replaces the initially inflated image. However, the substantive role of the international division seems to increase as it matures. Case histories of organizational change reveal that in the early stages of foreign involvements, the international division is often used as a service unit catering to the international aspirations of the product divisions, which jealously claim sole jurisdiction over all policy decisions. Thus, at this stage the international division is highly operations-oriented (concerned with foreign trade techniques, local laws, customs, fact-finding, etc.) and depends on the product divisions in what it may or may not carry out.

Its policy-making functions are strictly limited to consolidation and coordination of incongruous divisional practices and to suggestions to the product divisions. It can seldom commit the company or any product division in any substantive way. But unlike the subdivisional organs, this type of international division, illustrated in Figure 8-1, is not amenable to any product division's particularist policies; it is protected against any undue separatist influence by the involvement of the other product divisions and by its direct access to the top management.

As the foreign operations grow and mature, the international division shows a tendency to rise in the hierarchical structure. Simultaneously, key international

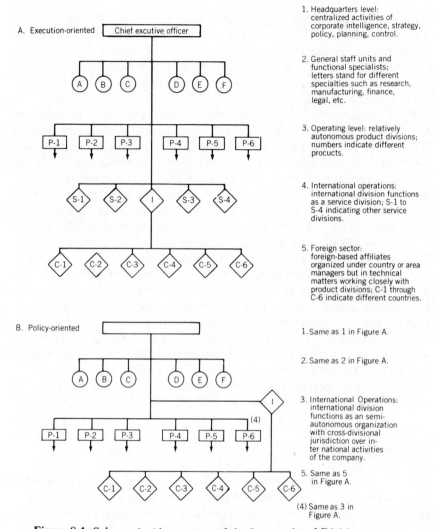

Figure 8-1. Schematic Alternatives of the International Division

policy functions are transferred from product division to the international division, the latter becoming synonymous with top management's organ for international affairs. While in the first stage the international division was conceived as a collective creature of the product divisions—a joint service unit comparable to traffic department or personnel department—it now has its primary identification with the supradivisional echelon of the firm. A schematic illustration of such a division is shown in part B of Figure 8-1. It might be added that the organizational charts of companies are seldom drawn so as to indicate the shift. Very commonly the international division is stuck in the chart on the same level with the product divisions, which creates the graphic illusion of equality between the international and the product divisions, a condition which research findings never have validated.

In all companies that use product-based divisionalization the potentially most difficult organizational problem is the relationships between the product divisions and the international division. Since the corporate command structure is built around product lines, introduction of an international division violates the basic schemes. What should be the position of the international division, and especially what power relations should it or could it have with the product divisions? How do you prevent the international division in such a setting from being reduced to a routine-burdened service organization to the product divisions, an appendix devoid of strategic influence and policy-making powers? These are questions to which no product divisionalized company can have easy answers. No perfect structural solutions exist for these problems. The nearest thing to a satisfactory solution is the model depicted in part B. But even here the international division, although under the protective eye of the top management, remains in many ways dependent upon the product divisions. This is particularly true if foreign-based factories are to use the manufacturing or engineering services of the domestic plants. How well or badly the international division functions in the product division setting depends, therefore, always on the cooperation and support it can get from the product divisions. Horizontal communication channels and interdivisional personal relations are thus crucial.

Territorial Divisionalization

It is a widely held misconception that the international division represents a natural extension of a territorially divisionalized company, which presents no special problems. Although superficial examination may show the international division as but one among several territorial divisions, and thus quite consistent with the basic structural scheme of the company, a close study usually reveals that this is not necessarily true. If the company has operations in several countries, the international division will differ significantly from the domestic territorial divisions in terms of diversity, managerial requirements, market conditions, etc. It may also differ significantly in size, either in population or geographic dimensions; for example, having jurisdiction over the entire world outside the home country. More fundamentally, in such a divisionalization is inherent a break in principles—namely, the rationale for the other territorial divisions cannot be the distinction between *domestic* and *foreign*, while for the international division the key criterion is foreignness and not the quantitative dimensions of the market or the locational relationships between sourcing and marketing.

Size of the International Division

Systems equilibrium theory requires that organizational subsystems seek equality of size or influence to have a balanced structure. If this theory is to be satisfied the international division, once established, would tend to grow until it has acquired equal size with other divisions of the company. The size is most likely measured in terms of either sales or investments, but could in special cases be expressed in terms of work force, profits, or some other statistic. It has also been hypothesized that the size of any new division is subject to a collective influence of the preexisting divisions of the firm. If the new division shows a rapid rate of growth the older divisions may act in concert to suppress this growth, their alliance solidifying as the newcomer starts approaching the size of the largest old division.

Neither hypothesis permits the international division to exceed the largest domestic division in size. In reality it often does. Many companies show much larger sales, investments, and profits from their international division than any domestic division; in some the international division equals or exceeds all other divisions combined. In most of these cases the international division has, in fact though not in name, become an international headquarters company.

International Headquarters Company Model

The difficulties inherent to the divisional arrangements have compelled industry to seek other structural solutions to its international problems. The international headquarters subsidiary company (IHC), a separate headquarters for foreign activities of the firm, seems to have provided the approach most acceptable to the majority of American companies.

From a purely legal standpoint, the creation of the international headquarters company might be conceived as the lifting of the international division out of the domestic corporate structure and elevating it to the status of an independent juridic personality with all the statutory organs, charter, and officers of an autonomous firm. Customarily the word *international* has been used to distinguish the subsidiary from the parent: Boeing International, General Electric International, Western Hotels International, Weyerhauseser International, etc. Its separate juridic status qualifies the IHC for a number of special privileges under internal revenue, foreign trade, foreign aid, and several other statutes and regulations. In certain instances, the legal advantages have been a major or even the primary reason for shifting to the international headquarters plan. More commonly they have constituted a secondary input, while the primary reasons have evolved around the strategies and operational efficiencies of the international sector of the parent corporation.

From the managerial point of view, the IHC company model goes beyond the divisionalization idea. Its scope is not limited to the domestic structure, nor are its operational capabilities subordinated to domestic divisions. Although it may serve the objectives of diversification—as to both product and market—it is not limited to this or any other objective of the domestic divisions; nor is it reducible to a routinebound service unit to the latter. Rather, the IHC company is an international headquarters prototype, a structural system for the administration of multinational foreign operations in the broadest meaning of the phrase: multinational corporate holdings, asset-producing activities, marketing, operating facilities, research, personnel, and organizational subentities, etc. The IHC may or may not be directly involved in operational activities. In large corporations it is often a company of companies, the central headquarters of a variety of different operating companies scattered throughout the world; in smaller ones, it is typically a hybrid between a holding-company-type policy and control center for a series of locally incorporated operating affiliates in different countries and an operating company engaged in managing the actual day-to-day operations of another series of affiliates.

Where fully developed, the IHC possesses a self-contained headquarters structure in all respects including trade and transfer arrangements with the divisions and domestic subsidiaries of the parent. As shown in Figure 8-2 the trilith enters the prototype immediately under the chief executive officer and separates from here down the entire hierarchy of the parent corporations from the international structure. In other words, it creates two completely separate structures, one for domestic affairs, the other for international affairs of the parent firm.

The two structures are linked on top in the office of the chief executive officer where the controls of both structures are housed. The chief executive heads both companies but often limits his activities in the international headquarters company to the traditional role of chairman. The operational synchronization between the two is carried out by a new corporate staff unit in the parent company, headed by a *contact officer* in a vice president's or equivalent rank. For greater effectiveness the contact officer sits on the boards of directors of both companies. In some firms he has been appointed to serve at the same time as the president of the IHC. This has had a tendency to introduce bias and to reduce communication between the two structures. In its pure form the IHC model does not tolerate such double assignments, and requires that the contact officer not be entangled in direct line responsibilities on either side. Not only does the mediation of all collaborations between the domestic operating units and the IHC belong to the contact officer's jurisdiction, he also must be broker and arbitrator in case of conflict and incongruities between the two systems.

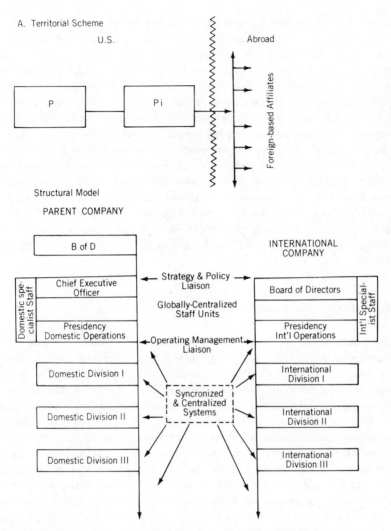

Figure 8-2. The International Headquarters Company Model

In other respects, the IHC company leaves the domestic structure quite unaffected. Like the international division, the IHC model prescribes for its internal organization a geographic breakdown, mostly by country. In larger firms the IHC company often takes on a multiple structure where some product organization may be superimposed upon the geographic principle. For example, within one diversified IHC company three subsets of operating subsidiaries exist: one for heavy equipment, one for scientific instruments, and one for consumer products. Although in each country and world region there are appropriate corporate organs having the general jurisdiction in the respective territory, the product groups are given a high degree of autonomy and are in many countries really subheadquarters for a number of their own specialized subsidiaries or other types of affiliates. In larger firms the international structural design often takes on a resemblance to gallaxies, with multiple centers, differentiated communication, channels, and multiple levels of managerial jurisdiction.

In practice the distinctions between the international division plan and the international headquarters company model are often difficult to discern. In many firms the heavily overused word *division* remains in the title of the organization long after its substance has been converted to the international headquarters company plan. This semantic difficulty has misled some observers to rate the divisional organization as the most common among American companies. Any substantive study will show this to be a mixing of geese and ducks. It is not so much the juridic form as the managerial content that distinguishes the international headquarters company from the international division.

The World Company Model

The organizational accommodation to the growing international impact upon corporate strategies has not stopped with the perfection of the dualistic structure which the international headquarters model represents. With it, however, a turning point had been reached. To this point, all the stages in the development of international organization—the subfunctional, the subdivisional, the divisional, and the separate international headquarters—have been based on the premise that domestic and international managements do not mix, and that organizational separation of the two is conducive to higher managerial proficiency and better corporate performance. As the logic of this premise dictates, each new stage has pushed the trilithic juncture to a higher hierarchical level, and effected the separation of the international from the domestic to consecutively larger and larger areas of the total organizational space. It has been an upward and outward movement; international expansion based on organizational separation.

From here on, the direction changes. The world company concept challenges the assumption of irreconcilability between domestic and international management. But the challenge is not motivated by the parochial naiveté "What is good at home is good abroad," but by the experience that the more discriminating approaches, greater intellectual awareness, and a more cosmopolitan orientation, which are required in international management, can also sharpen and revitalize the domestic sector of a company by raising the levels of social and cultural awareness and by reducing provincialism and other psychological rigidities resisting organizational adaptation to the ever-increasing tempo of change. The slogan could almost be reversed: "What is good in international management is also good in domestic management."

In the world company model, in its pure form, no distinction between the domestic and the foreign is recognized. That does not mean that the model is insensitive to territorially changing variables, such as cultural, economic, or political factors. Its principal aim is to place no structural limitation upon either the scope or degree of adaptation of the organization to the realities of different localities. Such adaptation is possible on both an inter- and an intranational basis, whenever the existing conditions make it desirable. Since the nature and extent of adaptation needed are determined by the territorial variation of conditions, the degree of adaptation in any particular aspect of the organization must be greatest in the localized activity areas and in functions that are immediately related to any particular or unique condition locally. Consequently, most of the adaptation requirements exist on the lower, primarily operating level of the corporate structure, and in principle, the need to adapt decreases along the vertical axes of the organizational hierarchy.

Due to trade barriers and political discontinuities, international boundaries often require organizational adaptation when transcended. A unit that combines corporate subentities from several countries into a single executive jurisdiction requires a greater degree of adaptation than an equal size unit whose components are all located in the same country. That is, a multicountry subsystem of an organization involves more adaptation than a unicountry unit on the same hierarchical level. This principle seems to hold on all levels and to apply to all functions. However, the degree of adaptation required tends to show interfunction variability, e.g., marketing requires more adaptation than production, and production more than engineering. But taken by itself each function presents a pattern that is consistent in that it requires less adaptation on higher levels of the organization and presents discontinuities and special problems when international boundaries are crossed.

Moving up its vertical axis, the model world company structure is to absorb the adaptations to different nationality and geographic conditions at its base, accommodate the resultant structural and operational diversities, and assimilate the pluralistic elements of the lower levels into an increasingly cohesive and unified whole at its top. In the higher echelons there will be neither any domestic vs. international dichotomy nor any country-by-country fractionation in the organizational structure. Theoretically, there is no nation-centeredness in any sense; but since under the existing political organization of the world the headquarters of a company must be domiciled in some country, there always is, in fact, a home country whose environmental constraints are an inescapable reality to the headquarters group of a world company.

From the top down, the world company model compels the headquarters executives to view their corporate roles from a global perspective, and to cultivate structures and objectives that enable the achievement of maximum growth and profitability in a worldwide context. The headquarters of the world company is, therefore, concerned not with national or international affairs but with world affairs. Its orbit is the globe, and conceivably in the future also the moon and outer space. Managerial problems peculiar to individual countries or certain groups of countries belong primarily to lower-level jurisdictions of the corporate structure, and are postulated to be at most only secondary inputs to the headquarters decision processes. Figure 8-3 shows the world company model. In its simplest form its command structure rests on the geographic principle, with area specialists occupying the key line positions. To this basic structure can be crafted elements of product organization, as well as functionally specialized units. How these combinations are best worked out depends on the specific circumstances of a particular firm. In terms of principles, such a composite design can follow the outline shown in Figures 8-3 and 8-4.

In the evolutionary chain of the international organization the world company model represents a return to unified structure. But this is not a backward movement. While the unification in the traditional foreign-trade-oriented firm resulted from subfunctionalizing and subordinating the international entities of the organization on a low hierarchical level and narrowly limiting the entire upper echelons to domestic business, the world company elevates the international and transnational responsibilities to the top of the structure and localizes individual country and regional problems on the bottom layers. Thus the evolutionary path has had both a horizontal and a vertical dimension, which has moved the international component along a spiral from the bottom to the top through various degrees of segregation of the domestic from the foreign, and ended in a full integration of the two in the central organs of the firm. In the process, top management has become totally internationalized and shifted from a nationalistic to a cosmopolitan role.

Spacial Structure

A corollary to corporate growth through international expansion is the multiplication of diversities and peculiarities that accompany each new country. Sheer size and physical distances in themselves will become a constrictive depressant as the company starts reaching for a truly global scope. To provide a structural basis for effective organizational solutions to these problems, a spacial distribution of the top management power and the concomitant territorial autonomy become at some point necessary. A monocentric multinational company, as shown in Figure 8-5, is conceivable only when the number of countries in the corporate realm is relatively limited; as the number increases the need arises for dividing the total corporate territory into geographic zones and establishing a zonal headquarters or *base company* for each. (Such a polycentric model is also shown in Figure 8-5.)

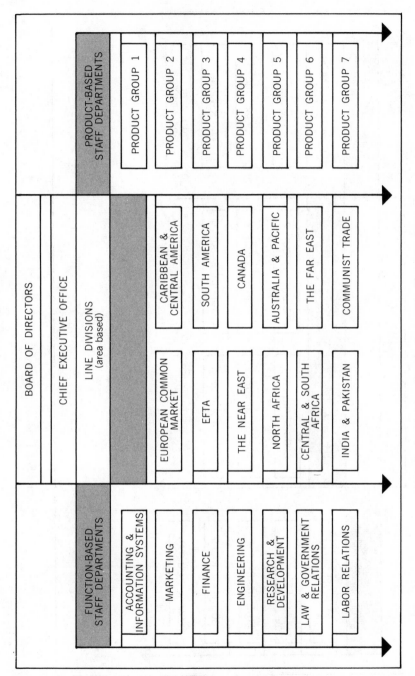

Figure 11
AREA-CENTERED WORLD COMPANY MODEL

Figure 8-3. Area-Centered World Company Model

Figure 12
PRODUCT-CENTERED WORLD COMPANY MODEL

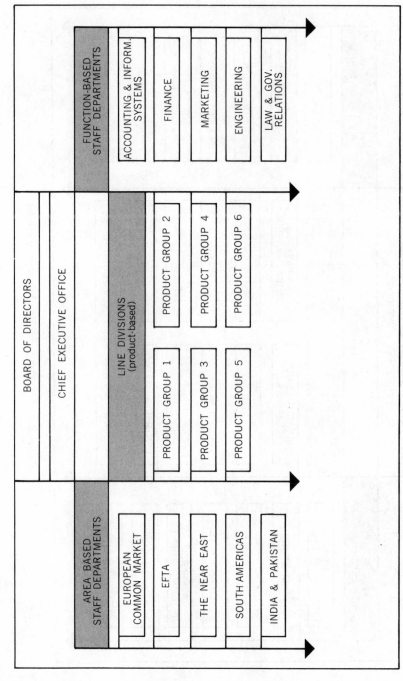

Figure 8-4. Product-Centered World Company Model

Explanations:
1. Each square represents a different country with its distinctive national culture.
2. headquarters company.
3. base company (headquarters for a group of affiliates).
4. affiliate companies.
5. headquarters line of command.
6. bass company line of command.

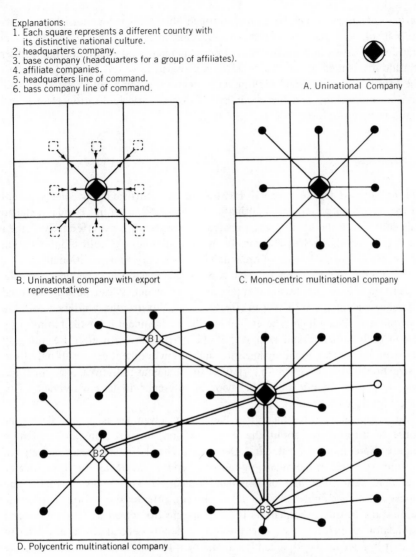

A. Uninational Company

B. Uninational company with export representatives

C. Mono-centric multinational company

D. Polycentric multinational company

Figure 8-5. Spacial Models of Multinational Corporate Organization

The base company concept can be utilized as an extension of either the international headquarters model or the world company model. Some companies have utilized the base company to perform the functions of the IHC, while keeping the structure of the parent company at home unchanged. In such a case the base company becomes an IHC located abroad. Depending on the region, certain advantages may be gained through this foreign location: better integration of top management and operations, greater financial flexibility in transferring assets and profits, and closer alignment with environmental realities outside the United States. These advantages must, however, be weighed against the loss of U.S. treaty and diplomatic protection, closer scrutiny by U.S. trade and tax authorities, and the possibility of unnecessary duplication of technical and routine procedures.

Polycentrism

During the past decade a general shift toward polycentrism has become apparent in the territorial patterns of multinational corporate structure. Fundamental to this shift is the theory that complicated systems work most effectively if their parts readjust themselves decentrally, with a minimum of central intervention and control, except in case of breakdown. This theory gains additional force for multinational organizational systems from the inevitable dependence of the organization upon its environmental forces, on which it can have but limited influence and then only if it can effectively and constructively interact with the environment. Being highly heterogenous, the environment is hostile to uniformities in both initiative and response of the corporation. An effective interplay between the multinational organization and its environment can result only from a structure that is capable of a variety of simultaneous initiatives, responses, and other types of organizational behavior in reference to its environment. This argues for decentralization.

In a typical multinational firm there is an advantage in a central clearing house of information about the gross situation, but decisions and execution require more minute local data. Deciding in headquarters means relying on information that is cumulatively abstract and to a greater or lesser degree irrelevant. Also, the line of command execution must apply standards and procedures that cumulatively do not fit the concrete, local situation. This is true because the central headquarters is by its nature first of all an accumulator and assimilator, sometimes also a synthesizer, and only secondarily a dispenser of what it has accumulated, assimilated, and synthesized from the total corporate realm. In mathematical terms, the headquarters functions as a producer and dispenser of analyses. The problems in different parts of the realm, however, depend on specifics and can therefore best be resolved only in terms of specifics.

But the advantages of widespread decentralization of a multinational company that a polycentric system represents is not limited to resolving immediate problems. A decentralized structure, at least to a point, engages more minds, and more mind, instead of a few headquarters executives. Instead of the few ideas and goals which the headquarters group can muster (the more centralized the structure, the more operationsbound and less idea-oriented the headquarters executives tend to be), a polycentric structure fosters creative inputs from much wider groups of its multicultural managerial corps. It mobilizes the latent intellectual resources of its field forces, which in a monocentric setting tend to remain dormant. The maxim that a society that distributes power widely is superficially conflictful but fundamentally strong and stable applies to the multinational enterprise perhaps even more than to political bodies. With their own peculiar abilities, aspirations, and criteria each affiliate, each country, continent, and professional grouping in the corporate totality can increase its contributory good to the company if a closer alignment and freer interchange is provided between the different parts of the corporation itself on one hand and between the various parts and their respective environments on the other. The shift toward polycentrism is propelled by this dual objective.

Managerial Orientation

The world view and philosophical attitudes do indeed have an impact upon corporate structure as well as the behavior of and policies issued by the structure. Documentation for this fact has been offered by this author in various writings before. None, however, has insisted that the managerial attitudes and points of view possess such omnipotence as in Perlmutter's scheme. While his argument makes plausible reading, it is contradicted by factual studies of multinational enterprise. The hard evidence of my own work leaves no room for doubt about the fact that managerial attitudes and ways of thinking are but one factor among many inputs that jointly produce the structure and activity patterns of a multinational or international firm. In case of conflict between the managerial attitudes and strategic necessities such as fighting off competitive attacks, utilizing previously unrealized opportunities, or achieving the company's growth objectives, management attitudes show much malleability and capacity to adapt. Individual exceptions to one side, corporate managers as a class show in general a greater aptitude to suppress their nonrational biases than most other groups in the society. Indeed, for the professional manager a prime principle and requirement is the ability to adapt to change and to the new conditions that change generates. Although this is more easily said than done, there is no escaping the fact that managerial attitudes are not constant but change with circumstances; they are typically the dependent variable in the total organizational equation, very rarely the independent one. Since many other factors impinging on corpoate form and activities are environmentally determined and thus are beyond managerial control, any conflict between the attitudes and the other factors will sooner or later compel a modification in the attitudes; the only alternative being a denial of corporate achievement by sheer stubbornness.

The argument that managerial orientation and attitudes are the primary causal factor in determining the organizational structure and behavior of international firms must be rejected on both empirical and theoretical grounds. Similarly, any implication that the managerial orientation issues a constant, unchangeable influence must also be discarded. But this is not to deny any influence to managerial orientation: it always has an influence, but one that is more often a derivative of the combined influence of other factors coacting or interacting with it than a causal one, and as such, its actual impact varies greatly with circumstances as well as among companies.

The questions of fixity and flexibility in managerial orientation are seldom reducible to personal prejudice or irrational psychological commitment; rather, they depend on information and aspirations that underline the orientation. A headquarters executive, when insisting that domestic practices be followed in foreign-based affiliates, does so not because of his psychological attitudes, but because his professional criteria are essentially information based. If all he has is information about the domestic scene, his criteria must necessarily be either domestic-oriented or pure conjecture. Provided with information about the contrasts between the domestic and foreign settings, the executive will, sooner or later, discover that modification of his domestic criteria will result in comparatively more efficient operations, and change his "attitudes" accordingly. As a rule, people who get set in their ways and dislike to modify their practices are a serious liability to any business organization, uninational or multinational, and should be removed from managerial positions.

The problem with ethnocentrism in international managements is primarily educational. The executive is inculcated with the values, views, and norms of his home environment. If his business experience also has been primarily limited to the domestic scene, there is no cause to wonder why he does not act from any other than an ethnocentric perspective. This is all he knows and understands. Given some systematic exposure to foreign area studies, a few years' assignments in other countries, and access to hard evidence on contrasts between the domestic and foreign situations, the executive will normally cease to cause any worry about undue nationalistic behavior.

Another way, and a much more useful one than the managerial attitude, is to study the corporate organization structures with a view to their capacities regarding different types of international behavior—which "corporate psychology" is natural to a particular structural design and which international managerial behavior can reasonably be expected to result from the design. This is quite a different matter from managerial attitude profile, unless we assume that attitude profile is automatically and accurately mirrored in organization structure. There is no evidence that this is the case; in fact, organizational studies point not only to significant time lags between any changes in management orientation and organizational structure but also to more frequent and wider movements in the orientation than in structure.

There is no such thing as a management attitude or orientation in the singular; the nearest thing to it in any multinational firm would be a consensus.

But then, whose consensus? Which executives' attitudes count, and how far down the hierarchial pyramid should we go? The executive cadre of any multinational firm represents a wide spectrum of attitudes on almost any significant corporate issue, especially organization and the relations of people in it. As in any other group a small majority of the executives hold strong opinions in a few matters but are quite uncommitted on most others; the majority is relatively uncommitted and open to persuasion, political or professional, in most matters. Any corporate consensus, therefore, tends to be highly volatile and responsive to business necessities as conceived by the executive body of the company.

9

Organization and Control of Affiliates

Each national affiliate in a multinational corporate structure constitutes a clearly differentiated subsystem with a considerable degree of autonomy, either recognized or unrecognized, plus unique characteristics deriving from its peculiar cultural environment. It would, therefore, be a gross oversimplification to visualize the organization of the various affiliates of a multinational corporation as simply extensions of the basic hierarchy of the parent firm. While all the affiliates are by definition part of the multinational corporate hierarchy, they are at the same time creatures of the indigenous national cultures and legal systems and, as such, never interchangeable or identical in either design or behavior. Conceiving of affiliates as nothing but extensions of the parent firm can lead to the perverted view that the decisive considerations are the organizational ideas and objectives of the parent, and that environmental forces can be ignored. The reality is quite the opposite: the organizational method and practices of the parent company, especially the latter itself—being the product of a unicultural experience—are often disfunctional in another country's culture, and require various degrees of adaptation or even complete redesign to be effectively employed. The purpose of this chapter is to identify the various sources of influence upon an affiliate's organization and to describe the consequences stemming from them.

Legal and Jurisdictional Differences. How the affiliates of a multinational company can be organized in different countries is first of all a question of law. To be admitted by a particular country the affiliate must qualify for a business license, and to do so it must comply with all legal provisions applicable to do business in that country. Since the laws of no two countries are identical, legal aspects of establishment must always be handled as a special case.

The visas for corporate entry into a country can be classified into four broad categories: first, the expatriate affiliate can qualify for a branch license; second, it can take the legal form of a subsidiary company created under the laws of the host country; third, it can be licensed as a joint undertaking between the parent multinational firm and an indigenous company or agency; and fourth, it can be an independent indigenous firm affiliated to the multinational company through entering into a licensing arrangement. With the possible exception of the last, the entry visas for expatriate corporate entities are subject to specific laws and regulations that are generally more restrictive, difficult to comply with than those which apply to goods, capital, or people. Known in law as *the right of establishment*, the treatment accorded to nonindigenous business entities by host countries is often subject to international agreements and commercial treaty provisions in addition to statutory and customary laws.

Branches

The simplest form of multiunit business operations is a firm with several branches. Although physically separate from the parent company and the other facilities of the firm, and regardless of its internal administrative autonomy, a branch is not an independent juridic entity from a legal standpoint. The law does not recognize the branch any more than it recognizes the existence of factory number two or a particular department in a firm. For legal purposes a branch is simply a physical extremity of its parent company. Since it does not have its own juridic personality, it cannot initiate any legal action such as court litigation, or be an object of one. For all legal purposes a branch is part and parcel of the juridic personality of its parent company, and its activities and actions are indistinguishable, under law, from the behavior of the parent.

In the domestic setting the branch is often the most convenient method of creating new operating centers or productive facilities that are physically removed from the existing plant. In the international setting this is not true. While in the domestic setting the legal status of the branch is of small concern, because the parent company remains responsible for any legal action taken either by or against the branch, in the international setting the lack of legal identity complicates matters greatly. When the branch is located in a different country than the parent company, there arises the jurisdictional problem of enforcing the host country's laws in reference to the branch as well as the branch's ability to benefit from the government services of the country of its location. Lacking its juridic personality, the branch is immune to outside legal action, as all such action must be directed against its parent. Since the parent, however, is located in a different country, the government of the host country of the branch would find itself in an intolerable situation of having an operating business entity within its territory over which it had no jurisdiction, and whose juridic embodiment was beyond reach outside the country.

Licensing of expatriate branch operations is therefore subject to the requirement that a qualified national citizen, either physical or organizational but in either case possessing a juridic personality, be authorized under a *power of attorney* or similar legal instrument to serve as a legal custodian of the proposed expatriate branch. The power of attorney conveys to the national citizen complete legal authority over the branch. In all matters of law, the custodian will be considered to be the legal embodiment of the branch. Referred to often as the *domestication of a branch*, the custodian arrangement creates additional uncertainties for the parent company which can be avoided by the use of other types of affiliates.

Even after being licensed the expatriate branch often remains suspect in the eyes of the local government and public and either overt or covert discrimination will be practiced against it. Its business license may require frequent renewal involving considerable expense; its taxable base may be so defined that the entire parent corporation—its assets or earnings—become liable to the host country's tax authority; and the regulation and governmental surveillance of the expatriate branch is often tighter than that of other types of businesses.

Because of discrimination associated with the expatriate branch, this form of organization is seldom found appropriate in multinational companies, except as subdivisions of an affiliate within the limits of a particular country.

Subsidiary

The second alternative open to a multinational firm is to set up its various national affiliates as separate *subsidiary* companies. This is done under the local laws of the country being entered. Thus, if it establishes a subsidiary in France and Brazil, it must abide by the business laws of France and Brazil respectively. The subsidiary may be a corporation, but could equally well take any other legal form of organization for which there is a provision in the law of the particular country. As pointed out elsewhere, in many countries, especially those under the Roman law system, there exist organizational forms other than the corporation which possess juridic personalities separate from their owners, and in which the owners' financial liability is limited to their investment in the enterprise. For example, German law provides for a limited liability company (G.m.b.H.), which resembles the U.S. corporation in all features essential to management and ownership, yet enjoys much greater freedom of action under law than does the German equivalent of the corporation (A/G). If a multinational company takes full advantage of the legal opportunities which the different organizational forms in various countries offer, inevitably the affiliates of the company will not all be corporations, but will constitute a mixture of many different forms.

Although the de jure and the de facto organizations in multinational companies are two distinct structures, the legal form of an affiliate can never be ignored as entirely irrelevant for management purposes. The juridic organis of the affiliate, especially after their statutory offices and officers, must always be somehow integrated with the actual decision-making systems of the corporate body. This must be done in such a way that there is no subversion of law or any sacrifice of operational efficiency. Obviously, the achievement of these dual objectives depends upon the nature of the statutory requirements as well as the operational conditions in the country concerned. The greater the incongruity between the two, the more difficult is their integration.

The Joint-Venture Company

In many countries the law permits the establishment of expatriate enterprises only if local nationals share in their control either by serving as officers or being investors of a specified percentage of the affiliates' equity. While the provision concerning officers is usually of lesser significance and does not often lead to the abandoning of a particular organizational form, the requirements of native participation in ownership can only be met either by selling shares in the host country stock market or, which is more common, entering into a joint venture with an indigenous firm or agency. In a number of countries the ownership requirements of expatriate enterprises are so formulated that it can be met only by owners who control large blocs of the stock. This seriously curtails the opportunity for public distribution of stock, and encourages joint venture arrangements. To enable the foreign company to contribute to the legally required capital, the parent may accept some existing assets such as industrial sites, land, facilities, machinery and equipment, production processes, or even patents and goodwill. All these can be assigned monetary values by mutual agreement. Cash contribution by the local concern can thus be varied to meet the particular situation. How far a parent company is willing to go in this respect in either direction depends on the alternatives available to the parties as well as the profit potential of the country concerned.

The organizational and behavioral aspects of the partly owned subsidiary companies and the joint venture companies are quite different in many ways. A subsidiary that derives part of its equity from selling stock to the general public in its country of domicile is not materially different from a wholly owned subsidiary, in that the cultural and social impact of the host country upon the organization is indirect and the integration of the affiliates with the indigenous society incomplete. As a rule the sociocultural effect depends on the nature of the stock ownership: if the stock is widely dispersed in small amounts the effect tends to be insignificant; if, on the other hand, the stock is owned by a small number of large stockholders, their voices will be heard. But in neither case is it likely that the minority stockholders will have any direct impact upon the operational and organizational behavior of the affiliates. As in the case of a wholly owned subsidiary, the partly owned affiliate remains for all managerial purposes, especially in its operational and organizational behavior, entirely subject to the parent company's control. Its adaptation and assimilation in the host country society differs in no significant respect from that of a wholly owned subsidiary, and for all practical purposes the discussion of the wholly owned subsidiary's integration into the host society is applicable to it.

The joint venture represents quite a different organizational relationship. Since its parent companies belong each to a different national, economic, ethnic, and cultural environment, there is a high probability of conflicting views and value judgments that must be reconciled. How difficult and serious these differences are depends upon the particular partners and countries involved. However the problem as such is universal for all international joint-venture enterprises. Like similar problems in nonbusiness organizations, such as church and military, it requires methods and techniques specifically designed to deal with it.

Coalition Type Management

The basic choice is between coalition and delegation. If the parent companies wish to prorate management control among themselves according to their ownership shares in the joint venture, they will be committed to a coalition administration of the venture. The resultant multinational management group will not only be imbued by the different national, ethnic, and cultural norms that guide the factions assigned to it from each country, but, being representatives of different firms, they will each bring to the joint-venture management their own parent company's point of view, objectives, and managerial practices.

The compounding of the cultural and managerial differences makes a coalition type of joint-venture management a highly conflict-prone proposition. Besides the cultural contrasts, the coalition will have to cope with a number of causes for dissension. First, there are environmental constraints. One partner may be operating only in its own country, while the other has international commitments. This may mean, for example, that the local partner is taxed by its government only, while the multinational partner is subjected to tax obligations in several countries; or that the local partner, being in tune with its native uninational environment, views any deviation from its own organizational and managerial behavior as undesirable, while the multinational partner, being subject to different influences in other countries, may regard such a point of view as highly eccentric.

Another source of dissension in a coalition management derives from the fact that each faction in the coalition must explain and justify to the other or others, as the case may be, its respective home office's decision and actions in respect to the operations of the joint venture; conversely, the decisions of the coalition must similarly be explained and justified to each parent company's home office. Under such conditions harmoniously unified and consistent management is difficult to achieve and psychologically demanding on the individuals involved.

Parental ownership ties and social responsibilities provide a further source of difficulty for the coalition. For example, family-controlled companies, typical in many countries, confront the nonfamily-owned American or European corporate partner with demands to make executive appointments from among the family membership, to declare and pay high dividends, to burden the joint-venture company with various consumptive needs of the family, or to divert some of its assets to meeting the social and cultural obligations that their standing in the society may require.

Inherent in any joint-venture enterprise is the question of divided profits. By committing itself to a joint venture each parent company denies itself the future opportunities for earning the full profit which the new enterprise is potentially capable of generating. In addition, the parents may perceive the future potentiality and the best ways of realizing it quite differently. When they become convinced that the full potential of the joint enterprise can not be achieved due to divergent parental views, the party or parties that are most disenchanted may begin to seek other avenues to tap the unutilized potential. In pursuit of this objective they will jeopardize the future of the joint-venture enterprise by either promoting policies of stagnation or by trying to maximize dividends to finance their separate facilities and operations deemed necessary to utilize the potential which in the respective parent's assessment is beyond the reach of the coalition-dominated joint-venture management. Experience shows that dissensions over the disposition of the joint-venture profit, especially regarding reinvestment and expansion allotments versus dividend distribution, are difficult to prevent. Naturally if all partners are equally disenchanted with the coalition stalemate the joint venture becomes simply a milking cow that is exploited strictly for short-term gains, in disregard of its future growth and long-term position.

A strained coalition has a strong impact upon both formal and informal organizational structure of the joint venture. It compiles compromises and inconsistent concoctions in the organizational design that not only encumber the internal administrative processes of the enterprise but also prevent its organization from becoming fully integrated with any of the parent companies. To the extent to which it remains unintegrated, it must of course suffer from the inability to utilize many of the processes and services that the parent organization could contribute. The factional tensions of the top management are mirrored in similar factions throughout the rest of the organization. There will necessarily be followers and defenders as well as antagonists and defectors of all factions of the coalition. If the joint venture is owned by several partners factionalization of its managerial corps may present a serious issue of employee morale and corporate cohesion.

Since the ownership of a typical joint-venture enterprise is limited to two or three partners, the factionalization is limited to the same number. This means that the differences and points of conflict are more easily definable and understandable, but it also means that the personnel, especially in the lower echelon of the organization, can draw more clear-cut demarcation lines between the different positions, which not only helps to internationalize the conflicting values involved but also sharpens and hardens the opposing positions if allowed to prevail over a longer period of time. But on the other side, the one-against-one and triangular factionalizations also facilitate the efforts to reconcile the differences. Professional business education and cosmopolitan management culture, with attendant value standards and behavior criteria, are also helping to resolve this type of problem. Several cases could be cited about joint ventures that, having been initially ridden by internal managerial dissension caused by factional rivalry in the top, ultimately turned out to be successful not only in achieving coherent and harmonious administration but also in pioneering in methods to overcome the traditional differences and in contributing to multinational managerial principles and practices.

Although much has been learned in the past twenty years about consolidating the interests and objectives of different partners to joint-venture enterprises, the coalition form of management still proffers greater organizational risks and managerial uncertainties than most companies can comfortably accept. Through the trials of past experience, industry has reached the decision to avoid the coalition type of management for joint ventures whenever and wherever another alternative is available.

Autonomous Management. The alternative to the coalition is to endow one of the parent companies to the joint venture with sole responsibility of its management and to limit the other partners' managerial involvement to long-range strategy decisions, such as product line, major investment expenditures, and other nonoperational goals and policies. Within this broad, long-range framework the managing parent will have complete autonomy in all matters of operational policies and methods, as well as organizational design and functioning. In more recent joint-venture agreements the provision for a managing partner company, or alternatively a clause for managerial autonomy of the joint-venture enterprise (its independence from all partners), is expressly provided.

The experience with the noncoalition type of joint-venture management has been generally better than with the coalitions. It has eliminated many of the sources of dissension, particularly those which are outlined above as peculiar to the coalition structure, and placed the joint-venture management very much in the same category with the management of any international affiliate in a multinational corporate context.

The only reason the noncoalition or managing-partner form of joint-venture administration has not become universal is the difficulty that many companies have in separating ownership from managerial controls. For the managing-partner form this separation is an absolute prerequisite. As long as the parents of a joint venture see managerial prerogatives as direct expression of ownership rights, nothing but the coalition administration is possible in a joint venture. For the student of business administration the concept of separation between ownership and management should not pose any intellectual or ideological dilemma: it has been expounded in American textbooks for many years. Yet in an international context even the American partners have exhibited extreme reluctance, particularly in the initial stages, to permit joint-venture management to operate in anything but ownership-determined frames of reference. Gradually, and often grudgingly, the superior wisdom of separating the two concepts has been accepted. It appears that the slowness of the acceptance is at least in part attributable to the fact that joint ventures have initially been negotiated and developed by people with narrow functional responsibilities, whose organizational talents and experience have been their least impressive credentials. However, as indicated above, the present state of the art in American multinational companies has risen above the ownership-management syndrome, and only the novice and managerially backward companies are still encumbered by its rigid applications in international joint-venture undertakings.

Joint-venture Practices in Europe. Outside of the United States the problem remains formidable. Even in Europe, where in many other respects managerial sophistication in international affairs is scintillant, an astonishing condescension and formalistic rigidity are typical in international joint-venture formations. A case in point is a recent joint venture between a Belgian and a German company. Both in the same technical-product line with different emphases, the two companies saw obvious advantages in a joint venture, which would strengthen both parent firms in such fundamental aspects as research, new product development, engineering, and competition on world markets. In all these and a number of lesser areas impressive numerical proof for the potential value of the joint venture was established. Both partners accepted the studies as convincing and the objectives of the joint venture as highly important. Yet despite such thorough research and documented prognostications, the joint venture landed immediately in an administrative swamp of a most unoperational organization format.

In the quest for a perfect power parity, the joint-venture agreement not only provided that both parents will have equal representation on the board of directors, but created also the principal executive organs—nine joint councils, or departments—and stipulated the exact numbers and positions to be occupied by the executives of each parent. They went even further. Taking a cue from the irrationalities of the big-power summit conference technique, they carried the misconstrued notion of national equality needs of the joint venture to the absurdity of fixing the seat of its board meetings in an insignificant and inaccessible town, its sole merit being its location equidistant between the headquarters of the two parent companies. Being oriented by the formal structure of the joint venture as distrustful and status-directed coactors, the two factions on the joint-venture management perceived their roles not as one of forming a cohesive, integrated whole, but as representatives and guardians of their respective parent companies' self-interest and investment vis-à-vis the other partner. The future of this particular joint-venture remains in doubt. Unless its organizational structure and managerial philosophy, including relationships with the parent companies are substantially altered, the advantages initially antici-pated from the joint venture can never see realization.

Joint-venture Practices in the Orient. The ownership-control syndrome has also presented a serious hurdle for Oriental enterprises, among which the Japanese have been pacesetters in most respects. Starting with a similar notion as the Europeans, the Orientals also have sought perfect equality among joint-venture partners. In their formula equality was to be achieved through equal ownership shares in the joint venture, which justified equal representation of each partner on the joint venture's board of directors. That such a formula will provide the highest possible probability for stalemate has not deterred its rather general adoption in the early years of Oriental joint-venture enterprises. When the inevitable stalemate materializes, the formula has generally not been discarded, but instead altered, in that the chairmanship of the board is distinguished from the rest of the board membership and endowed with the power to break any deadlock. This is done by giving the chairman's vote a greater weight than one. In case of a tie, the side on which the chairman votes will carry any particular motion. Most of the Japanese joint ventures which now are spread around the world are based on this formula. Only in very recent joint ventures has the separation of managerial control from ownership become evident. At the same time the autonomy of the joint venture has been increasingly emphasized, and it has become almost a generally recognized principle among the better-managed Japanese companies to view operational matters as more or less the exclusive domain of the joint venture's own distinct managerial cadre, and out of bounds for parent executive interference.

Social and Political Aspects. Compared to wholly owned subsidiaries, a joint venture enjoys a number of significant advantages, which derive from its social-political image as being a genuine part of the host society. Unlike their wholly owned subsidiary, the joint venture is seldom discriminated against as all foreign companies normally are. The discrimination against foreign firms is inherent in the concept of a sovereign nation which, in terms of its own logic, must promote and defend the interests of its citizens in preference over other people of the world. Since discrimination against foreign enterprise is therefore universal, it is important for an affiliate in a multinational corporate structure to avoid identification with foreign enterprise. The joint-venture arrangement provides an effective means for overcoming these discriminatory restrictions. Association with a native enterprise in a joint venture not only provides protection against negatively discriminatory governmental actions, but also places the affiliate in a position for seeking positive relief from burdensome domestic regulations. That is, through its joint-venture status the affiliate gains access to the full scope of the host country's governmental services. Governmental attitude is crucial for any affiliate, but especially in countries where central planning, socialization, and public regulation of their business activity are dominant. Import licenses, foreign-exchange controls, business and professional taxes, and work and residence visas to engineers, technicians, and managers are examples of so-called "routine controls" by which various governments can strait-jacket a foreign firm's operations. On the positive side are tax exemptions, tariff protection, low-interest loans, and other special privileges used by many countries as incentives for stimulating investment and industrial development. The friendliness of local government is therefore an essential precondition for the success of a new international venture, and the joint venture involving a native party provides a means for integrating the affiliate in its host's business system, yet leaving open opportunities for managerial integration with their multinational structure of the parent firm.

Being accepted as an integral part of the indigenous business system, the joint-venture enterprise commands a much greater degree of an affection and tolerance from the general public than would any wholly owned foreign subsidiary. Public goodwill is especially significant for the consumer goods industry and service firms such as insurance companies, banks, hotels, and common carriers, whose sales are directly related to public attitudes and acceptance of their product.

In labor relations, the joint venture can bargain with unions without being vulnerable to anti-American or antiforeign attacks, which often beleaguer wholly owned affiliates. It is not required to issue comparative, and often embarrassing, wage and salary data for all the operating facilities in its multinational structure, and there is evidence indicating that employee morale tends to rise as local capital enters a previously wholly owned enterprise. This seems to hold for white-collar as well as blue-collar employees. In a developing country where governments are supersensitive to foreign domination and strongly nationalistic philosophies dominate, the gains in morale derived from joint venture are potentially more significant than the gains in any other area.

Franchise Holders

A special kind of affiliate enterprise is represented by the franchise holders, who have been licensed to either produce or market the licensor's product. This relationship is always formalized in a written contract, which stipulates specific rights that are transferred from the licensor to the licensee, as well as the compensation, usually in the form of royalties, to be paid by the latter. The licensing arrangement in its pure form involves no capital investment. As such, it is quite different from any other parent-affiliate relationship. One might even question the appropriateness of the terminology of "parent" and "affiliate," especially the word "parent." Yet there is an undeniable operational linkage, managerial cooperation, jointness of purpose, and sharing of affinities between the two enterprises. There is also the dependence of the licensee on the licensor, in the sense that without the former's product, patent, or whatever property rights are licensed, none of the benefits could accrue to the licensee firms. Since there is no equity involvement, the arrangement is free from the ownership-control syndrome. Problems are solved and decisions are made on bases other than equity involvement ratios between the partners.

The history of international licensing affiliations is relatively free from interpartner managerial intrigue and dissension. This does not mean that everything in licensing arrangement management has been milk and honey. Far from it. But the difficulties that have existed are attributable to different reasons than ownership prerogatives.

Management of Licensed Operations. Before coming to them, it is helpful to make clearer the basic nature of managerial arrangements typically found in licensing arrangements. The solution to this problem has usually taken the course of least resistance: each partner doing exactly what he had been doing before, each remaining completely autonomous, and neither trying to dominate the other. This has been by far the most common formula in the early stages of any licensing agreement. In the long run, however, the noninterference principle has not always been easy to honor, and has tended to become a source of dissension. Typically it is the licensor who starts agitating for an operational integration of the two organizations. Its motives may be to increase the volume of business done by the licensee, to push for expansion and growth, and to push for adoption of operating methods and practices that have proven successful in licensor's own company. If there is not a ready and willing response from the licensee, the temptation to bring about the desired objective through various forms of involvement in the licensee's management and subtle forms of coersion become irresistible. Business history abounds with cases of cooperation gone sour and enmity replacing empathy where coercive tactics have been attempted. How much interference a licensee is prepared to tolerate is not only a matter of the economic interest involved, but also depends upon the environment and the character of the licensee company's internal culture.

Some firms react sharply to any attempt of overt pressure from the licensor, even though financial stakes in a licensing arrangement may be rather substantial, while others are tolerant, much more malleable, even though the stakes may be relatively low. But if the cultural condition and corporate philosophy are more or less comparable, the dependence of the licensee upon his licensing arrangements is of primary consideration for determining how much licensor involvement the licensee organization is prepared to absorb. More important than the total amount, although this is not irrelevant, is the proportion of the licensee's earnings that the licensed property rights represent. This, in turn, is a function of the size of the licensee organization: smaller and weaker licensees tend to be more malleable than the larger and stronger companies. However, this should not be interpreted that the smaller firms are to be preferred over the larger ones as providing potentially more efficient licensing relationships. The empirical evidence seems to indicate the contrary. Willingness to play by the licensor's rules and the ability to do so are two different things. Even more important, the licensor's strategies and ideas about achieving success in the licensee's country are often untested and based on mistaken assumption: they represent transplants from the licensor's home environment into a foreign situation, which may or may not be compatible with the exported practices.

Transitional Licensing

Licensing arrangements have proven successful and satisfactory organizational entities when the goals of the licensor are relatively limited and more or less clearly defined. This is usually true for small manufacturers, which use licensing to either supplement or replace export operations, or for larger companies, which wish to maintain the presence of their product in certain foreign markets that are considered to be on the periphery of corporate development and growth. In other words, the stability of licensing arrangements over a longer period of time has presupposed a relatively static business situation and no-growth or slow-growth aspirations. When these assumptions are not fulfilled, licensing relationships have shown a high incidence of deterioration, and in the long run failure.

To avoid the growth-restrictive tendencies of a permanent licensing arrangement, a temporary one can replace it, with the objectives to utilize the licensing relationships partly as a testing device to find out the mutual compatibility of the parties as well as the true market potential of the product or services involved, and partly or perhaps primarily as a self-generating source of funds for a more permanent facility to serve the long-range growth objectives. In its simplest form such a licensing arrangement would utilize either all or a very large part of the proceeds from the licensing operation after a stipulated number of years. The so-called *royalty and stock participation agreements* are specifically designed for a gradual conversion from licensing to equity joint-venture operations. They usually provide for a low or a declining royalty scale, plus a stock purchase commitment in a new or existing joint-venture establishment to succeed the licensing arrangement. The licensee acquires a partial ownership interest in the successor company through the stock purchases. In cases where local equity capital is not available in sufficiently large blocks to establish the joint-venture facility, it may be financed initially wholly by the U.S. licensor, and gradually converted into a joint enterprise by replacing part of the licensor's investment under a royalty and stock-purchase agreement.

Sources of Friction and Uncertainty. Both organizational design and the licensor-licensee relationship are affected by the exclusivity aspects of the typical licensing agreement. Virtually all licensing agreements contain certain exclusive rights. Some companies grant both exclusive production and distribution rights to the licensee for the host country or even for a number of countries surrounding it. Others grant exclusive production rights, but follow a policy of limited exclusivity or nonexclusivity in its distribution and marketing activities; still others may parcel out production rights on a limited exclusivity basis, but have strictly exclusive marketing territories and representatives. Which policy is followed is frequently not a matter of choice, but is dictated by the logic inherent in the situation. A thin market, for example, may leave no other choice for the licensee than to insist on a completely exclusive coverage; in a highly concentrated market, such as a large urban area, both the licensee and the licensor have more alternatives and a greater variety of arrangements are therefore natural.

A fundamental characteristic of all international licensing agreements is the so-called principle of mutual restraint: the parties contract to avoid interference with each other, in the sense that each will stay out of the other's market; the licensee promises to remain within his designated territory, and the licensor, while granting exclusive production or distribution rights to the licensee, also agrees not to compete with the licensee through other channels of distribution. The relationship between the two partners is subject to the relevant statutory provisions of both countries concerned. The laws relating to business practices, trademarks, patents, foreign relations, and competitive business practices are of particular significance. In case of the United States companies the antitrust laws are the potentially most troublesome. Their uncertainties and ambiguity have often acted as a depressant of international business activities, notably in deterring foreign companies from establishing joint operations, either equity or nonequity type, in the United States. Other legal requirements may also impede the operations of the affiliate in various ways, depending upon the intent and energy of the host government in administering them. Examples of foreign laws that can be generally restrictive include special status or commercial procedures dealing with are: (1) auditing authority; (2) terms of office for directors; (3) frequency of turnover of top management; (4) political stature of both directors and top management; (5) disclosure of financial statements; (6) degree to which the product is subject to distribution and price controls; and (7) degree of official protection afforded, such as legal monopolies and tax credits. In addition, of course, the host government has the power to block remissions or even expropriate the affiliate itself. Clearly the legal aspects are also significant in deciding among a licensing agreement, some form of joint venture, or a total commitment to a fully owned subsidiary.

10 International Managerial Communication

Nothing in multinational management presents a greater challenge than communication. Even in a purely uninational context, communication—the act of making ideas and opinions known to others—often causes serious problems. As Rupert puts it, "under normal circumstances it is difficult enough to communicate with people of a similar culture, but the problem is greatly complicated when one has to bridge the gaps between the minds of various peoples around the globe."[1]

The problem is not limited to the interpersonal sphere, but extends also to various intergroup relations, such as the interinstitutional, as represented by communications processes among the various affiliates of the firm, as well as the communications between the headquarters and the affiliates; and the international groupings that may overlap and sharpen some of the interinstitutional contrasts or be quite separate from them in an intrainstitutional setting.

The communication problem of a multinational firm could be structured in several different ways; the best way seems to depend on the purpose of the particular study. In this discussion we are guided primarily by two criteria: the structure of the available tool disciplines, such as accounting or linguistics; and the urgency of furthering the state of the art in the different aspects of communication, as reflected by the empirical record of failures in multinational corporate intelligence.

Inadequate or faulty communication seems to pervade most multinational organizations. Often problems go unnoticed because communication channels are too limited; for example, a conflict of values may go unnoticed because no communication is attempted, or perhaps more correctly, because the communication processes allow blind spots to exert in the organizational space. Proper communication may reveal problems as well as solve them. But communication can be used also for obscuring or camouflaging an existing problem by cajoling (creating) and conveying images that distort underlying realities. Not infrequently basic conflicts in values between the headquarters and affiliate executives are clothed over with a false aura of harmony and unison through various communicational contrivances designed to conceal the actual problems.

Multinational Communication Networks

The communication network of any multinational firm is a complex composite. Whether systematically planned or put together intuitively, this network is charged not only with the "normal" currents of management messages but also, and for our purposes more importantly, with the "supranormal" loads of a highly pluralistic organization. By the supranormal are meant the aspects of communication that are peculiarly characteristic to multinational companies; or, to use the definition by exclusion, that are atypical of uninational firms.

These supranormal information loads are our primary concern. Although they occur in an infinite number of different contexts it is useful to distinguish between interpersonal, intergroup, and interinstitutional communication, to better understand their nature and implications.

The *interpersonal* problem has for some time preoccupied many social scientists; psychologists, sociologists, and anthropologists. We conceded to these prior claimants the jurisdiction over the interpersonal communication, and dealt with it only in a supplementary way. In interpersonal cross-cultural communication there is very little that is peculiarly business-related or business-dependent. While this should not deter business scholars from studying the problem, it lends no particular incentive for such study.

The *intergroup* communication problem is more directly connected with the organizational context within which it happens to be housed. Interactions between the expatriates and indigenous executives, between various parallel-purpose groups such as the European marketing group and Latin American marketing group or the product X group in Germany and the product X group in Brazil, can hardly be either studied or understood without reference to the firm itself. The same is true about many intra-affiliate and intraplant groups, which may be less clearly differentiated yet distinctly different from those found in uninational companies.

The main focus of our research to date has been on the *interinstitutional* communication conduits. Since the purely international dimensions of managerial communication are inherently interinstitutional in character, they demand primacy in any logical progression from our present state of ignorance toward an understanding of the processes and problems involved.

By "interinstitutional" we mean the information channels between the different national entities in a multinational firm; that is, the vertical conduits between the headquarters company and the affiliate companies in different countries, and the horizontal conduits among the affiliates themselves. These are all transboundary conduits through which international managerial communications must pass. (It would be technically correct to argue that the interinstitutional, as here defined, constitutes but a particular variant of the intergroup classification. From a substantive standpoint, however, any lumping the two together would badly blur, if not conceal, much that is critical for any operational system.)

System Models and Design

If we visualize the totality of the multinational firm as the suprasystem and its headquarters and various affiliates in different countries as subsystems, the effect of the throughput capacity of the company's international communication channels upon the behavior and internal stability of the subsystem can be studied. The area of this effect is bounded at one margin by a model which permits a continuous transmission of maximum available information among all subsystems, and on the other margin by a model restricting interaffiliate information flows to the minimum, which may be defined in terms of legal requirements. In the latter case each affiliate would possess what might be called the "autonomy of necessity." Since there is very little information from the other entities of the multinational suprasystem, each affiliate must rely on its own devices for adapting itself to its environment and for determining its behavioral norms.

If we move to the other margin, where each affiliate is subjected to an unlimited pounding of international informational inputs from other affiliates and the headquarters, its ability to adapt to its own particular environment and to develop the behavioral norms that are appropriate for its stability and efficiency as a subsystem is obviously retarded, if not distorted. It remains open for debate whether an affiliate under such circumstances can ever achieve anything approaching a stable adjustment to or full integration with its national society.

Another polarity of systems models would distinguish between loose-knit and tight-knit communication networks. Neither is to be confused with a nonsystem, that is, a completely unstructured and unorganized communication. Any system implies a certain degree of restriction of communication among its members. To move from an unorganized to an organized state requires the introduction of constraints that replace random diffusion of information with established communication channels and processes designed to serve the organization's needs.

The findings of this study tend to discredit the loose-knit systems, which showed a generally much greater degree of toleration for fictitious imageries in place of factual information, and allowed basic conflicts of values between the executives in different affiliates to be clothed over with a false aura of harmony through improvisations contrived to conceal the actual problems. On the other hand, the superior efficiency of a more tight-knit system also requires a more competent staffing. Where the job is assigned to strongly ethnocentric and culturally unsophisticated personnel, the tight-knit systems also show a greater capacity for malcommunication and stereotypic bureaucratization of transboundary corporate relations.

The systems model that emerges as the most functional for the study of the multinational company as a suprasystem has these parts:

1. The institutional base structure consisting from
   a. headquarters company
      (1) as the central regulatory mechanism, and
      (2) as a particular kind of subsystem;

b. affiliate companies as distinct subsystems in their respective countries of domicile.
2. Coding and filtering mechanisms.
3. The numerical-technological systems overlay.
4. The linguistic-social systems overlay.
5. The multinational totality—the suprasystem.

Each rests on a different base and has its own peculiar logic and dynamics. Each also represents its own peculiar emotional investments in the other parts. All this makes each part highly dependent on the others. The dependence is often more covert than overt, especially in companies whose international acquisitions have outstripped their executive preparedness for multinational responsibilities.

Coding and Filtering Mechanisms

Misinformation and misinterpretation due to national differences are clear and ever-present dangers in all multinational companies which we have studied. In addition, interaffiliate and other intrafirm divergencies contribute to these dangers. For example, the information requirements of the headquarters company and the affiliates are not symmetrical. What the headquarters needs to know is often not what the affiliates want to reveal, and vice versa. The downward flow consists of explication of goals, indoctrination of ideologies, policy rules, specific task directives and task rationales (in relation to corporate objectives, other tasks, environmental dynamics, etc.), techniques, procedures, and feedback to affiliates about their performance.

A frequent failing in the headquarters' information exports is to use messages addressed to all affiliates irrespective of their countries of domicile; the result is information that is often too general and too remote from the actual conditions of the individual affiliates and the experiences of their managers to convey to them the action content which the headquarters intended.

On the other hand, affiliate information imports tend to be biased by the particularistic interests or the lack of capability of the affiliate involved. If it receives generalized or partial information that leaves room for interpretation and reduction to affiliate-relevancy by the resident management, the tendency is not always to seek the most authentic meaning of the message, but to pick either the one that best serves the particularist interests of the affiliate or the one that obviates the alternative judged the most dysfunctional to the affiliate's welfare.

Either end of a transboundary conduit can cause indefiniteness in the action content of the messages transmitted, which can seriously frustrate managerial effectiveness. Sermons and guidebooks urging all executives to augment generalized statements by appropriate affiliate-specific elaborations or applications probably help, but we failed to find any company whose managers had been able to surmount this problem on their own. The success was significantly greater in companies that had created "competent transboundary channels." This is not to be confused with the line of authority and responsibility concept. The key elements in these competent transboundary information channels are coding and filtering apparatus consisting of carefully designed and internationally sensitized structural entities at all subsystems: affiliates as well as the headquarters.

In the downward flow it is not always the absence of the filtering and coding apparatus at the headquarters which accounts for malfunctions in the information conduits. In many cases the structural step had been taken, but its personnel lacked the necessary cross-cultural sophistication or the transnational perspective to make it work. American- and French-headquartered companies seem to be particularly weak in top management's competency in this respect.

Upward Flows

Information exports of the affiliates are subject to two types of bias. First, the social system in many countries discourages factual communication with the person directly affected; the implied and indirect are preferred. Nationals of those countries find full and objective reporting difficult and distasteful. In much of the Orient, and elsewhere in various degrees, people are accustomed to telling their superiors only what they believe will please them, whether true or untrue, and to remaining silent about anything expected to cause displeasure. This principle is manifested in countless practices that at least in Western logic represent distortions of fact.

Second, there is a tendency for an affiliate to restrict its exports of information that could adversely affect the affiliate itself. Needless to add, the perception of the adversity need not be founded on fact.

The presence of expatriate managers can alleviate these biases, but never fully remove them. Only through systematic filtering and coding of the affiliate's information exports can consistent sufficiency and reliablity of affiliate reporting be insured. As in the headquarters, the coding structures alone do not suffice. Especially if the interests or behavioral norms conflict sharply between the headquarters company and an affiliate, structural channels may be blocked and information flows obstructed unless the channels are immunized against unilateral domination by explicit checks and balances. When the affiliates are left to design their own information linkages with the other organizational entities of the multinational firm, the resultant network would be characterized by a generally weak international linkage and an uneven pattern, with many asymmetric relationships produced by the lack of mutuality in the import and export propensities of the different affiliates. While each affiliate might then achieve a high degree of internal efficiency and balance, the company as a suprasystem would be both imbalanced and weak in the communicative capacity. Clearly the stability, balance, and efficiency of the multinational suprasystem is not the sum of the separately achieved internal equilibria of its various national affiliates.

Systems Adaptation

The most common multinational communication systems found have been engineered in the headquarters and imposed upon the entire multinational complex. Such unilateral attempts have never met with fully satisfactory results. Despite the applicability to it of a wide range of modern electronic machinery, managerial communication is not reducible to systems mechanics or network technology. Cultural and social dimensions of the communication process refuse to comply with technological criteria, and the unpredictable variabilities in external forces in a multicountry environment place almost forbidding demands upon any technical system, however perfect its design. The nationality, value system, world view, social position, and organizational rank, just to mention a few, that the various people occupy in the multinational organization space determine their perception and interpretation of incoming information and shape their conceptions of need and appropriateness of the information to be supplied to others. Every message emanating from one affiliate in the suprasystem needs translation not only linguistically, but also as to content, if it is to be effective in other entities of the system. (Readers unfamiliar with the theory of meaning are referred to Appendix I, pp. 151-153.)

Since a purely technology-based communication system lacks the capacity to cope with the cultural-social-human aspects of the multinational managerial communication process, it can become a self-inflicted rigidity that precludes organizational adaptation of the company to its heterocultural environment. Thus, in communication, as in most other spheres of the multinational corporation, the unilateral centralism is hardly preferable to the anarchic imbalance of complete affiliate autonomy. Regrettably, too many multinational companies find themselves in such indefensible polar positions.

To achieve a high degree of adaptation, goal orientation, and operational efficiency on a company-wide basis, the multinational suprasystem must somehow find the right combination of both of the centrifugal and centripetal tendencies. On the one hand, international communication systems and processes must provide enough connectedness for activities of one affiliate to trigger the necessary reactions in others, so that the contribution of all can be optimized; on the other hand, the affiliates must be provided enough separation from the rest of the corporate suprasystem for each to cultivate such particularist communication mechanisms as are required for an effective interaction with its local environment and internal balance, without jeopardizing the equilibrium and functioning of the suprasystem as a macrocosm.

In the world of contrasting cultures and conflicting national interests, no multinational firm can hope to achieve complete adaptation and equilibrium in all its affiliates. Perfection is impossible. But what is possible is a great deal more than either a headquarters-centered or an affiliate-centered system can provide. The key for an effective international communication system is effective coding and transfer organs for information exports and imports.

Numerical Information Systems

A multinational firm, like a uninational one, depends heavily upon numerical reporting. But unlike the domestic firm, it is torn between many conflicting requirements.

Accounting Systems

The most universal numerical information system is accounting. Although all countries utilize the double-entry principle, national accounting conventions and regulatory constraints are different in each country. Taxes, depreciation rules, retained reserve requirements, inventory evaluation, and "the accepted accounting philosophies" illustrate the most common variables of multinational accounting. Beyond this, accounting data are subject to indirect effects such as inflation rates, monetary and fiscal policies, and the general business conditions of a country, especially forecasts of future growth and other economic trends.

These contrasts pose difficult, often highly technical, problems for multinational companies. On the source level, the crucial accounting problems revolve around the question of which and how many accounting methods to use. On the use level, the critical question is: What do the data mean? Regarding the prevailing practices, many multinational companies endeavor to circumvent these difficulties by converting all financial data to U.S. dollars and American accounting expressions. This may rank high in the scales of American patriotism, but it does not increase one's information greatly. Typically, the conversion of figures is based on official exchange rates. Under the present IMF system, these rates are rather inaccurate and potentially misleading indicators of the real purchasing power represented by the data originating in different countries. Furthermore, the converted figures are difficult to evaluate and use for decision-making purposes, since the conversion process produces homogenized data in which the underlying national peculiarities and broader connotations of the data are lost.

Multiple Accounting Systems

Thorough studies of conditions, regulations, and national policies in each host country are a necessary precondition to any multinational accounting information system. When the contrasts among host countries are fully exposed, the likelihood dissipates that a *unicurrency* system limited on the headquarters country accounting conventions can meet the many different needs of accounting information of the multinational firm. Not only managerial, but also financial accounting may suffer perversions because of the unicurrency practice.

This leaves multiple or overlapping accounting systems as the only viable alternatives. By designing separate base systems for each country, local factors, both direct and indirect, can be taken in consideration and more meaningful records will result. The headquarters system, while used as a standard, is not imitated unless this can be done without violence to local factors. Thus, the base systems need not, and seldom can be fully integrated with one another. Coordination rather than integration should be the maxim on this level. Such host-country-oriented base systems assure the company completeness, authenticity, and affiliate relatedness in its basic accounting data bank.

For some special purposes, such as taxes, it may be necessary to have certain data reclassified and converted to the taxing country's format. This may give rise to any number of limited-purpose systems, all of which can utilize the base systems for their information inputs.

Typically, none of these is satisfactory for purposes of cost accounting, performance rating, or other operational control. Thus, a third type of system is needed to serve these purposes. This is in a sense a supranational system governed by operational information objectives of the firm, rather than laws, conventions, or conditions of any individual country.

In essence what we propose is a three-level accounting information model for multinational firms: (1) a host-country-oriented base system, (2) one or more limited-purpose systems, and (3) a managerially oriented supranational system. All three start with the same data inputs, but process them into different outputs to serve different functions.

Multinational Computer Systems

The major tool of modern accounting is the computer. But since its capabilities encompass a much greater realm than is needed in accounting as such, a computerized information system in business tends to take on a number of other data-processing aspects, such as various statistical and econometric processes besides accounting. From this derives the term *management information system*, as distinguished from accounting system. Computer software suitable for international use is still rudimentary and ominous problems remain unresolved. Yet all multinational firms studied utilize computers as instruments of corporate communication. The net contribution of these machines to international managerial understanding is not readily ascertainable. While they facilitate immensely the dissemination of quantitative data, they also introduce biases toward *uniformity* that tend to distort the meaning of the original data. This bias results first from the fact that the limitations of the system are not reflected in its output. For example, per unit production cost in different countries may have to be based on incomparable input data, due to such things as depreciation requirements, labor laws, and fringe benefits; but the computer outprint of the cost will conceal the underlying incomparability. Similarly, there are differentiating factors in each host country regarding almost any output data of the system: production per man hour, advertising efficiency, margins, sales force performance, etc. Such preinput and postoutput problems in a multinational enterprise demand more sophisticated and flexible information systems than those used in uninational firms.

A second source of the bias toward uniformity is the tendency among executives to use the computer data as the complete and final measure of the respective variable irrespective of the qualifications and limitations that may be applicable. This is due in part to the average executive's inability to fill in the gap that the computer system may have left, i.e., to cope with the international incomparability problems, and in part to the psychological pressure that any deviation from the systems standards exerts upon the individual decision-maker. Most likely to succumb to this pressure are executives who have become accustomed to computer systems in a one-country environment where underlying input data are quite similar throughout the system and the outprints, and therefore are relatively much more accurate indicators of the actual business realities than in a multinational context.

While computers are in general use by multinational firms, the concept of a multinational computer system is yet to be articulated. Progress to date has been limited to the engineering and technocratic aspects of computer use. Misinformation and misinterpretation remain, therefore, ever-present dangers in multinational computer systems.

Linguistic Aspects

Linguistic capability presents the greatest challenge in international managerial communication. It is no exaggeration to say that the typical American-headquartered multinational firm possesses no foreign language capability whatsoever—all its executive and technical personnel are strictly unilingual. Nothing can be communicated that is not in English. This subjects all transboundary communications of the firm to the tyranny of ignorance. It isolates the headquarters executives from the realities of affiliate companies, and retards the development of company-oriented constructive attitudes and personal loyalties among the indigenous personnel. Most companies exhibit agitated sensitivity on the language problem, but we found *none* that has taken decisive action to correct the deficiency in their managerial cadre.

A few companies are actually trying to correct the situation by subsidizing language study for executives. The typical arrangement covers the tuition and fees of an approved language program, and may also permit some company time to be used for attending the course. Both the coverage and intensity are left to the individual, and there is no concrete incentive for anyone to participate in the program. As a result, the more ambitious executives find more promising alternatives for their self-improvement endeavors.

Executives who do invest enough time in language study to become proficient find themselves rewarded with reassignment to the outposts, mostly in sales or procurement, where direct communication with local nationals is a critical necessity. Too often, these are dead-end jobs from which there is no access for further advancement. Thus, what appears initially as a promotion may in a longer perspective turn out to have been tantamount with reclassification from a regular executive career path to that of a technician or limited-function specialist. All in all, progress through these programs remains invisible to this observer.

A somewhat larger minority of U.S. companies seeks to remedy the language problem by employing multilingual foreign nationals to serve in crucial buffer positions between the parent company and the affiliates. This is self-deception. The multilingual foreigners are rarely endowed with any real executive authority, but serve more or less as errand boys for the headquarters people. Their contribution is limited mostly to routine communication problems. There is reason to suspect that at times they may even serve as amplifiers of the ethnocentric influences of the headquarters executives upon whom they so completely depend.

The large majority of U.S.-based multinational firms seems to believe that in time the problem will resolve itself. Their management, taking its cues from the traditional business school curriculum, refrains from any move to face the problem.

Finally, there is an undeterminable number of companies where the managerial culture puts a negative value on language knowledge. Acquisition of language facility thus becomes an impediment for an executive's international career. This kind of cultural perversion seems to derive from the chauvinistic fear that language knowledge renders one susceptible to unwanted and potentially dangerous foreign influences, which may induce the executive to "go native," that is, to lose his usefulness completely to the company. Viewed through an ethnocentric tunnel, it is better to remove such potential subversives from the seats of corporate power.

The Challenge of the Language Problem

To be able to use a foreign language in management communication one must have acquired command in not only vocabulary and syntax, but also in the underlying conceptual structure and the thought processes of the language involved. The standards for this ability are set by the culture to which the language belongs; as such it is an absolute and external standard, which no individual or institution can change. For this reason there can be no short cuts to linguistic facility: nobody can be made a linguist in a few easy lessons, nor can he be appointed to practice the language skill, the way people are sometimes appointed to be salesmen, supervisors, or managers with inadequate preparation. In the U.S. and Britain, where language instruction on the elementary and secondary school levels has been meager, the adult citizen lacks the fundamental knowledge and mental conditioning that the people in many other countries have acquired through a continuous language study on all levels of their schooling. Hence, it will require a very large and intensive effort in these countries before any truly multilingual managerial resource of significance can hope to emerge. In European and Japanese companies the prospects are brighter, but the problems are by no means solved.

Multilingual Communication

In the absence of a multlingual executive corps the multinational company must constantly communicate across different linguistic barriers. People in most national affiliates represent separate linguistic groups and messages flowing among them require either direct translation, or must pass through a triple process of being converted first from the sender's language into the headquarter language and then into the recipient's language. Errors and misinterpretations are possible at each step.

That errors can be completely eliminated from interlingual communication is doubtful. Errors can be *reduced*, through planned procedures and qualified interpreters attached to the communication system. The organization aspect was discussed above in connection with the need of coding mechanisms for information imports and exports; the language capability represents an important dimension of the coding organs.

From the substantive standpoint, linguistic conversion of managerial information is best accomplished by avoiding literal word-by-word translation, substituting a content-based interpretation. This process starts with transwriting the information content of the message, i.e., expressing the meaning of the message in the plainest and clearest statements of the recipient's language, regardless of the words and wordings used in the sender's language. The literary must be subordinated to the scientific to avoid ambiguity if the two conflict. Once this has been accomplished, the effectiveness of the message can be strengthened by recasting it into the most suggestive vernacular of the recipient country. The wordings of the message in the language of origin and the language of destination could be quite dissimilar after this process, yet the information is effectively communicated.

The tendency to use literal translation has been a basic weakness in international managerial communication. Its probable cause is the traditional methods of language instruction, together with the relative unsophistication of American executives in linguistic matters. A formal requirement of message transcription, where introduced, has invariably substituted content-based interpretation of messages for the traditional translation technique. In this process the emphasis is placed on language as a vehicle of transmitting accurate information rather than as an art of literary expression.

The lack of linguistic facility remains a critical blindspot in American managerial preparedness for effective multinational communications. In other aspects of communication some real progress has been achieved and further advances can be anticipated, partly through research in international business and partly through application or adaptation of domestic experiences. In the linguistic capability there has been no recognizable progress to date, nor is any indicated for the future. As more and more companies internationalize, the need for multilingual facility grows. So do the problems deriving from miscommunication.

The fact that the English language is widely taught in schools around the world cannot be expected to change the situation. Other people's knowledge of English is not a substitute for our own linguistic ability. The foreigners' knowledge of English can provide short-term relief, but not a long-term solution to any U.S. company's global communication problems.

To what extent the unilingual monolith of the American executive helps to ferment such resentment of multinational firms as conveyed by neocolonialism, foreign domination, and economic imperialism is beyond the limits of this study. However, history lends no support to the proposition that such attitudes will disappear without linguistic integration of the firm with its host society.

Appendix 10A: The Theory of Meaning and Coding

A. General Propositions

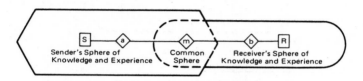

Communication can take place only if the sender's message falls in the receiver's field of knowledge and experience, as does ⟨m⟩ in the diagram above. If it falls outside the receiver's intellectual sphere, like message ⟨a⟩, it remains unintelligible to him. It can fall outside the sender's own sphere, like message ⟨b⟩, only as a result of an error or mutilation.

The boundaries of the common sphere are never sharp and smooth, but fuzzy and irregular, with multiple areas of partial communality surrounding the common sphere. Thus, excepting technical and linguistic errors, distortion-free communication is possible only in the relatively small sphere of complete communality of knowledge and experience. All messages that fall in one of the partial communality zones are distorted in proportion to the degree of noncommunality involved, for in such a case the sender is unable to formulate a message that the receiver is able to fully understand.

B. Uninational Communication

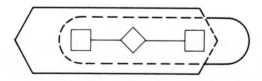

Here the sender and receiver of managerial messages have typically a large sphere of communality, and the possibilities for misunderstandings are small.

C. International Communication

Here generally the communality sphere is smaller and seldom complete. Three basic typologies exist:

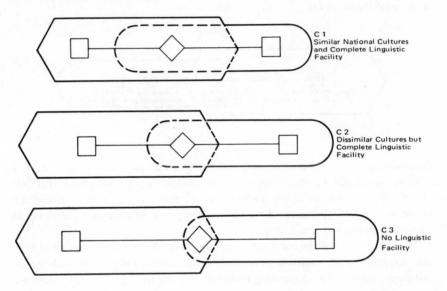

C 1
Similar National Cultures and Complete Linguistic Facility

C 2
Dissimilar Cultures but Complete Linguistic Facility

C 3
No Linguistic Facility

D. The Function of Coding

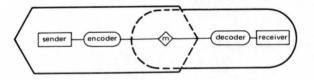

The purpose of coding organs is twofold: to insure that the message will fall within the sphere of an acceptable degree of communality if such exists, and to adjust the formulation (signals) of the message so as to enable its information content to pass from the sender's to the receiver's sphere of knowledge and experience without substantive change, if an acceptable level of communality does not exist.

In international managerial communication this process has three stages:

1. Sender (the headquarter's executive, for example) supplies the encoder with the substantive meaning to be communicated (facts, action desired, etc.).

2. The encoder formulates the message (signal), which is: (a) capable of transmission, and (b) fully understandable to decoder in the receiver's organization (foreign affiliate, for example).

3. The decoder reformulates the message, fully interpreting its substance to the receiver (the affiliate manager, for example).

11 Development of Multinational Executives

Every organization depends on a network of decision-makers who deal with the different problems of the various organizational units. Perhaps more than other types of economic organization, the multinational firm is in great need of flexibility in order to profit from its many opportunities and resources. Both the skills of individual managers and the managerial ideology embedded in the organization importantly affect organizational performance. The search for and cultivation of a managerial ideology that would maximize the aggregate effectiveness of its multinational structure is a basic need in all international enterprises. Being dependent upon an extensive network of alert, perceptive, and effective managerial decision-makers, a multinational organization can fulfill this need only through promoting organizational consciousness and creative interaction among individual members as well as groups that compose the network. If we accept the principle of ethnocentrism and acknowledge the limited ability of any one individual to ordain "the one best way," it should be clear that an effective organization must provide a mechanism for learning better ways. It should also be clear that if learning is to take place, its locus must be within the international corps of executives. Since the process of change and learning must start somewhere, perhaps the better place to start, and the one about which current research has learned something, is the managerial development process.

In this chapter the discussion centers on the process of developing international, particularly expatriate, executives. This process has three principal phases: recruitment, training, and promotion or advancement. Finally, we shall address the problem of providing improved knowledge about development.

Recruitment

Recruitment of Expatriate Executives

Cast in an idealized character type, the candidate for an international executive post is invariably described in some set of specifications that emphasize a flexible personality with broad intellectual horizons, attitudinal values of cultural empathy, general friendliness, patience and prudence, impeccable educational and professional (or technical) credentials—all topped off with immaculate health, creative resourcefulness, and respect of his peers. If his family is equally well endowed, all the better.

If business firms had in fact stuck to any such standard in their selection process, multinational business enterprise would still be a phenomenon of the future. Ideal people do not occur naturally—to the extent they exist at all, they are the result of a purposeful conditioning process. The objective of executive recruitment and selection, therefore, must be that of discovering those persons who have the capacities to grow along the path leading toward the idealized personality type if given the necessary training and incentives. The purpose of the selection process is to provide the inputs which are capable of refinement under the available training technology and incentive system.

Ethnocentrism

A manager who is assigned abroad takes his value system with him more surely than almost anything else. If this value system is purely a product of his native culture, his initial foreign experience is one of culture shock and value confusion. Even ideas about such elementary aspects of life as what is good or clean or honest or right or worthwhile, ideas that were learned when the individual was very young, become raveled and disarranged. These feelings cannot be violated without the individual feeling at least vaguely uncomfortable, insecure, or even profoundly offended. These moral reevaluations are not extinguished by hearing a lecture on cultural relativity. In a less-developed area these reactions are sometimes not clearly understood; the individual may believe that ignorance is the cause of the patterns to which he reacts unfavorably. But more is involved than values. We know from a good many experiments in psychology that an individual imposes meaning on everything he sees. It has been said that experience is something man projects upon the outside world. In the process of assigning meaning to the events of his life, the individual calls upon his previous experience and conditioning. When he confronts a different culture he will impose meaning on his observations, rather than feel that he does not understand. The pattern of meaning, however, will usually be the one he brought with him from home culture.

Fundamentally, ethnocentrism manifests itself in the individual's cultural inertia: his attempt to maintain the same patterns of behavior and modes of life that he had before moving abroad. He does this in the same way that he continues to follow the pattern of thought that he was conditioned to follow by childhood socialization in his native culture.

Expatriate American managers have shown a strong inclination to form inward-looking closed-enclave communities wherever sufficient numbers of families have been present. Their primary—sometimes their only—contact with the indigenous society has been with wealthy upper-class people of the host country. Only in rare instances have expatriate American businessmen learned the vernacular language of the country of their assignment. However, concerted efforts are now made by many firms to remedy this weakness.

In general, Americans like to think of themselves as open, friendly, gregarious, warm-hearted, generous, as guardians of charity and virtue; they try to respect the rights and feelings of others. However well intentioned, their ways can strike other peoples as naïve or meddlesome or even offensive. The important point we have learned is that any behavior taken out from its original culture context can be seen as wholly other than what the individual himself thinks it is.

An Italian executive says:

One of the major mistakes that American and German international combines make is that they try to impose the rules of the mother country on their foreign operations. They do so not only in the subsidiary's internal works, but also in their relations with customers. Some U.S. companies try to work in Italy on a fixed cost basis. . . . Fixed prices may be fine in the United States, but not in Italy. Whenever this happens, it is the headquarters, rather than the operating executives, who are being inflexible.

This quotation reflects two fundamental problems of ethnocentrism. First is the tendency of the headquarter's culture to get embedded in the affiliate organization overseas. Many analysts who recognize the principle of ethnocentrism as it applies to the individual manager and his behavior overlook the fact that culturally relative values, objectives, and procedures become embedded in the organization itself.

The second point is that ethnocentricity is not a one-way current. It is usually involved both in the activities of the multinational firm and in the perceptions and behavior of the host population. In the above quotation, the Italian executive exhibits his inability to conceive how any system other than negotiated or bargained prices can work in Italy. For him there is only one way, the Italian way.

This is not an isolated example. The principle is extremely important. When an executive leaves his home country and goes to work in another, he cannot expect host nationals to make any adjustment in their system of viewing things so as to understand the bias he brings. He will always be observed and understood (or misunderstood) in the terms of the indigenous culture.

Successful performance of the cross-cultural and interpersonal aspects of international executive work is a function of how well the executive is able to adapt his perception and behavior to the multinational environment. Adaptation must occur because, as explained earlier, the behavior patterns one learns for his own culture are not those that will make him an effective arbitrator among people with contrasting value systems. A person's sensitivity to his own value perceptions and cultural inertia—his ethnocentrism—are, therefore, significant indicators of his potential success as a multinational manager.

Technical Culture

The term *technical culture* is used here to refer to two important ideas: the technology that constitutes the operational system of a particular corporate culture, and the general level and types of technological skills—the technical credentials—with which the organization is endowed. Although the two are related—the first must always depend to a degree on the second—they are never the same. One does not need to know very much science or engineering to become intimately versed in the workings of the operational system of an organizational culture. It will suffice to be acquainted with the company and its policies, products, markets, and values—in short, its way of behaving and doing business. Mastery of such organizational technique is a very important executive skill. It is especially important for the stability of the organization and the predictability of change-introducing decisions. Its most universal reflection is the communication process. Verbal or written, communication within an organization always must be interpreted in terms of the organizational practices and policies of the company. In a monocultural environment, such as a domestic company, this organizational expertise may be relatively easy to acquire or may mistakenly so be conceived, since the knowledge and skill required are more elusive and less concrete as well as less standardized in a formal sense than are the skills in science and engineering *per se*. In international management, even the organizationally disinclined technocrats cannot escape the formidable complexities that the operational system of a multinational company embodies.

The level and types of technical credentials found in the organization are of importance for two reasons. Technical capacity is one of the most important elements leading to the acceptance of an international manager by foreigners. Rapid and easy acceptance by one's professional peers greatly speeds the process of fitting into the new circumstances. Furthermore, it eases acceptance by those with whom the individual must work in the organization. Of equal importance is the effect technical competence has upon one's own self-esteem and self-confidence.

One must be wary, however, of placing too much emphasis on the possession or acquisition of technical skills. While these are a necessary condition for successful managerial performance in the international sphere, they are not sufficient condition for success. Research on the effectiveness of technical aid missions to the developing countries has demonstrated that dissatisfaction with an expatriate's performance seldom comes from lack of technical expertise. The major source of failure is intercultural contrasts and attendant interpersonal skills. The major barriers to task accomplishment arise from the problems of communicating ideas and having them accepted and put into practice by the foreign host nationals, be they businessmen, bureaucrats, or peasants.

Home Office Executives

All managers of multinational functions or entities are not assigned to foreign locations. There is a significant difference between those executives of the multinational firm who remain at home in the headquarters and those who are stationed abroad. While the expatriate will have difficulty in adjusting his perspective and in adapting to the new culture, they will acquire a broader and more flexible frame of reference and, depending on the particular individual's aptitudes, become sensitized to both foreign and cosmopolitan normative systems. However, those who have remained in the headquarters at home have no hope at all for making such a change. The problem here is that those in the higher levels of the enterprise, senior headquarters executives and various functional specialists, will often be compelled to labor under the most culturally restricted personal experience.

This is important, because these are the individuals who will have the most profound effect on the establishment of corporate policy and practice. They will also be responsible for judging the upward mobility of other executives. By their power and because of their monoculture-based ethnocentricity, these higher-level executives can perpetuate the inflexible propagation of cultural values embedded in the headquarters organizational process, or retard the introduction of values that would liberate the organization's ability to respond flexibly to opportunities in its multinational environment.

Culture Fatigue

In preparation of people for overseas assignments the emphasis has been on helping the novice over the first hurdles and coping with the initial adjustment. These programs rest on the theory that the person's own ingenuity and ability to learn from experience will suffice after he has been settled into his foreign environment. This is not so. With stubborn consistency, greater difficulties have tended to surface in the later stages than in the beginning, after the initial shock for the novice. The second year, not the first few months, has proven to be the acid test of a typical U.S. executive working abroad. While he no longer is susceptible to culture shock, he now begins to suffer from something that is potentially more degenerative, *culture fatigue*. Culture shock is to a high degree attributable to the panic phenomenon, the natural fear of the unknown and the quite universal innate hostility toward strangers. In a sense, it is homesickness raised to an international exponential: a spontaneous, panicky revulsion and scariness that one might feel when he first sees unfamiliar ways or surroundings, not to mention new forms of poverty, disease, or human misbehavior.

Culture fatigue is not this kind of emotional disturbance. It does not occur immediately; rather it is something that may set in months after the person entered an alien social environment, but keeps growing in intensity as time goes on.

Culture fatigue is not unlike "battle fatigue," a well-known phenomenon of warfare that grows out of a protracted period of uncertainty and anxiety in hostile and dangerous surroundings. Battle experience itself is not a necessary condition for the symptoms to appear. The anxiety and uncertainty, the unfamiliar environment, and the extended period of time under which these conditions must be endured are the key factors.

While discussing the problem of culture fatigue it is important to acknowledge that the process operates not only on the individual who is sent to do the work, but also on the other members of his family. Indeed, the person most subject to culture shock is the wife. This fact has important implications for selection and training of persons abroad.

Training

Training of Expatriate Executives

A fundamental problem in training managers for international assignments is the scarcity of acceptable training material. Much of the material used in the usual management training programs, both in universities and in corporations, consists of culturally or nationally limited information. Questions of technique or theory could be universally applicable, but there is a great deal of institutional material and culturally limited assumptions in most management texts and guidebooks. To overcome this some companies have tried to develop their own-company-oriented textbooks and other teaching aids. To get first-rate materials, the cost of this approach is very high. Also, there has been the problem that the company-based materials are too inward-looking and narrow. Often such materials consist of case studies, which may not be the best medium for accomplishing the most important objectives of training for international management.

Managers who wish to be assigned to an overseas post may volunteer for consideration as posts become available. Some companies offer the volunteers a cultural conditioning program, which may also be extended to their families, before they are assigned abroad. Since family problems are a frequent cause of poor performance in overseas assignments, the volunteer system coupled with cultural preconditioning, including language study, greatly reduces the risk of unwilling family members becoming a problem to the expatriate. Even if the attrition rate during or after the program should be high, the overall result may still families, having learned about the problems and difficulties that beset the various foreign posts, can better understand the international realities of the company even if they decide to decline a foreign assignment. But more important, the processes of volunteering and cultural conditioning must necessarily lead to an increased selective efficiency and, in the absence of a wider recruitment base, can be of significant help in filling foreign posts.

In some cases too much glamour is connected with international assignments, which may lead to greater than necessary volunteer rosters. However, if the preconditioning program is properly constructed it should quickly demonstrate that the overseas assignments are not intended for vacation, and that people without serious interest and aptitude will find them overly demanding and frustrating.

Corporate Experience

Studies of the training programs used by established multinational firms based in the United States reflect different types of programs that are being offered. Three can serve as prototypic illustrations.

One company, a producer of office machines, focuses its training effort mainly on the product. A model course is conducted in its headquarters city, and traveling specialists move about to teach in the field. An aircraft company takes people who have finished its ordinary U.S. management program and rotates them through assignments in departments dealing with overseas operations. After that they are assigned abroad. A chemical manufacturer gives international executive prospects a quick briefing at the home office and sends them for language instruction to outside institutions. Trainees are then given an internship job overseas. Later, they will be called back, then assigned to positions of increased responsibility. A computer firm holds executive development programs in most host countries. From these local training programs, high-performing men are taken to the company's international executive development center in Europe.

Most other companies that have concrete programs for international executive development represent variations on these three themes. Common to all such programs is a heavy emphasis on company product and policy, and an inadequate treatment of behavioral and perceptual aspects. Some companies try to solve the cultural adaptation problem by indirection or even avoidance; that is, they include only very few people from the headquarters country in their international assignments, relying instead on third-country expatriates and local nationals, who are presumed to need no further cultural adaptation. That this ostrich technique has nothing beside possible psychotherapeutic value to recommend it should be self-evident.

Since the main objective of any international executive development program is the cultivation of those abilities and characteristics which are necessary for cross-cultural decision-making and leadership, product knowledge and organizational policy instruction can hardly accomplish the task. Instead, the emphasis should be on the broadening of perspectives, development of behavioral flexibility, the enhancement of learning capacity, and language facility.

The broadening of a person's perspective recognizes an enlargement of his perceptual system which can be achieved through diversification of learning experience, especially through greater awareness of differences in national cultures and social systems. To be real, the broadening of perspective must also lead to a greater perceptual flexibility—the ability to analyze a society and understand how it operates is more important than specific area knowledge, which can be gained relatively rapidly once one has the general grasp and an intuitive feel for life in a country.

A German expatriate serving as the general manager of a Latin American subsidiary of an European-based multinational company expresses his problem this way:

I came to this country with the idea of organizing the work here. After one year of struggling, I decided that I either had to abandon my organizational principles or go to a mental clinic. It is not possible to organize, plan and control your work the way you have learned at the home office. The key here is to improvise. Tactics are more important than strategy.

To this European executive the Latin American culture looks neither rational nor consistent. He finds his predictive abilities completely paralyzed and finds it impossible to plan, to systematize, or to control his organization because he does not understand the operational system of the host culture that is different from his own. The indigenous people living within that culture are able to perform these activities, but he is not. He had been assigned to his expatriate post ill-prepared and has not yet found his bearings in the new environment. Too many expatriate managers resemble this German executive.

A second aspect of one's perspective disguises clarification. In the long run we will find that those executives who have developed cultural awareness will have also acquired what might be called *cosmopolitan culture*—a personal analogue to the cosmopolitan company culture discussed earlier. From a nationalistic perspective they "lose their nationality." Their horizons will expand from the limitations of their national culture to a complex of several cultures or the whole world. As they are freed from dependence on a single national culture, they seem to gain the ability to think primarily of the company (and its cosmopolitan corporate culture) for which they work, and only secondarily of their original home country. Through greater cultural awareness, they gain strength for strategic decision-making and implementation of corporate goals.

Cultural Awareness

Although part of the cultural landscape in a general sense, geographic, economic, and historic descriptions of a country can at best provide but an introduction to understanding of its normative system and the resultant personality or behavior traits. For real understanding of culture we must be able to explain the social institutions, religious values and organizations, family and kinship system, and the status hierarchy of the country.

It is these variables that channel behavior and give a meaning and functionality to relationships. Knowledge of the patterns of interpersonal expectations prevailing among the local nationals is important, because the expatriate will depend on these patterns both in his own interactions and in attaining conformance for his managerial initiative, i.e., getting things done through the local people. Linguistic facility is the link between patterns of interpersonal expectations and the value-systems and reasoning processes that the local nationals use. The spoken language is merely a subset of the total communicative medium available and used by the native population. The very patterns of expectation are part of the communicative medium. Only when these patterns are shared or intellectually understood does the spoken language attain its full effectiveness. There are other languages, however, of a nonverbal nature—the paralanguages of time, location, exclusion, and emotion, which also need to be learned.

Behavioral Adaptability

The task of preparing people to work effectively in another country is never complete unless it includes the flexibility of attitudes and skills necessary to participate in another culture. Developing behavioral adaptability, i.e., the ability to behave in a mode consistent with another culture, is very much like learning to speak a second language.

As with learning a new language, so with learning a second culture. New habits must be acquired that may conflict with long-established ones. New impressions are continually misunderstood when they are interpreted in the context of the old and familiar. It is important to realize that learning to function in a second culture not only means acquiring a new set of responses to new cues, but also involves inhibiting other responses that have become habitual. Furthermore, many familiar cues mean something else, or nothing at all in the new situation.

No program of training can accomplish the full job of preparing people to fit in and participate successfully in a foreign culture. The process of learning can only be initiated; it must continue after the individual is on assignment. For a member of the international executive corps, the need to continue one's learning extends well beyond the terms of any particular assignment.

Human Relations Skills

Interpersonal skills are culture specific. If an executive learns how to interact successfully with individuals of a given culture, the specific behavior patterns that he finds successful there are not likely to be the ones that will be successful in his next assignment. Thus, specific learning about how to adapt to a given particular society is, in the long run, of less importance than the skill of learning how to adapt one's behavior to new conditions.

We might contrast the learning attitude with the closed mind of the rigidly ethnocentric individual. The latter goes to a new situation ready to evaluate and judge it. He is quick to identify any deviation from the familiar as something wrong, undesirable, incorrect, or foolish. On the other hand, an individual who succeeds in a foreign environment goes with the expectation that many things will be different; he assumes the attitude that he wishes to understand those differences. Together with this he takes a willingness to change his own behavior in order that he can perform effectively the job he was sent to accomplish in that new situation.

An important part of the NTL philosophy revolves around a role-set called "participant-observer" behavior. The basic idea is that while an individual cannot withdraw from the stream of life in order to observe what is occurring, he must take a learning attitude in his interpersonal relations. He must look for feedback as to the impact of his own behavior on others, and he must take the time to be very self-conscious about the effect of others on himself, as well as the motives that impel him to act. The aim of this self-consciousness is to understand oneself as a variable in the interaction process, and through this self-awareness to learn to adjust one's behavior to the requirements of new situations.

Third-country executives usually exhibit far greater behavioral adaptability than do Americans sent abroad. Not only do they make friends more easily, but they more quickly become integrated into the host society. Why are third-country nationals more effective in this regard? One reason may be that they have learned greater behavioral flexibility because of having to adapt to a number of different cultural-requirement sets. A further reason may be that they come with the expectation that they must learn new ways. They do not expect to be fully aware of everything that goes on in the minds of headquarters personnel, nor do they expect to be fully aware of everything happening in the host country. They are, therefore, much more likely to take a learning attitude toward both situations. This gives them greater behavioral flexibility and helps them to adjust to new situations more successfully.

Being able to establish an organizational norm of learning behavior will be crucial to the success of the international organization over the long haul. Earlier, we talked about the need to adjust internal policies to the environmental demands placed upon the organization. The key to successful adjustment along this dimension is continual and responsive monitoring of outside conditions, as they relate to the organization's operational requirements. Managers need to view themselves not only as effectors but also as receptors of informational feedback relevant not only to their own behavior but to the entire international organism of which they are a part.

Cross-cultural learning must be a continuing process. The need to learn does not cease, as long as the expatriate accepts an executive position. The company must help the individual maintain his learning attitude and to provide the means for its application. Some overseas programs follow the practice of recurring seminars or short courses after certain intervals.

Promotion

Up to the late 1960s American multinational companies had a tendency to follow the managerial slack theory in filling their foreign assignments. This meant that international positions were frequently staffed with people who in some way had become semiobsolete or ineffective as managers, and that the international executives were overlooked at the time of promotions and salary increases. It also meant that any younger man who accepted a foreign appointment seriously jeopardized his opportunities for advancement.

The majority of U.S.-headquartered multinational firms have done a sudden turnabout in this respect. The growth and relative significance of foreign-based corporate assets and earnings have made nonsense of the older practice of using international affiliates as dumping grounds for managerial slack or operating with the belief that the second-raters were good enough for affiliate appointments. Now the tables seem to have been turned, and the filling of affiliate posts has been sharply upgraded in importance. Indeed, many companies now consider nobody but the corporate elite for such assignments.

The managerial slack theory seriously undermines motivation in multinational business. If the men who are sent abroad do "die on the vine" and lose their mobility by virtue of their being out of the headquarters country, men who seek to be upwardly mobile will avoid such foreign assignments. Also, those who receive such foreign assignments will be more likely to leave the organization in search of opportunity elsewhere. Such conditions would severely restrain the organization's ability to properly staff its top management echelons with persons having sufficient international exposure.

Basic Plans: Promotion of executives in multinational companies follow three basic patterns, which are related to the strategies of the executive manpower system in use. The first pattern is national advancement. Here, the principle involved is that headquarters nationals may advance within the headquarters company, while overseas nationals have their opportunities limited to their own nation. A binational advancement strategy would be one allowing foreign nationals to be assigned to positions in the headquarters country. A multinational advancement policy would open the upper ranks of the headquarters organization to persons from all foreign areas, as well as the home country. Likewise, to the degree that the law allowed, local positions would be available to "third country nationals" or anyone who is properly qualified.

To a great extent, a truly international company can be judged by the way it promotes its managers, who are, in fact, its most precious asset. If a company's foreign activities are an integral part of its system of executive promotion, then all of the company's managerial talent should be available for international assignments. It seems important that upward mobility be allowed for international executives from whatever origin.

Improvement of Development Process

A major challenge for the multinational firm is to establish an organizational mechanism for learning how to improve its development program. A review of the literature upon which part of this report is based disclosed the fact that the bulk of the writings about international executive development are highly qualitative and impressionistic. To the degree that empirical evidence has been considered, it is the result of only the most casual observation. We are left with the unmistakable conviction that persons who are in charge of overseas operations do not think in terms of systematic evaluations of their results.

Only limited evaluation of the effectiveness of development programs is done, and what is done is largely anecdotal and unrepresentative. It is hard to see that there has been an accumulation of experience from one project to another within the same company. As a result, each new project starts at the same point of ignorance. We must admit that administrators are probably not trained to look for knowledge; but beyond that, it seems that they feel it would take too much time or money, or would interfere with the operation of the enterprise.

There are real problems in performing evaluations in a cross-cultural environment, and there are very few behavioral scientists who have significant experience in a worldwide setting. Researchers without such experience could hold behavioral assumptions that are extremely culturebound, and draw conclusions which reflect cross-cultural naïveté. If we hold the program of managerial development to be pivotal in its importance for the survival and effectiveness of multinational enterprise, the development program would be the place to incorporate a systematic procedure for study and research, so that today's efforts will give us better knowledge about how to conduct tomorrow's programs.

Executive Manpower Systems

As large and complex organizations multinational companies must possess systems for acquiring and cultivating manpower resources, especially executive cadres, commensurate with their needs. It is a well-proven rule that the more complex the environment in which the organization operates, the stronger the imperative for a systematized program of human resource management. In its highly diverse and pluralistic environment, the multinational company is particularly prone to crisis in the human sphere. The objective of this chapter is to explain how executive manpower systems have evolved in multinational companies, and to discuss the design and capacities of these systems.

The forms taken by executive manpower systems in multinational organizations are the result of the interaction of six important variables: the available managerial resources, the cultural contrasts, the sociopolitical parameters of countries constituting its multinational domiciles, the company's own organizational form, its corporate policies, and the composition of the executive corps. The first three factors are environmental and as such beyond corporate control. Changes in them are slow at best. In short-run situations they must be taken as given constants and corporate possibilities and imperatives defined accordingly. All adjustments or adaptations have to be unilateral; the company's measure of ultimate success being perfect adjustment to whatever their environmental parameters demand. In the long run a two-way adjustment is usually possible.

The form of an organization reflects the tasks it is set up to perform. These tasks relate to the opportunities it seeks to exploit in its environment, as well as the technology and resources with which it must work. These factors influence the distribution of authority, power, and information. They also determine the demands that will be placed upon the executive corps, which in turn specifies requirements for executive skills and qualities.

Corporate policies are those elements of planning, procedure, and practice which channel the work of the organization. Corporate policies are intimately related to the concepts of corporate culture and corporate climate, both of which will be seen to be crucial factors in the evolving world business organization.

The composition of the executive core is closely related to the value orientation, perspective, and often even capabilities of the firm. Internationalization of management has been generally much slower than acquisition of foreign-based facilities and the growth of multinational affiliate networks.

All the six factors are clearly interrelated. As the perspective of its management group becomes more internationalized, an organization will adjust its policies. Both of these changes will have an impact on the organizational form. More fundamentally, however, all three of these will be influenced by the three environmental variables that govern corporate activities relating to its human and material resources, markets, and strategic objectives.

Types of Multinational Executive Systems

One of the important dimensions of executive manpower systems is the source-nation of the individuals composing these systems. According to the source-nation criterion the systems can be classified into three types:

1. Expatriate transferees
   a. headquarters-country nationals
   b. third-country nationals
2. Host-country nationals
3. Supranational Executive Corps

Expatriate Transferees

In the early stages of its international growth, a firm usually tends to keep the management responsibility over its foreign-based operations in the hands of headquarters-country nationals, most of whom are transferred abroad and some exercising their power through "remote control." This is a system of exporting the headquarters executives and transplanting them as expatriates into the different foreign cultures where the company operates. Its appeal is twofold: first, simplicity of selection, appointment, and promotion, all of which can be achieved in a unilateralistic frame of reference without disturbing the established headquarters practices and routines; and second, the relative uniformity of backgrounds of all managerial cadres throughout the multinational structure—everybody is the product of the same national and corporate cultures and has reached his position by playing the same rules. (Needless to add, this system makes no provision for the indigenous variables of individual host countries with which multinational executives must cope.)

American-headquartered multinational firms seem to be among the most committed to the dependence on the expatriate transferee in their foreign-based affiliate management. The justification for this dependence has been researched by Professor Robinson whose work can be summarized in these points:[1]

the foreign enterprise is just being established (start-up phase);

the American firm wishes to develop an internationally oriented management for the parent company (that is, foreign assignments are seen essentially as management development);

no adequate management is available from other sources;

the American firm has surplus management toward which it feels responsible;

the American firm has no one sufficiently familiar with foreign environment to interpret communications from a non-American management;

virtually no autonomy is possible for the foreign enterprise because it is integrated so closely with operations elsewhere;

high-level technical skills of a nature that cannot be protected legally are carried by top management (for example, in a research-oriented service firm);

the foreign enterprise is seen as short-lived;

the host society is multiracial, and a local manager of either racial origin would make the enterprise politically vulnerable or lead to an economic boycott;

there is a compelling need to maintain a foreign image;

the American firm will be serving largely other American firms operating abroad, most of which are directed by United States nationals;

it is believed (most erroneously) to be desirable to avoid involving particular local nationals in management, because it would create dangerous animosities; for example, United States executives are reported to be in demand in Europe to manage multicountry operations involving supervision of managers of different European nationalities;

control is weak;

a United States national is simply the best man for the job, all things considered.

Third-country Expatriates

A variant of the expatriate system, often used as a complement to the headquarter nationals, is the third-country executive corps. The third-country executive is a citizen of country A, who works in country B for a company headquartered in country C.

In surveys by Business International, The National Industrial Conference Board, and the American Management Association, third-country nationals were reported to be more adept at integrating themselves into new situations and making friends in a foreign environment. Chorafas found a number of large companies to have a definite preference for third-country nationals in high management positions. Burroughs had only three Americans operating in divisions abroad. The rest of its overseas divisions were run by third-country nationals. The Italian subsidiary was run by a Frenchman, the French subsidiary by a Swiss, the Swiss subsidiary by a Dane, the Danish subsidiary by a Dutchman, the German subsidiary by an Englishman, and the Venezuelan subsidiary by an Argentinian. The versatility of third-country executives may indicate high mobility toward top management positions. For example, an established world business, Nestlé, has opened up top corporate posts for nonheadquarters nationals. Of the top eleven members of Nestlé's board of directors, six are non-Swiss.

Host-country Nationals

In companies that have been established internationally for a longer time there has been a clear trend toward the employment of an increasing percentage of local nationals in management positions. The reasons for this trend have been both economic and cultural, the need for knowledge and understanding the local environment, the rapid growth of overseas operations requiring speedy expansion of the management group, the increased ability to utilize individuals with different national backgrounds successfully in the corporate structure, and direct or subtle pressures by host-country authorities for replacing expatriate managers with indigenous employees.

The Supranational Executive Corps

By a *supranational executive corps* is meant a management pool composed of individuals from many national backgrounds who are thoroughly imbued by cosmopolitan corporate culture, which both balances and expands their national and international normative orientation, and who are available for assignment wherever their skills are required throughout the world. No company is known to have reached the stage where such an executive corps has in fact been fully realized. However, many have set this model as their ultimate goal and are pursuing policies and strategies to reach it. Some, such as Nestlé and Uniliver, are not far from reaching the ideal.

Organizational Evolution and Executive Manpower Systems

Organizational types tend to follow an evolutionary sequence beginning with the uninational organization and progressing stepwise toward the transnational type of organization. The dominant manpower strategy is related both to the stage and the direction of this evolutionary sequence. In Figure 11-1, this relationship is typified:

Clearly, there could be no world or multinational business organizations without a highly integrated corps of executives from different national backgrounds who are highly sensitized to cosmopolitan corporate values. Thus, as we see multinational enterprises evolving toward these all-encompassing forms of organization, we can understand a resultant dynamic influence toward the spreading and further refinement of cosmopolitan corporate culture and, its attendant, the proliferation of third-country nationals as members of a supranational executive corps.

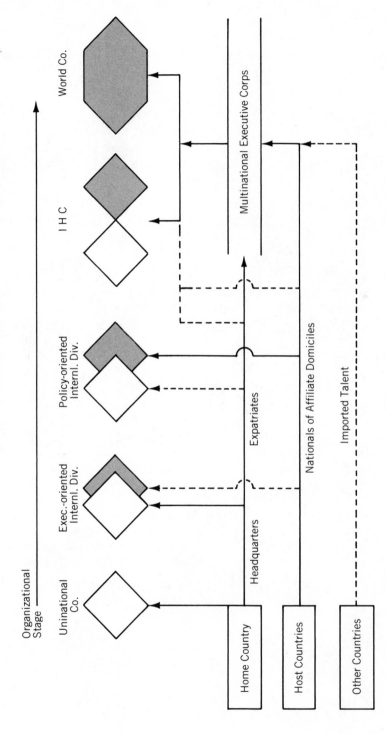

Figure 14
DOMINANT EXECUTIVE SYSTEMS

Figure 11-1. Dominant Executive Systems

12 Evaluation and Compensation of Multinational Managers

Even in a purely domestic setting most multiunit companies face difficult problems in evaluating the performance of their subsidiaries, branches, departments, or whatever the companies' subdivisions may be called. Dissatisfaction with budgets, standards, or any other performance criteria are voiced at one time or another in all companies; and human problems resulting from performance criteria, which are perceived as being "unfair," are well known to personnel managers and top management in all businesses.

In a multinational setting these problems have taken on new dimensions and become more complex. There is not only the question what should be the "right" performance criteria, right accounting principles, or right psychological measures, but also such issues as whether or not domestic profit standards should be extended into the international realm, and whether affiliate executives should be judged in the context of their particular countries or some regionalization of the worldwide operations should be adopted. In other words, should there be different performance criteria for each country, or should executives in "similar" countries be evaluated on some sort of composite basis, or go by a unitary profit standard.

Case studies indicate that a variety of different criteria are used by most companies in judging the executives of their overseas affiliates. These may be summarized as follows:

Financial results—usually measured in some type of profit figure (gross, gross less local taxes, net, etc.) of the affiliate or its subdivision for which the particular executive is responsible.

Growth results—reflected in the development of the affiliate or its respective subdivision in terms of size, efficiency, and maturity.

Organizational results—the ability to develop a harmonious internal environment with effective planning, communication, and control, and relationships among different groups, especially between expatriates and indigenous personnel.

Manpower development—the ability to develop indigenous people to fill the essential manpower needs of the company, in both the white- and blue-collar categories.

Environmental results—contributions to an effective integration of the affiliate with its host society on one hand and with the corporate culture and other affiliates of the company on the other hand. This includes not only the

173

understanding of the business environment in the host country, but also the executive's influence upon the environment, especially upon the elites of that society.

Personality profile—the executive's own involvement and adaptation to his international post; his ability to deal with new and unusual situations, and his capacity to learn from the experiences in the international assignment. Crisis behavior and the tenacity to withstand unexpected difficulties are often part of the profile.

Only in a purely subjective sense can such criteria be applied to evaluate the managers in different countries. Any objective attempt is wrought with forbidding complexities stemming from the countless differences in the operating environments of these managers. To get comparability, these differences must be identified and their differentiating effects eliminated by appropriate adjustments in the managers' performance records.

But even if a single indicator, such as profit, is adopted, the international setting imposes extremely complicating influences on its actual use. Measurement is difficult because of different factor inputs in different countries, differential inflation and exchange-rate movements, and time delays in reporting. Interaffiliate relationships frequently are far from as simple as they are in a uninational setting. For example, a factory in Argentina may produce certain specific parts for machinery that is to be assembled in Britain. The Argentine plant may have no alternative as to where it will sell its product. Similarly, the British plant manager may have no choice as to where it will obtain the parts. How is the price of transfer to be decided upon, and by whom—by either of the affiliates, or by someone above them? On this decision will hang the profit figures of both affiliates.

How can any standard be obtained for measuring managerial performance when one is operating through monetary frontiers, under differential rates of inflation, and within various-sized markets with different institutional arrangements, and widely varying cultural constraints. In every case there are important factors that are not under the control of the local management, and widely varying cultural constraints. There may be price controls, assets may need periodic reevaluation, the setting of depreciation allowances and exchange rates prevailing at any particular time may drastically affect profit or cost or efficiency measures. There may be problems as to the availability or cost of local loan funds, different legal requirements, and differences in business practice.

Time horizons, too, must be considered. Multinational companies need to look to the long run. Movements into the supranationally integrated markets such as the EEC, for example, are being made now in anticipation of market development that is expected over the next five to twenty-five years. United States firms are heading for Europe now because they want to be there before the expected growth occurs. At the moment their efforts may not be producing exceptional returns, but their commitment is for the long haul. Those firms which are established in the market will participate handsomely in its growth.

On what basis, then, can international executives' performance be evaluated? Before going any further toward an answer into this question it would be well to look at some other aspects of the problem. As was mentioned before, the culturally defined assumptions of management in the headquarters country tend to become embedded in the organization and extended overseas as the organization expands. When faced with the difficulty of measuring performance many firms end up relying on personal impressions: aggressiveness, tact, creativity, maturity, courage, and so forth. There are extreme problems of relativity in the perception of such personal qualities. Different observers of the same person might be expected to make different judgments as to these qualities. There is also some question as to whether these qualities have anything to do with long-run performance at all. The fact that these qualities are singled out is largely an artifact of American culture. In other societies some of these characteristics are defined differently; in still others, while defined in roughly the same way, these characteristics are thought to be dysfunctionally related to job performance.

Considerations like the above throw us back to the problem of trying to evaluate performance directly, rather than depending on such culturally limited judgments about intervening personality variables. All the objections raised initially make it difficult for us to look to profits as a measure of performance. Similarly, return on investment must be disqualified on similar grounds. More promising criteria are some kind of nonaccounting measures, such as market share, efficiency (measured as dollar or equivalent unit output per factor input), or quality and delivery performance. Even these measures have limited applicability and cannot be used as comparative devices. For example, market share measures would have no utility in evaluating the performance of the Argentine plant in the example above. Furthermore, these factors may be measuring only short-run performance, and for the international firm other things are of great interest. It is important to know how well a man is doing relative to the broadening of his perspective and his ability to communicate effectively in carrying out the organization's international work. Qualities like these are the ones which top corporate managers need to have: yet neither business nor the scholar have yet found a way of measuring them.

Compensation

Executive payment systems vary considerably from country to country.

A key difference in executive compensation between the U.S. and other countries is in the *perks* (perquisites). In Britain, for example, a senior marketing executive would be entitled to a company car, an expense account, financial assistance in his housing, extra holidays, subsidized lunch, and allowances for entertainment and travel. He might also get free or discount products for his private consumption and enjoy a paid membership in a private club as a part of his remuneration. However, he would have no stock options. The importance of perks and side benefits is greatest in those countries where higher incomes are heavily taxed, as it is in Britain and Sweden. It is interesting to note, however, that bonuses also are highly variable. The highest bonuses are paid in Germany, where they amount to roughly 20 to 35 percent of annual earnings for functional executives.

Other reasons for discrepancies include variations in tax laws and differences in public social services and standards—pensions, health care, education, and housing. Also, differences in the ownership affiliations of executives seem to be reflected in the compensation schemes—the owner executives being compensated through dividends and other allocations usually receive lower salaries than their nonowner colleagues.

Termination and transfer terms also vary. In contrast to American law, many other nations provide statutory protection for executive employees. In Belgium, for example, firing an executive requires two years' notice plus substantial extra compensation.

"It's a completely different enviornment than in the U.S.," reports John Alan James, president of Management Counsellors International, a Brussels-based consulting service.

Agreements that American executives assigned to Europe often work out with their companies—covering such matters as terms of stay and willingness to return to the U.S.—are of dubious worth in the eyes of European legal authorities. In Belgium, he notes, a court recently rejected such agreements as invalid.

Mr. James recalls a recent case in which an American executive, employed by a large U.S. concern, refused two transfers in succession—from Belgium to Spain and then from Belgium to the U.S. home base. When his employer moved to terminate him with minimal compensation after the second refusal, the matter was brought to a Belgian court. It ruled that the man was to get 2½ years' pay, including vacation money. The firing cost the company nearly $100,000.

Costly firing isn't limited to Belgium. Another U.S. company recently fired three men at its Italian subsidiary—an American, an Italian and a Frenchman. Each had been with the subsidiary for less than three years, but under Italian law each got severance credit for all service with the parent company anywhere in the world. Each man had, in fact, served the parent concern elsewhere. The settlement ordered by Italian authorities worked out as follows:

Each man got seven months' pay in lieu of having been given inadequate notice of termination, plus one month's pay for each year of employment anywhere in the world with the parent company, up to a maximum of 10 years' pay, plus 1½ months' pay for each year of service over 10 years.[1]

Salary Systems

From a rather chaotic beginning, the multinational companies have forged three standard approaches to expatriate compensation.

Headquarters Scale Plus Affiliate Differential

A foreign-service allowance, sometimes called *affiliate differential* or *post differential,* is applied to the regular salaries paid in the headquarters country. Thus the expatriate receives the regular salary for a particular type of work plus the post differential, which may include:

1. Cost of living allowance based on comparative indexes of food, selected consumer goods, and housing differentials;
2. Tax equalization adjustment designed to cover host-country taxes of the expatriate;
3. Hardship bonus or foreign-service premium as compensation for working abroad (usually 10 to 33 percent of salary);
4. Allowances for such family adjustments as extra expenses of children's education (private schooling, for example), periodic home leaves (two months per biannium), medical care, and cultural adaptation, for example, language training.
5. Compensation for inflation differential, currency devaluation, work permit fees, and other legal requirements of expatriates.
6. Expenses of complying with local business and professional customs, courtesies, and entertainment practices.

Some companies have broadened the post-differential concept to cover not only the extra costs and hardships, but also any extra gains and benefits which may be associated with a particular foreign assignment. This so-called *balance sheet method* includes all the extra benefit items as negative inputs to be deducted from the unadjusted total of the differential. For example, if an executive is assigned to a low-tax low-living-cost country, his take-home pay, as well as the real purchasing power of his salary, would be greater than in the headquarters country and a negative allowance to equalize his real earnings would be applied.

A number of companies seem to be either reducing or phasing out completely their affiliate differentials as reflected in the report below:

American corporations are taking a new—and very hard—look at the managers of their overseas operations. . . .

Some major firms have quietly begun to reduce the paychecks of their men in foreign outposts. Others are mulling such moves. . . .

Among recent developments:

—Hewlett-Packard Company has moved to eliminate cost-of-living allowances currently paid to some two dozen overseas executives. These allowances, which are being phased out over six years, run as high as $400 a month. The company also intends to end housing subsidies now granted Americans abroad. Another candidate for the ax: a yearly education allowance of up to $1,250 per child.

—Standard Oil of California has decided to slash premiums given its U.S. executives overseas to compensate them for the alleged difficulties of foreign living. Under the cutback, for instance, a man in Maracaibo, Venezuela, earning a base salary of $36,000 would net a premium of about 17%, down from 28% at present. The plan, which goes into effect July 1, will eventually affect nearly 300 officials.

—International Business Machines Corporation plans to cut sharply the huge premiums it currently pays to Americans sent to spots considered especially difficult because of health or other problems. Starting next month, for example, an IBM manager sent to Karachi would no longer get anything like the 40% hardship premium now paid on top of regular salary.

—Du Pont Company in the past two years has reduced the number of Americans in its foreign operations to about 300, a cutback of some 15%. Starting this month, in addition, the premium pay of many of Du Pont's overseas Americans will be cut. Under the plan, a man who received $400 a month as a foreign-service premium, on top of a $2,000 monthly salary, will get only $300 extra. After four years, the man's premium will be eliminated. . . .

R.E. Cogan, personnel director of IBM's World Trade Corporation, defends his firm's plan to trim premium pay in such places as Karachi by arguing that "some of the hellholes of the world aren't so hellish anymore." He adds: "People in the Peace Corps have been going to the worst places for no premium whatsoever." IBM currently employs some 800 American executives overseas, the official says.[2]

Under the headquarters plus system, the host-country executives are not entitled to the expatriate scale—neither the salary nor the post differential applies—but are compensated according to local salary standards. Thus it is a dualistic system based on strictly ethnocentric philosophy. The third-country expatriate represents an unacceptable dilemma for this system.

The Citizenship Salary System

This compensation scheme, also known as the *national origin system*, was develped to deal with the third-country expatriate problem. Instead of the headquarters country salary scale, this system specifies that each executive's regular salary be based on the scale of his country of citizenship or native residence. If the executive is assigned to a post outside his native country an appropriate affiliate differential will be added. Hence, American expatriate personnel are paid by U.S. standards, Frenchmen by French standards, and Japanese by Japanese standards, etc., regardless of where they are stationed. Each gets a different affiliate differential based on the comparative factors between his native country and the particular host country to which he is assigned.

This system appears to work reasonably well as long as expatriates at any particular affiliate originate from the same country, or if at least directly comparable positions at the same affiliate are not manned by people from countries with different salary scales. However, where such segregation of positions is not possible, as has been the case in more and more companies due to an increasing internationalization of the executive corps, the citizenship salary system becomes a source of serious dissatisfaction. Providing different salaries as well as different affiliate differentials for identical or very similar positions can neither go unnoticed nor be explained to the satisfaction of those discriminated against.

In certain extractive industries, where many affiliates are located in isolated company communities, the affiliate differential is equalized for all expatriates regardless of citizenship. The rationale for this so-called on-post-equivalency allowance is derived from the fact that all executives in such a company compound depend for the essential living requirements on company sources: company hospitals, company schools, and recreational facilities and programs. In practice this means that all the expatriates will receive the same affiliate differential that is applicable to the highest-income citizens.

The Global Compensation Scale

Companies that have become committed to move toward a supranational executive corps are now in process of replacing the two older compensation systems with globally applicable basic salary scales—the same salary for the same job irrespective of country—to which are added specific affiliate differentials, in which no on-post discrimination is permitted. This is to say that any pay in addition to the basic scale is affiliate-specific and job- or rank-specific, but completely immuned to the home country of the expatriate. Before such a single compensation system with its universally applicable scales and equitable treatment of all nationalities can be introduced, a global system of job classifications and rank orders must be developed. To date, no company appears to have completely succeeded in this effort. The difficulty lies in identification and measurement of internationally comparable elements in various executive assignments. Even in purely technical jobs the role expectations clash with the expatriate's home culture and the host culture where he works. Such variations increase rapidly when we shift the focus to positions where direct interaction with the host society is a large part of the job. As the host societies differ in countless ways, so do the demands on the managers whose responsibilities require direct interaction with the societies.

Another source of difficulty has been the lack of reliable data on which to base the computations of the various items in the affiliate differential. The most widely used source has been the U.S. Department of State, which publishes comparative living indexes for the purpose of determining foreign-service allowances for American diplomatic representatives abroad. The indexes cover food, housing, and certain consumer goods. Since the diplomatic posts are normally located in the capital or some other major city of the country, the State Department's information is often out of tune with conditions in industrial areas. The interregional differences in many countries seriously impair the usefulness of the State Department's data in determining affiliate differentials.

Although updated from time to time, the State Department indexes are often out of date, especially in countries that have high inflation or are undergoing rapid industrial and social changes. Disappointing experiences have induced many companies to seek better data by either going to international business research firms or, in a few instances, developing their own capabilities to do the job. At this writing, the slogan "equal pay for equal work" must remain only a distant objective for all multinational organizations. However, the trend is clearly toward a global system which, even if less than perfect, can offer material advantages over both of the discriminatory older approaches.

Indigenous Managers

Remuneration of local nationals has traditionally been governed by the prevailing standards of the host country. If a deviation from this standard occurred, it was a positive differential which was issued as an inducement to the best people to join the company or as an indicator of the company's progressiveness and concern with employee welfare. In size the differential was held in such limits as not to permit any serious upward pressure upon the prevailing salary standards of the country, which inevitably would have lead to an increase in cost. Nondisruption of the indigenous compensation standards became the cardinal rule and managerial salaries based on American standards unthinkable.

While still prevalent in the majority of multinational companies, the nondisruption theory has been divested from the moralistic aura in which it was preached in the 1950s and 1960s.

What the local salary standard actually is cannot always be determined. The exact job may not exist in the country or locality; salaries are kept secret and there are no published data; various fringe benefits, payments in kind, special bonuses, and other local practices may not be included in salary figures. Working conditions also vary widely, often contrasting sharply with those in the headquarters country. Thus, the local-standard approach of compensating native managers has left the headquarters a wide latitude of choices as to what the standard actually is. When the companies enjoyed a buyer's market, the standard was set more in terms of what other people were earning in the country involved than what a particular manager's duties and performances were. This meant that the native executive was often paid on a preindustrial, rural scale although he was performing industrial functions in an urbanized setting. In a seller's market, with the demand for native managers outstripping the supply, the indigenous standard has been undergoing a continuous redefinition and upward revision in the recent years.

Changes in the managerial mix on the affiliate level have contributed further to the upward revision of native managers' compensation. As long as the key executive positions were staffed exclusively by headquarters-country expatriates, no insurmountable difficulty arose. But when the third-country expatriates and indigenous managers started to be employed alongside the headquarters people, issues of executive motivation and employee morale inevitably became tangled with the compensation system. The local nationals, like the third-country expatriates, have maintained an unyielding opposition to any compensation system that expressly discriminates against them. Although many local nationals have accepted employment in positions where expatriates who are working beside them in substantially comparable assignments are paid significantly higher salaries, they have not ceased to pressure for an elimination of such discrepancies. With the demand for native managers increasing rapidly due to an accelerating internationalization of business, aided locally by enactments of statutory limitations for expatriate employment, the upward pressures to bring the native manager's salary to a par with that of expatriates has forced many companies to a grudging recognition that salary distinctions based on nationality are indefensible. The typical pattern now emerging is to allow a gradual upgrading of native manager salaries on a selective basis. A major American bank has recently established performance standards which, if met, will allow the particular local manager to be shifted from the local management status to the company's international executive corps. The reclassification of status is accompanied by adjusting his pay to the same basis as all the others in the international corps, including Americans. In return, the local manager must agree to go as a third-country expatriate to any other country where the bank may need his services. By structuring the system this way the bank hopes to be able to open the way for upward mobility out of the ranks of local nationals wherever it has affiliate offices. It is presumed in this case that any local manager promoted to the international executive corps will spend much of his remaining career in an expatriate rather than his native-country assignment. Since the ratio of expatriates to native managers has been small and constantly declining, this bank will still have the vast majority of its native managers paid on a lower scale.

A chemical company illustrates another rather typical modification of the traditional approach. In this case all native managers above a certain level are shifted from the local salary scale to the headquarters-country (U.S.) scale. The junior and lower-middle management personnel remains as before on strictly the national standard. The philosophy here is to provide an extra incentive for the native personnel for both self-improvement and job performance.

A third approach gaining increased application is to use the management by objective as a means of compensating native managers. By setting definite goals for different executive posts, and tying remuneration to degrees of achievement of these goals, performance rather than nationality becomes the focal consideration. However, this does not guarantee that differentiation between native and expatriate executives is, in fact, eliminated from the system. It does shift the emphasis to a more rational ground and opens a channel through which the system by its own dynamics can adapt itself to the rapidly changing conditions in most countries.

Studies of local salary structures of several countries disclose the tendency for managerial as well as other professional salaries to show strong upward pressure for lower-paid groups, and a relative stickiness for the privileged ones. The result is a narrowing of the range and an identification of the higher limit of the range as the norm for all. In the industrial countries this is already more or less an accomplished fact. In the developing countries, dependent upon the success with modernization, conditions have either passed or are approaching the point where the native personnel becomes more knowledgeable, confident, and both psychologically and financially mobile. In some developing countries recent progress has been unusually rapid causing the demand for native managers, and with it their self-appraisal, to skyrocket.

13 Taxation of the Multinational Company

Taxation is society's means of paying for governmental goods and services. As such, it is a worldwide phenomenon. Yet, each nation has its unique fiscal setting. The principles, policies, and practices of taxation show many diversities among countries. Due to the break of fiscal continuity at national borders, the multinational company is subject to highly heterogeneous tax requirements. Adaptation to this heterogeneity is a complex and conflict prone process. Vital interests of the firm as well as its host countries are involved.

A Framework for an International
Tax System

Figure 13-1 schematically contrasts the closed national tax system with the same tax system after it has been entered by the multinational firm. The national tax system, upon which the theory of taxation is built, is pictured as a closed loop. Given the objectives of taxation, as defined by national goals and policies, the taxing authority prepared laws and regulations designed to achieve the objectives.

The basis for the taxing authority's ability to do this is the sovereign right of each country to tax persons living within its borders. The jurisdiction of the tax is governed not by legal principles, but by political, economic, and administrative considerations. The laws and regulations will, in theory, be stated to conform with national concepts of equity and neutrality. These laws and regulations will be the basis on which persons within the country (including business firms) will compute their taxes and structure their business decisions to meet the requirements of the law and to minimize their tax bill.

The firm operating strictly within the country's borders will have little chance to maneuver around the laws and regulations. There may be some flexibility in the laws, such as the U.S. tax laws' allowance of several depreciation methods, installment reporting, capitalization or expense of different costs (interest, taxes, research expenditures, and mining and exploration expenditures), and capital-gains alternative-tax computations. But for the most part the decisions of the uninational firm will approximate the original objectives of the tax—at least, tax theory says they will.

But now enter the multinational firm. Given the same objectives of the tax system and the same concepts influencing laws and regulations, the multi-

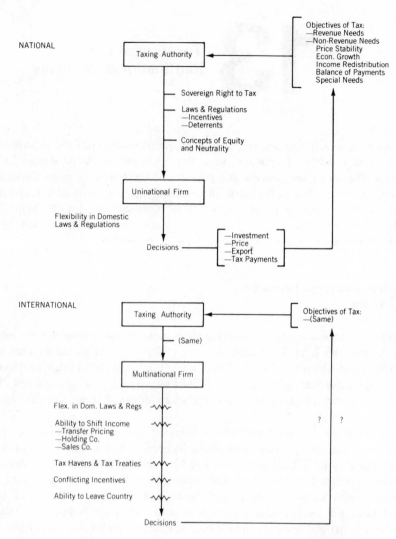

Figure 13-1. National vs. International Tax System

national firm will be subject to the same laws and regulations as the uninational firm. However as Figure 13-1 shows, the multinational firm has a whole array of alternatives available to it. These alternatives will open up the "closed loop" of the national tax system, by allowing the multinational firm to make decisions that the uninational firm could not even consider. Obviously the chances of the decisions matching the original objectives of the tax system are greatly diminished.

This is where the fun begins. The national tax authority will attempt to close the alternatives available for the multinational firm to circumvent the objectives of the tax system. The multinational firm will also be playing the game, by attempting to increase the available alternatives and open new loopholes as old ones are closed. Thus, the tax system and the multinational firm begin the interaction that will have a substantial influence on both.

John F. Kennedy expressed this indirectly in 1961: "Recently more and more enterprises organized abroad by American firms have arranged their corporate structures . . . so as to exploit the multiplicity of foreign tax systems and international agreements in order to reduce sharply or eliminate completely their tax liability, both at home and abroad."[1] This statement, which expresses why the U.S. enacted the 1962 Revenue Act with its provisions dealing with foreign-source income, merely states what any rational management of a multinational firm should be doing—taking advantage of the alternatives available to them.

This chapter will examine this interaction among multinational firms, their home-country tax systems, and their host-country tax systems. The main emphasis will be placed on the U.S. tax system, how it has been changed to cope with the multinational firm, how it has influenced the decisions of the multinational firm, and how the multinational firm has carried the effects of the U.S. tax system to other countries. Figure 13-1, schematically summarizes the interrelationships discussed. In the second section of the chapter the tax environment in other countries will be reviewed.

United States Income Taxes and the Multinational Firm

The U.S. tax law distinguishes between income from domestic sources and income from foreign sources. Foreign affiliates of American companies are subject to U.S. taxation if they contribute to the source income of the headquarters company. The legislation covering foreign source income has been amended at various times to meet changing conditions. This has been a process of piecemeal change. New, sometimes incongruous elements have been added which make the law inconsistent and self-contradicting in certain respects. The theoretical framework for the law rests on two fiscal principles: equity and domicile.

Equity on National Basis

The equity criterion requires that all taxpayers in similar situations be subject to the same rules. All U.S. corporations are taxed on all income, regardless where earned. Thus, if a U.S. company operates a branch abroad, the income of that branch will be fully taxable just like the income of any domestic branch. Equal treatment of domestic and foreign branches is theorized to neutralize any tax influence on location decisions: a company would neither increase or decrease its tax burden by choosing Kassel, Germany over Spokane, Washington. Consequently, the choice would be made on terms of true locational advantages rather than taxes. In reference to foreign companies doing business in the United States, this principle demands that they pay tax on all U.S. source income to be on equal basis with domestic firms, but not on their foreign source income.

Placed in an international rather than national context, the equity and neutrality concepts imply equal treatment of foreign-based affiliates of American firms and their native competitors in the different host countries. This is the position that certain foreign authorities and U.S. businessmen have advocated.

The equity and neutrality concept finds further expression in two rules:

1. *Avoidance of double taxation:* The foreign-tax-credit provision allows the headquarters company to deduct from its taxable income foreign taxes paid or deemed paid under Subpart F rules (to be explained later).

2. *All income taxed:* Rather than exempting foreign income from U.S. tax, the foreign tax credit rules include foreign income—as repatriated or Subpart F income in U.S. taxable income. Hence, the income is subject to at least the U.S. tax rate, for if the foreign tax rate is lower, only part of the U.S. tax will be eliminated by the foreign-tax credit.

Legal Domicile (Place of Incorporation)

The overriding criterion of the U.S. tax law has always been juridic domicile—country of incorporation. Domestic corporations are taxed on their worldwide income; foreign corporations are taxed only on their income earned in the U.S. A domestic corporation is defined simply as one incorporated within the U.S.; a foreign corporation is one incorporated outside the U.S.

This means that if the foreign-based affiliate of a U.S. company is not a branch but a separately incorporated entity under the host country's law, its profits would not be subject to American taxation unless and until transferred to the parent company in this country or distributed as dividends to its stockholders. Clearly, this concept runs counter to the equity and neutrality criterion. U.S. tax authorities have long argued that the principle of juridic domicile encourages companies to defer repatriation of earnings to postpone or to indefinitely escape U.S. tax obligation, and that for this reason the criterion should be dropped from tax legislation. However, Congress has not rescinded the juridic domicile principle as such and, formally at least, it construes to be the basic rule. Yet recent amendments to the law have emphasized the domestic equity and neutrality criteria and eroded the juridic domicile test to a rather hollow formality. The most critical damage to it was done by the 1962 Revenue

Act, which subjects U.S. company affiliates incorporated abroad to U.S. tax obligations whenever they engage in intracompany international trade in goods, factors, or services. Referred to as "Subpart F," this tax obligation applies to three types of affiliate income:

1. *Foreign holding-company income.* This includes dividends, interest, royalties, rents, and other distributions received from the ownership of stock or other securities in foreign enterprises, such as the subsidiaries of the affiliate.

2. *Foreign-base-company sales income.* This is income derived from purchases and sales transactions between affiliated firms or related parties where goods traded are both produced and sold outside the host country (legal domicile) of the affiliate. If, for example, a Finnish subsidiary of a U.S. company bought goods from its sister subsidiary in Switzerland and sold them to an Iranian buyer, the Finnish subsidiary would have earned base-company income.

3. *Foreign-base-company service income.* Income from services rendered to an affiliated firm in another county analogous to sales income above.

The Subpart F requirements place all foreign affiliates that interact across any national boundaries under U.S. tax obligation irrespective of where their profits originate or accumulate. The American headquarters company is taxed regardless of whether the affiliate profits remain abroad or are transferred to the U.S.

Only manufacturing affiliates that sell directly to third parties remain under the juridic domicile rule, and are not required to pay the U.S. tax until the earnings are transferred to the headquarters company in this country. Such isolated and localized operation defeats the inherent advantages of the multinational firm and is the object of bitter resentment by multinational organizations.

The conflict in substance between the juridic domicile criterion and the Subpart F imposition is unmistakable. Yet in form the conflict is evaded by the device of *deemed dividends*: if an affiliate's earnings remain abroad the Subpart F income is deemed to be distributed to the headquarters company, and must be included in its taxable income on an annual basis as if actually received. Thus by simply labeling the affiliate earnings "dividends" the law compels the headquarters company to pay taxes on income which in reality never has entered the U.S. national jurisdiction. The size of the deemed dividends is roughly related to the difference between the U.S. and the host-country tax rates: the bigger the difference the higher the distribution requirement. If the rates are nearly equal no deemed dividend income is taxed by the U.S.

The main purpose of the 1962 Revenue Act, which introduced the "deemed dividend" concept, was to discourage the accumulation of profits in tax-haven countries and to limit the use of "paper organizations" that have no business purpose outside of tax avoidance.

Tax havens or profit sanctuaries exist in countries that do not impose a tax on the foreign-source income of their domestic companies. A large number of countries fall in this group. Under the juridic domicile rule, if an American company established a subsidiary in such a country to sell goods made by the U.S. parent to third countries, the sales income of the subsidiary was untaxable in the U.S., and in the host country also, under the foreign source rule. If the earnings were paid out as dividends they became taxable as income to the parent; if, however, they were repatriated by liquidation of the affiliate, the U.S. tax was at the much lower capital gains rate. Inscrupulous use of the tax-haven technique spurred the enactment of the deemed-dividend concept. Now U.S. tax authorities go actually one step further—they do not recognize foreign affiliates as independent entities unless they have an actual substantive business purpose. Tax minimization is not considered a business purpose, and paper organizations set up to do this are subject to U.S. tax obligation.

These amendments, particularly the Subpart F, have caused concern in a number of host countries, which resent the fact that the U.S. extracts tax revenue from business profits earned in their countries. There have been threats of tax discrimination against American firms aimed at arresting that public revenue for the host country itself.

Exceptions

In the interest of U.S. foreign economic policy certain exceptions to the above rules have been granted. These include:

Western Hemisphere Trade Corporation. A reduced tax rate is available for corporations qualifying as a WHTC. Briefly, if over 95 percent of the gross income of a corporation engaged in Western Hemisphere trade is from sources outside the U.S., and if over 90 percent of gross income is from active conduct of a trade or business (as opposed to passive investment income), the corporation may qualify as a WHTC.

U.S. Possessions Corporations earning over 80 percent of gross income from trading in U.S. possessions.

Export Trade Corporation. If over 75 percent of gross income of a corporation is "export trade income," part of this income may be used to reduce Subpart F income.

Less-developed Country Corporation. The following are advantages of a LDCC:

Dividends received by a controlled foreign corporation from a LDCC are excludible from Subpart F income to the extent reinvested in less developed countries;

Dividends received by a U.S. corporation from a LDCC are not subject to gross-up;

A U.S. corporation does not realize ordinary income on the liquidation or sale of an LDCC if the stock has been held for at least ten years;

Securities of an LDCC are exempt from the interest equalization tax.

Controlled Affiliates

Since affiliation between domestic and foreign companies may range from nonequity contracted arrangements to complete ownership, it is necessary to distinguish between controlled and noncontrolled foreign affiliates to enforce the U.S. tax law. In the 1962 Revenue Act this distinction is made on the basis of ownership: if 50 percent or more of the equity capital of a foreign-based affiliate is owned by the U.S. parent company or other American stockholders, each of whom owns at least 10 percent of the total equity, the firm is considered American and its income is subject to U.S. taxation regardless of whether it is transferred to the stockholders or kept abroad; if less than 50 percent of the equity is owned by U.S. stockholders, or if their holdings are fragmentized into units of less than 10 percent each, the firm is considered foreign and its income is beyond the tax jurisdiction of the United States. For insurance companies the ownership ratio is 25 percent.

Attribution Rule

In determining the U.S. citizen's ownership percentage of a foreign firm, both direct and indirect ownership are considered. For example, if a U.S. firm owns only 5 percent of a French company's stock but at the same time owns a Swiss-based company which holds a majority interest in the French company, the U.S. company is *attributed* with a controlling (more than 50 percent) interest in the French company, and the latter company's income becomes taxable in the United States. Regardless of how roundabout the ownership relationship is and how many different foreign corporations are involved, the attribution rule still applies. Thus, organizational gimmicks cannot be used to circumvent the intent of the new law.

Influence of the U.S. Tax System on
Business Decisions: The Decision to
Enter Foreign Markets

Foreign operations are undertaken because they provide greater earning prospects than domestic alternatives. As taxes will affect the profits earned, their cost must be carefully determined in the location decisions. We will study the U.S. tax cost of foreign investment in three parts: the influence of the U.S. tax system on the structure of foreign operations, the influence of U.S. taxes on investment decisions, and miscellaneous influences of the U.S. tax system on the multinational firm.

Tax Influence on the Structure of
Foreign Operations

Export Operations. The simplest way a company can "go international" is to export its products. Export earnings are taxed just like domestic sales revenues. Thus, taxation is neutral with respect to exports. However, a firm can reduce taxes by utilizing a foreign sales company, such as a Western Hemisphere Trade Corporation or an Export Trade Corporation. Tax considerations would be the primary motivator in this form of organization, and tax savings would have to be weighed against additional costs of doing business through these special forms of organization.

Foreign Manufacturing Branch. A company can enter foreign markets by establishing a branch in a foreign country. Since the profits earned by the branch are wholly included in the taxable income of the parent company, again the U.S. tax law is neutral with respect to establishment of foreign branches. However, the host country, with its own concepts of neutrality, will be sure that this branch's income is taxed in its country just like that of any local firm. Thus, the branch faces taxation from both directions—and both based on neutrality!

Foreign branches have tried to avoid the U.S. tax by selling to related sales companies at little or no profit. However, Subpart F has essentially eliminated this "form vs. substance" organization and treats sales of a manufacturing branch as fully taxable no matter who the buyer is. As a consequence, foreign branches of a U.S. company have dwindled in number to a rarity.

Foreign Manufacturing Subsidiary. The juridic domicile rule has enabled foreign subsidiaries to shield their income from U.S. tax, although of course they are still taxable by the host country. This rule, though, can only be stated for foreign manufacturing subsidiaries selling directly to third parties. Once this manufacturing subsidiary sells to related sales companies in second countries, or holds investments in other subsidiaries, the Subpart F tax liability arises.

Foreign Holding Companies. A U.S. firm, rather than owning its foreign subsidiaries directly, can set up a holding company abroad. But since the provisions of Subpart F have generally eliminated the usefulness of holding companies, they will not be discussed here.

The U.S. tax law has encouraged U.S. firms to conduct their foreign operations through subsidiaries or partly owned affiliates in which they hold minority positions.

Investment decisions: The ability to defer taxes is equivalent to an interest-free loan of cash by the government. Thus, tax minimization and tax deferral are crucial aspects of a multinational firm's investment decisions. The tax considerations affect the following investment factors:

1. *Return on investment.* The return on any investment will be enhanced if U.S. tax liability can be avoided or the taxes deferred. To the extent that these possibilities exist, investments in foreign affiliates are more profitable (assuming a foreign tax rate below the U.S. rate) and tax neutrality is not achieved.

2. *Country of investment.* The U.S. tax factors influencing country selection are tax treaties with the country; the foreign tax credit's allowance of only income taxes as a credit (putting countries relying on indirect taxation at a disadvantage), whether or not the country qualifies as a less-developed country; and tax rates in the country compared with the U.S. rates.

3. *"Cost" of repatriation.* Any investment model must consider the cost to the parent company of recovering its investment. This can be accomplished through repatriation of earnings (subject to full U.S. taxation, with the foreign tax credit) or through sale of the stock of the foreign subsidiary (taxable at ordinary income tax rates or capital gains rates depending on the circumstances).

4. *Effect on U.S. financial income.* A multinational firm will present a consolidated annual report to shareholders. Foreign financial earnings, the foreign tax credit provisions, and differences between financial earnings and taxable income may make the effect of foreign subsidiaries on U.S. earnings-per-share very favorable. This can lead to increasing stock prices, which will enhance the parent company's ability to grow even larger through merger and acquisition. Thus, foreign investment decisions, because of the U.S. tax law, do enhance reportable financial earnings.

Other corporate decisions directly affected by the U.S. tax law include:

1. *U.S. accounting system.* Subpart F requires that earnings and profits of controlled foreign corporations be computed in a way consistent with the Internal Revenue Code's definition of earnings and profits. Thus, a multinational firm must be prepared to adapt the accounting system of its foreign subsidiaries to meet this requirement. This is another "cost" that must be considered when studying a foreign investment decision.

2. *Compliance costs.* In addition to the accounting system required, the Internal Revenue Service requires numerous reports of multinational firms. These reports are required under Subpart F, for reporting information on controlled foreign corporations and transactions involving stock of foreign corporations. Also, detailed records are required to support the foreign tax credit computation. Many authors have considered compliance costs to be the principal influencing factor of the 1962 Revenue Act on multinational firms not affected by the "tax haven" provisions.

3. *Country of domicile.* Some writers have suggested that if the U.S. tax authorities should decide to wage a battle against income deferral, this might be a great stimulus for the truly "multinational" firm to leave the U.S. as its country of domicile. If a firm is truly worldwide, it should choose as its home country the country most favorable to it. Taxation may one day become a chief impetus in changes of corporate nationalities.

Intracompany International Transfer Pricing

The most controversial issue of international taxation stems from pricing of intracompany international transfers of products and services. Due to tax differentials there is always an incentive for the international corporation to calculate the transfer price in such a way as to minimize the total tax burden for the firm. This can be achieved by minimizing the prices on transfers to countries with the lower corporate income tax and maximizing the prices on transfers to the high tax countries, thereby predistributing profits in a planned international pattern. The preplanned distribution pattern for profits need not and typically is not based solely on tax considerations, but is influenced by such other factors as currency values, exchange restrictions, political stability, and corporate growth requirements. Thus the tax element may be exceedingly difficult to both isolate and treat. The main counterforce for planned transfer prices is each country's desire to maximize its tax revenue under a given set of rules, especially to extract its full share from any international enterprise.

However, the multinational firm has at its disposal a range of "acceptable" transfer prices, which gives it a powerful tool in shifting considerable amount of income from one country to another. This range of acceptable comes about because of the difficulty in assessing the "true value" of the product and services transferred between subsidiaries of the multinational firm. Very often these are high unit value, special purpose subcomponents, produced, for example, in countries with low labor cost to be assembled elsewhere.

The U.S. tax law, as recently amended, requires that a *fair price* be used when any tangible property is transferred among related parties. The determination of the fair price continues to be a source of endless dispute. As a general principle the authorities regard transfer price fair if it is the same as what two independent firms would agree upon in a normal dealing "at arm's length" with one another. Three tests of arm's-length dealing have been specified: (a) the comparable uncontrolled price method, which utilizes the open-market price for the product transferred; (b) the resale price method, under which the final sales price of the recipient affiliate to unrelated parties minus a normal mark up is a fair transfer price for tax purposes; and (c) the cost-plus method, which takes the cost of producing the property and marks it up by "an appropriate gross profit percentage." If a market price exists for the transferred product the other methods are not admissible; and if a resale price exists, the cost-plus method cannot be used. The appropriate mark-up under (b) and (c) is determined by reference to transactions that do not involve related parties.

If these or any other rules are violated by a company, the U.S. tax commissioner is authorized to reallocate gross income, deductions, and credits among affiliated companies to reflect the full tax obligation of the combined enterprise. This can cause serious complications where an affiliate already has been taxed by the host country on income before the reallocation. The host country government not only resents external interference with its fiscal practices but also is insensitive to petitions for refunds or other adjustments based on reallocations required by the American tax authority.

The elaborate regulations and awesome powers of the U.S. Revenue Service have eliminated international tax evasion schemes that flourished in the 1950s, and have greatly complicated both the tax-planning and transfer-pricing problems of the multinational companies. However, they have not eliminated the managerial discretion and corporate flexibilities of utilizing international transfer pricing as a medium of tax minimization. No tax system, however involved, can be expected to fully incapacitate the transfer-pricing mechanism. Indeed, it appears that as a multinational firm matures and develops greater operational integration among its affiliates, the opportunities for employing the transfer price tend to increase sharply irrespective of national tax laws. This is true because much that is transferred among integrated affiliates does not consist of products for which there is either a marked price or a resale price but of semimanufactures and services, in various stages of completion, for which only the company itself has any direct use or value. This leaves the cost of production as the only conceivable pricing method. But what is the cost in a complex, interrelated system of inputs and outputs? It is first of all what the accounting system and valuation methods of the company show it to be. The authorities can nitpick, watch for accounting errors and even fraud. But they can fix or prescribe very little when it comes to the basic value relationships. The most any authority could hope for is to duplicate the record of all transactions of the firm—something which in practice is far beyond any cost horizon of the government itself. But even then the most decisive areas of managerial judgment as to the relative importance, opportunity costs, and methods of valuation of different input components in the overall production-distribution process cannot be assumed by the bureaucrats of the tax authority. They can never take the place of management as such. No amount of legislation and regulatory authority short of outlawing multinational firms can, therefore, prevent international transfer pricing from being used as a potent tool in business policy.

The Multinational Firm: Its Influence
on the U.S. Tax System

The U.S. tax system has a powerful influence on many decisions of the multinational firm; but it has also been influenced by the multinational firm. As U.S. firms have grown by establishing or acquiring foreign affiliates the U.S. taxing authority has sought new ways to combat the new problems that the multinationalization of business has caused.

The influence of the multinational firm has been felt primarily in two areas: tax revenues and fiscal principles.

1. *Revenue effect.* The ability of the multinational firm to defer taxes on its certain affiliates' income can be conceived as a reduction in U.S. tax revenue. The use of tax havens to defer U.S. tax was successfully limited by the Revenue Act of 1962. Possible changes aimed at eliminating deferral have been the subject of much debate for years. This discussion is certain to continue with the aim of further tax obligations for the multinational firm.

An additional revenue effect of the multinational firm is the increased cost of tax administration. The multinational firm presents new difficulties for the Internal Revenue Service. These include attempting to audit operations outside the U.S. and dealing with complex new regulations that no one readily understands. An entire new audit staff, the Office of International Operations (OIO), has been formed to attempt to deal with the complex international organizations of multinational firms.

2. *Fiscal principles.* The multinational firm has caused the U.S. tax authority to develop many complex rules to deal with it. Subpart F is one of the most complex provisions of the Internal Revenue Code. Yet there is still dissatisfaction with U.S. tax treatment of the income of multinational firms.

This dissatisfaction has led to pressure on the basic concepts underlying U.S. taxation. For example, the taxing authority has opposed the juridic domicile (place of incorporation) test and argued for the dominance of national equity and neutrality—that is, an end to deferral. On the other hand, business firms and others have argued for "international equity"—that is, freeing the U.S. firm to compete on an equal basis with other countries' businesses by providing permanent deferral of all foreign income, even income of branches of U.S. corporations. This concept of "true economic source of income" has been heard recently in discussions by tax and business people regarding proposals to limit the taxability of export sales (proposals for the establishment of domestic international sales companies).

Also, there has been increased discussion of *tax sparing.* As other countries find "tax holidays" a valuable incentive for increasing foreign investment, the U.S. must consider the possibility of foregoing the U.S. tax on earnings of subsidiaries in countries allowing tax sparing. These issues would hardly have arisen if it were not for the rise to dominance of the multinational firm.

Pressures are mounting to bring the U.S. tax system in close conformity with the rest of the world. For example, proposals have been increasing for the enactment of value-added tax to help relieve the reliance on the corporate income tax.

These pressures on the U.S. tax system will continue as long as the multinational firm has available to it the arsenal of alternatives unavailable to the uninational firm. As we have shown in earlier chapters, a number of these alternatives stem from inherent superiorities of the multinational firm and, as such, are beyond reach for the uninational companies. Consequently the strain on the national tax systems is not going to be easily reduced. Rather, it will continue indefinitely. As the U.S. tax system tries to pattern itself after the multinational firm, its influence is extended to a number of other countries. Ironically, the vehicle for this influence is none other than the multinational firm itself.

14 Society and the Multinational Firm: Conflict Analysis

Pessimistic critics of the multinational firm see in this new economic institution a dangerous potential for uncontrollable economic power which threatens the sovereignty of nation states. To these critics the operational and financial superiorities of the multinational firm over its uninational competitors are nothing but expressions of socially unaccountable corporate power, which have nothing to do with its inherent capabilities but result purely from its ability to escape the laws and other social controls of business in any particular country through its multiple domicile. This is to say that the multinational company gains its advantages and superiorities not by being more efficient in production, distribution, or organization of its affairs, but by being able to pick and choose from among many countries the one that offers the least resistance to its plans: the one where government regulations impose the least restriction and cost burdens upon the firm. By calculated assignment of legal parenthood to its different ventures, the company can bounce its social responsibility like pinballs from host country to host country in search of the highest score—the biggest profit from any particular investment undertaking through avoidance or minimization of social responsibilities. Such relative immunity to national regulation not only frustrates a nation's efforts to control its own economic destinies, but also tends to incapacitate its government in other spheres.

The regulatory immunity is only the first level of the pessimist's proposition. From here he moves to the deliberate exertion of active influence of the multinational firm on a nation's governmental functions. The mildest form of such active interference with a nation's governmental functions is perceived to be the most uncommon case where a firm may say in effect to a host government, "If you do not accommodate our requests we will move our operations to another country." The negative consequence of the move may be larger than those of the demanded regulatory relief and the government may feel itself compelled to comply.

The same tactic, choice of the lesser evil, can be employed in other ways. For example, the multinational firm may threaten to seek help from its headquarters country or some other host country's government, which in a particular situation may be both inclined and able to cause a diplomatic incident of such moment that the antagonistic government, considering its overall interests, may find it wiser to yield to the firm than to stand on its principle. While most governments officially want to stay out of private commercial arrangements—U.S. ambassadors are directed not to interfere in commercial negotiations unless

197

directed from Washington—none really seems to be able to claim a consistent record of not doing so. It is, therefore, not beyond the realm of possibility that either of these pressure tactics could be successfully employed by the multi-national firm in specific instances. However, past record of success with defiance of the national authority provides no encouragement to management to put the probabilities of success anywhere but very low.

From here the pessimist critic descends to the murky ground of sinister machinations, corruptive tactics, and political sabotage as asserted means for the multinational firm to strike down laws and regulations inimical to its designs. It is not clear from available evidence whether multinational firms are afflicted by any such antisocial tendencies more often than domestic firms. A random sample of headline-making corporate scandals during the 1960s shows the multinational companies to be much less subject to criminal violations than the uninational firms. Furthermore, the former's controversial involvements with national authorities were mostly related to the right of establishment or acquisition of preexisting indigenous enterprises to which the governments objected. These were often cases involving official discrimination against inter-national business rather than nondiscriminatory regulations. It would seem that no factual grounds exist for charging the multinational firm with any greater fallability in the social responsibility sphere than the domestic firms in any particular country. Indications are that the reverse is actually true, and this third level of the critic's charges can be dismissed. The first two, however, have been documented often enough to be taken as real, though admittedly exaggerated, tendencies which demand closer scrutiny.

The failure of governmental regulations to control the multinational firm have been interpreted variously as an impediment to social good which should be eliminated by eradicating its source—the firm itself—or as a reflection of social irresponsibility of international executives who maneuver their companies free from national control for the purpose of unabashedly defrauding and fleecing the public for the firm's enrichment. In this extremist view, international business is parasitic and devoid of any socially productive content. (It is usually left unsaid whether mankind's material requirements need to be provided for at all, or whether they will be derived from some occult source reminiscent of the biblical "manna from heaven" notion.) Since neither of these lines of thought rise above the level of righteous indignation, they provide no help in clarifying either the true state of affairs or the need for any change in it.

Factual Arguments

Several recent publications contain documentation of the difficulties that national governments have experienced in regulating the multinational firm.[1] The incidents of governmental helplessness range over a wide spectrum: local affiliates to adopt more aggressive export policies, to differentiate their products, to give wholehearted support to national economic objectives, to do research and develop new technology, to disregard the constraints imposed upon the firm by its headquarters country, to increase the voice of local nationals in strategic decisions, to remove the competitive superiorities over indigenous uninational firms, etc. The studies leave no room for serious doubt that national authorities have suffered frustration and their control system has been proven impotent by the problems and pressures associated with the presence of the multinational firm in their countries. Indeed, it is clear that most national governments that have tried to face it have registered mostly failures and very few successes in attempts to cope with the regulatory control of the multinational firm.

But why? Too often these attempts have been limited to pious rhetoric. Where action has been attempted it has been to deal with isolated instances on an ad hoc basis rather than any comprehensive, let alone systematic, attack on the problem. Despite much ado about the subject in many countries, there is as yet nothing that could bear the title "regulation of multinational firm." Nor is there any record that such regulation has ever been officially attempted. Yet this fact has not prevented the widespread belief that the nation state as such cannot be equal to the task: the powers of the multinational Goliath are so awesome that the governmental Davids had better give up before they start!

The reality is not quite so frightening. Failure to regulate is not synonymous with inability to regulate. In the absence of regulation the multinational company can hardly be blamed for utilizing the freedoms and opportunities available to it. That the domestic business controls may be rendered ineffectual in the process does not make the company any more socially irresponsible than other purposeful entities seeking the course of least resistance, but simply proves that the traditional regulatory controls are unsuited, inept, and inadequate for dealing with this new type of business institution. Take even such a simple matter as export policies of an affiliate. If the host country wants to force compliance with its national foreign-trade objectives there is nothing to prevent it from legislating that the affiliates of multinational firms domiciled in its jurisdiction align their export-import policies with those of the government. But as long as there is no such firm requirement, any amount of moralizing and castigating can produce little more than outlets for patriotic hot air. No managers can be expected to take their cues from political oratory or any other unenforceable external demands. If some did, their career paths might abruptly be changed.

The multinational company has moved into a regulatory vacuum that is not of its own making. The vacuum has been there all along, only no one before had the capacity to enter it and to use it as its operational arena. Once the government grasps the peculiar characteristics and capabilites of the multinational firm—which so far it has not, to any noticeable degree—it will come to realize that the regulatory vacuum is only an extension of its controllable realm and that it remains uncontrolled simply because of the government's own failure to work out the new designs and instrumentations of business regulation that are needed to guarantee that the desired social and political values are upheld by affiliates of the multinational firms in the country. As we shall see later, it may be wiser to establish international control mechanisms for certain aspects of this control than to attempt unilateral regulation. However, the problem is not inherently beyond the powers of the nation state, as erroneously implied by various writers.

Consequences

If governments are to succeed, as they sooner or later undoubtedly will, in perfecting meaningful regulatory systems to fully protect the national social interests, will this not neutralize the superiorities of the multinational firm? Will we then have arrived back at the neat simplicity of the orthodox theory where firms are firms whether uninational or multinational, where business is business whether here or there, and where the intuitively appealing assumptions of universality and complete substitutability prevail? And will the narrowly nationalistic prejudice of the pessimist critic not then have been confirmed?

No, not really. No regulatory system short of outright banning can completely nullify the operational and financial superiorities of the multinational firm. Their range could be narrowed and their categories possibly compressed by eliminating the possibilities for such manipulatory gains as now result from purely arbitrary or accidental loopholes in the business regulation of different countries. This would wipe out the tax-haven companies, profit oasis, and other formal shells to avoid local control, but would not materially alter the substantive operations of the multinational enterprise.

Although the international inconsistencies and a general lack of regulatory controls now contribute to the relative advantage patterns of the multinational firm, the primary source of its superiorities is not the regulatory jumble but the diversity and plurality inherent in its multinational business environment. Overregulation can regiment the multinational firm and arrest its productive utilization of the internation differences. This would be an undeniable social loss. But no regulatory system can ever remove the diversity and plurality from the multinational environment. They are the essence of the environment. The underlying economic, social, and cultural variations will not only remain but perhaps become even more pronounced after the shadows cast by the present confusion among the regulatory conditions which often counteract them have been removed.

While the current regulatory vacuum as such is bound to disappear and, let us hope, a sensible system of controls emerge, the range of choices available to the multinational firm will not necessarily shrink but merely be rearranged; in certain respects it could even increase. Whether any new regulatory vacuums favorable to the multinational firm will be created cannot be predicted. If not, the unchecked freedoms that supposedly exist in the present regulatory vacuum will be replaced by the relative freedoms of controlled environments that all have different risks, prices, or other resistances to overcome. This is hardly different from what is true even for a domestic firm, except in the numbers and types of alternatives. As a matter of managerial reality there never is a complete vacuum: resistance-free, no-cost, all-profit situations. The name of the game is the balancing of costs and returns from all possible choices. The more choices, the more opportunities for success, as well as for failure.

Conflict Causes

Social control of the multinational firm presents a snarled dilemma. Through its network of multiple domiciles and operating affiliates the firm can escape some important national regulations, thwart certain governmental policies, infuriate indigenous competitors and baffle the general public. To this ability to immunize itself against the conventional regulatory instruments of the nation state and especially its occasional excesses in transversing and defeating governmental objectives has become a major issue of international relations in our times as evidenced by an increasing body of publications on the subject. From this perspective the multinational firm is seen as the culprit, the broker of socially unaccountable powers, and even an evil instrument of neocolonialist exploitation of host-country societies. All this is no longer news. But it is a tunnel vision, onesided and often inflated by nationalistic bias.

From another perspective the problems and issues of regulating the behavior of the multinational firm appear altogether different. Besieged by divergent objectives and incongruous regulatory enactments of its various host countries, the firm is placed in multiple jeopardy, with no central judiciary to coordinate the chaos. Each host nation holds in its own right legal and political power over the firm. Each is thus empowered to impose official impediments and to inflict injury upon the firm's ability to function. Even if all the governments envisaged the contemporary multinational firm as a new progressive form of economic organization, rather than a façade to the old colonial exploitation, their uncoordinated efforts to cope with the new organizational phenomenon could still lead to strangulation of the firm as a multinationally functioning organ. Since some governments remain suspicious or even hostile to the firm, regulatory injury to it is not only a latent potential but an omniscient danger.

Unlike its relative immunity to certain national regulations, its exposure to multiple jeopardy which stems from the separateness and mutually contradictory character of the national regulations of its different host countries has somehow remained relatively untouched by writers on the subject. Our purpose here is not to attempt to counterbalance the record by an overstatement of the companies' side, but to impassionately unravel the conflict laden relationships as much as our present state of information permits. Hopefully, a more accurate and better balanced statement of the whole issue will emerge from the analysis.

Sources of Conflict

The conflict situations peculiar to the international relations of the multi-national firm can be usefully categorized by the interactions from which they arise. Basically there are six interacting systems with nine clearly identifiable relationships among them. They are depicted in Figure 14-1. To avoid generalities, the United States is assumed to be the home country for the headquarters company; each relationship is dissected and its conflict-prone aspects evaluated with that assumption in mind. To the extent to which other home countries such as Japan or the United Kingdom have different regulations and public policies, the specific facts would differ, but in principle and scope the problem areas would remain the same between their multinational firms and public authorities.

The conflicts between the multinational firm and its different host countries may occur on several different planes. They may involve primary objectives, secondary activities, or purely coincidental specifics. It is neither necessary nor typical for the conflict on one level to be parallel with corresponding conflicts on other levels. It is quite common for conflict on any given plane between the multinational firm and the nation state to coexist with concordant interests on other planes. Cooperation and accord in macrodecisions, for example, provides no guarantee that the firm and the state will not contraposition themselves in certain microdecision areas.

The relationship is never a matter of pure conflict or pure cooperation, but a dual process of simultaneous conflict-cooperation resolution. Any equilibrium between the conflicting and coinciding tendencies derives not from any mechanistic adaptation, but from interaction, negotiation, and other processes of exercising the powers each side can apply. Unilateral resolution of conflicts between the nation state and the multinational firm can hardly be expected to produce rational results: if the state merely dictates the norms for corporate policy or if, at the other extreme, the company seeks to counterpose its own strategy—including that of nonparticipation—to national policy, no true resolution of the conflict is possible.

The resultant situation is likely to lead to an enlargement and aggravation of the discord which sooner or later will require new measures, usually at a greater cost to the society. That this lesson has not been fully learnt by all businesses is reflected in the refusal of several major companies to negotiate with host

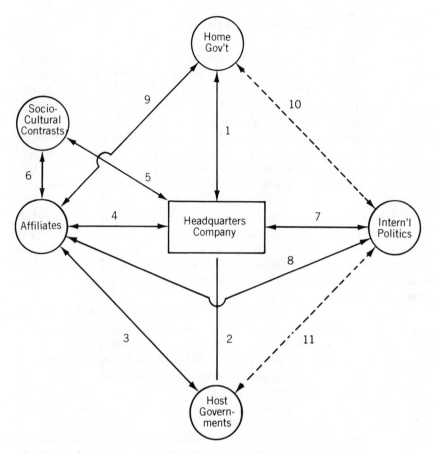

Numbers refer to basic relationships from which different types of conflicts may arise.

Figure 14-1. Conflict Analysis Model for Multinational Firms

governments when changed political or economic conditions in the country have demanded revision of established relationships, or to redress long-existing grievances by nationals against the firm.

Since the conflicts invariably turn on issues of value priorities, their rational solution presupposes axiological analysis as a basis for harmonization of the discordant positions. The natural relationship between the host society and the multinational company is not effective isolation or independence, as was sought by the colonial enterprise, but an active interdependence with multiple linkages, mutual interactions, tensions, bargaining, and conflict resolution through adaptations to new realities on both sides.

Home Country vs. Headquarters Company

The regulatory measures of the United States that either directly or indirectly conflict with the interests of the multinational firm range over a wide spectrum.

1. *Financial and foreign exchange controls.* Restrictions on direct foreign investments, profit repatriation requirements, limitations on reinvestment of affiliate earnings, regulation of international credit transactions, and company balance of payments guidelines, all not only limit the firm's ability to follow economic dictates of the market but also jeopardize its relations with host countries whose capital formation, economic growth, and balance of payments are negatively affected to the extent to which the U.S. restrictive measures are successful.

Even such an apparently innnocuous measure as the interest equalization tax of 1963 can cause a significant reaction. It not only discouraged many potential investors from buying foreign stocks but also encouraged many Americans to liquidate their foreign stock holdings and replace them with domestic stocks. As a result stock prices in Europe dropped, despite rising real profits and an extraordinary economic growth.

2. *Taxation of foreign-based and foreign-incorporated affiliates' income*, which again reduces the capital available to the firm as well as the host nations of its affiliates. (For a full discussion of the tax issue see Chapter 15.)

3. *Foreign aid, food for peace, and technical assistance programs*, which at times subsidize projects in competition with multinational firms.

4. *Extraterritorial application of U.S. Export Control Act* to foreign affiliates of the firm, by holding the headquarters company liable for their compliance with destination restrictions and validated license rules, with restrictions on sales of strategic materials, technical data, unpublished technology, and other export controls. That these interfere directly with the affiliates' ability to market their output and to acquire inputs in most advantageous markets is self-evident. But since the host countries rarely share the U.S. objectives for these restrictions, and since their own export trade as well as foreign economic policies are countermanded by the extraterritorial impositions of the U.S. trade regulations, pressures for retaliation again jeopardize the company's position and productivity.

5. *Extraterritorial application of the U.S. Trading with the Enemy Act* parallels that of the Export Control Act. This act prohibits American citizens from transacting any business with nationals of enemy countries, currently including China, Cuba, North Korea, and North Vietnam. Applied to the multinational firm, it makes all foreign affiliates of it bound by the same restriction. The loudest protests against the extraterritorial application of this law have come from Canada, where many American subsidiaries have either discouraged or flatly refused to fill orders from the U.S.-embargoed countries. But in Europe and Latin America official indignation is rising. In Belgium an

affiliate was ordered not to deliver rice harvesting equipment to Cuba, despite normal trade relations between Belgium and Cuba. Refusal of the order necessitated cutbacks in the affiliate's labor force and seriously marred its public image. In France both a computer maker and a truck manufacturer were compelled to refuse sizeable orders from China. This flew in the face of the French government's objective of having friendly trade relations with China.

6. *Extraterritorial application of U.S. antitrust laws and policies.* These laws not only restrict the firm's freedom to mergers, acquisitions, and joint ventures in disregard to the host country's own laws—the U.S. rules have also been applied to reduce a firm's foreign-market share, deemed to constitute monopoly by U.S. Justice Department Anti-Trust Division, and is even more keenly aimed against any cooperative arrangements between the firm's affiliates and other foreign firms, which the American authorities' regard as criminal in intent by definition. Also, foreign affiliates of U.S. firms have been forced to give information to American courts and instructions have been issued by American authorities to non-U.S. firms regarding their market behavior, licensing, and exclusive distribution agreements.

The conflict of objectives becomes especially evident in the two investigations against the firms Gillette and Litton Industries which have purchased the enterprises Braun A/G and Adler-und Triumpfwerke in the German Federal Republic. In both cases the U.S. authorities wanted to determine whether the U.S. companies restrict competition on the American market by acquisition of firms in Europe. However, with these transactions it was the German and the European markets which were mainly affected. The two cases appear especially paradoxical, as the acquisition of the two European enterprises by American firms did not become the object of instructions or conditions of national or European authorities but U.S. authorities. Should the American authorities or courts have insisted on reversing one of the transactions, then the freedom of European enterprises to sell their property to American companies would have been limited.[2]

American courts have refused to define except in highly ambiguous terms the limits of their foreign antitrust involvement. As a textbook rule the U.S. courts are supposedly to refrain from impairment of the international relations, but in practice they have insisted on compliance by foreign affiliates with their edicts and interpretations, unless confronted with express mandates of foreign governments. The mere fact that an act is not in violation of the host country law, and an exhortation of repercussions, have been so far disregarded.

7. *Home country's insistence that its law and policy be favored in company's foreign operations.* This general proposition is evidenced by the incidence cited above as well as numerous other litigations on all aspects of business affairs. The same tendencies, though not as persistent, are reflected in the British, French, and Japanese official attitudes toward their multinational firms. It appears that until international conventions are established to curb the extraterritorial

applications of national laws and policy by the home countries of headquarters companies—conventions that may take decades to negotiate and ratify—the multinational firm will remain exposed to conflicting legal sanctions and can succeed only to the extent to which neutral surfaces and compromises can be found. Inescapably the multinational firm is forced to become the international carrier of its home country's laws and policies for extraterritorial implementation. This is an inherently contradictory and potentially self-defeating role. When the recipient host countries react to home country controls, the company is always caught in the middle and drawn into costly and protracted litigations with both governments. Insult to injury is often added by news publicity portraying the firm not as the victim but the villain, the notorious instrument of the home country's imperialistic designs or the unpatriotic betrayer of home-country interests.

Host Government vs. Headquarters Company

Several areas of host government action against the multinational firm were indicated in the previous section. In addition there are four others:

1. *Control of affiliates.* In some countries the law has always required that foreign ownership of certain types of firm, such as public utilities, steel mills, real estate, vital consumer services, arsenals, etc., be limited to a certain percentage of equity, or that specially restrictive procedures be followed in licensing any foreign-ownership participation. In others, especially in certain developing nations, the rules are now being tightened and requirements for partial indigenous ownership established to previously wholly owned affiliates of foreign firms. At this writing, for example, the government of Guyana has decreed that the wholly owned bauxite subsidiaries of American and Canadian aluminum companies be reorganized as partly owned enterprises, in which the government itself would be a major shareholder.

This is typical of the trend in most extractive industries, whose practices have lacked the flexibility necessary to meet the contemporary expectations of the host nations. While a preexistent ownership limitation may be resented, it is seldom a source of a real conflict unless a firm endeavors to subvert it through its own political initiative (support of legislation, contribution to favorable candidates, etc.). A change in ownership requirements, on the other hand, is always conflict-ridden. If the change is toward restriction, the multinational firms affected resist it in self-defense; if the change involves liberalization, nationalistic elements in the host country will force the issue. In either case the firm cannot escape the pressures.

Control of affiliate activities is sometimes sought also by requiring that local nationals serve as its directors. Conflicts arising from this requirement are in essence very similar to those arising in connection with the ownership rule.

However, since the statutory organization, as explained in Chapter 9, can be relegated to more or less formalistic rituals while the substantive matters are vested in managerial organization, two questions arise: Is the dual organizational structure now so commonly used by multinational firms a subversion of host-country controls and, as such, an illegal or antisocial practice? and Is managerial efficiency, a generally accepted prerogative of the firm, to be subjected to nationalistic constraints, which are quite unrelated to the objectives of the firm? Both questions are explosive, and no doubt will figure in headlines in future court litigations and international negotiations.

2. *Market behavior expectations.* The policy directives which the head-quarters issues in reference to its affiliates' basic behavior patterns are of great interest to the host society. First, will the affiliates be directed to function in harmony with the host nation's objectives and policies that are in conflict with U.S. antitrust laws? And second, if they do not, how will the various indigenous publics, particularly the local businessman and consumer, react to the affiliates' alien behavior? If this behavior deviates drastically from the local norms—for example, if the company's pricing policy disregards established pricing practices of the country or the firm shunts participation in industry self-regulation for fear of U.S. antitrust violations—the ire of the local groups may be aroused against the company. To what action this might lead varies with the particular circumstances and countries involved.

In early cases such disruptive market behavior of affiliates was sometimes successfully defended in the name of economic progress: the American methods were to repay for any initial damage multifold by ultimate elevation of marketing efficiency and consumer satisfaction in the country. Although still attempted, this tactic seems to carry progressively less conviction and the affiliates are faced with local initiatives to block or even roll back the transplantation of U.S. practices in the host countries.

3. *Actions against both the headquarters company and local affiliate.* Typically the host country deals with the multinational firm as such rather than with the headquarters or the affiliates as separate entities. Since the affiliate is within its jurisdiction, the government often directs all its actions, including those intended against the headquarters, to the affiliate as a matter of practical convenience or necessity. Hence, clear distinction between host-country-head-quarters-company relations from host-country-affiliates relations is neither possible nor particularly important. Actions which usually go against either the headquarters or the affiliate are included in the next section.

Conflict Between the Host Government and
the Affiliate of the Multinational Firm

The affiliate of a multinational firm, however welcome by the host government as a source of employment, income, and economic growth, has certain needs that governmental policies and regulatory authorities either frustrate or prevent from being adequately met.

The government takes its cues from its perception of the national interest for which no universal definition exists. Different countries and even succeeding governments of the same country cling to their own perceptions of what does and does not serve the national interest. The affiliate's prime commitment is to the corporate interest as perceived by the top management of the headquarters company. Except for the rare coincidence where the two happen to coincide completely, there is always an area of potential conflict between the best interest of the host country and the best interest of the affiliate. In some aspects these respective interests are identifiable in concrete economic terms, in other aspects they arise from ideological or other purely attitudinal presuppositions. In a deeper sense the value judgments nearly always lie at the root of the national constraints circumscribing the affiliate, while the business calculus is more apt to take its formulations from the internal logic of the firm or a multinational corporate system.

We could simplify matters by distinguishing between inherently objective—the factually demonstrable—aspects of self-interest, and the ideological or attitudinal aspects of it that defy concrete explanation. But if this clarifies or confuses the real conflicts, it is not readily apparent. There is always the danger that the concrete tends to overshadow the subtle and intangible in disregard of their respective influence on the real situation.

1. *Balance-of-payments pressures.* Being an integral part of an international organization, the affiliate of a multinational firm is inherently an instrument of international transfers. It may trade in money, securities, goods, services, information, property rights, jobs, and other economic values. Inevitably, then, the affiliate's presence affects the balance of international payments of its host country. If the host is not a major trading nation the affiliate's international dealings may play a very significant role in the nation's payments position. Also, hopes or expectations for improvement of payments position tend inevitably to focus on the affiliate as the source and instrument of bringing it about. Invariably, the improvement involves deficit reduction. Import purchases by the affiliate are therefore resisted, regardless how necessary they may be for the affiliate's business viability. This applies not only to the imports of finished goods but also to all input goods, regardless of their level of refinement, as well as to information, services, and other in-transfers the affiliate may require.

Exports, by the same token, are a blessing to monetary authorities, who tend to view anything but a constantly increasing volume as suspect on the part of the affiliate. Official surveillance and prodding have been particularly characteristic in reference to affiliates whose own earnings of foreign exchange are insufficient to balance its foreign payments. Although these pressures vary from country to country, being particularly pronounced in smaller and less developed countries, they are never completely absent even in such industrial powers as, for example, West Germany and Japan.

Managerial awareness and sophistication in the balance-of-payments area has enhanced significantly since the mid-1960s. It is no longer exceptional for corporate planners and policy-makers to project the balance-of-payments effect of their decisions and to take into consideration any anticipated governmental reaction to the projected results. In many firms the zero-effect criterion now has been adopted as the minimum requirement for any major international expansion: unless the foreign exchange earnings of the venture equal its foreign-exchange requirements, the program either will be abandoned altogether or advance agreements negotiated with the authorities to guarantee not only the supply of the projected exchange deficit but also freedom from future governmental reprisals.

How reliable such advance guarantees are depends more on the country and its future governments than on the legal instruments involved. In the industrial countries there is little to fear. In the developing countries contractual agreements between the governments and private international firms are often regarded as symptoms of undue foreign influence—neocolonialism, in the nationalistic jargon—and unilateral changes in them can net a new government handsome political dividends. This is a new reality that has rendered utterly unsatisfactory the strategy of privileged positions that many companies, particularly in oil and other extractive industries, have been following to this time.

The zero-effect criterion serves to protect the firm against any special privilege changes in the future, and must therefore be regarded as preferable to any preferential treatment contracts. The only safe exceptions to this rule include projects whose benefits are rated by the host-country authorities as significant enough to justify the projected foreign-exchange expenditure. In practice, such projects fall mostly into governmentally adopted economic growth plans rather than purely private initiative.

The problems would be simple if the balance-of-payments effects of major corporate decisions could be readily ascertained. In most cases they cannot. Cases where the firm operates a number of integrated affiliates in the same host country where the exchange expenditures of some may be linked with the exchange earnings of others can be particularly complicated. The net balance-of-payments effect of any particular decision can, therefore, be a subject of interpretation, that is objective conflict, rather than concrete measurement. Since in addition the political officials often lack the necessary education to be able to understand the financial intricacies of multinational business, the conflicts in this area must be regarded as practically perpetual, despite many new techniques and formula for their resolution. Venture capital has always accepted risk and uncertainty, be it commercial or political, and this we can safely assume to be continuous in the future. Hence, there will always be firms that will disregard the zero-effect criterion and stake their fortunes on the hope of being able to persuade authorities to regard their other contributions as ample justification for any balance-of-payments deficit they may cause.

2. *Capital transfer restrictions.* Although a particular aspect of the balance-of-

payments problem from the host country's standpoint, official restrictions on international capital transfers deny the multinational firm the capacity to optimally allocate its capital resources throughout the world. There is a real cost to the company in complying with these restrictions. Unlike other costs, the transfer restrictions produce no benefit for the firm and, as such, are subject to not only the inherent tendency of a firm to minimize cost but also to the philosophical aversion against punitively counterproductive arbitrariness.

It appears that governmental and corporate minds have never really met on this issue. Each has remained in its separate orbit and no progress toward a resolution of the central issue can be reported at this writing.

3. *Public revenue requirements.* Only the rear guard of the colonialist enterprise still debate whether an affiliate should or should not contribute to public finance on the same basis as purely indigenous firms. For others the argument has now advanced to the question of defining and measuring what these contributions ought to be. Besides taxation, which was separately discussed in Chapter 13, the public finance conflicts between the affiliate and the host government include the whole area of the firm's effect on the infrastructure and essential public services. Not only the rates to be charged for public utility services required by the affiliate, but in many countries also the creation of the needed infrastructural capacity such as sewage systems, electric power plants, and transportation facilities, may provide cause for collision between the national and corporate interests. Again, the developing countries and other small economies are the most conflict-prone. With an undeveloped or small infrastructural capacity and inadequate financial resources for expansion, these governments must necessarily ration the use of utility services to avoid the politically intenable situation where a few foreign firms exhaust a large share of the available supply, leaving much of the local need unsatisfied. If price alone was used this would often be the result.

Any nonprice rationing is inherently a political act, which except in a purely autocratic ruling always involves balancing the many divergent demands upon the rationing public authority. Persuasion, bargaining, and power politics all are natural attributes of the rationing process. It would therefore be indefensible naïve for any multinational firm to proceed on the premise that it cannot influence the outcome and to assume a completely passive role in this process. While some affiliates could succeed in spite of it, this behavior certainly would have to be classified as misguided and contrary to the best interest of the firm.

Factual observations leave little room for any fears about the passivity of multinational firms in exerting their influence on host governments in the area of public finance. On the contrary, the evidence points to the excess of corporate lobbying and other political manipulations designed to influence host-country regulatory bodies. This excessiveness is likely to boomerang: it trades the credibility and long-range good of the corporation for the immediate or relatively short-run regulatory favors, which tends to overly politicize the affiliate's presence and make it progressively more suspect of antinational behavior.

4. *Foreign trade regulations.* All countries regulate transboundary trade activities in some form. Customs tariffs, quotas, and various export and import licenses apply to the affiliate of a multinational firm just the same as to domestic companies. But unlike its uninational domestic counterpart, the multinational firm can in certain respects circumvent the trade controls, and to that extent substitute its own trading policy for that of the host government. The main instruments for doing this are transfer pricing, drawbacks, and possible revealed earnings of foreign exchange.

Through appropriate transfer prices ad valorem duties, value-based quotas, and export-import taxes can be often reduced to levels significantly lower than those applicable to the uninational traders. Drawbacks, the ability to recoup the import duties paid when transferring a product such as a subassembly or part to a sister affiliate in another country, may allow multinationally integrated affiliates to trade at essentially no import duty liability. For example, an affiliate imports product X on which it pays a given amount of duty; after adding value to the product by manufacture and possible addition of other input goods, it exports its output to a sister affiliate abroad, which entitles it to obtain a refund of the original import duties paid. If the value added by the affiliate was significant and the export volume substantial, the questions of reductions or even eliminations of the import duty may arise as possible areas of common interest and cooperation between the firm and the nation. Since cooperation and conflict are interlocked processes this possible harmony of objectives can just as readily become the source of disharmony if governmental and corporate values or interpretations rest on different premises.

This possibility is not limited to reexporting but applies to any affiliate with a demonstrable surplus in its own foreign-exchange balance. Depending on the host country's needs, the surplus represents bargaining power that the firm can use to gain relief from various foreign-trade restrictions. The fact that the chances for favorable results to the firm vary with the country only adds to the possibility for strife and uncertainty as to what is a rational initiative.

Beyond the border controls, national foreign-trade policies may impose destination controls and financial requirements including credit limits, risk insurance practices, and means of payment (currency, instrument, etc.) rules. These, too, can place the company and the government on opposite sides. Particularly bad have been the quadrangular quarrels involving the contrarities between the trade controls of the host country and the headquarters country.

If both nations are content to limit their policy jurisdiction to the business firm actually domiciled in its borders, the affiliate and the headquarters can each adapt its trading to the national policy of its respective domicile, and there is cause for conflict only to the extent to which the headquarters insists on centralization or commonality in business policy. The facts show this to be a rather frequent cause of difficulty for multinational firms. Yet much angrier confrontations have arisen from the attempts of national authorities, especially the U.S. government, to impose their controls extraterritorially upon the affiliate through sanctions against the headquarters company.

So far the host countries' reactions to this have fallen short of concrete countermeasures, though the rhetoric in such countries as Canada, France, Sweden, The United Kingdom, and even West Germany has revealed a swelling acrimony toward the extraterritorial application of American policy. By all indications, including the U.S. government's inflexibility, this practice will continue to harbor the sources of potentially violent conflicts between the multinational firm and its various domiciles.

5. *Requirement to operate within host country's domestic framework.* As corporate citizens of their host countries, the affiliates of multinational firms are expected by public authorities to govern their behavior by both the economic and social policies of the country. Pursuance of centrally planned goals and abstention from activities contrary to it are taken for granted. Wage and salary policies are expected to comply with established norms; hiring, firing, promotion, pension, family allowances, and innumerable other aspects of employment may be similarly subject to either statutory rules or customary practice, deviation from which bears the mark of unethical or antisocial behavior. Pricing, advertising, and selling methods may also be subject to legal norms or moral expectations peculiar to a specific host country.

Such national constraint structures not only are hostile to any globalization of corporate behaviors, but also cause conflicts between the affiliate and the society by the interfering with optimization processes in the internal economics of the multinational firm. This is to say, the compliance with the host-country domestic policy and custom extracts a price from the firm that in theory at least is equal to the difference between results achieved and those of an economic optimization model free of the socioeconomic national policy constraints.

6. *Fears of foreign hegemony.* More illusive yet no less real are host-country fears that stem from unofficial public perceptions that the affiliate of a multinational firm might be the agent of foreign domination and mutilation of the domestic order. These fears take many forms. The best documented are those of the Canadian government, whose task force research shows that in twelve of nineteen major industries, affiliates of multinational firms constituted more than half of existing firms, and that in some fields (petroleum, rubber, primary metals, transport equipment, chemicals, nonmetallic minerals) foreign enterprises represented oligopolistic concentrations that dominated the market. In Australia, France, and the United Kingdom the affiliates of American companies have also become conspicuous by their relative size and/or market share in different industries. In other European countries the picture varies in specifics, but the pattern reemerges again and again. The affiliates of the multinational firms, most but not all of which are U.S. headquartered (other

headquarter countries are U.K., France, Switzerland, W. Germany, Holland, Belgium, Japan, Sweden, and Italy) tend to hold strategic power in a number of industrial sectors.

Recent researches into the reasons for a fear of foreign domination have added to the nationalistic inferiority complex by showing the profitability of the affiliates to significantly exceed that of their indigenous competitors. This has been the case in all countries where such studies have been made.

Why the profitability of the affiliates has been higher has been answered in two ways. The strongly nationalistic element has seen in it proof of the excessively materialistic behavior and the industrial robber-baron philosophy of the multinational firms. The less ideology-bound interpretations have attributed the high profitability of the affiliates to subsidies from the headquarters company and sister affiliates in the form of advanced technology and management know-how. In a narrow sense this may be true in specific instances. Generally speaking, however, the higher profitability derives from the operational superiority of the multinational firm, as we have explained earlier in discussing its motivities.

Most host governments have so far shown considerable ambivalence in their official reactions to the increasing presence of the multinational firm. While typically intensively preoccupied with the matter in its administrative and regulatory agencies, the cabinet-level policy statements have been cautiously void of direct references to the multinational firm. To interpret this restraint as an official indifference toward the hegemonic powers of foreign affiliates would be to completely ignore the deeds of the government in contrast to its lack of words. The officials' unofficial rhetoric can be taken as providing the script for the officially unarticulable concerns and countermeasures. Most countries have too much to lose to openly confront the U.S. with charges of economic domination. Moreover, the economic advisors are only now unlearning the narrow precepts of the neoclassical foreign-trade theory as the guide for international economic relations. However, as the pressures build up and a more rational explanation of the multinational firm behaviors become available to official policy-makers, a positive articulation of national problems and policy responses are certain to follow. This time is practically upon us.

Headquarters—Affiliate Conflicts

The pressures and restrictions imposed upon the affiliate by the host society either by overt or covert controls seldom can be disposed within the affiliate's own organization. Much of these are transmitted to the headquarter company.

1. *Indirect influences.* In certain cases, such as obtaining government licenses, access to resources, etc., the burden of the transmission is to gain the headquarter's consent for the deviations from company policies which the local

controls necessitate, or to elicit help in attempts to overcome the host-country restrictions. This may broaden the point of impact from the affiliate to both the affiliate and the headquarters, but it rarely affects the substance of the conflict. The exceptions occur only in completely decentralized multinational structures, where the headquarters is ill-prepared to actively intervene in any of the affiliate's activities.

2. *Direct opposition.* Certain other types of host-country controls, however, pit the affiliate directly against the headquarters company. These are usually the regulations or customs that somehow reinforce the affiliate's particularist ambitions in contrast to the total corporate interest. Self-determination as to pricing, managerial promotions, compensation plans, contract negotiations, industry affiliations, and similar problem areas fall into this category.

To plead local restrictions for the revision of headquarters policies or for the support of own initiatives is a common tactic of affiliate managers. When such pleas are strictly a tactical maneuver and when an articulation of existing realities is not always readily apparent, elements of both are often present.

3. *Home office skepticism.* Headquarters executives, therefore, have no simple way to handle such pleas. They are the men in the middle of a threeway conflict. As elaborated earlier, the headquarters management as a body is charged with potent ethnocentric inertia which the international executive corps must constantly combat. The home government's demands for extraterritorial application of its national policies imposes the requirement to reject any notion of complete affiliate autonomy and encourages centralization of headquarters policies conceived in the context of home-country environment. This means disregarding host-country conditions and particularities from which derive the affiliate's particularistic problems as well as possibilities.

4. *Pivotal leverage.* As the third vector of this triangular field of force, the affiliate becomes in essence the pivotal entity. Only through it can either the headquarters company or the host government concretely test their conflicting policy expressions. From its pivotal position the affiliate management derives power it would not otherwise have: it can either facilitate or complicate matters by its chosen behavior, and thus greatly influence the final performance. If the affiliate's top people are temporary expatriate transferees from the headquarters company its self-assertion may be minimal. But if its top management is composed of local nationals with long tenure, the politics of the situation assumes greater force: the affiliate is not likely to be above playing both ends against the middle to enlarge its own discretionary powers.

5. *Plurality of host environments.* The headquarters must, of course, guard against purely autogenic expansionism of the affiliate. The bigger the number of countries and affiliates in the firm the higher become the possibilities of tensions between headquarters and the affiliate. Part of the reason for this is simply statistical. Greater plurality of national environments creates greater diversity of intercountry differences, which reduces the number of companywide com-

munalities and requires more delegation in one form or another to the affiliates in the particular situations.

6. *Divided corporate loyalties.* Each national entity in the multinational corporation has different citizenship and owes, at least officially, its first allegiance to its respective country of domicile. But to serve the corporate interest, each must also accommodate the aspirations of the other host countries, and particularly the home country of the headquarters company. Whenever serving the interest of one host country goes against the interest of the other, the corporate family is subject to intracompany international stress. Complete loyalties of all affiliates to their host countries become impossible. At times of international tension among the host countries the intracompany stresses due to divided loyalties increase accordingly. Since the headquarters company must adjudicate how the ultimate "disloyalties" should be distributed among the affiliates concerned, it tends to become in the eyes of the affiliate the adversary to their particularist point of view. It is in the context of this relationship that the loyalty conflict between the headquarters and the affiliates often occurs.

7. *Divided managerial loyalties.* On the personal level the divergent loyalties of affiliate managers and headquarters executives may further aggravate the problem. If the affiliate manager is a local national, he is emotionally committed to the host society, and may find it psychologically difficult and morally degrading to pursue policies which he perceives as nonsupportive of the legitimate expectations of the host society. Thus the indigenous manager may find his personal loyalties at variance not only with the loyalties of headquarters executives but at times also with the best interest of the affiliate in which he exercises managerial authority. The expatriate manager of the affiliate is in no better position. Being himself a citizen of another country, yet responsible for the conduct of a corporate citizen of the host country, he has a particular dilemma whenever the two citizenships happen to demand different behavior.

8. *Limitations of image promotion.* To relieve such intracompany international tensions the headquarters companies tend, over time, to strive toward an apolitical stance. Company magazine editorials of multinational firms commonly argue how irrational it is for a headquarters company to profess loyalty to any single nation while being part of a multinational hierarchy of companies around the globe. This claim of complete political detachment is hardly realizable. As we have pointed out earlier, certain loyalties are simply not negotiable, and if not voluntarily acquiesced, the state will use its powers to compel compliance. Furthermore, many of the prophets of the denational or loyalty-neutral concept of corporation have shifted with apparent ease from their executive suites to cabinet positions and become the guardians of the national prerogatives over its corporate subjects. In the U.S., for example, the federal government has always drawn its heaviest contingent of officialdom from among executives of big business. This has confused but by no means eliminated the loyalty conflict between the multinational firm and the federal government.

On the affiliate level overt political indifference may be precluded by its relative economic importance or simply by high public sensitivity concerning foreign enterprises. Instead of neutrality, the typical affiliate strategy calls for a low silhouette: remain in the background and move with the main stream. This, of course, provides no real solution to the loyalty conflict.

Sociocultural Contrasts

Running mainly along the political frontiers and often accelerated or complicated by linguistic boundaries, the indigenous cultural systems of each host society, including that of the headquarters, cut across all levels of human relations in the multinational firm. Person-to-person relationships, interactions among technical, professional, and managerial groups, all are subject to the cross-cultural tensions and pressures where transboundary contacts are involved. They run in both directions. The native personnel of the affiliate asserts its cultural tendencies, generating resistance to headquarters ethnocentricities as well as counterpressures to supplant their own values to those of the multinational firm. From the headquarters issue technocratic centralism and other culture-blind practices, which perpetuate the conflict.

For strict technical analysis the conflicts that the sociocultural contrasts create for the headquarters pose different problems to management than those created for the affiliate. However, since their ultimate resolution can be achieved only by bridging both sides of the problem, we shall take the short cut of enlisting them under one heading. The reader is referred to Chapter 5 for the general perspective of cross-cultural forces in multinational organization. Here we will limit the presentation to highlighting the main conflict areas.

1. Headquarters pressures for sociocultural continuity—often mistaken for morality and rightfulness—in affiliate operations and behavior. Through its superior power the headquarters organization can impose its home-country norms upon the affiliates, whether accepted or resented.

2. Pressures from host-country nationals to mold corporate behavior to indigenous patterns and norms, especially the value and status crises of affiliate managers who become alienated from the native society but are unable to join the headquarters country society. The results are either anomie in various degrees or the tendency of affiliate managers to "localize" headquarters methods, priorities, and practices to suit their own sociocultural aspirations.

3. Differences in problem-solving and decision-making styles.

4. Deviations in negotiating practices and in settlement of disputes.

5. Host society's countermeasures, especially covert punitive actions against culturally deviant behaviors. These actions may be directed against the affiliate as a corporate citizen, against indigenous managers as sociocultural perverts, or against expatriate executives as foreign agents.

6. Inadequacy of linguistic facility on either side to communicate without misunderstandings and misinterpretations in qualitative ideas and social nuances.

The concept of cosmopolitan corporate culture (see Chapter 5) appears to offer the only viable proposition for an ultimate reconciliation of these conflicts.

International Politics

Host-country foreign policy is a major source of external influence upon the transboundary activities of the multinational firm. In some countries, such as Spain, this influence may be rather direct and restrictive; in others, such as Switzerland, it is indirect and subtle; but it is always there.

In the contemporary world foreign policy is rarely made by unilateral action of any one country. Rather, it results from a process of multilateral international interaction in which the outside world participates in a rough correspondence to each country's importance to the nation promulgating the policy. That is to say, the substance of foreign policy in our times must be viewed as a synthesis of multilateral inputs, adaptations, and adjustments that evolve with changes in international relations, and not as a unilateral expression of any country.

While many other forces figure in the international policy process, military-industrial power constitutes its central axis. The immense concentrations of the military-industrial power in two supernations has dwarfed the capacity of most other countries to assert their own influence on world relations in the recent past. The struggle for international supremacy between Moscow and Washington created a bipolar world in which the mutually antagonistic drives of the two supernations could either completely nullify or vastly magnify the international initiatives of smaller countries. Appearances of sovereignty aside, the contemporary world is an organization not of equals but of unequals.

Making of foreign policy, therefore, in typical host countries requires that great importance be attached to the reactions and possible countermoves of the supernations as well as other countries affected. From the national interest standpoint the basic rationale of a country's foreign policy is to attain what is possible under the given realities of international forces. Since the most insistent realities in the recent past have been the bipolar political tensions between the U.S. and the U.S.S.R., each other country has, in various degrees, endeavored to shape its own foreign policy so as to optimize the effect of this polarization. The sudden rise of many self-proclaimed neutral nations whose "neutrality" has fluctuated with not only the politics of foreign aid but also with any new turn in strategies of Washington or Moscow underscores the force of the bipolar tensions. The developed countries have shown no greater resistance to such opportunism than the economically underdeveloped countries. The sterile theatrics of Mr. Palme marching in an anti-American street demonstration in Stockholm instead of conceiving concrete policies which he, as Swedish Prime

Minister, had full powers to put in effect is a case in point. The fact of the matter is that appearances and substances of foreign policy have in all host countries drifted farther and farther apart. At the same time the external political currents have tended to increase in dominance and implicate individual country foreign policies in all parts of the globe.

The main currents of contemporary international politics that have greatly affected multinational business expansion might be grouped as follows.

1. *Moscow-Washington polarity.* As illustrated in a number of legal rules concerning foreign trade and investments that were discussed earlier this world political polarity has had numerous business relevant manifestations.

2. *Conflicting attitudes toward China.* For the U.S. business, China was a nonentity until the 1971 preliminary relaxation of the twenty-year embargo. At this writing the rapprochement between Peking and Washington is only a probability, about which any prognostications remain highly speculative. Should it materialize, its effect on world business would be enormous. The purely economic potentialities for trade and industrial cooperation seem very impressive. But the modes and conditions for utilizing the potential remain mysteries. That neither the typical ownership nor the control pattern of multinational firms will be acceptable to the Chinese seems certain. Resolution of the conflicts in philosophy as well as administrative techniques is the arena where ultimate success or failure will be decided.

In the meantime the removal of the embargo will help to eliminate several conflict areas which in the past have plagued the affiliate operations of U.S. firms in many countries; namely, all the situations where the affiliate could legitimately do business with China under its host country's policies but was held in violation of headquarters country's policies. The emergence of China as an active trading partner of the U.S. is likely to cause a tidal change in international political currents. The present bipolar axes will be replaced by a tripolar or multipolar base structure, opening new avenues for international interaction.

3. *Arab-Israeli conflict.* In the Near East international business has for years been confronted with Arab-Israeli conflict, which has severely curtailed any normal operations, not to mention growth. This situation seems certain to remain completely antagonistic to multinational enterprise until the political problem has found a permanent solution.

4. *Neocolonial fears.* In the developing countries the political environment of multinational firms suffers from contamination by fears of exploitation, covert influences on government policies, and corrupt officials. Corporate insensitivity to these perceptions, even if unfounded, can hardly protect the firm against harassment by the political authorities. Conflicts arising from this situation are potentially lethal, as the expropriations of many affiliates have shown.

To survive in those countries, multinational business must learn to do what it so often has failed to do: namely, to identify its policies and programs with those of the host nation and to demolish its traditional image of a reactionary uninterested in the development and modernization of the country. Perhaps this image applies primarily to the older multinational firms in extractive industries. The relative newcomers in manufacturing, distribution, and science-based industries have experienced no such drastic and disastrous conflicts with the political authorities as have befallen their forerunners in extractive industries. It is not clear if this difference is attributable to the increasing scarcity of the natural resources on which the extractive industries so completely depend or to the legacy of the colonial era from which their corporate norms derive.

5. *Malbehaviors of other firms.* One of the worst political pollutants of the international business environment has been the unscrupulous malbehavior of a few enterprises. Among the most notorious was the webb of mutual funds in Europe engineered by an American of questionable repute. As a result of its machinations, restrictive national regulations were put in force in a number of countries aimed at preventing foreign firms from entering this and similar activity. Though less publicized, there have been a number of incidents of similar malbehavior in many other branches of business. Even when no concrete regulation has resulted from such malbehavior, it has invariably poisoned the atmosphere for ethical companies active in or wishing to enter the country.

6. *The emerging North-South axes.* Athwart the East-West field of political tension lies the North-South polarity, that is, the conflicting goals of the rich and the poor nations. Through the U.N. Trade and Development Conferences the backward countries have been building slowly but insistently a united front against the economic hegemony of the industrialized North—both capitalist and communist. A key point in their platform is redistribution of the gains from international trade and investments on a nonreciprocal basis.

Already the North has felt compelled to yield to some degree to this southern initiative. For example, tariff concessions and controls on direct investments clearly differentiate between developed and developing countries. However, in a longer perspective there seems no escaping from the conclusion that the pressure from the South has so far reached only its incipient phase. As it gains power and momentum, it will force both the East and the West to revise their policies as both are subjected to the same pressure. As an illustration: the U.S.S.R., which originally cosponsored the UN resolution calling for the creation of the Trade and Development Conference over the express opposition of the Western industrial countries, was compelled to switch sides soon after the first conference convened and the developing countries staked their unqualified claim against all industrial countries, capitalist and communist alike.

Multiple Jeopardy of the Multinational Firm

In the chapters on motivities we analyzed how the multinational firm can benefit from its diversified multitude of separate national environments. In this chapter it has been stressed that due to its presence in many countries, the multinational firm can, in pursuit of its corporate interest, circumvent or even contravene certain policies and regulations of individual host countries. But still our focus was on the extraordinary powers and behaviors of the multinational firm, and our vantage point that of an outsider to the firm.

If we now reverse the focus and view these problems from the point of view of the firm, a different proposition emerges. It can be capsuled in two phases:

1. As a static short-run profile the firm is confronted with several types of incongruous conditions and requirements including these.

a. differences in constitutional principles
b. different statutory laws
c. conflicting public policies
d. variations in regulatory principles and administrative practices
e. different sociocultural norms and patterns

Compliance with the requirements in one host country can mean a direct violation in another. This is an ever-present danger. The multinational firm can rarely act confident that it is not desecrating either the overt or covert code of corporate behavior in one or more of its host societies.

2. In a dynamic long-run context the firm's predicament worsens as the host societies assert their political power to compel the company to comply with whatever a particular country conceives as not supportive of its national best interest. This not only means new or stricter controls, but may also lead to such constrictive excesses as legislation prohibiting foreign involvement in an industry, sector, or region, and forced reorganization or even expropriation of the company's affiliates. Since such antifirm measures can originate simultaneously in any and all of its host countries, the multinational company is literally placed in multiple jeopardy. It can be punished by many "courts" and many times over as each host country enacts its own regulatory requirements and to mold the activities of the firm.

The full magnitude of the multiple jeopardy problem cannot yet be assessed. As pointed out before, the host governments have so far ventured their consternations in political oratory, and little purposeful effort has been made to produce actual regulatory systems to cope with the multinational firm. Indications are, however, that such preliminaries are about to be succeeded by concrete action. Several governments have commissioned task force studies and other investigations to inform legislative authorities on the ways and means of dealing with the situation. As long as each country goes its own way, the internation incongruities and regulatory contradictions are very likely to become even greater than now.

As a consequence the multiple jeopardy of the multinational firm will be greatly magnified. This pessimistic prognostication has a very high probability of becoming true. Things will become worse, perhaps much worse, for the multinational companies before permanent relief can be foreseen. Only if several countries act in concert, harmonizing and coordinating their regulatory systems, can there be any real hope for reduction of the multiple jeopardy risk. To date there is no indication that such international cooperation is in the offing.

15 Labor Conflict

The rise to dominance of the multinational firm has triggered a shift in the relative power positions of management and labor. In labor's view the shift represents a retrogression. The long-range strategy of the labor movement to countervail big business with big unions worked admirably in most industrial countries, notably in the United States, until about 1960. By effective organization and concentration of labor influences into large, well-disciplined unions, a sufficient counterweight to management power had been created to allow unions to bargain from a position of strength. An approximate balance of power had been achieved. While not an Eden of bliss in democratic context, it did put the organized worker in a privileged and even an elitist stratum relative to unorganized labor. From the historic perspective this was a triumph for the worker's welfare and a testimony to the movement's mission and leadership. The countervailing power of mangement and labor had become a reality in the United States by the midcentury and has henceforth been recognized as a condition of normalcy both in theory and national policy.

From partisan points of view it is possible to argue that the balance was never really achieved, or that it was overachieved, creating labor's hegemony. Both partisans can cite specific unions and industries where one or the other type of disparity exists. But these are exceptions. The partisans can also argue about the methods—accuracy of measurement—what the best indicators of relative power are, but they can hardly contest the fact that collective bargaining has not only worked, but worked to the near exclusion of alternative systems of resolving employer-employee conflicts in the industrial realm. Any shift in this balance of power in management's favor signals to labor leaders a retreat to the frontiers of weakness—a return to subservience and subordination that the movement can neither accept nor endure. To labor, therefore, the multinational firm is not a villain or culprit of the normal management sort, but an antagonist of an entirely new and mortally menacing variety. Against it, a total struggle seems to be American labor's resolute response.

The Causal Proposition

Multinationalization has created for management new motivities and flexibilities that have greatly enhanced its bargaining power vis-à-vis labor. Since the sourcing base of the multinational firm knows no national boundaries—it can draw anywhere in the world the capital, technology, raw materials, ideas, and manpower that it needs—management is not dependent on any one country's labor supply or labor union's policies, but can choose from among a number of potential hosts for any particular operation. In the short run, this new managerial disgression may be limited by the relative immobility of investment in given facilities—the sunk cost constraint—but in the long run nearly all operations become locationally tradable. More significantly, all new investment, whether for replacement or for expansion of plant capacity, is internationally footloose and will seek domicile wherever the comparative advantages happen to lie.

To labor unions this international mobility of the multinational firm portends an ominous doom. Though international in ideology, the unions have failed to acquire any international operational capabilities of their own. Their organization and policies have remained strictly national or subnational. There has never been an international labor union, nor any international collective bargaining, not to mention any international labor contract as such. The rather exceptional circumstances of American-Canadian union relations to one side, labor internationalism has been almost entirely a surface pigmentation, its action content being limited to convention oratory, expressions of solidarity, and the International Labor Organization (ILO), an United Nations agency concerned largely with comparative statistical data on wages and working conditions in different countries.

Behind its rhetorical façade of international brotherhood, the labor movement in the U.S. as well as other free countries has erected its organizational and operational structures for purely domestic capacity.[1] Whether the cause for this has been ideological self-deception or practical necessity—the dependence on legislative definition and governmental enforcement of union rights—cannot be argued here. However, the fact that the labor unions organized and built their powers as an integral part of the nation state's internal apparatus explains both their past successes and prospective problems.

Having focused its efforts on countervailing the powers of the domestic firm, labor scored impressively by achieving equivalence, if not dominance, at the bargaining table. But its narrow focus missed the broader scene. As the international expansion of business in the 1950s and 1960s started converting domestic companies into multinational firms at an accelerating rate, labor's domestic entrenchment provided no possibility to match the enlargement of managerial powers. Thus a disparity gap was opened. Given the continuation of the multinationalization of business, the disparity is certain to increase as long as labor unions remain uninational in scope and capacity. Labor's leadership rejects this new reality as a perversion of normal relationships. Its remedy is a massive economic legislation to restore and preserve union power.

Grand Strategy of American Labor

The prospect of being confronted with a potentially invincible management power has stirred the American labor unions into a concerted action to undo the multinational firm. This effort is exerted from a number of different perspectives, which encompass not only union interests, but also the national welfare and international relations. A simultaneous thrust from many intersecting and overlapping plains, the new labor strategy is to derive reinforcement from broad segments of the society and to yield a convergent thrust against the multinational enterprise. Congressional enactment of labor's program would thus be an ultimate certainty. This factor of identifying labor's interest with the national interest axiomatically isolates the multinational firm as antithetic to the public good. However, convincing substantiation, not to mention factual proof, for labor's claim remains to be provided. Some of its aspects may never be resolved, except in philosophic terms, but others will have to be objectively sorted out from a nonpartisan point of view before any final conclusions can be drawn. Thus, the confrontation between organized labor and the multinational firm is neither avoidable nor readily forgotten. It is only beginning, despite the massive energies already diverted to it. The conflict turns on a composite of complex issues for which no foreseeable resolution lies in store.

Domestic Issues

Spokesmen for American labor cite a long list of domestic and international difficulties which they attribute to the emergence of the multinational firm. These assertions can be systematically summarized in seven main charges:

1. *Export displacement.* The multinational firm (MNF) displaces U.S. exports with foreign-produced goods, thereby decreasing domestic employment and payrolls, causing the U.S. trade balance to deteriorate and depressing economic conditions at home.
2. *Technology drain.* The MNF exports American technology to exploit low-cost foreign labor, depriving the American worker from his rightful opportunity to share in the utilization and rewards of these transfers.
3. *Investment depressant.* The MNF's investments abroad deplete capital resources needed for domestic economic growth which undermines new job creation in the American economy. Together with technology transfers foreign direct investments represent an exportation of jobs: the displacement of American labor with foreign labor.
4. *Import substitution.* The MNF substitutes imports from its affiliates in

low-wage countries for American-made goods. These imports not only cause unemployment and idle plant capacity at home but, being sold at U.S. prices, yield excessive profits, at the expense of labor in both countries involved.

5. *Price manipulation.* The MNF manipulates transfer prices to improve the international allocation of its assets. This tends to undermine domestic stability and to thwart national economic policies.

6. *Tax evasion.* The MNF, through a closed-circuit intracompany trading system, can shift its activities, resources, and earnings across national frontiers among its affiliates to minimize its total tax liability and to escape its lawful contribution to public revenue. As a high-tax and high-price country, the United States is singularly vulnerable to this loss.

7. *Payments disbalancing.* The MNF's independence from and frequent circumvention of the normal channels for international trade and finance has inflicted the United States with a chronic balance-of-payments deficit which, besides its stagnating effect on domestic conditions, has debased the dollar as the key currency and materially contributed to the disintegration of the international monetary system.

This in conspectus is American labor's case against the multinational firm, or so the labor leaders have put it forth. For good measure, the threat to host-country sovereignty, brain drain, and clandestine political machinations are used as rhetoric wrappings for the seven-prong charge. But this is strictly for oratorical effects. As we shall see later, a substantive analyses of the broader international issues may counterpoise more often than corroborate the labor's contentions. Furthermore, the sought-for remedy being anti-MNF legislation, which by juridic necessity is limited to the U.S. national jurisdiction, labor can expect no practical payoff from pursuing the host-country criticisms of multinational business.

As to the remedy itself, the trade union leadership seeks far-reaching new legislation to regulate and harshly suppress multinational business operations. It envisages the creation of a federal foreign-trade and investments commission to license and supervise transnational capital transactions; to restrict outward transfers of technology by subjecting patentholders to governmental licensing and by prohibiting any foreign production of the patented product; and to extend U.S. tax liability to all foreign affiliates of American firms, by eliminating the deferred tax status of foreign earnings as well as the foreign tax credit.

Thus, labor's objectives translate into an ultraprotectionist legislative offensive that could cut wide and deep. To management these legislative objectives of labor signify not only the demise of multinational business operations, but also the beginning of governmental expropriation of the managerial freedom to independently act in reference to investments, deployment of technology, and corporate involvements.

If enacted this bill would politize international investment decisions of the private sector; reduce remittances of foreign earnings to the U.S.; delay foreign investment decisions to a point where they would no longer be timely; reduce the demand for supplier parts; and, in general, increase rather than reduce unemployment. Equally, if not more important, is the fact that the establishment of an investment review commission for foreign direct investments could lead to the establishment of a commission to review and pass judgment on domestic private investments. In effect, this would further the process of socializing U.S. business and industry.[2]

This quotation capsulizes the management's counterargument. The haste to read into the unions' legislative demands an imminent socialization of domestic investments serves to underscore the apprehension and alarm with which the strictly domestic businesses, the uninational firms, have assessed their own competitive horizons against the superiorities of the multinational firm. Though constantly inciting many to start their own international ventures, the multinational firm remains a potential threat to the firms that have not yet reached the threshold of international expansion. For self-preservation they must suspect, if not counterpose, the multinationalization movement. Hence, the house of management is divided against itself along the uninational-multinational line. How serious this division is is not clear. Many areas of ignorance concerning the nature and motivities of multinational firms have obscured and obstructed the delineation of the two spheres of corporate interest. Despite a widespread research attack on this ignorance many aspects of the multinational firm continue to defy analytically exhaustive explanations.

The areas of ignorance leave much room for conjecture and speculation. In which side's favor will weigh the realities concealed behind the current ignorance is the question. For labor even the mere possibility of being able to split the employers' unity holds promises of glory. If the uninational business sector sided with the unions either overtly or covertly the multinational sector would stand isolated and exposed, its resistance to political control greatly reduced. Labor's strong appeals for patriotism are to evoke the necessity of all domestic sectors; business, labor, and government, to domesticate the multinational firm.

For the multinational sector the possibility of any division of the managerial front forebodes incalculable risks. But there is very little short of competitive self-restraint against the domestic sector that it can do to assure an unified stand—thence the ideological behest in defense of private enterprise prerogatives rather than practical, hardheaded "business approach."

This is not the sector's only difficulty. Whether the multinational companies collectively can be labeled a sector at all, in any other than purely statistical sense, is debatable. At least no common stance, no explicit articulation of either the sector's own stand or its response to labor's offensive have yet appeared.

The international corporate stance today is too often self-contradictory: the company professes to support international economic freedom, actively lobbying for the national treatment principle in host countries, but in the U.S. legislative halls it pleads for protectionist restrictions, citing exceptional hardship as justification. The hardship to be avoided is foreign competition in the U.S. market. Hence, the strategy is to have it both ways: unhindered access to foreign markets and exclusion of import competition from the domestic market for monopolistic privileges. The import restrictions would hamper but little the MFN's own international operations; their full effect will fall on the traditional foreign traders, thus further enhancing the MFN's relative advantage over the uninational firm. This duality in international strategy undermines the social image of the multinational firm as such and makes unlikely any consistent and analytically defensible sectoral strategy analogous to that of organized labor.

The Overall Perspective

To put the issue in its proper perspective we must retreat from the partisan frontier to a neutral ground. What can we objectively say about labor's charges against the multinational firm? Clearly, there are a number of questions concerning the factual record; much of the relevant data is not yet available and much of the rest is incomplete. There are also many genuine conflicts of interest between the host societies and the multinational firm, as we diagnosed in Chapter 14. Add to this a very considerable, though yet undefined, area of ignorance of the new international linkages and motivities that the multinational firm has brought into play, and there remains no room for doubt that many aspects of the confrontation between American labor and the multinational firm require a vast amount of further research conceptual articulation, and social interpretation before any analytically complete resolution of the conflict becomes possible.

However, recognizing the complexities of the problem and the limitations of what we know is not to negate the existence of promising approaches toward a constructive solution. Indeed, one must remain within the limits of what is known and objectively definable. The fact that our understanding of the multinational firm is considerably less than complete does not put this subject into any different category from other economic issues; they all involve some degree of indefiniteness and ignorance.

The antimultinational stand of labor rests on two principles of doubtful validity: first, the assumption that the conflict represents a zero-sum proposition in which the gains of one party necessarily require an off-setting loss to the other. This static notion underlies the labor arguments both on the micro (union vs. firm) and macro (American vs. other countries) levels. Productive gains resulting from the multinationalization of a firm are thus not only denied, which as we have seen in Chapters 3 and 5 is in itself an inadmissable omission, but they are portrayed as indicators of loss to the unions and the nation. By such perverse logic any growth of a multinational firm that is not parallel by similar growth of labor and the U.S. national economy represents an oblique diversion from the latters' wealth. From this distorted premise black-and-white implications follow mechanically.

Labor's second argument is narrowly nationalistic, if not xenophobic. It embraces protectionism as the path to American economic hegemony and advocates international economic discrimination not only in wages but in all other costs and prices. How under such an ultranationalistic policy American industry could attain competitiveness in the world market is left obscure. Why other nations would accept without retaliation American protectionist policies also remains unexplained. All empirical evidence to date argues against any submissive cooperation of other countries. The trend in the contemporary world is unmistakably away from the old spheres of influence concept and toward an international democracy based on equality and mutuality in a multilateral context. Discriminatory practices, therefore, are certain to incite resentment and retaliatory measures by other countries.

The Factual Record

Taken individually, indictments by labor against the multinational firm can be objectively judged only in terms of available facts. Each indictment as summarized above carries an important enough charge to demand a point-by-point analysis. In this discussion we shall follow the same order as we did on p. 000.

Export Displacement

Multinationalization, as a rule, causes a company's exports volume to increase rather than to decline (see Chapters 2 and 3). The increase is attributable to the comparative advantages that a firm derives from becoming structurally integrated with its different host economies when it acquires a multinational structure. This gives it a better information base and a more realistic perception of the needs and opportunities, as well as the risks and uncertainties, in foreign markets.

New products can more readily be conceived, market tested, and introduced to meet the consumption requirements of specific countries, and American lines modified and adapted for the same end.

The organizational capacity and sourcing flexibility (including moving with rapidly changing local conditions) of the multinational firm adds a special dimension to its marketing prowess. Factual proof of this can be found not only in numerous case histories but also in the aggregate export data assembled by the U.S. Department of Commerce. These data show that some 45 percent of aggregate exports of parent companies have consisted of finished goods to be marketed by their foreign affiliates. Thus, the very substantial increase of component parts, subassemblies, and other semimanufacturers that has resulted from the establishment of manufacturing affiliates abroad has been paralleled by continued growth of finished exports of the parent companies. For many firms the establishment of foreign-based affiliates has proven a real stimulus to their traditional exports, due either to the complementary effect of the added local product varieties or simply to a more effective marketing than they were able to achieve without their local affiliates.

Labor's assertion that the reports of semimanufacturers could be assembled in this country and exported as finished goods is almost totally lacking in factual merit. Neither the implication that nothing more than assembly of U.S.-made parts is done by foreign manufacturing affiliates nor the assumption that the foreign societies are exact replicas of the U.S. permits any serious contemplation of this assertion.

Technology Drain

This is probably the most elusive charge to either support or refute. Technology has no concrete dimensions, and therefore is immeasurable as an economic aggregate. Moreover, technology is perishable; it cannot be packed and stored for future use without a serious risk of obsolescence.

Lacking any comprehensive statistic, figures for research and development (R&D) expenditures and the royalties and fees subaccount in the balance of payments are often used as indicators for the technology sector. These can be dangerously misleading. A dollar spent on R&D need not result in the same output of new technology in country A as it does in countries B, C, or X. Factual indications reflect wide international variations in research productivity. Furthermore, the institutional structure, orientation, and type of research activities seem to have a significant bearing upon the cost-output relationship of new technology.

The myth of an increasing technology gap between the U.S. and other nations sprung from a simplistic extrapolation of the R&D statistics of the 1960s. The setbacks of American products in world competition in the early 1970s demolished the myth and made room for the current cry of an overhanging technology debt for this country. However, this reverse gap notion is no less psychology-based than its predecessor. Neither has yet been analytically demonstrated.

If there had been a massive outflow of technology from the U.S. parent companies to their foreign affiliates, most of it would be reflected in the balance of payments. For the period of 1964 to 1969 the royalty and fee payments to U.S. parents from their foreign affiliates totaled only $2.5 billion, while payments for managerial services reached nearly $4 billion. Since the managerial services consisted primarily of organizational, marketing, personnel, and especially intracompany international integration activities, they represent increased exports of invisibles rather than a loss of technology as such. At best only a small portion of this know-how could have found domestic application.

Foreign critics contend that these acquisitions have provided the U.S. parent with a bonanza by transferring to it the technological resources which the acquired foreign firm had derived primarily from the publicly funded university research of the host countries.

The foreign critics' argument is not wholly without merit. In continental Europe, for example, the principal research apparatus of the society has been the university system. Indifferent to immediate applicability of findings, the European university researchers have focused on fundamental knowledge. Their findings and inventions have often provided the new knowledge from which commercial applications can be derived with relatively small developmental cost. This is to say, the European companies have been able to start their product and engineering developments on a higher technological threshold than typical U.S. firms.

If this bonanza theory should be proven valid, it would put the U.S. multinational firms into the net import column for technology and expose the labor charge of technology drain as totally unsupported. But even if the bonanza theory were totally rejected, there is no evidence that the multinational companies have caused a drain on U.S. technology which has decreased domestic employment.

Contrary to labor's contention, direct foreign investments of the multinational firms draw but a fractional share of their capital input from this country. Normally, the exported capital serves only as seed money in the developmental stages of the multinational structure. (See Chapters 4 and 5 for explanation of financial motivities.) Much of the subsequent accumulation abroad results from either retained earnings—which usually are wholly foreign-sourced—from fundraising in the foreign financial markets.[2] The outstanding foreign debt of 339 U.S. companies approximated $12 billion in 1971.

The fundamental reason for private business investments is anticipated return. Capital gravitates to the localities where the availability and cost of other factors meets the investor's return expectations. Unless a project promises to yield a return commensurate to the risks involved it will not be funded. This applies equally to domestic and foreign investments. If a company is artificially restrained by governmental controls from developing a profitable project abroad and finds that acceptable investment opportunities do not exist at home, its excess cash will be placed in short-term securities and, more important, no additional funds will be raised. Regulatory restriction of foreign direct investment, therefore, will not necessarily result in an equivalent increase in domestic investment. It would, however, decrease world investment and retard the growth of the companies affected. Furthermore, in many cases, U.S. companies have invested abroad to retain their markets. Here the choice has not been between domestic and foreign opportunity, but between making the direct investment or losing the foreign sales. Unless these protective investments were made, a negative impact on U.S. labor market would have been axiomatic.

It is relevant to add also that the employment trends have been upward in the U.S. industries which have made the largest direct investments. Their growth at home compares very favorably with that of the domestic sectors.

Import Substitutes

Multinationalization has not resulted in any disproportionate increase of imports from foreign affiliates. Excluding Canada (because of special relationships) affiliate-sourced imports in recent years have approximated 10 percent or less of U.S. total. Compared with the very substantial exports to the affiliates which we discussed earlier, these imports appear insignificant indeed, the net effect of the intra-company international trade on the U.S. trade balance being clearly positive.

Data are not available to get a reading of parent-affiliate trade for foreign multinational companies. Their increasing investments in the U.S. have been a growth component in this country's labor market and its economy as a whole.

Sectoral studies point to the fact that U.S. direct investments abroad originate primarily from industries with low imports. Conversely, the industry groups with the smallest foreign holdings tend to belong to the high import category (shoes, textiles, liquors, etc.) These statistics seem to imply that the domestically oriented industries tend to provide actually a greater pull for imports than do the international enterprises. The underlying cause for this tendency is relative inefficiency of the strictly domestic industries, which makes imports from foreign producers profitable.

Payments Disbalancing

The chronic deficit in the U.S. balance of payments has made this a politically hypersensitive issue. No convincing explanation of the reasons for the deficit has yet emerged. The complexly multivariate relationships, compounded by doctrinaire assumptions of the nature of international economic relations, are responsible for the lack of an adequate explanation of the problem. Thus the field has been left open for speculative hypotheses and partisan assertions.

Direct foreign investment has been construed by protectionists, including union labor, as a major cause of the U.S. deficits. Objective evidence conflicts with this charge.

To start with, international investments flow both in and out. The inward investments of foreign firms neutralize for the balance-of-payments purposes an equivalent amount of outward investments by U.S. companies. Thus, in any short-run interval, the net balance-of-payments effect of new international investments is the difference between the two opposing flows. Since the outflows has been greater (the net balance increased from $1674 million in 1960 to $4067 million in 1970), the protectionist argument is valid in the short term.

However, direct investments are inherently *long-term* undertakings. Their pay-back period extends over the multiyear life at the projects, which may span decades. Therefore, the only economically meaningful way to measure the balance-of-payments effect of a direct investment is to juxtapose the original outward investment with the cumulative total of dividends and other in-transfers to which the investment gives rise during the entire life of the project.

Between 1960 and 1970 the remittances of foreign affiliates, as shown in the U.S. direct-investment account, generated a total capital inflow of over $50 billion and a *net cumulative credit* to the balance of payments between $11 and $12 billion. In the last few years the foreign exchange earnings produced by direct investments have constituted the biggest positive element for the U.S. balance of payment.

This is to say that in aggregate the remittances by foreign affiliates have made a basic positive contribution to the American balance of payments not only in long run but also in the short run on a continuing basis. To suppress direct foreign investments for the purpose of reducing payments deficits is, therefore, self-evidently counterproductive.

If governmental regulation suppressed further multinationalization of American firms while encouraging inward investments from abroad for short-term balance-of-payments relief, the future balance-of-payments position of the U.S. would suffer as a result. As the American holdings abroad leveled off while foreign holdings in the U.S. increased, the result would be an increased outflow (remittances to foreign headquarters firms) against a stationary or declining inflow to the U.S. headquarters firms. Clearly an uninviting proposition.

It does not seem that American labor's current predicament would be remedied by a governmentally decreed divestiture by multinational firms of their affiliates abroad. The sources of the problem lie elsewhere.

In its role as a factor of production, labor can adopt either of two courses. It can be essentially dynamic, supporting rapid change with the objective of increasing national output and hence welfare—accepting, as a price, the occupational and personal dislocations which must inevitably accompany rapid change. Or it can adopt an essentially static attitude giving up income but avoiding many of the costs of dislocation. Organized labor now seems to have chosen the second approach. . . . The most important shift in the U.S. political constellation on trade policy is organized labor's move to the protectionist camp. . . .
As the most visible embodiment of rapid change, the multinational corpo-

ration has become a special target of organized labor . . . another underlying cause of labor's change of position in its decreasingly representative nature as the overall U.S. labor force grows primarily in the services rather than goods-producing sector. [Only 25 percent of U.S. labor is unionized.] Most goods producers are unionized and most service producers are not. . . . Moreover, labor has not moved quickly enough in organizing the fast-growing high-technology industries as those industries have developed their share of the U.S. economy. This factor is also crucial for trade, policy, since it is the high-technology industries which can compete effectively in the world market.[3]

Ideological Dilemma

International solidarity has long been an ideal of labor movement. Confronted with the same problems and striving for the same goals provided the parallels for workers' organizations in all countries. Devoted to collective action as counterforce to exploitation, labor unions from the start aspired for cooperation and communication with their brothers, regardless of country. This community in goals and conditions was translated into a flaming internationalism when Karl Marx at the ripe moment coined his classic slogan: *"Proletarier aller Länder vereinigt euch"* (proletarians of all countries unite). Henceforth the movement's ideology has embraced internationalism as a cardinal virtue, which its leaders of all political persuasions have universally shared.

The new ultranationalism of American unions represents a sharp break with this tradition. And more than philosophy is at stake. Labor unions in countries hosting the affiliates of U.S. multinational companies find the American unions' present protectionist offensive aimed more against them than the companies. This confrontation between the American and the host-country unions remains an unpredictably dangerous source of potential conflict on the multinational business scene. How the U.S. society disposes of the current offensive by American labor against the multinational firm will have a direct bearing on the size and nature that this negative force may play in future multinational business relations.

Notes

Notes

Preface

1. Jack N. Behrman, "The Multinational Enterprise: Its Initiatives and Governmental Reactions," *The Journal of International Law and Economics*, Vol. 6, No. 2 (January 1972), p. 215.

2. *The Wall Street Journal* (April 18, 1973), p. 20. © 1973 Dow Jones & Company, Inc. All Rights Reserved.

3. "The New Competition from Foreign-Based Multinationals," Special Report, *Business Week* (July 7, 1973), p. 56.

4. Jack N. Behrman, op.cit., p. 221.

5. National Association of Manufacturers, *U.S. Stake in World Trade and Investment*, New York: 1973, p. 1.

Chapter 1
The Multinational Firm

1. David H. Blake, Preface, *The Annuals of the American Academy of Political and Social Science* (September 1972), p. ix.

2. A.H. Clausen, "The Internationalized Corporation: An Executive's View," *The Annual of the American Academy of Political and Social Science*, September, 1972, pp. 12-21.

3. U.S. Department of Commerce, Office of International Investments, *The Multinational Corporation, Studies in U.S. Foreign Investment*. Washington: U.S. Government Printing Office, 1972, p. 7.

4. Yair Aharoni, "On the Definition of a Multinational Firm," *Quarterly Review of Economics and Business*, Vol. II (Autumn 1971).

5. Neil H. Jacoby, "The Multinational Corporation," *The Center Magazine*, Vol. III. No. 1 (May 1970).

6. Endel J. Kolde, *International Business Enterprise*, Rev. Ed., Englewood Cliffs, N.J.: 1973, p. 143.

Chapter 3
Operation Motivities of the Multinational Firm

1. See Endel J. Kolde, *International Business Enterprise*, Second Ed., Englewood Cliffs: Prentice-Hall, 1973, pp. 394-405.

2. Ibid., pp. 161-68.

3. "An Auto Industry Starts Coming Apart," Special Report, *Business Week* (February 21, 1970), p. 51.

4. Paul A. Samuelson, "International Trade and Equalization of Factor Prices," *Economic Journal* (June 1948).

5. Robert E. Baldwin, "The International Firm and Efficient Economic Allocation, International Trade in Inputs and Outputs," *The American Economic Review* (May 1970), p. 430.

6. John H. Dunning, "Technology, United States Investment, and European Economic Growth," *The International Corporation*, a symposium edited by Charles P. Kindleberger, Cambridge: M.I.T. Press, 1970.

7. Baldwin, op.cit., p. 430.

8. Ibid., p. 431.

9. Ibid., p. 433.

10. Ibid., p. 434.

11. Endel J. Kolde, op. cit., pp. 152-53.

12. Ibid.

13. Ibid., p. 154.

14. Louis T. Wells, Jr. (ed.), *The Product Life Cycle and International Trade*. Boston: Harvard University Press, 1972, pp. 11-15.

15. Statement by E.M. Windt, President Eaton Yale and Tone, quoted from *Marketing Insights* (February 9, 1970), p. 1.

Chapter 4
Financial Motivities: Concepts and Causes

1. Charles P. Kindelberger, *International Economics*. Homewood, Ill.: Richard D. Irwin, 1968, p. 390.

2. Eli Shapiro and Francis J. Aeartlov, "The Supply of Funds for U.S. Direct Foreign Investments," *The International Corporations*, Charles P. Kindelberger, ed., Cambridge,: MIT Press, 1970, p. 123.

3. H.G. Grubel "Internationally Diversified Portfolios" *American Economic Review*, Vol. LVIII, No. 5, Part I (December 1968).

4. Harry Levy and Marshal Sarnat, "International Diversification of Investment Portfolios," *American Economic Review* (September 1970), pp. 668-75.

5. David K. Eitman and Arthur I. Stonehill, *Multinational Business Finance*, Reading, Mass.: Addison-Wesley Publishing Company, 1973, p. 192.

6. Judd Polk, Irene W. Meister, and Lawrence A. Veit, *U.S. Production Abroad and the Balance of Payments: A Survey of Corporate Investment Experience*, The Conference Board: Special Study, 1966.

7. U.S. Department of Commerce, *The Multinational Corporation* Washington D.C.: U.S. Government Finding Office, 1972. This report in fact comprises three studies: *Policy Aspects of Foreign Investment by U.S. Multinational Corporations; U.S. Multinational Enterprises and the U.S. Economy;* and *Trends in Direct Investment Abroad by U.W. Multinational Corporations, 1960 to 1970*.

8. Ibid.

Chapter 5
Financial Motivities: Managerial Environment

1. Jack N. Behrman, *National Interest and the Multinational Enterprise*, Englewood Cliffs: Prentice-Hall, 1970, p. 46.

2. Gunter Dufey, "The Eurobond Market: Its Significance For International Financial Managements," *Journal of International Business Studies* (Summer 1970).

3. Charles E. Saltzman, "Current Trends in the International Securities Market," The Conference Board, *Record*, Vol 7 (May 1970).

4. H. Lee Silberman, "The Euro-Commercial Paper Capter," *Finance* (October 1970), pp. 23-26.

5. Stoubaugh, *Money in the Multinational Enterprise*, New York: Basic Books, 1973, pp. 49-74.

6. Behrman, op. cit.

7. Endel J. Kolde, *International Business Enterprise*, Englewood Cliffs, New Jersey: Prentice-Hall, 1973, pp. 166-167.

Chapter 6
Culture Context of Multinational Organizations

1. Konrad Lorenz, *On Aggression*, Toronto, New York, London: Bantam Books, 1970, p. 240. Originally published by Harcourt Brace Jovanovich.

2. Margaret Mead, "Anthropolitical Data on the Problem of Instinct," *Personality in Nature, Society and Culture* (Clyde Kluckhohn and Henry Murray, ed.), New York: Alfred A. Knopf, 1953, p. 115.

3. Geoffrey Gorer, "The Concept of National Characters," (Clyde Kluckhohn and Henry Murray, ed.), op.cit., p. 251.

4. Lorenz, op.cit., pp. 79-80.

5. *See Harvard University Program on Technology and Society*, Project descriptions, Annual Reports, 1966 through 1970.

6. Lewis C. Gawthrop, "The Environment, Bureaucracy, and Social Change," *Environmental Settings in Organizational Functioning* (ed. by Negande), Kent, Ohio: Comparative Administrative Research Institute, Kent State University, 1970, p. 21.

7. F. Champion Ward, "America the Resilient," *The Journal of Higher Education*, Vol. XL, No. 6 (June 1969), p. 425.

Chapter 7
Structural Members and Factors of
Multinational Organization

1. Warren G. Bennis, "The Coming Death of Bureaucracy," *Size Up*, Bulletin of the International Imede Association, No. 29 (December 1969), p. 11.

Chapter 10
International Managerial Communication

1. Anthony E. Rupert, "Communicating in a Growing International Organization," *Proceedings of the 14th International Congress for Scientific Management*, p. 231.

Chapter 11
Development of Multinational Executives

1. Richard D. Robinson, *International Management*, New York: Holt, Rinehart & Winston, 1967, pp. 73-74. The reader is referred to Robinson's critical comments on these points.

Chapter 12
Evaluation and Compensation of
Multinational Managers

1. *The Wall Street Journal* (March 12, 1973) p. 6. © 1973 Dow Jones & Company, Inc. All Rights Reserved.
2. Ibid., January 8, 1973, pp. 2, 11. © 1973 Dow Jones & Company, Inc. All Rights Reserved.

Chapter 14
Society and the Multinational Firm:
Conflict Analysis

1. Foreign Ownership and the Structure of Canadian Industry, Ottawa: Privy Council Office, 1968; Jack N. Behrman, *National Interest and the Multinational Enterprise* Englewood Cliffs: Prentice-Hall, 1970.
2. Raimer Hellmann, *The Challenge to U.S. Dominance of the International Corporation*, Cambridge: Dunellen, 1970, p. 226.

Chapter 15
Labor Conflict

1. David H. Blake, "Trade Unions and the Challenge of the Multinational Corporation," *The Annals of the American Academy of Political and Social Sciences* (September 1972), pp. 36-38.

2. National Association of Manufacturers, *U.S. Stake in World Trade and Investment: The Rule of the Multinational Corporation* (mimeographed), p. iv.

3. C. Fred Bergsten, "Crises in U.S. Trade Policy," *Foreign Affairs* (July 1971), pp. 621-23. Copyright 1971 by Council on Foreign Relations, Inc.

Bibliography

Bibliography

Abegglen, James C. *The Japanese Factory*, Glencoe, Ill.: The Free Press, 1958.

Abegglen, James C. "Subordination and Autonomy Attitudes of Japanese Workers," *The American Journal of Sociology*, Vol. 63, No. 2 (September 1957), pp. 181-89.

Aharoni, Yair. *The Foreign Investment Decision Process*, Cambridge: Harvard University Press, 1966.

"American Business Abroad, The New Industrial Revolution," Special Issue of *Saturday Review* (November 22, 1969).

American Labor's Role in Less Developed Countries, Ithaca: New York State School of Industrial and Labor Relations, Cornell University, 1959.

American Management Association (ed.), *International Management Information Systems: Approaches to Design and Implementation*, New York: 1967.

Annals of the American Academy of Political and Social Sciences: The Multinational Corporation (September 1972).

Anderson, David S. "Communications Problems of Financial Reporting," *The Journal of Accountancy*, Vol. 115, No. 4 (April 1963), pp. 59-64.

Ansoff, H.I. *Corporate Strategy*, New York: McGraw-Hill, 1965.

Argawala, A.N. "Socialist Economy with Private Backbone," *Columbia Journal of World Business* (Spring 1966).

Baker, R. "Taxation in the E.E.C.," *Taxation and Operations Abroad*, Princeton: Symposium Tax Institute, 1960.

Balandier, G. "Comparative Study of Economic Motivations and Incentives in a Traditional and in a Modern Environment," *International Social Science Bulletin*, Vol. VI, No. 3 (1954), pp. 372-87.

Baldwin, George. "Brain Drain or Overflow," *Foreign Affairs* (January 1970), p. 358.

Baldwin, Robert E. "The International Firm and Efficient Economic Allocation, International Trade in Inputs and Outputs," *The American Economic Review* (May 1970).

Ball, G.W. "Multinational Corporations and Nation States," *The Atlantic Community Quarterly*, Vol. V, No. II, (1967).

Ball, George W. "Making World Corporations Into World Citizens," *War/Peace Report* (October 1968).

Ballon, Robert J. *The Japanese Employee*, Rutland, Vt.: Charles E. Tuttle, 1969.

Ballon, Robert J. *Joint Ventures and Japan*, Rutland, Vt.: Charles E. Tuttle, 1967.

Barber, Arthur. "Emerging New Power—The World Corporation," *War/Peace Report* (October 1968).

Barber, Ph. J. "Les Entreprises Internationales," *Analyse et Prévision* (September 1966).

245

Barber, Richard J. "Big, Bigger, Biggest-American Business Goes Global," *The New Republic* (April 30, 1966).

Barr, Andrew. "The International Harmonization of Accounting Principles," *Federal Accountant* (November 1967), pp. 1-17.

Bata, Thomas J. "Communicating in Growing International and Decentralized Organizations," *Proceedings of the 14th International Congress for Scientific Management*, Rotterdam: Rotterdam University Press, 1967, pp. 226-30.

Behrman, Jack N. *National Interests and Multinational Enterprise*, Englewood Cliffs: Prentice-Hall, 1970.

Berelson, Bernard. *The Behavioral Sciences Today*, New York: Harper & Row, 1964.

Bertin, G.Y. "L'investissement des Firmes Étrangères en France," Paris: P.U.F., 1963.

Bertin, G.Y. "Les Rapports Entre L'etat National et l'Entreprise Étrangère," *Analyse et Prévision* (juillet-août, VI/1968).

Bienen, Henry. "An Ideology for Africa," *Foreign Affairs* (April 1969), pp. 545 ff.

Bivins, K.K., and Greene, J. *Compensation of Overseas Managers: Trends and Guidelines*, New York: The Conference Board, 1969.

Blough, Roy. *International Business, Environment and Adaptation*, New York: McGraw-Hill, 1966.

Brewster, Kingman, Jr. *Antitrust and American Business Abroad*, New York: McGraw-Hill, 1958.

Brooke, M.A., and Rim, H.L. *Strategy of Multinational Enterprise Organization and Finance*, London: Longmans, 1970.

Brown, Courtney. *World Business, Promise and Problems*, New York: Macmillan, 1970.

Browne, Dudley. "Differences Between U.S. and Foreign Reporting," *Financial Executive* (January 1963), pp. 20-23.

Buckley, W. (ed.). *Modern Systems Research for the Behavioral Scientist*, Aldine Publishing Company, 1968.

Business Taxation, The Report of the President's Task Force on Business Taxation, Washington: U.S. Government Printing Office (September 1970), pp. 34-82.

Byron, George D. *Profits from Abroad: A Reveille for American Business*, New York: McGraw-Hill, 1964.

Carroll, Mitchell. "How EEC Tax Strategists Plan to Counteract U.S. Competition," *Business Abroad* (December 1970), 95:7+/.

"The Challenge of Multinational Business," Editorial, *Fortune* (August 15, 1969).

Choi, Anthony C.D. "Translation of Foreign Operations: A Survey," *Management Accounting* (April 1968), pp. 28-30.

Chorafas, Dimitri N. *Developing the International Executive*, New York: The American Management Association, 1967.

Clark, D.G. *The Industrial Manager*, London: Business Publications, Ltd., 1966.

Cracco, Étienne. *International Business–1970, A Selection of Current Readings*, East Lansing: Michigan State University, 1970.

Crozier, Michael. *The Bureaucratic Phenomenon*, Chicago: University of Chicago Press, 1964.

Dale, Ernest. "The Effect of New Information Technologies on Management Structure and Development," *Proceedings of the 14th International Congress for Scientific Management*, Rotterdam: Rotterdam University Press, 1967, pp. 238-46.

Daniels, John D., and Arpan, Jeffrey. "Comparative Home Country Influences on Management Practices Abroad," *Academy of Management Journal*, Vol. 15, No. 3 (September 1972).

de Windt, E.M. speech by, "The Role of the Multinational Company in the World Marketplace," Eaton Yale & Towne, Inc., 1969.

de Windt, E.M., Ford, Henry, II, and Norris, Robert M., Multinational Issues of *Public Relations Quarterly*, Part I, Winter 1971; Part II, Spring 1971.

Dearden, John. "Decentralization and Intra-Company Pricing," *Harvard Business Review, XXXIII* (July/August 1955), p. 65.

Demonts, R. "La Recherche dans la Firme Plurinationale et sa Propagation," *Economie Appliquée*, Paris (octobre-décembre, 1967).

Dill, William, R. "Environment as an Influence on Managerial Autonomy," *Administrative Science Quarterly*, Vol. 2, No. 4.

Donner, Fred G. *The Worldwide Industrial Enterprise*, New York: McGraw-Hill, 1967.

Drancourt, N. "Entreprises Transnationales Contre Étatisme Industriel," *Entreprise*, (22 mars 1969).

Dubin, Homans, and Mann, Miller. *Leadership and Productivity*, San Francisco: Chandler Publishing Co., 1965.

Duerr, Michael G., and Greene, James. *The Problems Facing International Management: A Survey*, National Industrial Conference Board, New York: 1968.

Dufey, Gunter. *The Eurobond Market: Function and Future*, Seattle: Graduate School of Business Administration, University of Washington, 1969.

Dunning, John H. "Technology, United States Investment, and European Economic Growth," *The International Corporation* (Charles P. Kindelberger, ed.), Cambridge: M.I.T. Press, 1970.

Dymsza, William A. *Multinational Business Strategy*, New York: McGraw-Hill, 1972.

Easton, David (ed.), *Varieties of Political Theory*, Englewood Cliffs: Prentice-Hall, 1966.

Eckman, Donald P. (ed.). *Systems: Research and Design*, New York: John Wiley & Sons, 1961.

Edwards, Ronald. "New German Tax Action Requires Immediate Action by U.S. Taxpayers" *Journal of Taxation* (November 1967).

Eitman, David K., and Arthur I. Stonehill. *Multinational Business Finance*, Reading, Mass.: Addison-Wesley, 1973.

European Community Information Services. "Tax Harmonization in The European Community," *The International Accountant*, London, Vol. 38 (October 1968).

Evan, William M. "Indices of the Hierarchal Structure of Industrial Organizations," *Management Science*, Vol. 9, No. 3 (April 1970).

Farmer, David H. "Source Decision Making in Multinational Company," *Journal of Purchasing*, Vol. 8, No. 2 (February 1972).

Farmer, Richard N., and Richman, Barry M. *Comparative Management and Economic Progress*, Homewood, Ill.: Richard D. Irwin, 1965.

Farmer, Richard N., and Richman, Barry M. *International Business: An Operational Theory*, Homewood, Ill.: Richard D. Irwin, 1966.

Foreign-affiliated Enterprises in Japan, published by and for Ministry of International Trade and Industry, Tokyo: 1969.

Form, William, (ed.), *Industrial Relations & Social Change in Latin America* Gainesville: University of Florida Press, 1965.

Froomkin, Joseph N. "Management and Organization in Japanese Industry," *Academy of Management Journal*, Vol. 7, No. 1 (March 1964), pp. 71-76.

Gabriel, Peter P. *The International Transfer of Corporate Skills: Management Contracts in Less Developed Countries*, Boston: Division of Research, Graduate School of Business Administration, Harvard University, 1967.

Gennard, John. *Multinational Corporations and British Labour*, London: British-North American Committee, 1972.

Gloor, M. "Le Multinationalisme d'une Entreprise Suisse," *Revue économique et sociale* (fevrier 1969).

Goode, Richard. "Reconstruction of the Foreign Tax System," *Readings in Taxation in Developing Countries*, ed., Richard Bird, Baltimore: Johns Hopkins Press.

Gott, R.C., "La Société Internationale et la Croissance Économique," *Revue de la Société d'Études et d'Expansion*, Bruxelles: (mars-avril, 1969).

Gorer, Geoffrey. "The Concept of National Character," *Personality in Nature, Society and Culture* (Clyde Kluckhohn and Henry Murrey, eds.), New York: Alfred A. Knopf, 1953.

Green, Michel. "New Model Multinational Bank," *The Banker*, Vol. 121, May 1971.

Grubel, H.G. "Internationally Diversified Portfolios," *American Economic Review*, Vol. LVIII, No. 5, Part I (December 1968).

Gunther, Hans (ed.). *Transnational Industrial Relations*, London: Macmillan, 1972.

Haire, Mason, Ghiselli, Edwin E., and Porter, Lyman W. *Managerial Thinking: An International Study*, New York: John Wiley & Sons, Inc. 1966.

Hall, Ed. T. "The Silent Language in Overseas Business," *Harvard Business Review* (May/June 1960).

Harding, S. "Financial and Accounting Problems Peculiar to International Business," *International Accountant*, London (June 1968).

Harding, S. "Financial and Accounting Problems Peculiar to International Business," *Accountant*, London (January 13, 1968), pp. 45-51.

Harvard University Program On Technology and Society, Annual Reports, 1966-70.

Hass, Jerome. "Transferpricing in a Decentralized Firm," *Management Science* (February 1968), pp. B310-B331.

Hayden, Spencer. "Communications and Control Problems in Overseas Operations," *Personnel*, XXXXV, No. 4 (July-August 1968), pp. 22-29.

Hayden, Spencer. "Organizational Problems in Overseas Operations," *Personnel*, XXXXV, No. 2 (March-April 1968), pp. 15-25.

Hayden, Spencer. "Problems of Operating Overseas: A Survey of Company Experience," *Personnel*, XXXXV, No. 1 (January-February 1968), pp. 8-21.

Heath, Dwight B. (ed.). *Contemporary Cultures and Societies of Latin America: A Reader in the Social Anthropology of Middle and South America and the Caribbean*, New York: Random House, 1965.

Heilbroner, Robert L. "The Multinational Corporation and the Nation-State," *New York Review of Books* (February 17, 1971).

Hellmann, Rainer (trans. by Rust). *The Challenge to U.S. Dominance of International Corporation*.

Henley, Donald S. "Multinational Marketing: Present Position and Future Challenges," *1972 Combined Proceedings* (Baris and Bocker, ed.), Chicago: American Marketing Association, 1973.

Henning, Michael A. "An International Business Guide to the U.S. Tax Reform Act of 1969," *Business Abroad* (March 1970), 95:15+.

Henriquez, Urena Pedro. *A Concise History of Latin American Culture* (trans.), New York: Praeger, 1966.

Hill and Knowlton, Inc. *Handbook in International Public Relations*, New York: Praeger, 1967.

Hirshleiger, Jack. "On the Economics of Transfer-Pricing," *Journal of Business*, XXXIX (July 1956), pp. 172-88.

Hitchin, David. "Foreign Government Influences on Purchasing Policies," *Journal of Purchasing* Vol. 12, No. 2 (August 1967).

Hoselitz, B.F. "The Recruitment of Management in Underdeveloped Countries," *International Social Science Bulletin*, Vol. VI, No. 3 (1954), pp. 433-43.

Human Problems of U.S. Enterprise in Latin America, Ithaca, N.Y.: Conference Report, Cornell University, 1956.

Hymer, Stephen. "The Internationalization of Capitol," *Journal of Economic Issues*, Vol. 6, No. 1 (March 1972).

Hymer, Stephen H. "Direct Foreign Investment and National Interest," *Nationalism in Canada* (P. Russell, ed.), Toronto: McGraw-Hill, 1966.

Hymer, Stephen H. "The International Operations of National Firms: A Study of Direct Investments" (unpublished doctoral dissertation), Boston: M.I.T. Press, 1966.

The Impact of U.S. Foreign Direct Investment of U.S. Employment and Trade—An Assessment of Critical Claims and Legislative Proposals, National Foreign Trade Council, New York: (November 1971).

Jacoby, Neil H. "The Multinational Corporation," *The Center Magazine*, Vol. III, No. I (May 1970).

Kapoor, A., and Brub, Phillip D. *The Multinational Enterprise in Transition*, Princeton, N.J.: The Derwin Press, 1972.

Katz, D., and Kahn, R. *The Social Psychology of Organizations*, New York: John Wiley & Sons, 1966.

Kaufman, O. "Problème Structurels de l'Internationalisation des Entreprises Européenes et Américaines," *Analyse et Prévision* (avril 1969).

Kaufman O. "Internationalisme Européen et Multinationalisme Américain," *Revue Économique et Sociale* (mai 1969).

Kelman, Herbert C. (ed.). *International Behavior*, New York: Holt, Rinehart and Winston, 1965.

Kindelberger, Charles P. *American Business Abroad*, New Haven: Yale University Press, 1969.

Kindelberger, Charles P. *The International Corporation*, Boston: M.I.T. Press, 1970.

Kluckhorn, Florence Rockwood, and Strodtbeck, Fred. *Variations in Orientations*, Evanston, Ill.: Row, Peterson & Co., 1961.

Kolde, Endel J. "A New Trend in International Trade Policy," *The Korean Business Journal* (March 1969), pp. 92-100.

Kolde, Endel J. "The Functions of Foreign-Based Affiliates in the Administrative Structure of International Business," pp. 155-83 in *Revue Économique et Sociale* (Special issue entitled "A Symposium on Business and Education"), Lausanne University, Switzerland (December 1962).

Kolde, Endel J. *International Business Enterprise*, second ed., Englewood Cliffs: Prentice-Hall, 1973.

Kolde, Endel J., and Richard E. Hill. "Conceptual and Normative Aspects of International Management," *Academy of Management Journal* (June 1967), pp. 119-28.

Konzli, R. "La Politique de Rumeneration du Personnel dans les Entreprises Internationales Operant en Europe," *Revue Économique et Sociale*, (aout 1968).

Kraayenhof, Jacob. "International Challenges for Accounting," *Journal of Accountancy* (January 1960), pp. 34-38.

Krause, Walter, and Mathis, John F. *International Economics and Business: Selected Readings*, Boston: Houghton Mifflin, 1968.

Kuznets, Simon. "International Differences in Income Levels," *Economic Change*, New York (1953), pp. 216-52.

Lange, Oscar. *Wholes and Parts: A General Theory of System Behavior*, (Trans. by E. Lejea). Oxford: Pergamon Press, 1965.

Lawrence, Paul R., and Lorsch, Jay W. "Organizing for Product Innovation," *Harvard Business Review*, Vol. 43, No. 1 (January-February 1965).

Leavitt, Harold J. "Unhuman Organizations," *Harvard Business Review*, Vol. 40, No. 4 (July-August 1962).

Levy, Haim, and Sarnat, Marshall. "International Diversification of Investment Portfolios," *American Economic Review*, Vol. 60, No. 4 (September 1970).

Lipset, Seymour, and Salari, Aldo (ed.). *Elites in Latin America*, New York: Oxford University Press, 1967.

Litvak, I.A., and Maule, C.J. "Conflict Resolution and Extraterritoriality," *Journal of Conflict Resolution*, Vol. 8, No. 3 (September 1969), pp. 305-19.

Litvak, I.A., and Maule, C.J. "The Union Response to International Corporations," *Industrial Relations*, Vol. 11, No. 1 (February 1972).

Litwak, Eugene. "Models of Bureaucracy Which Permit Conflict," *American Journal of Sociology*, Bul. 67 (September 1961).

Lorenz, Konrad. *On Aggression*, Toronto, New York, London: Bantam Books, 1971. Originally published by Harcourt Brace Jovanovich.

Lynch, John. "Determination of Earnings and Profits of a Controlled Foreign Corporation," *Taxes—The Tax Magazine* (April 1967), pp. 263-83.

McCarthy, Mary. "A Guide to Exiles, Expatriots, and Internal Emigrés," *The New York Review of Books*, Vol. XVIII, No. 4 (March 5, 1972).

McKean, Roland. *Efficiency in Government Through Systems Analysis*, New York: John Wiley & Sons, 1968.

Michalet, Charles Albert and Delapierre, Michael. *La multinationalisation des enterprises francaises*. Paris, France: Centre d'Etude des Techniques Economiques Modernes, 1973.

Maisonrouge, Jacques G. "The Evolution of International Business," speech, IBM World Trade Corporation, at meeting of American Chamber of Commerce in the Netherlands, June 5, 1968.

"The Man Who Makes It One World for IBM," *Business Week* (July 18, 1970).

Mason, Edward S. (ed.) *The Corporation in Modern Society*, Cambridge: Harvard University Press, 1959.

Massie, Joseph, and Luytjes, Jan. *Management in an International Context*, Harper and Row, 1972.

Mieszkoski, Peter. "Carter on the Taxation of International Income Flows," *National Tax Journal* (March 1969), 22:97-108.

Morgan, Lee L. "The Win-Win Situation: How U.S. Investment Abroad Benefits the U.S. as Well as the People of Host Countries," speech before 58th National Foreign Trade Convention (November 16, 1971), Caterpillar Tractor Co., Peoria, Ill.

Morrison, Thomas. "Taxation of International Investment," *Accounting Review* (October 1966).

Mosson, T.M. *Management Education in Five European Countries*, London: Business Publications Ltd., 1965.

Moulyn, A.C. *Structure, Function and Purpose*, New York: Liberal Arts Press, 1957.

Moyer, R. "International Market Analysis," *Journal of Marketing Research* (November 1968).

"The Multinationals Ride a Rougher Road," *Business Week* (December 19, 1970).

National Association of Manufacturers. *U.S. Stake in World Trade and Investment: The Role of the Multinational Corporation*, New York: 1972.

National Industrial Conference Board. *Appraising Foreign Licensing Performance*, Business Policy Study No. 128, 1969.

National Industrial Conference Board. *Obstacles and Incentives to Private Foreign Investments*, Business Policy Study No. 130, 1967-68.

National Industrial Conference Board. *Obstacles to Private Foreign Investment*, Vol. 1, New York: 1969.

"Nationalism Sets Boundaries for Multinational Giants," *Business Week*, No. 2076 (June 14, 1969), pp. 94-96.

Negandhi, Anant R. (ed.). *Organization Theory in an Interorganizational Perspective*, Kent, Ohio; Kent State University Press, 1972.

Nehrt, Lee C. *International Finance for Multinational Business*, second ed., Scranton, Pa.: International Textbook Company, 1971.

"On the Way: Companies More Powerful than Nations," *U.S. News & World Report* (July 19, 1971).

Okun, Bernard, and Richardson, Richard W. *Studies in Economic Development*, New York: Holt, Rinehart and Winston, 1961.

Osgood, Charles E. "Cross-Cultural Comparability in Attitude Measurement Via Multilingual Semantic Differentials," *Current Studies in Social Psychology*, New York: Holt, Rinehart and Winston, 1965.

Osgood, Charles E. "Studies on the Generality of Affective Meaning Systems, *American Psychologists*, 1962, pp. 10-28.

Osgood, Charles E., Suci, G.J., and Tannenbaum, P.H. *The Measurement of Meaning*, Urbana: University of Illinois, Institute of Communications Research, 1957.

Parizeau, J. "Les Prix Internationaux," *Revue d'économie politique*, Paris (juillet-aout, 1967).

Parks, F.N. "Survival of the European Headquarters," *Harvard Business Review*, (March-April 1969).

Perlmutter, Howard V. "Super-Giant Firms in the Future," *Wharton Quarterly* (Winter 1968).

Perlmutter, Howard V. "The Tortuous Evolution of the Multinational Corporation," *Columbia Journal of World Business*, Vol. IV, No. 1 (January-February 1969), pp. 9-18.

Perrow, Charles. *Organizational Analysis: Sociological View*, Belmont, Calif.: Wadsworth Publishing Company, 1970.

Polk, Judd, Meister, Irene W., and Vest, Lawrence A. *U.S. Production Abroad and the Balance of Payments: A Survey of Corporate Investment Experience*, New York: The Conference Board, 1966.

Prakash, Om. *The Theory and Working of State Corporations*, London: Allen & Unwin, 1962.

Reinoud, H. "Impact of New Technologies on Management Effectiveness," *Proceedings of the 14th International Congress for Scientific Management*, Rotterdam: Rotterdam University Press: 1967, pp. 247-53.

Robbins, Sydney, and Stabaugh, Robert B. *Money in the Multinational Enterprise*, New York: Basic Books, 1973.

Robertson, Roland. "Strategic Relations Between National Societies: A Sociological Analysis," *Journal of Conflict Resolution*, Vol. 12, No. 1 (March 1968), pp. 16-34.

Robinson, Richard D. "The Global Firm-to-Be: Who Needs Equity?" *Columbia Journal of World Business*, Vol. 3, No. 1 (January-February 1968).

Robinson, Richard D. *International Business Policy*, New York: Holt, Rinehart and Winston, 1964.

Robock, Stefan, and Simmons, Kenneth. *International Business and Multinational Enterprises*, Homewood, Ill.: Richard D. Irwin, 1973.

Robinson, Richard D. *International Business Management*, New York: Holt, Rinehart and Winston, 1973.

Root, Franklin. "Foreign Constraints on U.S. Business Abroad," *Economic and Business Bulletin*, Vol. 7, No. 2 (September 1967).

Rose, S. "The Rewarding Strategies of Multinationalism" *Fortune* (September 15, 1968).

Rostow, Walt, "The Stages of Economic Growth," *The Economic History Review* (August 1959).

"A Rougher Road for Multinationals," *Business Week* (December 19, 1970).

Rupert, Anthony E. "Communicating in a Growing International Organization," *Proceedings of the 14th International Congress for Scientific Management*, Rotterdam: Rotterdam University Press, 1967, pp. 227-30.

Sagara, Morijii, Yamamoto, Kazuo, Nishimura, Hirohiki, and Akuto, Hiroshi. "A Study on the Semantic Structure of Japanese Language by the Semantic Differential Method," Japanese Psychological Research, Vol. 3, No. 3 (1961) pp. 146-56.

Saltzman, Charles E. "Current Trends in International Securities Market," *The Conference Board Record*, Vol. 7 (May 1972).

Samuelson, Paul A. "International Trade and Evalualization of Factor Prices," *Economic Journal* (June 1948).

Seiler, John A. "Toward a Theory of Organization Congruent with Primary Group Concepts," *Behavioral Science*, Vol. 8, No. 3 (July 1963), pp. 190-98.

Shelling, Thomas G. *The Strategy of Conflict*, Cambridge: Harvard University Press, 1960.

Shepard, Herbert R. and Blake, Robert R. "Changing Behavior Through Cognitive Change," *Human Organization*, Vol. 21 (Summer 1962).

Silberman, H. Lee. "The Europ-Commercial Paper Caper," *Finance* (October 1970).

Singer, H.W. *International Development: Growth and Change*, New York: McGraw-Hill, 1962.

Social and Labor Aspects of Economic Development, Geneva: International Labor Office, 1963.

Sorofin, Pitirim A. "Sociology of Yesterday, Today, and Tomorrow," *American Sociological Review* (December 1965), pp. 833-43.

Stanley, Alexander O. *Handbook of International Marketing*, "International Marketing Section," New York: McGraw-Hill, 1963.

Steiner, George Albert, *Multinational Corporate Planning*, New York: Macmillan, 1966.

Stobaugh, Robert B. "The Multinational Corporation: Measuring the Consequences," *Columbia Journal of World Business* (January-February 1971).

Stock, Leon. "Tax Planning of Foreign Operations," *Management Information System*, Institute of Management Sciences, Monograph 1 (January 1960), pp. 86-91.

Stopford, John and Wells, J.T. *Managing the Multinational Enterprise*, New York: Basic Books, 1972.

Stroller, David S., and Van Norn, Richard L. *Design of Management Information System*, Institute of Management Sciences, Monograph 1 (January 1970), pp. 86-91.

Surrey, Stan. "The Implications of Tax Harmonization in the EEC," *Taxes* (June 1968).

Szule, Tad. *Latin America*, New York: Atheneum, 1966.

Taiguri, Renato. "Value Orientations and the Relationship of Managers and Scientists," *Administrative Science Quarterly* (June 1965), pp. 39-51.

Tanaka, Y., and Osgood, C.E. "Cross-culture, Cross-concept, and Cross-subject Generality of Affective Meaning Systems," *Journal of Personality and Social Psychology*, Vol. 2, No. 2 (1965), pp. 143-53.

Tax Foundations, Inc. *Tax Harmonization in Europe and U.S. Business*, 1968.

Tax Institute of America. *Taxation of Foreign-Source Income*, Princeton: 1966.

Teague, Burton W. *Compensating Key Personnel Overseas*, The Conference Board, 1972, Conference Board Report No. 574.

Terhune, Kenneth W. "From National Character to National Behavior: A Reformulation," *Journal of Conflict Resolution*, Vol. 14, No. 2 (June 1970).

This Is Teleconference, Seattle: Boeing Company.

Tugenhat, Christopher. *The Multinationals*, London: Pelican Books, 1973.

U.S. Department of Commerce, *The Multinational Corporation*, Studies of U.S. Foreign Investment, Vol. 1 (March 1972).

United States Tariff Commission. *Operation of the Trade Agreements Program* for years 1958 and 1971.

Useem, John and Ruth, and Donoghue, John. "Men in the Middle of the Third Culture: The Roles of American and Non-Western People in Cross-Cultural Administration," *Human Organization*, Vol. 22, No. 3 (Fall 1963), pp. 169-79.

Van Geothem, Pierre. *The Americanization of World Business: Wall Street and the Superiority of American Enterprise*, New York: Herder and Herder, 1972.

Veliz, Claudio (ed.). *Obstacles to Change in Latin America* (papers from London Conference on Obstacles to Change in Latin America, 1965), New York: Oxford University Press, 1965.

Vernon, Raymond. *Sovereignty at Bay*, New York: Basic Books, 1971.

Vernon, Raymond. *Sovereignty at Bay: The Multinational Spread of U.S. Enterprises*, New York: Basic Books, September 1971.

Vice, Anthony. *The Strategy of Takeovers: A Casebook of International Practice*, New York: McGraw-Hill, 1971.

von Bertalanffy, Ludwig. "General Systems Theory: A New Approach to Unity of Science," *Human Biology* (December 1951), pp. 303-61.

Ward, Champion F. "America the Resilient," *The Journal of Higher Education*, Vol. XL, No. 6 (June 1969).

Washburn, N.F. (ed.). *Decisions, Values, and Groups*, New York: Pergamon Press, 1962.

Weathers, Milledge W. "Some Implications of the GATT Rule Governing the Treatment of Domestic Taxes and International Trade," *National Tax Journal* (March 1970), 23:102-11.

Weintrants, Leon. *International Manpower Development*, New York: Praeger, 1969.

Wells, Louis T., Jr. (ed.). *The Product Life Cycle and International Trade*, Boston: Harvard Graduate School of Business, 1972.

Wilkins, Mira. *The Emergence of Multinational Enterprise: American Business Abroad from the Colonial Era to 1914*, Cambridge; Harvard University Press, 1971.

Wilkinson, Theodore L. "Worldwide Auditing Standards and the World Economy," *Price Waterhouse Review* (Winter 1967), pp. 7-13.

Woodward, Joan. *Industrial Organization: Theory and Practice*, London: Oxford University Press, 1970.

Yoshino, M.Y. *Japan's Managerial System*, Boston: M.I.T. Press, 1968.

Yoshino, M.Y. "Minimizing Conflicts in International Joint Ventures," *Financial Executive* (November 1968).

Zabilka, Gladys. *Customs & Culture of the Philippines*, Rutland, Vt.: Charles E. Tuttle, 1963.

Zawodny, J.K. *Man and International Relations*, Vols. 1 and 2, San Francisco: Chandler Publishing Company, 1967.

Zuelke, R.C. "How to Hire Employees for Foreign Assignments," *International Management* (January 1965).

Index

Index

About the Author

E.J. Kolde is Senior Professor of International Business in the Graduate School of Business Administration, University of Washington. He received his undergraduate education at the National Military Academy and Tallinn Technical University (Estonia), the D.H.S. degree from the Stockholm School of Economics, (Sweden) and the M.A. and the Ph.D. from the University of Washington. Professor Kolde has been a visiting professor at Harvard University, Lausanne University Management Development Institute (Switzerland), the University of California at Berkeley, the University of British Columbia, Cranfield Institute of Technology (England), and Kobe University of Commerce and Sophia University (Japan). His research and advisory activities extend to many parts of the world. He is the author of numerous publications, including the MacKinsey prize article, "Business Enterprise in a Global Context," which has appeared in several books and journals; and *International Business Enterprise* (Prentice-Hall, 1968 and 1973).

TABLE 2.9
Landownership With and Without Lot Owners,
by Township, 1793–1796

ship	Taxable Population	Number of Landowners	Percent Landed	Lot Owners	Percentage of Landownership When	
					Lots Excluded[a]	Lots as Landless[b]
	311	149	47.9	35	41.3	36.7
	362	136	37.6	17	34.5	32.9
hem	173	108	62.4	9	60.4	57.2
ind	315	164	52.1	7	51.0	49.8
	463	196	42.3	6	41.6	41.0
	281	137	48.8	6	47.6	46.6
	241	147	61.0	15	58.4	54.8
	256	138	54.9	13	51.4	48.8
	156	84	53.8	7	51.7	49.4
on	111	80	72.1	65	32.6	13.5
	360	211	58.6	45	52.7	46.1
	341	227	66.6	5	66.1	65.1

g lot owners from both the taxable population and the landed population.
g lot owners from the landed population only, thereby increasing the number

the county seat town of Washington, which now had
township jurisdiction, obviously the greatest impact
d. From a landownership percentage of 72.1, the per-
falls to 32.6 when lot owners are excluded and to 13.5
t owners are considered landless. Furthermore, thir-
the fifteen people who did own acreage in addition to
wn lots owned outlots of small acreage around the
hey were, in fact, still lot owners, the same as those in
ring Strabane and Canton townships who also owned
None of these people were farmers. Only one man on
shington assessment owned a large farm. Tavern-
John Dodd had 204 acres plus his town lot. The sec-
gest acreage was 56 acres and three lots belonging to
n proprietor, John Hoge. Thus, the appearance of

be added that the amount of livestock in western Pennsylvania was below the levels of older, more established regions. This would considerably reduce the cleared acreage needed for hay, pasture, and grains. Nevertheless, if the figures for Springhill Township in 1783 are at all typical, there was little surplus agricultural production in western Pennsylvania at the close of the Revolution.[14]

The land patterns of the 1780s, therefore, reveal a new, subsistence-level, agricultural society in various stages of development. The river regions had been developed the most; many border regions had scarcely been touched. Most settlers had moderate landholdings, but very few had advanced to commercial farming. A significantly large percentage were landless, making it necessary for small farm clearings to support more than the owner's family. Western Pennsylvania, at the close of the Revolution, clearly had not risen above a subsistence level.

Land Patterns of the 1790s

By the mid-1790s, the land patterns of western Pennsylvania had changed significantly. Confronted by great population growth, the percentage of landownership had declined, and acreage figures were significantly smaller. A few people had been able to concentrate larger holdings, but a new type of property—the town lot—gave rise to a class of smallholders at the other extreme. There was a marked lowering of all median acreage figures, but it was offset by sufficient increases in cleared acreage to allow an important degree of commercial agriculture. Because of the population growth during the decade, a new county—Allegheny—had been erected in 1788 out of Washington and Westmoreland, and another new county—Greene—was to be carved out of southern Washington County in 1796. A number of township divisions had also occurred in response to the growing population. The edge of the frontier had been pushed further west and north, and significant settlements such as Thomas Ryerson's existed in the border regions. These exposed areas were still subject to

Indian raids that were only troubling memories elsewhere in the region due to the uncertain military results in Ohio early in the 1790s. Thus, after a decade of steady growth, western Pennsylvania showed considerably more maturity than it had in the 1780s.

One change in the land patterns from the 1780s was a small decline in the percentage of landownership. (See tables 2.1 and 2.2.) The decline was 3 percent to an overall 59 percent and was about the same in both Fayette and Washington counties.[15] The decline in landownership is also evident in each region, and particularly so in the border townships. These border townships were generally undeveloped in the 1780s, but the impact of continuing settlement had a marked effect upon them. For example, in Smith Township in Washington County, 89.5 percent of the settlers owned land in 1784. By 1793, it had been divided into two townships. The eastern one, still bearing the name Smith, now had a landowning percentage of 70.9, nineteen percentage points lower. The western part of the old township, now called Hanover, had a percentage of 86.0, a figure much closer to the 1784 percentage. This type of graphic change confirms the basic pattern that as new regions became settled their percentage of landownership dropped sharply. This undoubtedly had happened in the river townships and, to a lesser extent, in the interior townships prior to the 1780s. The comparative statistics indicate that this process had now slowed considerably in the river townships by the 1790s, but still showed some life in the interior townships and was very much in evidence in the border regions.[16]

An important new factor affecting the distribution of land in western Pennsylvania in the 1790s was the appearance of town lot owners, the first indications of urbanization. The lot owner with a fourth- or a half-acre lot was a much different property owner than even the small farmer with fifty acres. Persons who owned no other land than their town lots made up 3.7 percent of the landowners in Washington County and 9.5 percent of the landowners in Fayette County. The statistical importance of these people can be illustrated by the simple fact that the overall decline in the percentage of landownership should have been doubled—6.1 percent, not 3 percent—if these lot owners had been landless (table 2.8).

The appearance of town lots h
upon the individual townships in v
oped. For example, in Luzerne Tov
age of landownership increased i
47.9 percent. The reason was i
gained proportionately more land
cause Luzerne now contained th
which forty persons—thirty-five
land—now owned town lots. If tov
from consideration, the Luzerne p
41.3 in 1796, or if persons with on
landless, the percentage of lando
only 36.7 percent (table 2.9).

The same thing can be illustr
where the percentage of all landov
would have been 52.7 if town lot
consideration, or only 46.1 if lot o

TABLE 2
Landownership, With and V
by County and Regio

County/Region	Taxable Population	Number of Landowners	P L
Fayette	2,473	1,158	
Washington	4,969	3,232	
TOTAL OR OVERALL PERCENTAGE	7,442	4,390	
River	2,692	1,395	
Interior	2,762	1,590	
Border	1,988	1,405	
TOTAL OR OVERALL PERCENTAGE	7,442	4,390	

a. Excluding lot owners from both the taxable p
b. Excluding lot owners from the landed popul
ber of landless.

Region/To

River
  Luzern
  Spring
  E. Beth
  Cumbe
Interior
  Frankli
  George
  Chartie
  Strabar
  Canton
  Washin
Border
  Bullski
  Greene

a. Exclud
b. Exclud
of landless.

less. I
separa
occurr
centag
when
teen o
their
town.
neight
outlots
the W
keepe
ond la
the to

town lots in the landownership percentages of the 1790s obscures important changes that were taking place. Luzerne's 1796 percentage of landownership does not mean that nearly half of the population were landowning farmers. Instead, only 37 percent had such lands; the remaining landowners of Luzerne were town dwellers.

Another basic change in the land patterns of the 1790s was a decline in the size of landholdings. (See table 2.3.) The inclusion of town lots at the bottom of the land spectrum was one factor causing smaller acreages, but other causes were more important. The growth of families and some early subdivision of lands among children reduced acreages. Also, many persons, as if following the example of Edward Cook, sold portions of their lands to the many new settlers who had entered the region, and many speculative holdings had been sold off. This basic pressure of a growing population on a fixed quantity of land was the major cause of the small acreage figures for the 1790s.[17] The median acreage dropped from 200 to 140 acres over the course of the decade. Modal acreages, which in the 1780s were 300 acres in all categories, were just as uniformly 100 acres in the 1790s. Mean acreages exhibited somewhat less change due to a few very large speculative holdings. Thus, in both counties, similar changes occurred. The rate of change was definitely greatest in the border regions and more moderate in the interior and river regions. Yet, in these two latter regions, the typical landowner now owned a scant 120 acres.

The full distribution of landholdings for the 1790s gives further evidence of the trend toward smaller acreages (table 2.10). Every decile except the last indicates smaller acreages, and the gaps between deciles grow more precise, with fewer 50- or 100-acre jumps. The first decile, which includes lot owners, contains acreages so small as to cast doubt on whether they could support any real farming population, and in Fayette County, nearly 20 percent of the landowners make up this category.[18] Whereas two out of three landowners in the 1780s held less than 300 acres nearly five out of six held less than 300 acres in the 1790s. The 300-acre tract declined in number from 160 to 72 in Fayette and from 491 to 191 in Washington,

TABLE 2.10
Acreage by Deciles,
Washington and Fayette Counties, 1784–1796

	Fayette		Washington		Total
Decile	1785	1796	1784	1793	1790s
1	1–50	L–2	1–70	L–47	L–40
2	50–100	2–50	70–100	47–70	40–64
3	100	50–83	100–110	70–100	64–100
4	100–150	83–100	110–150	100	100
5	150–200	100–131	150–200	100–140	100–140
6	200	133–170	200–250	140–170	140–170
7	200–300	170–200	250–300	170–200	170–200
8	300	200–270	300	200–250	200–254
9	300–320	270–332	300–400	250–350	255–340
10	320–2,200	332–4,200	400–4,700	350–40,000	340–40,000

Note: L = town lot.

but the 100-acre tract increased in number from 115 to 134 in Fayette and from 390 to 526 in Washington.[19]

Two contradictory trends occur among the top decile of landowners. On the one hand, this last decile now begins with a smaller acreage; like Edward Cook, many of the largest landowners had subdivided their holdings. On the other hand, a small group had been able to increase their holdings, and the size of the largest holdings was much above that of a decade earlier. Thus, while the major trend was toward smaller holdings, a few were able to consolidate and increase their holdings. For example, eleven tracts in these two counties now exceeded 2,000 acres, whereas only five in the whole region had been as large in the 1780s. A number of the largest holdings were absentee owned, but there were also local residents who held very large tracts of land, and Thomas Ryerson, a newcomer since the early 1780s, owned the largest tract of all, 40,000 acres! No one else was even close to the size of his acreage on the southwest border of what would be the new and sparsely settled Greene County.

This consolidation may also be observed by comparing the growing gap between the top and the bottom deciles of landowners. As table 2.5 indicates, the top 10 percent of landowners increased their control over the land from approximately 26 percent to approximately 35 percent by the 1790s. At the same time, the bottom decile of landowners dropped from controlling approximately 2 percent of the land to less than 1 percent. The substantial consolidation that occurred over the decade cannot be denied, but it was not an abnormal increase. Merle Curti found that in the new frontier county of Trempealeau, Wisconsin, in 1860 and 1870, and in a control group of much older Vermont counties, the comparative percentages of land owned by the top docile was approximately 38 percent and by the bottom decile, generally under 1 percent, in both places.[20] By comparison, therefore, the land consolidation in western Pennsylvania had not quite attained these levels, but it was rapidly moving in that direction.

As in the 1780s, focusing attention solely upon the landowners obscures the very sizeable minority of landless individuals. Attention given to the median taxable individual and his status also reveals important changes. The median taxable person in Fayette and Washington counties was now a fifty-acre landowner, and in the river townships, he was a town dweller. (See table 2.6.) Fayette County, in 1796, scarcely a full generation away from wilderness, presented the amazing and paradoxical situation of a newly emerged frontier society in which the typical settler was already landless.

Closer examination of the median taxable person reveals two other important facts. First, although the amount of cleared acreage had more than doubled since the 1780s, enough to allow median landowners to begin some commercial farming, the fifty acres owned by the median taxable person left him at a subsistence level. Second, an examination of median taxable individuals reveals a very important new development—the spread of nonagrarian occupations, especially in Fayette County.

Cleared acreages in the 1780s were estimated at about 10 percent of a settler's land. Therefore, the median landholder with 200 acres had cleared some 20 acres, and the median taxable person with 100 acres had cleared perhaps 10 or so acres. How much had the situation improved since then?

Three Fayette County townships showed cleared acreage in 1796. Washington and Tyrone townships, the river and interior townships on the northern border, had 22 and 20 percent of their land cleared, but Luzerne, a central river township, had 35 percent of its land cleared. Collectively, cleared land totaled 25.5 percent.[21] If the 25 percent figure is used, it appears that settlers had cleared another 15 percent of their land.

Translating these percentages into specific examples must be done with care because the increased percentage of cleared land has to be applied to smaller holdings. Statistically, the median landowner of the 1790s now had 35 acres (25 percent) of his 140 acres cleared, compared with 20 (10 percent) of 200 acres in the 1780s; the median taxable individual now had 12.5 acres (25 percent) of 50 acres cleared, compared with 10 (10 percent) out of 100 acres in the 1780s. The smaller acreages reduce the impact of more cleared land on these statistical models. The actual situation of the median landowner may have been a bit better than the statistical model as seen in table 2.11. Three of the men had enough cleared acreage to move beyond the 40-acre subsistence level, and John Sherrick, in particular, had the cleared-land requirements for commercial agriculture. Charles Porter's small livestock holding suggests

TABLE 2.11
Median Landowners,
Washington, Tyrone, Luzerne Townships, 1796

Township/ Landowner	Acreage		Livestock	
	Total	Cleared	Horses	Cattle
Washington				
Samuel Burns	125	15	0	1
Peter Miller	125	25	0	4
Tyrone				
John Sherrick	200	80	3	5
Luzerne				
Charles Porter, Sr.	106¾	45	0	1
Abraham Merritt[a]	107	53	3	6

a. Merritt's cattle included two oxen; he also had a still.

that he, too, had enough cleared land for some commercial farming, while Abraham Merritt's whiskey still suggests interests beyond simple farming.[22] Only the two settlers from Washington Township still lacked enough cleared acreage to rise above subsistence farming.[23]

On the other hand, the amount of land cleared by the median taxable individual with fifty acres was surprisingly small. There were forty-nine persons in Washington, Tyrone, and Luzerne townships who owned fifty acres or less, but only one had as much as thirty-five acres cleared. Two had thirty acres cleared, six had twenty-five acres cleared, and three more had fifteen to twenty acres cleared. The median cleared acreage among twenty-five persons owning fifty acres or less in Luzerne was seven acres; among twenty persons in Washington, it was four acres; and among four in Tyrone, it was two acres. No person with fifty acres of land in these three townships had enough cleared land to rise above subsistence level. It must be added that eighteen of these forty-nine were nonfarming people, including the owners of three small, unseated (unsettled) tracts. Most were artisans, plus a mill owner, tavernkeeper, storekeeper, and tenant. More than a third, therefore, clearly had nonfarming incomes, and perhaps others did also. Nevertheless, persons called *farmer* who had nineteen of fifty acres cleared, or thirty of forty, or seven of thirty, or twenty-five of thirty-nine, as was the case in Luzerne Township, were destined for subsistence farming. By the 1790s, therefore, cleared acreage in western Pennsylvania had increased measurably. Some median landowners could venture into commercial farming. The median taxable person, in Fayette County, at least, no longer possessed enough land for viable commercial farming, and many of them were increasingly turning to nonagricultural pursuits.

This trend toward nonagrarian occupations is clearly evident among the list of median taxable inhabitants in each township in Fayette County (table 2.12). All of them were apparently artisans or laborers. The one man who did possess enough land for subsistence farming was actually a tailor and had been the local constable the year before. Two others were artisans owning town lots in Connellsville. Wagoner Jacob

TABLE 2.12
Property of Median Taxable Persons by Township,
Fayette County, 1796

Township/ Median Taxable Person	Acreage	Livestock		Value ($)
		Horses	Cattle	
Bullskin				
John Livingston, tailor	2 lots	0	0	160
John Lyon, blacksmith	2 lots	0	2	210
Franklin				
Jacob Wolfe, wagoner	0	4	0	160
Georges				
Nicholas Walker	0	0	2	16
German				
Archibald White	0	2	0	42
Walentine Waylin	0	1	0	36
Luzerne				
"Black George," "industrious"	0	0	0	0
Springhill				
John Workman, single free-man	0	0	0	0
Jacob Shoemaker, single free-man, mechanic	0	0	0	0
Tyrone				
Samuel Story, laborer	0	0	2	12
Washington				
Garret Rittenhouse, tailor	41 acres	1	0	49

Wolfe worked at Isaac Meason's ironworks, where he also apparently resided. The median taxable person in Tyrone was designated a laborer, only to have the designation crossed out. He may have been a common laborer, or perhaps a drifter with no specific trade. George, the free black from Luzerne, lived with a small colony of free blacks near Crawford's ferry, an important crossing point on the Monongahela. He, too, was probably a common laborer and was termed "industrious" to differentiate him from another black named George, who was termed "lazy." The two median taxable individuals from Springhill were both single freemen; one had an unspecified trade, and the other probably lived with a landed family of the same name. Those from German and Georges townships may have been tenant farmers, hired hands, or common laborers. Only the one from Georges may have had a landed family to depend on.[24]

Comparison of these median taxable persons of the 1790s with those of the 1780s clearly identifies the changes that occurred over the decade. The number of landless persons increased, and acreages declined. The average settler was no longer a small farmer in Fayette County, although he was in Washington County. Livestock holdings remained small, and the overall economic status of the median taxable settler as measured by landownership was lower. Nonagrarian occupations appeared in significant numbers.

Thus, the changes in the land patterns that occurred between 1783 and 1796 indicate the speed with which the frontier was disappearing in western Pennsylvania. The percentage of landownership declined and acreages became perceptibly smaller. Town residents were an important new factor. Common laborers and artisans—not landowning farmers—were the typical settlers in some townships. By the 1790s, a differentiation of economic functions was occurring; upper and lower classes were being sorted out; the class structure was maturing. One very important part of this transformation was the growing polarity within society and particularly the emergence of a small group of wealthy economic leaders.

3　The Concentration of Wealth

A SMALL CLASS of wealthy individuals provided the driving force for the transformation of western Pennsylvania after the Revolution. By the 1790s, they had come to dominate the class structure of the region. They controlled a larger share of local wealth. They formed a small group of landowners who increased the size of their large holdings contrary to general trends. And they established the businesses and industries that created new forms of wealth in the region. A growing division between the richest and poorest deciles of the population clearly illustrated this trend.

Isaac Meason, Fayette County iron magnate, provides one of the most graphic examples of this wealthy elite. Like Edward Cook, Meason came to the region in the first wave of settlement in the early 1770s. By the late 1790s, this former Virginian had become the wealthiest man in Fayette County and its largest landowner except for the owner of one speculative tract in the mountains. Meason acquired a large tract of land and registered eight slaves in the early 1780s. He later purchased the estate of Thomas Gist, the old Ohio Company guide, then entered into the iron industry in the early 1790s; the business flourished. His firm soon employed 10 percent of the population of his township, and many artisans lived on his land.

Political influence paralleled Meason's economic rise. He served one term in the state legislature in the 1780s and served on the state executive council in 1783. In 1791, he became an associate justice of the county courts. Meason contributed conspicuously to both trends discussed in this chapter. He greatly increased the size of his landholdings, participating in land consolidation with the other largest landowners. Also, he was a leading industrialist, creating new forms of wealth in addition to land.[1]

This wealth that increasingly came to be concentrated in the hands of the economic elite involved several components. Land was the major source of taxable wealth. Significant accumulations of land continued to occur in the border townships, and some accumulation occurred elsewhere, but it was definitely less noticeable in the river townships where early settlement was concentrated. Business enterprises, when added to landholdings, normally indicated significant wealth. Mill owners, in particular, formed a group large enough to be studied, and most of them were found among the top levels of the class structure. Owners of slaves also formed a sizeable group, and like the mill owners, they tended to be persons of wealth. Livestock was almost universally owned, but the wealthier people owned more, and perhaps of better quality. All of these forms of wealth generally were held by a few and, in combination, contributed to the growing concentration of wealth evident in the 1790s in western Pennsylvania.

Total Taxable Wealth

There can be no doubt that the wealthiest citizens of western Pennsylvania were richer as a class in the 1790s than were their counterparts in the 1780s. The amount of total taxable wealth controlled by the top 10 percent of taxable inhabitants increased over the decade by approximately 3 percent in Washington County and 7 percent in Fayette County. By the mid-1790s, the wealthiest decile of taxable persons in Washington County controlled 37 percent of that county's wealth, and in Fayette County, a similar group controlled 50 percent of the wealth. In the 1780s, this elite controlled more than 40 percent of the taxable wealth in eight townships, but in the 1790s, they controlled more than 40 percent of the wealth in fifteen townships. In five Fayette County townships, they controlled more than 50 percent of the wealth. At no time in either decade did they control less than 29 percent of the wealth of any township. The peak concentration occurred in the mid-1790s in Springhill Township, Fayette County, where the wealthiest decile owned 58.8 percent of the wealth (table 3.1).

On the other hand, at no time did the poorest decile ever control as much as 2 percent of the taxable wealth in any township. There were only three cases in either decade of the poorest decile controlling more than 1 percent of the total wealth. By the mid-1790s, the percentage of wealth controlled by these people dropped to zero in several townships. Thus, in terms of total taxable wealth, a definite trend toward a class structure with greater extremes of wealth was clearly evident. As might be expected, the greatest concentration of wealth came in the river townships and in certain northern interior townships. These were the regions that generally had the most landless persons and were the first to develop large-scale enterprises. There seems to be little doubt, therefore, that the intensity of settlement in a township was one of the factors that contributed directly to the growing diversity and matu-

TABLE 3.1

Mean Percentage of Wealth of the Richest and Poorest Deciles of Taxable Population, by Region and County, 1784–1796

Region/County	Richest Decile		Poorest Decile	
	1780s	*1790s*	*1780s*	*1790s*
Border				
Washington	31.7	33.5	1.02	0.54
Fayette	42.3	(a)	0.02	(a)
Interior				
Washington	33.1	38.1	0.59	0.32
Fayette	44.4	50.4	0.26	0.07
River				
Washington	39.2	40.6	0.23	0.14
Fayette	43.2	50.0	0.13	0.04
TOTAL				
Washington	34.7	37.3	0.61	0.34
Fayette	43.4	50.9	0.15	0.05

a. Since the records for Wharton Township, one of two Fayette border townships, are missing for the 1790s, a comparison figure would be misleading. The individual percentages for these two townships are: richest: Bullskin, 44.3–55.8, Wharton, 40.3–(missing); poorest: Bullskin, 0.04–.00, Wharton, 0.00–(missing).

rity found in the western Pennsylvania class structure in the 1790s.[2]

The Pattern of Land Accumulation

Many of the largest landowners in western Pennsylvania participated fully in the trend toward greater accumulation of wealth that caused increased disparity within the social structure. The wealthiest decile of landowners increased their aggregate control over the region from approximately 25 to 33 percent. To understand this process further, two groups of the largest landowners, those who owned 400 acres and those who owned larger tracts, have been studied and their actions over time compared. Although these groups combined do not coincide precisely with the top decile of landowners in either period, they provide a satisfactory approximation for studying their actions.[3]

Two basic facts stand out from these surveys. First is the startling revelation that nearly 90 percent of the largest landowners of the 1780s took no further part in the land consolidation that occurred between the 1780s and the 1790s. Rather, new settlers comprised the greatest proportion of the largest landowners in the 1790s. Second, the geographical distribution of these new landowners confirms that the greatest opportunity for advancement was in the more remote townships and that the maturation of the class structure made it more difficult to climb to the top elsewhere.

With regard to the first observation, only 11.7 percent of the largest landowners of the 1780s added to their holdings over the decade. (This includes the thirty-two landowners known to have increased their holdings and the one who probably did.) Nearly 75 percent failed to participate, including approximately 45 percent who had smaller holdings (35.9 percent were smaller and 8.4 percent probably smaller), and another 30 percent who disappeared completely (table 3.2). Among landowners of the 1790s, the largest single group among the leading landowners were new men who had entered the area since the Revolution. Thirty-nine percent of

TABLE 3.2
Changes in Status of Largest Landowners and
Origins of Largest Landowners of the 1790s by Region,
Washington and Fayette Counties, 1784–96

Changes/Origins	Border		Interior		River		Combined Counties	
	No.	%	No.	%	No.	%	No.	%
Changes in status, 1784–96								
Larger	13	9.7	12	17.6	7	8.5	32	11.3
Same	15	11.2	9	13.2	11	13.4	35	12.3
Smaller	44	32.8	25	36.8	33	40.3	102	35.9
Gone	45	33.6	17	25.0	23	28.1	85	29.9
Status unclear	17	12.7	5	7.4	8	9.7	30	10.6
Probably larger	0	0	0	0	1	1.2	1	0.4
Probably same	3	2.2	0	0	2	2.4	5	1.8
Probably smaller	14	10.5	5	7.4	5	6.1	24	8.4
TOTAL	134	100.0	68	100.0	82	100.0	284	100.0
Origins of 1793–96 Landowners								
New landowners	86	50.3	30	29.4	19	26.0	135	39.0
Large in 1780s	42	24.5	33	32.4	28	38.4	103	29.8
Improved from 1780s	37	21.7	31	30.4	19	26.0	87	25.1
Probably improved	6	3.5	8	7.8	7	9.6	21	6.1
TOTAL	171	100.0	102	100.0	73	100.0	346	100.0

the large landowners of the 1790s were new settlers. Another 31 percent, however, were local residents who had increased their holdings sufficiently to climb into the ranks of the largest landholders. The final 30 percent were those leaders who had maintained their status over the decade. For people of means and ability, there was still considerable opportunity to enter the region and move to the top of the socioeconomic ladder, contrary to the general pattern of smaller landholdings and more landless persons.

Nevertheless, this pattern of opportunity was not uniform. The areas of greatest land accumulation were the border and southern interior townships. The least opportunity to accumulate more land existed in the river and northern interior townships. Border townships were the most newly settled areas and had many absentee speculators. In the 1790s these townships had lower percentages of early settlers with large acreages or settlers who had significantly increased their acreages. These border regions were thus attractive to settlers like Thomas Ryerson, who accumulated a vast 40,000-acre holding on the southwest border of Washington County.

For interior townships, the patterns were more varied. The greatest opportunity for new settlers existed in south-central Washington County. Less oppportunity to become a large landowner existed in the other interior townships with greater early settlement. The more heavily settled river townships had the least opportunity, and the fewest number of very large landowners. The greatest portion of large landowners in the river townships were the leaders of the 1780s who remained, followed by those who had acquired enough additional land to climb into the top ranks. Only nineteen new persons were able to come in and acquire 400 acres or more in these river townships, and the same also held true for the northern interior townships of Washington County, where only four new major landowners appeared. It is again evident that opportunity tended to follow the settlement pattern from river to border, from the center to the edges. Becoming a major landowner in the 1790s was easier in the newer areas, but more difficult in the settled, stable areas.

This may be further illustrated by comparing these landowners on the basis of the size of their holdings (table 3.3). The 400-acre landowners and those with more than 400 acres did not behave in the same manner. More of the largest landowners disappeared by the 1790s, especially in the border areas, where the turnover of speculative holdings was greatest. More of this group decreased the size of their holdings, but the greatest change (64 percent including probable owners) came in the river townships, while the least change came in the border townships. Also, a greater number of the largest landowners were able to increase their holdings, but very few were in the river townships. On the other hand, the staying power of the 400-acre landholder was four times that of his larger neighbor. Twenty-three percent of the 400-acre holders still had their full tract, but only 5.5 percent of those whose holdings were above 400 acres did.

TABLE 3.3

Changes in Status of 400-Aces Landowners and
Landowners with More Than 400 Acres by Region,
Washington and Fayette Counties, 1784–1796

Changes in Status 1784–1796	Border		Interior		River		Combined Counties	
	400 Acres	Above 400	400 Acres	Above 400	400 Acres	Above 400	400 Acres	Above 400
Larger	6.0	13.4	11.8	23.5	10.5	6.8	8.6	13.8
Same	16.4	6.0	23.5	2.9	23.7	4.6	20.1	4.8
Smaller	28.3	37.3	32.4	41.2	21.1	56.8	27.4	44.1
Gone	26.9	40.3	23.5	26.5	34.2	22.7	28.1	31.8
Status unclear	22.4	3.0	8.8	5.9	10.5	9.1	15.8	5.5
Probably larger	0	0	0	0	2.6	0	0.7	0
Probably same	4.5	0	0	0	2.6	2.3	2.9	0.7
Probably smaller	17.9	3.0	8.8	5.9	5.3	6.8	12.2	4.8
TOTAL	100.0	100.0	100.0	100.0	100.0	100.0	100.0	100.0
N	67	67	34	34	38	44	139	145

This pattern seems to reflect a basic difference in motivation between the two groups. The 400-acre tract was the normal limit in Virginia-controlled areas prior to 1780 and in
Pennsylvania after 1784. Many persons able to take this full
allowance were people of means whose primary motive was to
establish a viable farm. Those aggregating more than 400
acres exhibited a speculative bent, acquiring additional lands
and selling excess lands when profitable. This difference in
motivation also tended to be associated with the degree of
settlement in a given region. The ability of a person to acquire
large landholdings was greater in the less-settled regions and
less so in the more established river townships. By the 1790s,
the largest landowners in the older townships found fewer
new lands to add to their holdings, but the continuing population growth presented excellent opportunities for them to
dispose of their excess lands.

In summary, these surveys of the largest landowners indicate that much of the land consolidation that occurred between
the 1780s and the 1790s resulted from new landowners in the
border townships, not from increases by the great landowners

of the 1780s. Some of these new landowners, as the next chapter will indicate, had acquired very large speculative tracts, but there were also new residents who bought large acreages. Upward mobility for some local residents was also possible, and 31 percent of the larger landowners of the 1790s had increased their holdings enough over the previous decade to become major landowners. Together, these new landowners and the earlier settlers who acquired more land comprised 70 percent of the great landowners of the 1790s. The landowning elite of the 1780s had neither the power nor the continuity to keep out new members. The area was too new; too many opportunities still existed. Nevertheless, the fluidity of the early years of settlement was passing. It existed as it had originally, only in the border townships. In the river townships, fewer people could now purchase very large estates, and the remaining great landowners were better able to dominate. Class lines, insofar as landownership defined them, were hardening; opportunity to own large tracts was declining. In these older areas, few lands remained to be claimed. The pressure of population—due both to births and to newcomers—forced land subdivision. Other things were also beginning to compete with land as the major indicator of wealth. The fact that three of the new major landowners of the 1790s were local, industrial enterprises indicates where much of the new opportunity lay and what the future had in store.

Business Enterprise and Other Forms of Wealth

The most significant forms of alternative wealth were the various frontier enterprises such as gristmills and sawmills, ferries and distilleries, and by the 1790s, nascent industries, especially in iron. Slaves and large herds of livestock also were concentrated in the hands of a few. All these additional forms of wealth were closely integrated with landownership to create the concentrated wealth of the 1790s. In order to indicate the close interrelationship among these forms of wealth, the largest landowner in each Fayette County township is compared to the person who had the largest tax valuations. Then, three of these forms of wealth—mills, slaves, and livestock—are surveyed to place their owners within the class structure. It will be evident that mills and slaves were concentrated in the hands of the wealthy and that only a few people had large herds of livestock.

The comparison of the largest landowners with the wealthiest persons in each Fayette County township clearly exhibits the close interrelationship between land and other taxable wealth (table 3.4). (Washington County, with trends less pronounced than Fayette County, did not illustrate this as well.) Land was no longer the only guarantee of wealth. The manner in which land was developed was becoming important also. Some sort of business enterprise was joined with land by the richest settlers in every township, with the exception of Bullskin, where unseated, speculative lands were the major form of wealth exihibited by the richest taxpayer. In half of the townships, the largest landowners were not the wealthiest citizens. Even where the largest landowners were the wealthiest citizens, they also had various enterprises intimately connected with the land. As the economy of western Pennsylvania matured, land became less important as the fundamental source of wealth and livelihood, both to the very rich and to the growing body of landless poor.

The background of these economic leaders of Fayette County illustrates this consolidation process. For example, in Georges Township, Prescilla Rees was the widow of Jonathan Rees, who had been one of the county's wealthiest millers for several years. He had substantial acreage, but his mills were the real source of his wealth. John Hayden was in the process of becoming an ironmaster. His first attempt in partnership with John Nicholson of Philadelphia, who served a term as state comptroller, had failed, and he had just sold his bloomery to Jonathan Hayden. (It is interesting that Jonathan Rees once owned the bloomery land.) Hayden persevered, and by 1798 his property totaled 3,458 acres and was valued at $10,680. Indicative of the value industry added to his land, Hayden's 38-acre tract containing his furnace was worth $5,000, and a 57-acre tract with a forge, $500. In addition to other lands, he had over 2,600 acres of mountain land worth only fifty cents an

TABLE 3.4

Largest Landowner and Wealthiest Person, Fayette County Townships, 1796

| Township/Person | Land | | Livestock | | Mills | Other Taxable Wealth | | Slaves | Total |
	Acres	Value ($)	Horses	Cattle		Stills	Other		Value ($)
Bullskin									
Johnson and Co.	4,200	1,050	(unseated)						1,050
Edward and Owen Jones	1,800	5,400	(unseated)						5,400
Franklin									
Isaac Meason	3,200	—	17	2	2		iron	1	10,864
Georges									
John Hayden	2,248	398		1	1				472
Priscilla Rees	620	1,000			x				1,000
German									
Andrew Long	500	2,000	4	12	1			1	2,425
Andrew Rabb	400	1,500	4	7	3	4			3,943
Luzerne									
Reason Virgin	450	3,600	2	3	1				3,723
Rees Cadwallader	255	6,484	2	13	3		town	2	7,614
Springhill									
Philip Pearce	631	3,365	8	3		2		1	3,795
Tyrone									
Turnbull and Co.	1,069	—					iron		1,950
Washington									
Edward Cook	600	—	3	10	x	x	11 buildings	3	5,060

Note: With the change in tax laws beginning in 1796, assessors no longer always listed each enterprise separately but, instead, often lumped land, buildings, and improvements into a single sum. Thus, where the 1796 assessment is not specific, but some form of wealth is known to have existed immediately prior to or immediately after 1796, it has been so indicated by x. The Georges Township information is for 1795 and was listed in pounds but has been converted into dollars at the going rate of £3 = $8. Dollars were used on the assessments for the first time in 1796.

acre. Economic leaders in German and Luzerne townships also illustrate the increased value business enterprise added to land in comparison to large-scale farming. Andrew Rabb, who was a prominent miller and the county's largest distiller (he had four stills totaling a 600-gallon capacity compared to a normal still of 40- to 75-gallon capacity), easily exceeded the wealth of Andrew Long, a farmer with a larger tract of land. Likewise, Rees Cadwallader had only moderate acreage, but as proprietor of a river town and owner of three mills (gristmill, sawmill, and fulling mill), he easily outdistanced leading landowner Reason Virgin.[4]

In Springhill, Philip Pearce had a pair of stills in the 1790s, but land remained the major factor in his leading position. However, if Albert Gallatin's personal estate (350 acres) and his company's lands (550 acres) were combined, he would have been the largest landowner in Springhill in 1796. Furthermore, with his new gun works added to his glass plant, plus the proprietorship of New Geneva, which he was just then laying out, he soon would be unquestionably the townships' wealthiest citizen. The county's wealthiest citizen in the 1780s, who was still doing well, was Edward Cook. As noted earlier he came to Fayette County before the Revolution, opened a store, and quickly moved into other enterprises. He owned, at various times, mills, stills, slaves, one of the earliest stone houses, and some 3,000 acres of land. He also served in elective local and state office, the military, and the county judiciary. He and Gallatin both played major roles in the Whiskey Rebellion, and they were among the most influential men in the county.[5]

Turnbull and Company in Tyrone, the first iron furnace west of the mountains, was in production by 1789. The fact that this company was the wealthiest taxpayer and the largest landowner in its township is indicative of the new kind of wealth that appeared among the economic leaders as western Pennsylvania matured. John Hayden and Albert Gallatin were in the process of accomplishing the same thing, and so was Isaac Meason, perhaps the county's outstanding example of an enterprising individual. The company of Meason and Dillon was begun in the early 1790s, and their Union furnace was the second one west of the mountains. Meason, like Cook, came early and quickly established himself on a large tract in Tyrone Township. He soon expanded his lands, and transferred his activity to Franklin Township, where he bought most of the deceased Thomas Gist's estate. Gist had been an early guide for the Ohio Company, and his property became the Meason home place. Gallatin's Swiss friend, John Badollet, marveled at Meason's activity in 1793 as he "reflected that a dreary solitude had been changed in the space of a year into a place of activity where perhaps a hundred souls where [sic] kept busy and fed."[6]

By 1796, Meason employed a tenth of the taxable population of Franklin township on his 3,200 acres, but he further increased his holdings that year. In 1797, his 600-acre furnace tract, though worth just a dollar an acre for the land, was worth another $8,600 with the furnace and mills on it. He was also developing a 300-acre site on the Youghiogheny River (value $1,800) into the town of New Haven. Another 300-acre tract (value $300) had a forge and a sawmill on it worth $500, while a small gristmill stood on another 500-acre tract. In addition, there were 900 more acres from the Gist estate and 1,700 acres of mountain land. Meason's total lands in 1797 were 4,600 acres, worth $12,000, and his total taxable wealth was $22,684. Just the value of his twenty horses ($1,200) was seven times the value of the total wealth owned by the township's median taxable person, and his county tax for 1797, $31.44 ½, was five times as great as the next richest person, who paid $6; and six times as great as the next five, who paid $5 each. Certainly, Meason personified, and the other economic leaders participated in, the successful development of business enterprises that greatly enhanced personal wealth and contributed most significantly to the growing concentration of wealth that occurred between the mid-1780s and the mid-1790s.

Among the other forms of taxable wealth, one group of entrepreneurs who can be charted over a period of time and placed within the class structure are the millers (table 3.5). Thirty Fayette County millers have been ranked in terms of their comparative wealth.[7] In 1785, only ten of these thirty

TABLE 3.5
Percentage of Millers in the Top Decile of Landowners
and Tax Valuation, by Region,
Fayette and Washington Counties, 1785–1796

County by Region	Top Decile 1785			Top Decile 1793–1796		
	Township Land	County Land	Value	Township Land	County Land	Value
Fayette						
Border	33	33	50	67	67	67
Interior	44	44	67	67	67	83
River	27	27	33	42	42	83
TOTAL	33	33	47	52	52	81
Washington						
Border	—	—	—	25	29	42
Interior	—	—	—	27	22	54
River	—	—	—	29	20	63
TOTAL	—	—	—	27	23	54

millers were among the top decile of landowners in either
their township or the county, yet fourteen (47 percent) were
in the top decile in total wealth. Between 1785 and 1796, nine
of these millers disappeared. Of the remaining twenty-one,
eleven (52 percent) were now within the top decile of landowners in their township or the county, and seventeen of the
twenty-one (81 percent) were now within the top decile in
valuation. Eight of those who disappeared were not ranked in
any top decile, but the ninth to disappear was Thomas Gist,
the county's largest landowner in 1785, who had died. It is
evident, therefore, that the mill owners of Fayette County
participated in the trend toward consolidating wealth both by
eliminating their smaller, possibly less efficient rivals, and by
improving their own position. Their counterparts in Washington County probably did likewise. At least the majority of the
ninety-six millers in Washington County were also, by 1793, in
the top decile in tax valuation.

In both Fayette and Washington counties, large landholdings were not necessary for a miller to do well financially.
Many were economic leaders but not among the largest land-

owners. In Fayette, in 1785, the median miller had only 200 acres, the same size as the county's median acreage. Six millers had 100 acres or less; seven of them had 500 acres or more. On rare occasions, a miller had as few as two acres, but the very largest landowner in Fayette County in both 1785 and 1796, and in Washington County in 1793, had mills.

Land, therefore, was not necessarily important in gaging the economic status of a miller. George Tobin, for example, had only 75 acres, but his name frequently appeared in the county court proceedings, and he was a well-known member of the merchant community. Jonathan Hill had only 105 acres in 1785, yet Hill was sued and brought suit perhaps more than any other person in Fayette County. He speculated in mountain land, and in spite of numerous judgments against him, was taxed for 550 acres ten years later. Men like Hill and Tobin were probably merchant gristmillers, purchasing grain, then grinding and barreling it for shipment. Unlike the merchant miller, there were local millers who normally ground grain for their neighbors for a percentage of the grain or flour. A number of early millers probably did this, but commercial milling became increasingly important.[8]

The fact remains, however, that owning a mill demanded a certain amount of capital, and grain mills, being more permanent structures than sawmills, required a considerable investment. In Fayette County, gristmills were valued from £40 to £150 in 1785, and in Washington in 1793 from £5 to £400. (Some of the great variations in value are undoubtedly due to the lack of uniform assessment procedures.) Sawmills required less capital and ranged in value from £20 to £50 in Fayette and £2 to £100 in Washington. Those fulling mills that had been estabished were approximately equal in value to the sawmills, ranging in value from £15 to £60. In general, then, mill owners were among the wealthiest individuals in western Pennsylvania; and along with the large landowners, and the new industrialists, they were the economic leaders of the region.

Slaves were another form of taxable wealth closely associated with the economic leaders (table 3.6). Slavery was, officially, a dying institution in Pennsylvania during the period

TABLE 3.6
Percentage of Slaveowners in the Top Decile of Landowners
and Tax Valuation, by Region,
Fayette and Washington Counties, 1785–1793

Region	Top Decile, Fayette 1785			Top Decile, Washington 1793		
	Township Land	County Land	Value	Township Land	County Land	Value
Border	20.5	29.5	63.6	28.6	24.5	75.5
Interior	27.3	24.2	60.6	30.6	26.7	70.0
River	42.8	42.8	57.1	38.7	51.6	74.2
TOTAL	25.0	28.6	61.9	31.8	32.7	73.6

under study. Nevertheless, it still had some strength and generally signified concentrated wealth. Pennsylvania enacted a gradual abolition law in 1780 which required the registration of all slaves or they would become free. No slave child born after March 1780 was officially considered a slave, but rather was considered to have the same status as a four-year indenture until age twenty-eight, at which time he or she would become free. The law was not enforced in much of western Pennsylvania until after the boundary dispute with Virginia was settled. Once a settlement was reached, dissident settlers were given until 1 January 1783 to register their slaves and comply with the law.[9] Thus, 795 slaves were registered in Westmoreland County (which then included Fayette) and another 443 were registered in Washington County by 1783. Both Edward Cook and Isaac Meason, for example, registered slaves. Many slaves remained throughout the course of the next two decades. The 1790 census listed 834 slaves in all of western Pennsylvania, and the second census still listed 431 in 1800. In 1790 in Fayette and Washington counties there were 282 and 265 slaves, respectively; and by 1800, there were 92 and 106, respectively.[10]

The available tax assessments for Fayette County listed 163 slaves in 1785, while the Washington assessments contained 154 slaves in 1793.[11] Slaves appeared in every township except two: Wharton, the mountain township in Fayette County, and Franklin, a sparsely settled, southern interior township in Washington County. Most of the slaves were in the river townships—50 percent of those in Washington and 55 percent of those in Fayette counties. Most slave owners had only a single slave or, at most, two or three. Only ten Fayette County residents were taxed for more than three slaves in 1785, and only two Washington County residents were taxed for more than three slaves in 1793.[12]

Slaves were obviously not an important source of labor; there were very few plantations where slave labor was a prominent factor. For the most part, slaves seemed to serve as domestics or as farm laborers for some of the better-off yeomen. Nevertheless, slaves were expensive. They ranged in value from £10 to £40 or more. To own a slave demanded some wealth. In fact, most slave owners were among the wealthy class. Fully 68.5 percent of all slave owners were among the richest 10 percent of the settlers, although less than a third of them were among the top 10 percent of the landowners. Slaves in western Pennsylvania, therefore, were not owned because large lands demanded their labor, but rather they were owned for domestic service or farm help, and, undoubtedly, for status. Slave ownership, therefore, also indicates concentrated wealth.

The final form of wealth found on the tax assessments, livestock, was fundamentally different from mills or slaves. The latter were owned only by a few people, and these owners tended to be definitely upper class. Livestock, on the contrary, was the most widely owned form of property, surpassing even land in the breadth of its ownership pattern. The concentration that occurred here, therefore, involved property affecting a broad spectrum of people.

Two basic trends stand out with regard to livestock. First is the fact that very few people owned large herds of livestock in either decade, and the upper limits in the size of herds did not vary greatly. Neither was there much difference in the number of persons with large herds—ten animals or more—although there was some increase in those owning six, seven, or eight. However, the vast majority of people, approximately 90 percent, owned two or fewer horses and three or fewer cattle. Owning a large herd was reserved for a select few (table 3.7).

TABLE 3.7

Percentages of Taxable Population Owning Livestock, by Size of Herd, Washington County and Fayette County

Size of Herd	Washington County				Fayette County			
	Horses		Cattle		Horses		Cattle	
	1784	1793	1784	1793	1785	1796	1785	1796
0	16.2	22.5	24.7	19.6	21.1	34.5	28.7	28.8
1	28.0	33.8	19.2	23.0	26.9	32.6	22.3	30.3
2	37.2	33.3	28.1	31.1	34.8	23.8	25.5	21.0
3	13.0	7.5	14.9	15.4	10.0	5.4	14.0	9.5
4	4.1	2.1	7.5	6.5	4.9	2.2	5.6	5.2
5	0.8	0.6	2.9	2.5	1.1	0.8	2.0	2.5
6 and over[a]	0.7	0.2	2.7	1.9	1.2	0.7	1.9	2.7

a. Herds of livestock ranged as large as: Washington County: horses, 1784 to 13, 1793 to 10; cattle, 1784 to 16, 1793 to 20. Fayette County: horses, 1785 to 12, 1796 to 17; cattle, 1785 to 15, 1796 to 13.

The second trend, perhaps a surprising one, is that in spite of an obviously improving agricultural situation, the numbers of animals owned by the settlers did not increase significantly. In fact, an increasing percentage of people did not own a single horse in the 1790s, but a greater percentage of people than before now owned a few cattle. In Fayette County, for example, only 21.1 percent of the taxable population had no horses in 1785, but 34.5 percent had no horses in 1796; 82.8 percent had two or fewer horses in 1785, but 90.9 percent had two or fewer in 1796. The same trend was evident in the Washington County figures for horses. On the other hand, the figures for cattle indicate that the number of people owning at least a cow or two increased by a few percentage points in each county.

Some care is necessary in analyzing these numbers, however. In both counties, an increasing number of people at the bottom of society could not afford the basic means of transportation, a single horse. Cattle ownership, an indicator of subsistence agriculture, did increase. More people owned a cow or two in the 1790s. Since only "horned cattle" were taxed, this indicates that more lower-class people had breeding livestock, and the yearly increase could be used for meat without destroying future productivity. Especially in Washington County, the proportion of people owning no cattle at all declined over the decade. Thus, the figures for horses confirm the trend toward a more stratified society, but the figures for cattle suggest that those on the bottom were better able to deal with their lower position.

Thus, the socioeconomic maturity evident in the concentration of other forms of wealth is not as prominent in livestock. Because livestock was owned by so many, overall trends must be viewed carefully. Nevertheless, the same small proportion of the population that had large herds in the 1780s still had them in the 1790s. For example, the very wealthiest individual in each county in the 1790s also had the largest herd of livestock. Isaac Meason in Fayette County had seventeen horses; Thomas Ryerson in Washington County had twenty cattle. Furthermore, fifteen of sixteen persons owning more than five horses in Fayette County in 1796 ranked in the top decile in total taxable wealth. In Washington in 1793, seven of ten persons owning more than five horses ranked in the top decile. Large herds simply indicated wealth in both decades. To own more than two horses or three cattle at either period almost automatically placed one in the top decile of all livestock owners and signaled significant wealth.

Other forms of taxable wealth were not as clearly associated with the upper classes. Ferry owners, tanners, and stillers, for example, ran the gamut in economic status. These people were as likely to be landless as to have large landholdings. When they were wealthy—like the owners of large herds of livestock—they tended to be the same landowners, millers, slave owners, and industrialists already singled out as the economic leaders of western Pennsylvania. It was this small, dynamic group of economic leaders who were most responsible for the growing concentration of wealth that spearheaded the transformation of western Pennsylvania between the 1780s and 1790s. Two other groups, landlords and town proprietors, were also economic leaders. The roles they played in the maturing economic and class structures were important ones, each worthy of individual discussion in the next two chapters.

4   *Tenancy and Absenteeism*

> I told them I would make them a last offer and this
> was—the whole tract at 25 S. pr. acre, the money to
> be paid at three annual payments with Interest;—or
> to become Tenants upon leases of 999 years, at the
> annual Rent of Ten pounds pr. Ct. pr. Ann . . . they
> then determined to stand suit for the land.[1]

THIS ENTRY from the diary of George Washington in 1784
introduces the highly interrelated subjects of absentee ownership, landlords, and tenants. The existence of tenancy is not
in question; it is the extent and the characteristics of tenancy
as an important factor in the transformation of western Pennsylvania that are the concern of this chapter. Washington had
tenements in both Fayette County and Washington County.
Among the motives for his 1784 trip to western Pennsylvania
were to inspect his lands, deal with unfavorable tenant relationships, and explore a transportation link between the headwaters of the Potomac River and the Monongahela and Ohio
rivers. As the diary makes clear, the people on his land in
Washington County disputed his claim to the land, and rather
than become long-term tenants, they chose to go to court.
Ultimately, Washington received a favorable ruling, but he
never was able to follow up his court victory and reclaim the
land. Washington was clearly an absentee landlord, but was he
typical? Probably not. Landlord-tenant relationships proved
to be widespread in western Pennsylvania, but wealthy absentees were not the primary reason for its existence. Rather,
tenancy was a solution for the increasing number of landless
people coming into the region as it matured. The relationship
was a mutual one, providing land for the landless and major

improvements to undeveloped land for the landowners, both local and absentee.

Tenancy

Discussing tenancy in western Pennsylvania during the 1780s is like describing an amorphous cloud; it is obviously there, but its size and shape are nearly indeterminable. Perhaps this is why earlier commentators have either played down the existence of tenancy or ignored it altogether. Nevertheless, more recent scholarship clearly recognizes the existence of tenancy and is beginning to define its scale and role in early American development.[2] The assessments of the 1780s only hint at the existence of tenancy. Not until 1796 do the tax assessments begin to reveal its true size. Neither Washington County nor Westmoreland County assessments for the 1780s, published in the *Pennsylvania Archives,* give any indication of landlord-tenant relationships. Only the original returns from Fayette County in 1785 give indication of such relationships. These appear in five of nine townships and are indicated by entries such as the following from Franklin Township:

Samuel Boden—2 horses, 2 cattle	£15
landlord's part—300 acres, good land	£120
Joseph Hall—1 horse, 2 cattle	£10
landlord's part—150 acres, medium land	£45

By these and similar designations, sixty-nine cases of tenancy have been discovered in these five Fayette County townships. In three of the five townships—Franklin, Springhill, and Washington—the number of landlords was 15 to 16 percent of the landed population, while in the other two—German and Georges—landlords were only 7 and 9 percent of the landed population, respectively. Collectively, these landlords accounted for 12.8 percent of the landed population in the five townships. Assuming the other four townships also had tenants, but possibly expecting fewer tenants in the two mountainous border townships, a reasonable estimate of the number of landlords would be 10 percent of the landed population. An estimate of the number of tenants living on these landlord tracts would be 6.2 percent of the total population of Fayette County. The extent of tenancy in Washington and Westmoreland counties was probably similar to or a little less than in Fayette County, since they had fewer landless persons.[3]

The 1793 manuscript returns for Washington County also have only scattered suggestions of tenancy. No *landlord's part* designations appeared in Washington, but the term *estate* was used in seemingly similar circumstances. The 1796 assessment for Strabane Township confirms that these estate markings were probably the means used in Washington County for indicating landlord's parts. Take for example the Strabane entry of Nathaniel Burdoo, a farmer. He was assessed for two horses and two cows, value £28. His entry also included 100 acres, 20 cleared, and two cabins, value £200; then comes the phrase "Estate, Morgan, Phila[delphia]."[4] There were, in 1793, eighty-eight estate or similar entries in Washington County. Here, too, they were not uniformly spread throughout the county. Five townships—Peters, Somerset, Strabane, Morris, and Donegal—accounted for fifty-seven of the eighty-eight indications of tenancy, while ten townships had no indications at all. In these five townships, 8.6 percent of the landowners were landlords, while 5.6 percent of the total population in these townships were tenants. These figures are a little less than the estimates for Fayette County in the 1780s but close enough to suggest that the kind of tenancy indicated by these notations was fairly uniformly spread throughout western Pennsylvania, at a rate for landlords of perhaps 10 percent of the landed population, and for tenants, of 5 to 6 percent of the total population.

These early indications of tenancy prove woefully inadequate, however, in the face of certain returns in 1796. Two townships in particular, one in each county, present full accounts of the number of renters and tenants. In these two townships—Cecil in Washington County, (where George Washington had his dispute with local squatters on his land) and Luzerne in Fayette County—the tenancy rate for the total population was four times the 5 to 6 percent rate mentioned above. Twenty-five percent of the taxable population of Cecil

Township were listed as tenants in 1796, and 20.9 percent of the taxable population in Luzerne were termed renters. There was no indication in the years immediately preceding 1796 that tenancy existed in either township in such quantity. In 1794, thirty-seven adults in Cecil Township were landless. Two years later, seventeen were gone, but seventeen of the remaining twenty now appeared as tenants. Sixteen of their seventeen landlords had been in the township in 1794; only one was new. Of the other three landless people of 1794, one was a tailor still landless in 1796, and the other two had acquired land; one had 270 acres of unseated land, the other had 100 acres, apparently obtained from his father. For example, in 1794, Benjamin Carter and Nicholas Cassidy were landless residents, but were gone by 1796. However, James Craig and Francis Henry, also landless in 1794, appeared in 1796 as tenants, respectively, of John Donald, the owner of 400 acres, and Samuel Logan, the owner of 200 acres. These two landlords each had a second tenent, both artisans, a reed maker and a cooper. Considering that every other township had its share of landless persons with no apparent means of support, and that these people appeared in 1796 in Cecil and Luzerne as tenants, one must conclude that the incidence of tenancy was much higher than previously thought.

The issue becomes even more complicated when we examine the assessment for East Bethlehem in 1796. The East Bethlehem assessor specified those who were inmates, defined on the assessment as "persons who have no land in s[ai]d township." Of 270 taxables on the list, 104 inmates and 37 single freemen comprised the landless population. The assessment did not indicate who was a tenant, but did specify occupations. Forty-seven of the inmates and six of the freemen were farmers, including three who added a trade to farming. Thus, 37.5 percent of these landless appear to be tenant farmers, 19.7 percent of the taxable population. The farmer-inmates almost all lived on land owned by farmer-landowners. A few lived on absentee-owned land, or land of widows or the aged or an occasional artisan who had a tenant maintain his farm. Thus, it appears again that something like 20 percent of the population of a township could be classified as tenant farmers. Many of the other inmates were artisans or laborers living with landed persons in the township. This detailed information on inmates also suggests a complex society, where a variety of renting, trading work for living space, or working shares existed. The true nature and extent of these interrelationships can never be fully known, but easy generalizations about frontier society are no longer possible.[5]

If approximately 20 percent of the taxable population of western Pennsylvania were tenants, this adds a significant new perspective on the class structure. First, it helps explain the status of a number of the landless persons in the region. In addition, it raises the immediate question as to why earlier indications of tenancy were so inadequate. Finally, since tenancy was so widespread, it makes questions concerning the status and condition of these settlers that much more important.

Scattered evidence suggests that the reason for the discrepancy in the amount of tenancy indicated on early assessments and those of 1796 was simply that these earlier tenancies probably involved absentee landlords only, while the 1796 ones included all landlords, absentee and local. Local officials had no difficulty keeping records straight and collecting all taxes due when the landlord was local, because such a landlord would be charged for his land and cattle like everyone else. However, with absentee landlords, a specific notation probably seemed necessary to some officials. Under the law, the local tenant was responsible for the taxes due on an absentee landlord's land. If the absentee did not pay, the tenant was liable for the tax. The tenant, in turn, was protected by law to the extent that he could deduct these taxes from his rent, or could recover them by debt action in court for which the landlord had to pay the costs.[6] Therefore, the problem of trying to collect all the taxes legitimately due county governments from absentee landlords seems to be sufficient reason for these special notations on some assessments.

Other evidence corroborates this conclusion. In the example of an estate in Strabane Township in 1796 given earlier, the landlord was Morgan and Company of Philadelphia. There were, in fact, three estate tracts belonging to Morgan on that

1796 return. Two of the tenants on these lands appeared on the 1793 Strabane return with estate designations, while the third was landless. The two landless inmates in East Bethlehem in 1796, who were listed with estates of 660 and 350 acres in 1793, were, in 1796, living on the land of Joshua Gilpin of Philadelphia and Thomas Cooper of Hartford County, Maryland.

Among the 1785 tenants with landlord's part designations in Franklin Township was Gilbert Simpson, who was in partnership with, and the agent of, George Washington. As we have seen, it was partially to dissolve this unsatisfactory partnership and to check on other tenements in western Pennsylvania that Washington made his 1784 trip.[7] Also, the assessment for Washington Township, Fayette County, identified many of the landlords charged with these lands. Of eleven so identified, none were township residents. (There might be one exception if a Captain Matson is Peter Matson, but this is doubtful since Peter was not assessed for any land.) A couple of these landlords lived in neighboring Franklin and Menallen townships. One was a minister from Westmoreland County, and another, renting three tracts, was a leading citizen and county officer in Washington County. Thus, the terms *landlord's part* and *estate* apparently indicated absentee ownership.

On the basis of these bits of evidence, therefore, it seems likely that the tenancy indicated prior to 1796 involved absentee landlords only. If such designations were distributed with reasonable uniformity, the above approximation from the 1780s—that one landowner in every ten was a landlord—now becomes that one landowner in ten was an absentee landlord whose tenants comprised 5 to 6 percent of the total population. In addition, however, it has been shown that another 15 to 20 percent of the taxable population of 1796 were also tenants, but on land owned locally. If 20 or more percent of the population were tenants in 1796, probably more than 5 to 6 percent were tenants in the 1780s. Because there was a higher percentage of landed persons and a smaller population, tenancy may not have reached 20 percent in the 1780s, but it very probably doubled the 5 to 6 percent rate. A total tenancy rate, therefore, of 12 percent in the 1780s and of 20 percent in the 1790s can serve as reasonable estimates.[8] One caveat, however, is that most of these examples come from the more developed areas and may overstate the amount of tenancy found in the border regions. Nevertheless, it is clear that the maturation process in western Pennsylvania involved an increase in tenant relationships.

What sort of relationship existed between these tenants and their landlords? Was tenancy an adequate means of livelihood? Was tenancy an aid or a restriction to social mobility? Here again, evidence is fragmentary, but some tentative conclusions can be drawn.

Little is known of the official relationship that existed between landlord and tenant. The few cases involving prominent absentee landlords do provide some guidance. In the case of George Washington, definite long-term leases were offered to those occupying his land in Cecil Township. He had a specific agreement with Gilbert Simpson, who was chief tenant on his land in Franklin Township, Fayette County. In the case of Joshua Gilpin, who had tenants in Luzerne and East Bethlehem townships, specific rent amounts were established. Likewise, in a case from Bedford County, specific terms for seven-year "improvement" leases were spelled out by the agent on behalf of the absentee landlord.[9] Undoubtedly, each landlord-tenant relationship had specific terms, and rents occasionally were even specified on the assessments. Nevertheless, the bond between landlord and tenant must have been fairly loose, benefiting the landlord by having his land cleared, and providing the tenant with a temporary means of livelihood. The turnover of tenants was very high. Legal action to maintain a tenant contract or for damages for breaking a lease were virtually unheard of in the county courts. Had the institution of tenancy been a formal, highly structured one, surely some legal indication would remain in the court records, but none has. In the fluid frontier society, apparently both landlord and tenant accepted tenancy as a loose arrangement.[10]

One explanation may be found in the agreement Joshua Gilpin had with his tenant Henry Harlan. Visiting Harlan's tenement in Luzerne Township, Gilpin noted in his journal the amount of rent, then stated: "But [he] has laid out all the rent for 11 years in improvements." Apparently, rents did not necessarily return to the landlord, but were spent on the property by the tenant. Washington failed to reap profits from Simpson's tract in Franklin Township and, in fact, he periodically had to advance additional funds to Simpson. He was disappointed that his tenants had shown little inclination to undertake meaningful improvements. He complained that his mill in Franklin Township that Simpson built was deteriorating and would bring in little income. His Washington County lands were occupied by several families who disputed his title to the land. Even though he successfully undertook ejectment proceedings against them, he received no long-term benefit. Israel Shreve, who later rented the Washington tract tenanted by Simpson, wrote that the lands had been "rented for repairs only."[11] For any landlord, a tenant could just turn up "gone" one morning, as Andrew Dehaven of Somerset Township apparently did in 1793. Landlords clearly benefited from improvements made by tenants, but the problem of making a tenant concerned about property that was not his own faced every landlord, and for an absentee like Washington or Gilpin, the problems were compounded. Thus, rents based on improvements over which landlord and tenant could disagree provided a very subjective basis for a binding legal contract.

The relationship between tenants and local landlords is even more cloudy. One travel account suggests the kind of relationship this was. A "Swiss Farmer" stated that "very many landowners lend their lands to people who are careful and hardworking in return for half the yield, and in addition furnish them with cattle and agricultural implements."[12] Clearly, this is the basis of the *inmate* relationship. A number of landless families lived and worked the lands of local owners, but letters are lacking to explain the exact relationship. From the assessments, however, it is clear that not only farmers but also artisans and laborers lived as inmates. Their status seems just the same as that of tenants living on absentee-owned land.

The condition and social status of tenants is also difficult to pinpoint. Some renters were apparently well-off. A few were landowners who, for some reason, also rented a second tract. A 300-acre landowner in Georges Township rented another 150 acres; a miller in Springhill rented the land for his mill. Gilbert Simpson had a small tract of his own besides the 300 acres he rented from George Washington, and Simpson could even afford to own slaves. He was assessed for five, but at least two had been sent with him by Washington. Nevertheless, most of the tenants were poorer people. The great majority had little taxable property—perhaps a horse or two and one or two cows. What little can be discovered about their rents suggests that they were fairly high. Rents ran about £10 to £15, and for some tenants, were approximately equal to the value of their taxable personal property.[13] A tenant required to pay £10 or £12 but having taxable property of his own (primarily livestock) worth only that or less obviously was not in a strong capital position. Furthermore, considering the amount of cleared land available to a tenant—fifteen to twenty acres—and the estimates of subsistence needs and crop yields that have been developed by historians, a tenant probably made an adequate living but had a very narrow margin for a bad year.[14]

Insolvent debtor petitions to the county courts indicate that persons were forced into bankruptcy for being unable to pay debts smaller than a £10 annual rent. Nine such petitions came before Washington County courts in early 1795. Of the six for which a specific amount was stated, four were for debts of £10 or less, one for £16, and one for £26. Thus, considering all these factors, the economic condition of tenants in western Pennsylvania was tolerable, probably adequate to provide a basic living. Some probably did well. Many could provide for their family at a rough subsistence level, but the system allowed little margin for error, misjudgment, or a poor harvest.

Tenancy was an uncertain means to social advancement. One indication is simply the narrow economic margin, as indicated above, under which most tenants operated. Also indicative is the great difficulty encountered in trying to trace tenants from one assessment to another. For example, of the twelve tenants indicated in Cecil Township in 1784, only two could be found a decade later, both perhaps now with their own land. Of forty-six tenants in Cecil in 1796, only eighteen were there two years earlier; twenty-eight were new. In trying to trace these forty-six tenants through wills, only one could be found.[15] Of seventeen tenants found in Morgan Township in 1796, only seven were there in 1793. Georges Township, Fayette County, had no 1796 return, but the one for 1795 contained thirteen landlord's parts. In tracing these both forward and backward, eleven of the thirteen were not in the township for a decade, and eight of them not more than six years. Joshua Gilpin's tenant, Henry Harlan, was a landless weaver in Luzerne Township before becoming a tenant for eleven years at the time of Gilpin's 1809 visit.[16]

It is perhaps enlightening to discuss a few of these Georges tenants for whom sufficient information is available. Levi Wells was the one person who lived in the township for more than twenty years. He first appeared on the tax list in 1783, when Fayette County was still part of Westmoreland County, and he was assessed for 50 acres of land. When he appeared on the first available Fayette County roll in 1787, he had 170 acres. He maintained that approximate acreage through 1795, when 160 acres were charged as his landlord's part. Beginning in 1798, and thereafter until he "moved" in 1803, Wells had 100 acres of land. During these last years he was termed a farmer three of four times, and once a weaver. Thus, for most of his years in Georges Township, Levi Wells appears to have rented 170 acres. By the late 1790s, however, he may have been able to purchase 100 acres of his own (or was able to rent only that much). His farming apparently did not provide sufficient income since he also did some weaving. Renting provided Levi Wells with an adequate living, may have allowed him to become a landowner, and thus afforded modest social advancement.

Two others fared less well. John Wood first appeared on the tax list in 1793 with 200 acres, undoubtedly the same 211 acres charged to his landlord in 1795. By 1798, unlike Wells, he was assessed for no land. He may no longer have been renting a farm, since the 1799 assessment listed Wood as a shoemaker, and he was marked "moved" in 1800. Probably Wood was primarily an artisan inmate who rented land and farmed as a secondary occupation. He never acquired land as Wells may have done, and there is no indication of any social advancement for John Wood. The same was true of Jacob Gard. He first appeared in 1795 renting 400 acres. In 1798, he, like Wood, was assessed for no land, and in 1799 was termed a farmer, even though he had no land of his own. He continued in this same status through 1805. In 1806, Gard was simply listed as laborer, and by 1808, he was gone, although several other Gards, all poor, remained in the township. Significant social mobility was denied all three of these tenants, and their stories are probably typical of many others.

What then can be concluded from these fragmentary bits of evidence about the status of tenants on the western Pennsylvania frontier? First, tenancy was a common occurrence. Probably 20 percent of the population were tenants by the mid-1790s. Second, for most tenants, the condition of tenancy was a short-term matter, an expedient they did not intend to continue indefinitely. The lack of court cases and the great turnover among tenants indicate that tenancy was not usually a permanent condition, at least not at this stage of development of a frontier community. Third, tenancy was probably a beneficial arrangement for both landlord and tenant in a newly settled region. For the lower-class tenant, it was a means of livelihood through which he undoubtedly hoped to improve his position, gain land, or save enough to purchase land on the next frontier. Considering the close margin on which tenants operated, it is problematical how many ever achieved this goal. For the landlord, whether local or absentee, tenancy was a good means of getting his wilderness land improved. There could be conflicts of interests, however, as Washington discovered. Tenants, with their eyes toward the west, were not overly anxious to maintain someone else's property, and more than one landlord awoke to find his tenant gone. Finally, it does not appear that tenancy provided a means for upward social mobility, at least not for many at this period in the region's development. A few did become landowners. Since there is no doubt that tenants were geographically mobile, others probably were able to save money and buy land in Kentucky or Ohio and advance up the social ladder. The true extent of advancement is unclear. Tenants do not appear to be trapped or hopelessly debt ridden, but rather footloose; they were at least basically provided for and, perhaps, even a bit optimistic. Nevertheless, few rose in western Pennsylvania society. As a group, their stay brought little noticeable social or economic advancement. Perhaps as many moved on from frustration as from hope.

Absenteeism

The absentee landowner and the land speculator played important roles in the development of western Pennsylvania, serving as active catalysts for change. The extent of this activity, however, like the extent of tenancy, is difficult to determine. For the 1780s, the assessment records do not contain enough consistent information, and by the 1790s, although more information is available, the record is still not complete. Fortunately, "A list of the Taxes of the Unseated Lands of Washington County for the Year 1789" has been discovered, which helps fill in some of the gaps. Nevertheless, determining the full extent of absenteeism requires some roundabout calculation.

In this discussion, the term *absentee* is normally used to refer to a person owning land but not residing within a given township. An absentee, therefore, could reside across the border in a neighboring township, or across the state in Philadelphia. It has been impossible to divorce absenteeism from speculation in this discussion. Therefore, since speculators are not always outsiders, those cases of obvious speculation (that is, multiple holdings) within a given township are also included.

To determine the true extent of absenteeism in western Pennsylvania, three different categories of landowners must be considered. The first of these categories is the absentee landlords specifically identified by the landlord's part and estate designations. Since they have been fully discussed, nothing more needs to be said about them here other than to reiterate that 69 of them were found in the 1780s and 104 in the 1790s.[17] A second category of absentees and speculators contains the owners of unseated (unsettled) lands. Because more is known about this group, an extended discussion of these speculators, their interests, and problems will be undertaken in conjunction with the 1789 tax list of unseated lands. The extent of these unseated lands, as well as that of other absentee categories, as reported on the assessments is summarized in table 4.1.[18]

Although both of these first two categories are easily identi-

TABLE 4.1
Absentee Ownership by Category of Landowners,
Western Pennsylvania Counties, 1783–1796

Category/ County	Absentee- Owned Tracts	Percentage of Total Tracts	Absentee- Owned Acres	Percentage of Total Acres
1780s				
Landlords	69	1.5	13,495	1.3
Westmoreland	—	—	—	—
Washington	—	—	—	—
Fayette	69	1.5	13,495	1.3
Unseated tracts	362	8.0	140,626	13.2
Westmoreland	192	14.0	72,600	22.0
Washington	158	6.8	64,426	11.5
Fayette	12	1.5	3,600	2.1
No livestock	308[a]	6.8	80,754[a]	7.6
Westmoreland	133[a]	9.7	30,819[a]	9.3
Washington	122[a]	5.3	37,380[a]	6.7
Fayette	53[a]	6.5	12,555[a]	7.4
Total 1780s	739	16.3	234,875	22.1
1790s				
Landlords	104	2.3	20,658	2.5
Washington	88	2.72	17,706	2.8
Fayette	16	1.38	2,952	1.4
Unseated tracts	206	4.7	138,062	16.6
Washington	161	5.0	118,137	18.9
Fayette	45	3.9	19,925	9.7
No livestock	153	3.5	22,145.5	2.7
Washington	117	3.6	19,800	3.2
Fayette	36	3.1	2,345.5	1.1
Total 1790s	463	10.5	180,865.5	21.8

a. These figures are 75 percent of the actual number and actual acreage based on estimates derived from the 1783 census of three Westmoreland townships.

fied, they were not uniformly reported. Therefore, a third category has been used to pick up those not reported. This includes many of the tracts without specific designation but on which no livestock was reported. Justification for this third category comes from the census that accompanied the assessment returns for three Westmoreland County townships in 1783. There were forty-three tracts without livestock in these three townships, but on only nine was there any population, a total of ten persons. Significantly, six of these ten people were single freemen, young men, perhaps hired as laborers making the first modest improvements on the land. This means that approximately 75 percent of these lands accounted for no population, and were presumably absentee owned. Using this census information as a guide, an estimate of 75 percent of all such tracts without livestock has been assumed to represent absentee landowners in the 1780s. Thus, out of 410 actual tracts without livestock in all three counties, 308 have been added to the known landlord and unseated tracts.

For the 1790s, no local census associated with an assessment was available as a guide. Therefore, such information as occupation, single freeman status, name comparison, known facts and a measure of intuition have been used to delete from the list of all 327 landowners without livestock in Fayette and Washington counties those persons who were obviously or probably local residents in the 1790s.[19] The results of this complicated methodology also may be found in table 4.1. From these three categories of absentee landowners—the landlords, the owners of unseated lands, and the owners of lands without livestock—a composite estimate of the extent of absenteeism in the western Pennsylvania frontier can be obtained.

One primary trend stands out in this composite. Although the proportion of persons who were absentees declined significantly over the decade, the proportion of land controlled by those absentees held steady due primarily to larger unseated holdings. The reason for this would seem to lie in the stage of development represented by the respective categories. Both landlords and many of the owners of lands without livestock represent absenteeism at a later stage of development than owners of unseated land, who by definition were owners of virgin lands. Owners in the former two categories had improved holdings. Some of their lands were worked by hired labor or were farmed by tenants. In some cases, their lands represented investments in new towns and, in a few cases, they were investments in some enterprise in neighboring townships. On the whole, these two categories of absentee landowners were indicative of a more developed stage of frontier speculative and investment enterprise, a stage that occurred after lands had been initially settled, subdivision of lands had begun, and the buying and selling of improved property had been initiated.

By contrast, the owners of unseated lands were the initial speculators, the people who purchased large tracts of land with the hope of selling them off or renting portions to settlers making their way into these virgin lands. It comes as no surprise that, with few exceptions, unseated lands appeared overwhelmingly in the western border townships, the eastern mountain townships, or in the southern townships of Washington County, while the other two absentee categories appeared mainly in the remaining interior and river townships (table 4.2).

The peak of speculative activity apparently occurred in the late 1780s and early 1790s, but it was on the decline by the mid-1790s. The "List of the Taxes of the Unseated Lands of Washington County for the Year 1789" contains 300 unseated tracts that year, compared with 158 on the assessments of 1784 and 161 on those of 1793 (table 4.3). (Even if some or all of the tracts without livestock in Washington County were unseated, it would not bring the 1784 or 1793 totals up to 300.) Apparently, as settlement grew in western Pennsylvania, making it an attractive investment, and as the nation's general economy recovered in the latter half of the 1780s, speculation increased in western Pennsylvania. By the mid-1790s, however, settlement had expanded into most of the region and new opportunities for this type of speculation declined. Such a pattern of speculative activity would closely follow the pattern for the rate of population growth discussed in chapter 1, peaking about 1790 and then declining, but still showing considerable strength by the end of 1796.

TABLE 4.2
Distribution of Absentees by Type of Holding and Region,
Fayette and Washington Counties, 1784–1796

	Washington				Fayette			
	1784		1793		1785		1796	
	Number	Percent	Number	Percent	Number	Percent	Number	Percent
Absentee landlords								
Border	—		21	23.9	—		1	6.25
Interior	—		45	51.1	31	44.9	14	87.5
River	—		22	25.0	38	55.1	1	6.25
TOTAL	—		88	100.0	69	100.0	16	100.0
Lands without livestock								
Border	62	50.8	30	25.6	24	45.3	17	47.2
Interior	29	23.8	67	57.3	17	32.1	3	8.3
River	31	25.4	20	17.1	12	22.6	16	44.5
TOTAL	122	100.0	117	100.0	53	100.0	36	100.0
Unseated lands								
Border	158	100.0	132	82.0	12	100.0	36	80.0
Interior	—		28	17.4	—		6	13.3
River	—		1	.6	—		3	6.7
TOTAL	158	100.0	161	100.0	12	100.0	45	100.0

In terms of the number of acres held in unseated tracts, however, there was no decline, only constant increase, like the pattern of concentrated wealth described in chapter 3. In 1784, 158 unseated landowners in Washington County held 64,000 acres, an average of 405 acres each. The 300 unseated landowners of 1789 owned 158,000 acres, an average of 527 acres each. Moreover, the 161 unseated landowners of Washington County in 1793 held 118,000 acres, or an average of 733 acres per landowner. (Excluding Thomas Ryerson's 40,000 acres, the 1793 average was 488 acres.) This consolidation can be seen in two examples. In Finley Township, only 6 of 126 tracts in 1789 were larger than 400 acres; but in 1793, 7 of 42 were. In Greene Township, 20 percent of the unseated tracts exceeded 400 acres in 1789, 30 percent in 1793, and 60 percent in 1796.

TABLE 4.3
Taxes on Unseated Lands, by Region,
Washington County, 1789

Region	Unseated Tracts	Percentage of Total	Unseated Acres	Percentage of Total	Taxes (£)
Border	267	89.0	151,668	96.0	121.10. 5
Interior	19	6.3	3,507	2.2	4.17.11
River	14	4.7	2,753	1.8	3. 5. 3
TOTAL	300	100.0	157,928	100.0	129.13. 7

Note: There is reason to doubt the precision of this tax list. David Redick, Washington County lawyer and agent for certain eastern speculators, signed a notation on this tax list to the effect that he would pay his clients' taxes, but first he wanted to procure a list of holdings from each client because he found it "impractacable to know wheather they have any of these lands taxed by this list so incorrect has the returns been made. He observes some tracts here which he knows to be Seated." Redick should know, for he had 8,000 acres on the list himself, second only to the 30,000 acres of Robert Morris and Company.

Thus, absenteeism in various guises was a very real factor on the western Pennsylvania frontier, and it had not yet lost its influence by the mid-1790's. A sizeable increase from 280 to 366 absentees in Washington County offset a decline from 134 to 97 in Fayette. Increases in the designated categories of unseated tracts and landlords offset a decline in tracts without livestock, and increased overall absenteeism in the interior townships offset small declines in the other two regions. Fewer tracts without livestock perhaps indicated the increasingly settled state of the region. Certainly, the growth of towns, opening up a whole new area of speculative activity, was indicative of a more settled place. The quantity of unseated lands, however, still gave a strong frontier flavor.

Several other questions need to be answered concerning these absentess. First, who were they? Where did they come from? How did they acquire and maintain their lands? What problems beset speculators, and how much profit could they make? In answer to the first of these questions—Who were the absentees?—it can be stated that they were as likely to be western Pennsylvanians as outsiders. The task of identifying all absentees is obviously insurmountable, but certain assessments do give us some idea. Three such townships, Bullskin in Fayette and Greene and East Bethlehem in Washington contained eighty-eight absentees and speculators in 1796 who can be divided according to place of residence into the five categories.[20] From these figures it is clear that the majority of speculators came from within the region itself, but that a strong minority of about 40 percent came from completely outside western Pennsylvania, about half of them from Philadelphia (table 4.4).

What attracted people to speculate in western Pennsylvania land was obviously the lure of profit, and many of them probably made the profit they were looking for—but there were pitfalls. If turnover of land is any indication, there was a ready market for unseated land. In Greene Township, for which the fullest figures are available, the turnover of unseated lands was more than 50 percent within three to four years, indicating that opportunities for selling unseated lands were good (table 4.5). How much profit could be made? A hypothetical example will illustrate the possibilities. A speculator in 1784 bought a 400-acre tract of land, the new legal maximum allowed that year, and paid £3.10 per 100 acres, the price set for land in western Pennsylvania by the land office.[21] If one can assume a fairly constant tax rate of 5s. annually, the rate levied against 400 acres on the 1789 list of unseated lands in Washington County, a speculator could acquire and hold

TABLE 4.4
Place of Residence of Absentee Landowners,
Bullskin, Greene, and East Bethlehem Townships, 1796

Place of Residence	Bullskin	Greene	East Bethlehem	Total
Outside western Pennsylvania	14	12	6	32
Neighboring counties	11	3	3	17
Neighboring townships, same county	14	4	5	23
Same township	7	1	—	8
Unknown	8	—	—	8
TOTAL	54	20	14	88

TABLE 4.5
Turnover of Unseated Lands,
Greene Township, 1784–1796

Year	Number of Tracts on List	Number Remaining In		
		1789	*1793*	*1796*
1784	33	5	3	1
1789	29	29	12	6
1793	30	—	30	12
1796	20	—	—	20

his 400-acre tract ten years for an outlay of £16.10 plus any legal or agent fees he may have had. If he could sell the land at just 1s. per acre (£5 per 100 acres), he would almost certainly at least break even, and by the 1790s, his chances of doing that were good. In 1793, unseated lands in the border townships of Washington County were assessed at £5 per 100 acres, and often more. Seated or settled tracts were often assessed at two or three times more. Since assessed valuation was often below market value, there is little doubt that a speculator's chances for profit were reasonably good.

Shedding further light on this matter of profit are the lands sold by the sheriff in execution of legal judgments. Local residents were in a better position to know about these real estate bargains than distant speculators, and they undoubtedly made some shrewd investments. Absentee speculators often engaged a local person of means to act as agent for them. Local officialdom was in a particularly good position to spot an advantageous deal. Ephraim Douglas, prothonotary of Fayette County, was able to pick up 300 acres in Tyrone Township for the bargain price of £5, while John Clark, Esq., of Franklin Township obtained 200 acres for £30 in October 1790. Lawyer Hugh H. Brackenridge of Pittsburgh obtained 1,386 acres in September 1791 for the sizeable consideration of £500 at a sheriff's sale, but a fellow member of the bar, David Redick of Washington, paid only £13 for a tract of unknown size in Hanover Township in 1793.

Major speculators also took advantage of these sales to satisfy judgments or make good investments. Levi Hollingsworth of Philadelphia, for whom Redick acted as agent, obtained 2,705 acres of improved land in Nottingham township for £1,070 in satisfaction of a £7,454 debt owed him by Dorsey Pentecost, a speculator in his own right. Isaac Meason, iron magnate of Fayette County, in 1789 obtained 1,050 acres from the estate of Thomas Gist for £165.10 (£134 for 430 acres of excellent land that became the Meason homestead, and £31.10 for 620 acres of mountain land). In 1791, he obtained 604 acres (300 acres for £200 and 304 acres for £300) in Franklin and Tyrone townships for £500.[22] Local residents and officials were also quick to pick up town lots. A list of the owners of outlots in the townships surrounding the town of Washington reads like a who's who of county officialdom. It included Judge Alexander Addison; lawyers David Redick, David Bradford, Thomas Scott; Town Proprietor John Hoge; State Senator Dr. Absolom Baird; Assemblyman Thomas Stokely; County Recorder of Deeds and Register of Wills James Marshel; and County Treasurer Andrew Swearingen.

The above land prices include not only some bargains, but they also strongly indicate the appreciated value of improved land. Isaac Meason's 1791 purchase of 304 acres at about £1 per acre was twenty times the £5 per 100-acre break-even price of the hypothetical speculator. Little wonder that absentee owners or even local residents were willing to have tenants on their land. A few years' work by a tenant obviously would increase the value of any land appreciably. In addition, tenants were resident agents. There was no possibility of tax delinquency, because tenants were legally liable for taxes on absentee-owned lands, taxes which they in turn could legally deduct from their rent, as noted earlier. Tenancy, therefore, was a means both to gain greater profits for the land speculator and to avoid some of the problems of absentee ownership, not to mention a possible source of income in itself.

There were, however, problems confronting the speculator or absentee. The most obvious was the possibility of making a bad investment. Those made by onetime state comptroller John Nicholson, in partnership with John Hayden in Georges Township, failed to prevent his bankruptcy. The failures of prominent national figures like Robert Morris and James Wilson, largely because of land speculations gone bad, are well known.[23] It has already been noted that George Washington failed to make profits from his western Pennsylvania lands.

Uninvited tenants or squatters were certainly among the problems confronting Washington and other absentees. Squatters prevented the landowner from obtaining rents from legal tenants, made improvements the value of which the absentee might never obtain, and could conceivably deprive him of his title to the land. The squatters on Washington's lands, rather than purchase at his price or become tenants, decided to stand suit for the land. Such procedure naturally involved the speculator with court costs if he lost (£2 to £4 was the typical cost of ejectment proceedings in western Pennsylvania courts), legal fees, and lost rents from the delay. Not all legal contention over land was caused by squatters. Many clashes over title came from duplicate grants of the same land, the rival ambitions of other speculators, and legitimate confusion and uncertainties over boundaries in a new territory. The number of ejectment proceedings in the county courts—654 of them in Westmoreland, Washington, and Fayette counties through 1795—gives some indication of the extent to which squatters and contested titles caused specualtors, as well as local settlers, difficulty.[24]

Taxes were another problem, particularly for the person living outside western Pennsylvania. Such people often employed local residents of position to act as their agents. Thus Stephen Gapen, who owned 4,000 acres himself in 1796, acted as agent in Greene Township for such people as Jared Ingersol; Zachariah Connell, town proprietor with 1,800 acres, acted for Johnson and Company in Bullskin Township; lawyer David Redick acted as agent for at least four other people besides Levi Hollingsworth of Philadelphia. George Washington had three different agents—first Gilbert Simpson, then Maj. Thomas Freeman, both of Franklin Township, Fayette County; and then Col. John Canon of Canonsburg, Chartiers Township, Washington County—to oversee his various holdings in western Pennsylvania. Joshua Gilpin was still using agents for his business in 1809.[25] The duties of these agents were to keep the speculator informed about taxes and potential sales, to pay taxes, to collect rents, to guard against squatters and court suits and, perhaps most important, to recruit new tenants for the land if the landlord did not send out his own tenants. The services rendered by these agents, therefore, were vital to the absentee speculator, and the changes made in the state's tax laws in 1795 made them even more important.

During the decade before 1795, speculators in western lands could count on having their tax-delinquent property advertised in the Philadelphia papers, and on a series of stay laws postponing delinquent sales, which made the possible loss of property remote. In 1786, following the first taxation of unseated western lands in 1785, the legislature passed a law requiring county officials to send descriptions of delinquent unseated lands to the state treasurer, who would advertise such lands in one or more Philadelphia papers for two months before returning the list still delinquent to local officials. As early as 1789, however, the state was unhappy with the system and, in anticipation of changes, it passed the first of a series of stay laws on delinquent western lands. The following year, advertising was extended to twenty-six weeks. Not until 1795 was a new system worked out. Thereafter, delinquent unseated lands would be advertised on the local level only and sold after three years of delinquency.[26]

Finally, in April 1796, the state admitted that the 1786 law was a complete failure, that advertising cost more than it ever gained, and it returned the remaining old delinquent tax lists to county officials for collection in accordance with the new provisions of the 1795 law. All previous laws delaying the sale of delinquent lands more than six months or necessitating advertising outside the local county were voided. The whole problem, therefore, was dropped back on county officials, and speculators would henceforth have even more need for local agents to oversee their investments.[27]

Whether the state played a role or not, delinquent taxes were no small problem, as the list of delinquent taxes for Allegheny County, 1794, indicates. The *Pittsburgh Gazette* of 31

May ran a list of delinquent taxes containing approximately 800 names—two full newspaper pages of four columns each. Most tracts were 200 to 300 acres, but multiple holdings of five, ten, or twenty tracts by one person were common. The great bulk of these delinquent taxes and multiple holdings lay in the donation lands west of the Allegheny River, which had been set aside in 1780 to compensate soldiers for the currency depreciation that occurred during the war.[28] Speculators now owned most of these, but this situation should not be seen as typical of the whole region. Nevertheless, in the regularly constituted townships of Allegheny County, a number of delinquent lands were reported. In the town of Pittsburgh, eleven lots were delinquent, as were seven tracts in Pitt Township. The western border area of Allegheny County, Moon Township, had forty-three delinquent tracts in its first district and nineteen in its second. These included tracts of 2,600 and 3,600 acres, the latter belonging to Peter Muhlenberg.

Thus speculation in western lands did have its difficulties. Problems of squatters, taxes, tenants, agents, and judicial proceedings could cost money or even cause loss of the property. Unwise investment could ruin a man, as the classic examples of Robert Morris and James Wilson show. However, land speculation could also be profitable, and with prudent attention to one's holdings, profit, perhaps even large profit, was very likely. Speculators and absentee owners performed an important function in providing opportunity for some of the landless to obtain tenant tracts and in providing some early capital for frontier development. As this chapter has shown, there was a symbiotic relationship between tenancy and speculation. Certainly there was no lack of persons willing to take the plunge. The turnover of lands was rapid. Numerous investors from distant places and many of the local economic leaders found investing in western Pennsylvania land inviting. Their activity was an important influence in transforming the early settlement and class patterns of western Pennsylvania.

5 Town Development

ONE OF THE most potent forces in the transformation of western Pennsylvania was the beginning of urbanization. By the 1790s, town lots were appearing on the local assessment records with growing regularity. In Fayette and Washington counties, there were seventeen towns by the middle of the decade. There is no necessary contradiction between the frontier experience and urban processes. One was part of the other from the beginning. It is clear that towns performed a number of vital functions for society early on.[1]

Behind the establishment of each town was a town proprietor, the entrepreneur who platted the town at some strategic place on his own property and sold off lots to willing purchasers. (Some county seat towns vary from this process, as will be noted later.) In western Pennsylvania, these town proprietors were among the most active and most enterprising men in the region. We have already noted that Albert Gallatin, Isaac Meason, and Edward Cook were town builders at some point in their careers. John Canon, proprietor of Canonsburg in Chartiers Township, Washington County, was another who was typical of the group.

John Canon was one of those successful men who came to the region early, located some of the best land along Chartiers Creek, and prospered. He arrived in 1773, took up land under the authority of Virginia, patented three 400-acre tracts, and acquired others at various periods. In 1784, he was assessed for 800 acres and, in 1793, he was assessed for 700 acres plus another 1,000 of unseated borderland. He apparently built a mill as early as 1781, although it is not noted on the early assessments published in the *Pennsylvania Archives*. By the 1790s, he had both a sawmill and a gristmill. Canon was also a slave holder. His prominence was indicated early when he was appointed a justice of the peace, first for Augusta County and then for Yohogania County under Virginia jurisdiction, before the boundary dispute was settled. He was sent to the Pennsylvania state legislature in the early 1780s, and again in the early 1790s. Pennsylvania also made him a justice of the peace as early as 1784, and again in 1791.

Canon's prominence is further indicated by the fact that George Washington made him his personal agent to oversee the general's affairs shortly after his 1784 trip to western Pennsylvania. Canon's lands were not far from the disputed lands Washington was litigating in Cecil Township. Canon also had military experience in the Indian wars, early ties to Ohio trading companies, and was a major influence in establishing an academy in Canonsburg in 1791, a forerunner of Washington and Jefferson College. In 1787 he platted the town of Canonsburg and immediately attracted to his town a physician, a shoemaker, a tanner, a tavern keeper, and Craig Ritchie, one of the county's most successful merchants, among others. By the time of his death in 1798 at age fifty-eight, Canon was indeed one of the region's premier citizens. His experience was similar to that of other proprietors. They were wealthy, powerful men, and the towns they founded played a prominent role in the maturing process rapidly occurring in western Pennsylvania.[2]

As noted in chapter 2, the appearance of town lots in the 1790s introduced a new category of landowners who affected the land patterns in two different ways. First, they provided a new, inexpensive form of land that kept the percentage of landownership higher than it would have been otherwise. Second, by adding their negligible size to the total acreage, they contributed to the trend of smaller overall acreages and the growing polarity between the top and bottom deciles of landowners. More important, however, were the functions towns performed and the services that came to be clustered in them. Therefore, it is important to know who bought lots and lived in these towns. What was the class structure of these earliest towns? What kind of political or economic influence did towns have at this early date? Did a disproportionate number of political or economic leaders live there? What cultural benefits centered in towns? Answering these and related questions will indicate the significant role these small urban centers played in the growth and development of western Pennsylvania.

Western Pennsylvania Towns and the Town-Building Process

Before considering the impact towns had on the frontier society of western Pennsylvania, it is necessary to identify the towns and to understand something about the process of town building in western Pennsylvania. By 1796, there were nine towns in Fayette County and eight in Washington County.[3] It is hardly surprising that border townships had the fewest towns—four, compared with six in the river townships and seven in the interior townships. A summary of these towns and their locations may be seen in table 5.1 and in the maps in appendix B.

All towns were located on a source of water, nine on rivers and eight on smaller streams. Several river towns were also at the mouths of tributary streams, and three were very near tributary streams, which gave them second sources of water for human needs and industrial power. Only Hopwood and Washington were very close to the headwaters of their respective streams, but Hopwood, at the foot of a mountain, had swiftly flowing water. Water was also a source of transportation for the river towns and for Canonsburg, at certain times of the year.

All the towns had important road connections to the major centers. Five towns were on the early road network that became the famous National Road. In the case of Bridgeport, located across Dunlaps Creek from Brownsville, one did have to cross the bridge to reach the road. Connellsville and New Haven were on the opposite side of Stewart's Crossing, which had been an important crossing point on the Youghiogheny since the days of Gen. Braddock, and was now a state road. Monongahela, then called Parkinson's Ferry, was located where the Glade Road from Bedford to

TABLE 5.1
Location of Towns Established in
Fayette and Washington Counties by 1797

County/ Town	Township	Date	Location River[a]	Creek[b]	Road[c]	Industry Site[d]
Fayette County						
Uniontown	Union	1776	—	o	p	ml
Brownsville	Menallen	1785	M	m	p	—
Haydentown	Georges	1787?	—	h	l	ml, i
Hopwood	Union	1791	—	h	p	—
East Liberty	Franklin	1792	Y	—	l	—
Connellsville	Bullskin	1793	Y	—	p	—
Bridgeport	Luzerne	1794	M	m	p	ml
New Haven	Franklin	1796	Y	—	p	—
New Geneva	Springhill	1797	M	m	s	G
Washington County						
Washington	Separate	1781	—	h	p	—
Canonsburg	Chartiers	1787	—	o	l	ml
Fredericktown	East Bethlehem	1790	M	—	l	—
Greensboro	Greene	1791	M	—	s	—
Carmichaels	Cumberland	1792?	—	o	s	—
Burgettstown	Smith	1795	—	h	t	ml
Monongahela	Nottingham	1796	M	m	p	—
Waynesburg	Greene	1796	—	o	t	—

Note: The town of Washington had its own separate jurisdiction. Also, present-day names and spellings have been used for the towns regardless of their original or subsequent names.

a. River: M = Monongahela River; Y = Youghiogheny River.
b. Creek: o = located on an important creek; h = at the headwaters; m = at the mouth.
c. Roads: p = on a princiapl state or interstate road; s = on an important secondary road with interstate connections; l = on an important local road connecting local centers; t = terminal points of local roads connecting with local centers.
d. Industry: ml = mill site; G = Gallatin's enterprises, (store, mill, glassworks); i = iron forge.

Washington crossed the river. Three of the towns lay on important secondary roads south into Virginia. Two of them, New Geneva and Greensboro, lay on what Albert Gallatin called "the nearest portage from the western waters to the Potowmack and the Federal City."[4] Others were on important local roads; Canonsburg was on the road from Pittsburgh to Washington, and East Liberty on the road from

Uniontown to Greensburg. Only two border towns lacked through transportation, having instead local roads that connected them to central areas of the county.

A number of towns were at mill sites, and mills and local industry seemed to be significant factors associated with early town foundings. Water, of course, attracted the mills, but around some mills a cluster of activity developed, such as at Haydentown or Burgettstown. Generally, however, industry came to the towns, not towns to the industry. The one major exception may be Gallatin's town of New Geneva, which was laid out directly in conjunction with his glassworks. New Geneva, in its early days, was the closest approximation to an industrial or company town in the region. Yet, even here there was a cluster of settlement before Gallatin formalized it.[5]

The process of establishing a town in western Pennsylvania was much different from the well-known pattern in New England. Towns were not established by a corporate body, and the state legislature took no part in the process. Instead, the normal pattern was for an individual proprietor such as John Canon to plat a town on his own land and to offer lots for sale to the public on his own initiative. Sometimes a public lottery was used in the selection of lots, and after newspapers were established in Fayette and Washington counties in the late 1790s, town lots were advertised in the newspapers.[6] Town lots were of various sizes, and sometimes of irregular shape, but generally they contained one-fourth of an acre. Lots in Greensboro were one-half an acre in size, and in Washington, the size was about one-third of an acre.[7] Lots in Uniontown, Burgettstown, Haydentown, and Brownsville were one-fourth of an acre, and lots in New Geneva were a little under one-fourth of an acre.[8] Bridgeport lots varied from around one-fourth to one-fifth of an acre, while those in Connellsville varied from one-fourth to one-sixth of an acre.[9]

In addition, surrounding the towns were large lots called *outlots*. These lots served as pasture for the livestock of town dwellers, as future room for town expansion, and as investments for interested persons. The size of outlots varied greatly. In Connellsville, the proprietor set aside 100 acres divided into outlots of 1 to 4 acres to be used "for pasture."

An outlot sold to John Clark in Bridgeport was somewhat more than 1 acre in size. Shopkeepers Isaac Jenkinson and Jesse Townsend each owned a 4-acre outlot in Fredericktown, in addition to their several town lots. Around the town of Washington, lots were even more varied in size. In Strabane Township, lots of 1, 5, 7, and 10 acres were found, as well as two lots totaling 13 acres and two totaling 15 acres.[10]

The plats of these towns generally lacked distinction. As John Reps shows, there was a strong European planning tradition brought to America, and some colonial cities were well planned. However, this tradition was generally lost in the private, largely speculative town processes of the frontier. The grid pattern of town development, derived by running a straight line and laying off lots, was so easy that most proprietors had little concern for natural factors or contours, or such features as town squares or parks. Brownsville did incoporate a public square off of Front Street along the river, and Connellsville set aside a public landing. Gallatin, perhaps because of his European background, incorporated a public square into his New Geneva design. Natural conditions gave Uniontown its bent "elbow" street that became Main Street. But Haydentown was little more than lots laid out along the road intersection. Hopwood was a formal grid platted along the main road, and East Liberty was a little grid on the bluff above the Youghiogheny. Burgettstown was platted also along the road, and Canonsburg developed along two intersecting roads near Chartiers Creek. By far the best community plan was Waynesburg, the new county seat of Greene County. It was platted as a typical grid, but it retained a wide commons along the northern boundary a couple of blocks from the center of town. This has been retained and still provides a delightful green space several blocks long.[11]

The cost of town lots and their assessed value also varied. Henry Beeson sold lots in Uniontown for 40s. in 1776 and £5 Pennsylvania money in the 1780s, but his brother Jesse had to pay £7.10 for a lot in Bridgeport a decade later. Lots in Connellsville and Canonsburg, however, sold for only £3, and in Greensburg, lots were 45s. Burgettstown lots were advertised as selling for only $4 to $6 (£1.10–£2.5).[12] The assessed value of unimproved town lots in Washington County in 1793 ranged from £5 to £7.10. In Fayette County, unimproved lots ranged in value from $10 to $30 (£3.15 to £11.5) in 1796.

The purchaser of a town lot was under certain obligations beyond his purchase price. In nearly every case, quit rents or ground rents were due annually, although in some cases they could be eliminated by paying a lump sum. Most quit rents were a half a dollar (3s. 9d.), and in Hopwood, the rent could be paid in coin or with a bushel of wheat, which normally sold for 4s. Occasionally, the quit rent was higher, such as the whole dollar required in Washington and Canonsburg.[13] Lot owners were often required to build on their lot within two years. In Hopwood, five years was the allowed time span, and in Fredericktown, owners of multiple lots had to erect only one house for every two lots owned within the two-year period. Houses had to be of a minimum size, in some cases sixteen by twenty-four feet, but in others eighteen or twenty feet square was permissible. The chimney was always required to be constructed of brick or stone.[14]

Town proprietors had certain obligations, too. They promised to issue a clear deed. Access to drinking water and to any public landing was guaranteed. Proprietors normally gave townsmen free access to their own neighboring lands for building stone, lumber, firewood, and coal, if any was near. At times, proprietors imposed stipulations upon certain enterprises. No distillery or ferry was allowed in Fredericktown, and no ferry could be established at Connellsville.[15] Although these early town plats lacked distinction, there was scarcely a plat that did not designate one or more lots for public use, usually for an educational or religious use. Some proprietors even guaranteed financial support for education. Zachariah Connell, for example, pledged his first four years of quit rents to erect a school and meetinghouse, and Thomas Hopwood also made a sizeable pledge toward an academy in his town. John Canon, however, seized an opportunity to establish an academy in Canonsburg a few years after platting the town, when an early educational venture in neighboring Washington fell into difficulty after a fire. Thus, the proprietors were interested in making their towns attractive to purchasers and in insuring that the basic needs of the townspeople would be met. Only in that way could their ventures prosper.[16]

There is little doubt that town proprietors desired their towns to prosper. They were, as has been noted, some of the most important and enterprising men in their counties. The typical town proprietor was a middle-aged, well-established settler. As table 5.2 indicates, most of them settled in western Pennsylvania in the 1770s or early 1780s, usually a decade or more before they laid out their towns.[17] Almost invariably the proprietor was a member of the landed economic elite, ranking in the top decile of his township in both land and total taxable wealth.[18] Many of them had other business interests. Nearly all who did owned mills like John Canon; Rees Cadwallader owned three mills of different types. Isaac Meason and John Hayden were ironmasters as well. Albert Gallatin owned a glassworks and was building a gun works, while Joseph Parkinson was a merchant and ferryman. Their economic positions made them prominent citizens and gave them

TABLE 5.2
Characteristics of Town Proprietors,
Washington and Fayette Counties, 1793–1796

Proprietor/Town	Settled	In Top 10 Percent of		Other Business	Political or Military Service
		Land Value	Tax Value		
Rees Cadwallader, Bridgeport	1783	no	yes	yes	no
Zachariah Connell, Connellsville	1770	yes	yes	yes	yes
Joshua Dickerson, East Liberty	1770	yes	yes	yes	no
Albert Gallatin, New Geneva	1786	yes	yes	yes	yes
John Hayden, Haydentown	1781	yes	yes	yes	no
Robert Peoples, Haydentown	1788?	no	no	yes	no
Isaac Meason, New Haven	1770	yes	yes	yes	yes
George Burgett, Burgettstown	1773–80	no	no	yes	no
John Canon, Canonsburg	1773	yes	yes	yes	yes
James Carmichael, Carmichaels	pre-1784	yes	yes	no	yes
John Hoge, Washington	1782	yes	yes	no	yes
Joseph Parkinson, Monongahela	1770	no	no	yes	no
Elias Stone, Greensboro	pre-1784	yes	yes	no	no
Frederick Wise, Fredericktown	1770	no	no	no	yes

opportunities for political office. Connell held local office, while Gallatin, Meason, Canon and John Hoge all served as high as the state level; Gallatin attained national prominence. At least five of these men had military experience in addition to, or in lieu of, political experience.[19]

The Role of the Towns in Frontier Society

The small towns on the western Pennsylvania frontier played several important roles in that society. They served as trading centers, gathering together a variety of skills and services in one place. The towns also provided opportunities for common laborers and dependent people to achieve some economic status and security. Town real estate became a new source of investment, replacing the dwindling supply of unseated lands and gave an opportunity for some of the poorer members of society to become property owners for the first time. For some towns, providing the services of government was a most important role. Finally, towns in general promoted the only veneer of intellectual and cultural activities covering the general crudeness of frontier life.

Probably the most important functions of nascent frontier towns was to provide a marketing center for the exchange of goods and services. Here, in one convenient place, a variety of skills, professional services, and market opportunities were gathered. Many towns had milling facilities in or near them, but they also drew together artisans and professional people.

Uniontown, for example, had approximately twenty artisans and shopkeepers by 1783, just seven years after its founding and in spite of the war. By the mid-1790s, although the exact number of artisans is unknown, Uniontown had added such new trades as potters, tailors, a breeches maker, a silversmith, and a brewer.[20] Brownsville had more than a half-dozen merchants and shopkeepers by the mid-1790s, and its important river location made it one of the most important boat-building centers in all of the West.[21]

Travelers' reports at the turn of the century indicate that these towns were continuing their growth. Brownsville, by

1803, included the first paper mill west of the mountains, a ropewalk, a brewery, and several other manufactures, while its port facilities provided a commercial outlet for some two-dozen mills situated within a few miles of the town. Union-town, by 1803, was doing such a large mercantile business that traveler Thaddeus M. Harris believed it was the most flourishing town west of the mountains with the exceptions of Wheeling and Pittsburgh.[22] Six years later, Joshua Gilpin reported that Brownsville, together with Bridgeport, had 300 houses, many containing stores, taverns, and tradesmen. He noted eighteen stores in Brownsville itself and reported that Dunlaps Creek between the two towns was "lined with mills & houses."[23]

The growth of Pittsburgh and Washington also centered in trade and manufacturing. Pittsburgh's unique river location determined that its early life would be dominated by traders. George Washington found the town primarily inhabited by "Indian Traders" in 1770. Fourteen years later, in 1784, Dr. Schoepf found that Pittsburghers were still making money by dealing "extortionately with strangers and travelers" who interrupted "their comfortable sloth." However, the same year, Arthur Lee found "a great deal of small trade carried on," with the local shops taking in "money, wheat, flour and skins." Industry became increasingly important in Pittsburgh and provided, by the end of the century, the real basis for its spectacular growth from a lazy town of traders to a major western city.[24]

The town of Washington developed more rapidly than Pittsburgh apparently did, and for its first decade or more, it was Pittsburgh's greatest rival. In 1792, *The American Museum or Universal Magazine* reported that Washington had a greater variety of artisans and retailers than Pittsburgh. Twenty-three different types of skills were listed for Washington as against only seventeen for Pittsburgh, although Pittsburgh did have about 20 percent more artisans practicing fewer trades. Both towns could claim such nonessential trades as a clockmaker and a silversmith, whose clientele were undoubtedly drawn from the upper levels of society. The town of Washington reminded James Elliot of his Massachusetts home. This soldier of the Whiskey Rebellion found it to be "a considerable town, consisting of framed buildings, clapboarded, and chiefly painted red, except the court house and two or three other buildings which are stone." He found the town "very pleasing to me, as it resembled a New England town." Rev. John Heckewelder, in 1792, found Washington contained "60 well-built houses," and in 1797 he wrote, "It contains about 200 houses all of which are two stories high." By 1798, Washington could boast sixteen retailers and more than thirty persons dealing in mercantile pursuits, in addition to ninety-three artisans and tradesmen, including such new trades as Windsor chair makers and coppersmiths.[25]

It is unfortunate that detailed tax information was so lacking for these major towns, but an examination of the smaller towns indicate what probably occurred initially in the larger towns. Here again, merchants, artisans, and industry were important. In Canonsburg, for example, a doctor, two merchants, a shoemaker, a tanner, a cooper, and a tavernkeeper were among the first twelve to purchase lots. In Haydentown, a tailor, a joiner, and a blacksmith were among the first lot purchasers to be identified. Merchant Isaac Jenkinson was probably the leading organizer of Fredericktown following the untimely death of proprietor Frederick Wise. Possibly no town in western Pennsylvania owed its beginnings more directly to industry than New Geneva, Albert Gallatin's town built primarily to house the employees of his glass works and gun works.[26] Only three small towns—Bridgeport, Connellsville, and Fredericktown—can be studied in detail (table 5.3). Their assessment data reveal that 14 percent of lot owners were engaged in various mercantile pursuits. Another 37 percent were skilled artisans, and in Fredericktown, fully 50 percent were artisans. A small professional class in these towns already owned 6 percent of the lots. There can be little doubt that serving as a center for the distribution of goods and services was one of the earliest and most important functions of these frontier towns.[27]

A second important role played by the towns was to provide economic opportunity for the lower classes. The precise

TABLE 5.3

Lot Owners, by Occupation,

Bridgeport, Connellsville, Fredericktown, 1796

	Bridgeport		Connellsville		Fredericktown		Total	
Occupation	Number	Percentage	Number	Percentage	Number	Percentage	Number	Percentage
Professional	2	5.0	4	7.1	2	7.1	8	6.4
Mercantile	5	12.5	6	10.7	6	21.4	17	13.7
Yeoman	1	2.5	3	5.4	0	0.0	4	3.2
Dependent	11	27.5	13	23.2	1	3.6	25	20.2
Artisan	16	40.0	16	28.6	14	50.0	46	37.1
Speculator	5	12.5	14	25.0	5	17.9	24	19.3
TOTAL	40	100.0	56	100.0	28	100.0	124	99.9

influence that towns had upon poorer people is nearly impossible to determine. Nevertheless, dependent persons who lacked skills or a profession comprised 20 percent of the lot owners in these three small towns. A few of these dependents were widows. Widow Mahaffey of Connellsville and her two sons, both without apparent skills, each owned a lot in Connellsville. The town probably provided more opportunity for common labor for her sons than would living in the hills of Bullskin Township, and for her, the town probably meant security not found in a lonely cabin.

To "Black Bobb," the river town of Bridgeport offered the opportunity to become a property owner—probably for the first time in his life—as well as a place for him to find employment as a common laborer. In the town of Washington, another black laborer, Ignatius Hewitt, was able to buy a lot, but fellow laborer, Shadrack, was not so fortunate. Several lot owners were young single freemen. Towns gave some of these young men opportunities for work and their first stake in society. Most single men of the towns, however, did not own property. In the town of Washington, for example, twenty-three of the thirty-one landless were single men. Many of these young men probably joined those who moved on to the next settlement. Others, however, stayed, found worthwhile jobs, and became permanent town residents. For all of these laboring dependent people, an important consideration must have been the low initial cost of a town lot compared with the cost of beginning a small farm. Towns gave the unskilled opportunities for both employment and property ownership that they may not have found elsewhere.

New towns served a third function in frontier society— they opened up a new form of real estate investment, particularly in townships where settlement had claimed virtually all of the unseated land. Speculators were attracted to this low-cost property as readily as the lower classes. In fact, 22 percent of the lot owners in the three small towns of Bridgeport, Connellsville, and Fredericktown were speculators. In the town of Washington, only 7 percent of the lot owners were speculators, but the list of persons owning the larger outlots around the town was full of investors, many of them local leaders. In the three small towns, a few investors were yeomen who may have bought to establish a son in a trade, or they bought just to make a profit. Other speculators lived outside the township. In Bridgeport, for example, speculators included a Brownsville businessman, two residents of neighboring Menallen Township, and two Washington County residents. In Fredericktown, speculators included the president judge of the Western Pennsylvania Judicial Circuit, Alexander Addison, an eastern speculator with large holdings in the border townships, and residents of the town of Washington, of neighboring Cumberland Township, and of Fayette County. The same was true of Connellsville, where residents of Washington and Westmoreland counties, one from New Jersey, and a Uniontown justice of the peace were among the lot owners.

The low initial price attracted many persons to town lots, but for an investor, the potential value was equally important. That these lots appreciated greatly was evident in a case brought before the Washington County Court. Merchant John Acheson sold a lot he owned in the town of Washington to Samuel Acklin in October 1789. Acklin was to pay annually a minimum of £3.7.6 in marketable beef, pork, wheat, or whiskey; £3 went to Acheson and the rest paid the quit rent. Upon payment of £50 (£40 if Acklin could pay it off within a year) a deed would issue.[28] What improvements Acheson may have made before selling were not stated, but the appreciated value was obvious. In 1793, when many lots in Washington were assessed for £7.10, Samuel Acklin was assessed for a £40 lot. In neighboring Strabane Township, £40 was the assessed value of farms ranging from 100 to 250 acres. New towns, therefore, did provide excellent opportunities for investment, and a number of enterprising people took part, no doubt gladdening the heart of each town proprietor in the process.

A few towns served as the seat of local government, another very important function. Being a county seat not only meant that the merchants, artisans, laboring people, and speculators would come to town, but also that many others had to come to the county seat to avail themselves of the various services of government. People came to probate a will or to record a deed. Hunters came to collect a bounty on wolves or squirrels, and millers came to register their flour brands.[29] Many interested citizens came to visit old friends and to learn the latest news during the quarterly sessions of court.[30] Still others came to the county seat to initiate or to answer a suit for some alleged wrong, to collect a debt, to petition insolvency, or to pay taxes. Some voters, too, had to come to the county seat for elections.[31]

Considering the many people guaranteed to come to a county-seat town, and considering the speculative, enterprising mentality of the proprietary class, it should not be surprising that the choice of county seats was contested. In nearly every case, the selection of the county seat involved some planning on the part of enterprising men. Only Pittsburgh was a truly important town when it was designated county seat of Allegheny County in 1788. Located at the western edge of Westmoreland county, Pittsburgh had long felt itself unduly subservient to the county seat, Hannastown, thirty miles to the east. The burning of Hannastown in 1782 and the subsequent internal struggle within Westmoreland County over the location of a new county seat gave Pittsburghers their opportunity. Pittsburgh lawyer Hugh H. Brackenridge had been elected to the legislature in 1786 partially on a platform promising to make Pittsburgh a new county seat. Brackenridge's political differences with his fellow Westmoreland representative, the powerful William Findley, also may have influenced the struggle. Within a few weeks, the bill creating Allegheny County, with Pittsburgh as its county seat, made its appearance in the legislature, and Findley and Brackenridge, ostensibly for other reasons, crossed political swords. Pittsburgh, however, was simply too important to be denied.[32]

Uniontown also had been established before the need for a county seat arose, but apparently not without some hopeful design toward the future. Within two years after Henry Beeson settled in 1767, Alexander McClean, a surveyor and later the county's reigster of wills and recorder of deeds, suggested to Beeson that the site would be suitable for a county seat. After first building a mill, Beeson laid out the town in 1776. It languished during the war, but when the need for a new county seat arose in 1783, Uniontown was the only logical choice.[33]

In Westmoreland and Washington counties, the choice of a county seat was even more the result of strong-willed men. When Westmoreland County was erected in 1773, the house of Robert Hanna on Forbes Road was designated as the site for holding court; Hanna was made a justice of the peace and placed on a five-man commission to select a permanent site. The "strong-minded Irishman of great shrewdness" saw to it that the commission never found another site. However, the burning of Hannastown in 1782 and the location of the state road a few miles to the south thwarted Hanna's design. Still, a second commission and then a third could not agree on a new site. The commissions deadlocked; members complained about not receiving notices of meetings; petitions supported both sides. After months, new commissioners broke the deadlock when three prominent men worked out a solution personally beneficial to themselves. William Jack and Christopher Truby, both county officials, agreed with their neighbor and commission member, Michael Rugh, to sell two acres of land to the county for public buildings for the nominal sum of six pence. Jack and Truby would then also mark off sixty acres of their own land into town lots and sell them to the public, while Rugh oversaw the court construction. The two commission members from the southern part of the county went along, but the two from the northern part refused to have anything to do with the proceedings. Nevertheless, Greensburg became the county seat, and Hannastown never rose from its ashes.[34]

Washington presented another case of predesign. The original proprietor, David Hoge, resided near Carlisle in Cumberland County and never came west. Hoge had earlier purchased the Washington site, used during the Virginia period as a central meeting place. When, in 1781, talk was that a new county would be erected, Hoge had a cabin built on the site. As he apparently had hoped, the legislature designated his cabin as a meeting place for the county courts, and the fact that his brother Jonathan was a representative from Cumberland County may have been decisive. In any case, Hoge immediately had lawyer-surveyor David Redick, his nephew-in-law by marriage to Jonathan's daughter, lay out the town. Lots sold quickly, and the town was begun. The family connections of David Hoge, with his brother in the legislature and his brother's son-in-law on the scene in Washington County, undoubtedly facilitated the whole enterprise. Since Hoge did not come to the new town, he sent his sons John and William, to whom he sold the proprietorship in 1785, and they became the resident proprietors.[35]

Waynesburg appears to have been the only county seat that had no enterprising proprietor. Rather, when Greene County was erected out of Washington County in 1796, five trustees were instructed to choose a site within five miles of the center of the county. They chose 160 acres of the 350-acre Thomas Slater farm, bought it for $2,376, and laid out 201 lots. The only building on the site was Slater's own cabin. Only one of the trustees was from Slater's township, and two of the trustees lived in Washington County, not the new Greene County. Perhaps the legislature had learned from past disputes.[36]

Thus, in many ways, the vital function of dispensing justice on the frontier created towns ex nihilo. The services performed by such towns so insured their growth that shrewd men were anxious to benefit from them. However, providing justice was not limited solely to the county seats. Towns were the logical centers for dispensing justice on the township level too. The Union Township justice of the peace was the Uniontown tavernkeeper Jonathan Roland; the Chartiers Township justice of the peace was the Canonsburg merchant Craig Ritchie; the East Bethlehem Township justice of the peace was the Fredericktown merchant Isaac Jenkinson. Towns per se were logical centers for providing the services of local governments.

In 1784, Ephraim Douglas, the new county court officer for Fayette County, cried out that "this Uniontown is the most obscure spot on the face of the globe,"[37] and there is much evidence of the crudity, the roughness, and the difficulties that faced new town dwellers. Nevertheless, these little towns also provided the only centers of cultural activities, relieving the coarseness of frontier society. Towns provided a major source of news, information, and contact with the outside world. Rev. Robert Ayers and many of his neighbors came to town at court time to learn the latest news. Publishers sought out towns as logical locations of the first newspapers. The *Gazette* was established in Pittsburgh in 1786, and for nine years it alone supplied the region with news. By the end of the century, however, Washington had established two newspapers, and Uniontown had one. In Greensburg, a newspaper was published in both German and English, and Pittsburgh had added a second paper.[38]

Town dwellers were also more likely to be better read and better versed on contemporary problems. Rev. Ayers read the *British Literary Magazine* at the home of Mr. Brooks in Uniontown; he borrowed a book after having dinner at the home of lawyer John Young in Greensburg. To get his fifteenth volume of the "Encyclopedia," he "went to town," presumably to Brownsville, or perhaps Uniontown. The location of "Jackson's Bookstore," where he stopped on his return trip from performing a marriage, is unknown, but it may have belonged to the same Jackson who established the papermill in Brownsville.[39] The little town of Fredericktown led all others in establishing a library. As early as 1793, the secretary of the Library Company called members together in the library room to elect officers.[40]

Towns often provided leadership in contemporary issues. One of the two Democratic societies that sprang up in Washington County during the Whiskey Rebellion years of 1793 and 1794 was centered in the town of Washington. The other one was more broadly representative of the countryside, but was centered around the site of Parkinson's ferry, which soon became the town of Monongahela. Less violently political in its goals was another society organized in Washington in February, 1789; The Washington Society for the Relief of Free Negroes, and Others, Unlawfully Held in Bondage. Imbued with the wave of patriotism sweeping the country that year, the founders of the society found a parallel for seeking the freedom of all Negroes in the way that America had "asserted her rights" and "fought for her own liberty." The membership of the society was a virtual who's who of the Washington County officialdom.[41]

Interest in higher education also centered in the towns. In 1787, the state granted a charter for an academy in Pittsburgh and the next year set aside 5,000 acres of land for the use of the school. In Washington County, Presbyterian ministers were the leading influences in turning local elementary study into the basis for the Washington and the Canonsburg academies. The county courts of Washington County, in 1788, ordered that all future bench fees collected by the courts would be paid to Washington Academy, and the following year the school opened with twenty some students.[42] When fire destroyed the Washington Academy facility, John Canon provided land to establish an academy in his town in 1791, apparently incorporating the early educational work of Rev. John McMillen into the Canonsburg Academy. The piqued Washingtonians soon rebuilt their own institution. Meanwhile Methodist Bishop Francis Asbury established a school in Uniontown in 1792. Pittsburgh had a school for young ladies by 1786, and it had an evening school—perhaps a forerunner of adult education—as early as October 1793.[43]

Common education was not lacking, but it was less centered in the towns. Some town proprietors did try to provide for the beginnings of education, as noted above, but with dubious success. Rather it was the clergy of the local churches, many in rural areas, who provided much of the rudimentary education. Also, a number of schoolmasters taught the young—those who could afford to pay—in most townships.[44]

Perhaps the only major form of early cultural life not exclusively located in the towns was religion. There were some churches established in the towns—a Baptist church in Uniontown, an Episcopalian church in Brownsville, a Lutheran church in Greensburg. During this period, however, "religion was a predominantly rural institution, with churches mainly in the open country."[45] The four most prominent clergymen in Washington County—Presbyterian ministers Thaddeus Dod, Joseph Smith, John McMillan, and Matthew Henderson—all served rural congregations, and there were rural Presbyterian churches in Fayette and Westmoreland counties and rural Lutheran churches in German Township and Westmoreland County.[46]

As for the fine arts—music, dancing, and the theater—
little can be found in these early years. Pittsburgh had a music
teacher in the 1790s, and one minor Washington official was a
schoolteacher and music teacher. There were some hints of
dancing beyond the country dancing of common people. Social dancing among the leading families of Pittsburgh was just
making its appearance during the last decade of the century,
although lawyer Brackenridge did rhapsodize about "halls
lighted up with splendor, ladies and gentlemen assembled,
various music and the mazes of the dance," as early as 1786.
Both Washington and Pittsburgh had traveling theater troops
during 1790, but there was very little beyond this until the
nineteenth century. Support of these fine arts demanded
wealth and the emergence of a social leisure class. Such pre-
requisites did not yet exist in the small towns of western Pennsylvania in the eighteenth century, and they did not exist in
quantity in the major towns of the western frontier until the
second and third decades of the nineteenth century. Western
Pennsylvania towns had a class structure in the eighteenth
century, but they did not contain the wealthy leisure class
necessary to support the fine arts.[47]

The Class Structure of Western Pennsylvania Towns

The new towns that grew up on the western Pennsylvania
frontier began to demonstrate a class system very early on. In
these early days, the lines between classes were not precise.
Many of the new businessmen, for example, played a dual
merchant-artisan role. Others added a political dimension to
their economic pursuits. Poorer artisans were little distinguished from general laborers. Furthermore, with a tax system largely oriented to land and agrarian forms of wealth, the
exact status of a given town resident could be hidden. Merchant inventories were not necessarily reflected in the value of
the building and lot which housed them. Nevertheless, a meaningful general description of these early towns is possible, and
it reveals that they followed, for the most part, the patterns of
their larger, more sophisticated urban brethren.[48]

The class structures of four towns in particular—the three smaller towns of Bridgeport, Connellsville, and Fredericktown in 1796, and the county-seat town of Washington in 1793—have been delineated for this study (table 5.4).[49] The most obvious feature of these towns is the dominant postion of the professional and mercantile classes. These two groups consistently had the greatest taxable wealth and normally included members of the richest decile of taxable persons in each township. The town proprietor was, in every case, in the top 10 percent, and Benjamin Wells, the hated revenue collector of the Whiskey Rebellion and a Connellsville merchant,

TABLE 5.4
Taxable Wealth, by Occupational Categories,
Bridgeport, Connellsville, Fredericktown, 1796

Town/ Occupational Category	*Number*	*Percentage*	*Range*	*Taxable Wealth*	
				Median	*In Top 10 Percent*
Bridgeport					
Professional	2	5.0	440–7,614[a]	—	1
Mercantile	5	12.5	60–5,104	351	1
Yeoman	1	2.5	1,025	—	0
Artisan	16	40.0	41–703	121	0
Dependent	11	27.5	60–570	250	0
Speculator	5	12.5	70–100	100	0
Connellsville					
Professional	4	7.1	245–2,034[a]	1,058	2
Mercantile	6	10.1	20–3,640	375	2
Yeoman	3	5.4	335–778	600	0
Artisan	16	28.6	10–505	165	0
Dependent	13	23.2	10–360	45	0
Speculator	14	25.0	20–1,250	80	1
Fredericktown					
Professional	2	7.1	194–480[b]	—	1
Mercantile	6	21.4	125–1,060	148	1
Yeoman	0	0.0	—	—	0
Artisan	14	50.0	2–228	53	0
Dependent	1	3.6	87	—	0
Speculator	5	17.9	7–60	15	0

a. Amounts given in $.
b. Amounts given in £.

was the fourth person in the professional class to rank among the top decile in small towns. A leading merchant or two also usually ranked among the top decile in taxable wealth. In Bridgeport, it was the brother of the proprietor, who was a miller. In Connellsville, it was a merchant and a forge owner, and in Fredericktown, it was a merchant. The few yeoman farmers who owned town lots for whatever reason also tended to be above average in total wealth, but it was their farm acreage, not their town lots, that normally provided the wealth. The exception was John Rice Connell, the proprietor's son, who had three highly valuable lots in addition to his 100 acres.

The laboring classes formed the greater portion of the class structure of these towns. On the whole, artisans tended to be better-off than dependents, the exception in Bridgeport notwithstanding. A few artisans had above average wealth. Blacksmiths, millwrights, and certain members of the building trades tended to lead the list, but the numbers in each trade were so small as to make generalizations hazardous. The wealth of dependents did not range as high as that of artisans. These people lacked any particular occupational skill. There may have been an unlikely gentleman here or an undetected speculator there, and there were a few widows. Considering their generally low economic status, however, the great majority of them probably fell into the common laboring class of the towns.

The town of Washington, although it was almost as large as the other three combined, did not have a significantly different class structure (table 5.5). In fact, the particular nature of Washington as a county seat intensified the dominance of the professional and mercantile classes. Six of the eleven persons in the top decile of this self-contained township were in the professional classes, and the other five were in the mercantile class. At the very top was town proprietor, John Hoge, whose taxable wealth was over £1,200. He was followed at some distance by lawyer David Bradford, leader of the Whiskey Rebels (£319), County Treasurer Andrew Swearingen (£221.10), lawyer James Ross (£156.10), President Judge Alexander Addison (£132), and lawyer Thomas Scott (£129.10).

TABLE 5.5
Taxable Wealth, by Occupational Categories,
Washington, 1793

Occupational Category	Number	Percentage	Range (£)	Taxable Wealth Median (£)	Taxable Wealth In Top 10 Percent
Professional	16	14.4	8–1,216.10	123	6
Mercantile	20	18.0	8–296.10	76	5
Artisan	24	21.6	0–120.10	26.10	0
Dependent	43	38.7	0–121.10	8	0
Speculator	8	7.2	5–60	20	0

The county's register of wills and recorder of deeds, James Marshel (£129), just missed inclusion in this group by 10s. The fact that the median wealth of the professional group was only £6 below the cutoff line for the top decile indicates the economic strength of this governing class.

There were also several persons of wealth in the mercantile category. Tavernkeeper John Dodd led the mercantile group largely because he was the only town resident with a large landholding—204 acres. Another tavernkeeper, Hugh Wilson, followed with £181.10; merchants Blakeney, Cunningham, and Clark completed the top decile, with taxable wealth ranging from £142 to £158.5. Merchant David Acheson and tavernkeeper John Purviance were the only other persons with taxable wealth above £100, and from these leaders, the wealth of the mercantile group declined to certain small retailers and several tavernkeepers with modest wealth. Six ranged from £51 to £92, and seven more ranged from £8 to £41 in taxable wealth.

Among artisans, a tailor had the greatest wealth, followed by a shoemaker and an artisan of unknown trade, all with more than £100 of taxable property. From these three, artisan wealth fell off to a cabinetmaker with £66 of taxable wealth, and three artisans with £46, £51, and £53. Four more artisans had property worth £30 to £40. The dependent classes were headed by a widow with property worth £121.10. Five other dependents had property valued at £40 to £80. None of the rest had more than £30 of property. Twelve dependents were single freemen with no property, and twelve others were taxed for the value of a horse (£8) or less. Those few absentees who owned lots had only small holdings. One owned as many as four lots, another had two, but the rest had only one lot each. Thus, in this new county-seat town, which in 1793 was only twelve years old, a definite class structure based upon occupational groupings had emerged. The government leaders of the county and several leading merchants clearly headed the class structure. They were followed by skilled artisans and then the dependent classes. The few speculators probably had little real economic influence on the life of the town.

Towns provided a greatly disproportionate number of political leaders in comparison to the rest of the county. In a study of thirty-six principal political leaders who collectively held more than 120 major offices and numerous minor posts—twenty-six men from Washington County and ten from Fayette County—36 percent came from towns, especially county seats.[50] By contrast, town dwellers made up only 6 percent of the total population. Towns contributed six times their proportional share of political leaders. To be sure, several county officers moved to the county seat after being elected and maintained land elsewhere. For example, James Marshel, sheriff and then register of wills and recorder of deeds for Washington County, continued to hold 1,400 acres in Cross Creek Township. Others, however, located in the town first, then developed political careers. Two lawyers, two merchants, a doctor, a tavernkeeper, and the town proprietor—all from Washington—developed political careers after they settled in the county seat. Towns, particularly the county seat, provided would-be political leaders with the opportunity to become known by a broad range of people and to make the contacts necessary for political success.

The influence of these new towns did not distort the occupational patterns of neighboring townships. In the early stages, their influence seldom passed beyond the borders of the townships within which they were located. Numbers of merchants, artisans, common laborers, even local politicians lived in all townships, and the overall proportions of these occupational groups in townships with new towns was not significantly different from those in townships without towns. Where towns existed, there tended to be a few more professional people. Yeomen farmers were more concentrated in the townships without town development. Around Washington, it is true, the townships of Canton and Strabane had only seventeen and nine artisans respectively, when a more normal number would have been about thirty. Also, West Bethlehem Township had only thirteen artisans, while East Bethlehem, with its small river town, had eighty-nine. In a township like Franklin in Fayette County, however, where large numbers of artisans lived, the presence of Isaac Meason's iron plantation, not the tiny town of New Haven, was the cause.

Within a given township, however, the influence seemed more direct. In the large, mountainous township of Bullskin, for example, one-half of the professional, mercantile, and artisan classes owned lots in Connellsville. In the river township of Luzerne, 20 to 25 percent of the mercantile and artisan classes owned lots in Bridgeport. Six of seven cordwainers in Bullskin and Luzerne townships owned town lots. The only property owned by carpenters, tailors, tanners, bricklayers, and boat builders in these two townships were town lots. How many artisans lacking taxable property also may have lived in these towns cannot be said from the assessment data. In Fredericktown, however, where five mercantile people and fourteen artisans owned lots, an additional seven propertyless artisans and two propertyless mercantile clerks (a total of nine inmates) also lived in the town and resided with property owners. Similar situations undoubtedly existed in the other towns.

Towns had a particularly great influence upon professional people. Scarcely any lawyer lived anywhere but in the county towns. Although townships without towns had physicians, the single physicians in Bullskin and Luzerne townships lived in town. Tavernkeepers and innkeepers were concentrated in towns. For example, ten of twenty-seven tavernkeepers licensed by the Washington County courts in 1792 were from the town of Washington, and altogether the town of Washington apparently had fourteen tavernkeepers in 1793. In 1795, Westmoreland County limited the number of taverns in the county to thirty-four, but eight were designated for Greensburg alone.[51]

Thus, within the given townships, towns were major forces for change even in the early years. They definitely attracted the professional, mercantile, and artisan populations within the township. They also acted as trading centers; they contained most of the cultural life that existed; they performed the many services of government. A significant number of the major political leaders came from these early towns. In function and, to some extent, in class structure, these early towns were already quite different from the surrounding countryside. Town dwellers were making an impact on the transformation of western Pennsylvania society far in excess of their small numbers.

6   The Occupational Structure

BY 1796, western Pennsylvania had been settled for approximately one generation. Fifteen years had passed since the Revolution ended, and nearly that much time had elapsed since Indian hostilities had threatened the core of the settled region. With the signing of the Treaty of Greenville in 1795, all Indian threats to the area were gone. With the signing of the Pinckney Treaty in 1796, the river system was open to New Orleans trade. Western Pennsylvania still retained a frontier flavor in the mid-1790s: a number of land speculators remained, farms were only partially cleared, and border regions were still sparsely settled. Nevertheless, a definite aura of sophistication now pervaded the region. The rapid rate of population growth had slowed, and the amount of absentee ownership had passed its peak. Emerging economic leaders had founded industries, and proprietors had platted new towns. It is well, therefore, to take a close look at this society in 1796 to determine just how far the transformation of western Pennsylvania had proceeded. How large was the artisan class? Were yeoman farmers able to produce surpluses for trade? How did the dependent classes survive?

A thorough study of the occupational diversity and the class structure in 1796 is possible because of important changes in the tax laws. The law of 1795 forced local assessors to thoroughly revise their procedures for 1796. Now occupations were listed for each taxable person, and buildings, cleared acreages, and rental information were often listed. These data allow for the study of most of Fayette County in 1796, supplemented by data from several townships in Washington County.[1]

In surveying the occupational structure of Fayette County, all occupations have been organized into six categories: professional, mercantile, yeoman farmers, various dependent classes, artisans, and absentee speculators.[2] Three of these categories contain 90 percent of the population, while the other three shared the final 10 percent. The largest group is not the yeomen, the landowning farmers. Instead, the various dependent classes make up the largest single group, 43 percent of the taxable population, compared to 31 percent for the yeomen. Artisans are a distant third, constituting 16 percent of the population. Among the smaller categories, the mercantile group is 4 percent; absentees are almost another 4 percent; and the professional class is nearly 3 percent of the population. We will examine the three small categories first, then examine in greater detail each of the large categories. Table 6.1 summarizes this occupational structure for Fayette County.

The Professional Class

The smallest occupational category is professional, which includes only sixty-four persons. These sixty-four people divide into two groups: thirty-four government officials and thirty other professionals. In several instances, assessors did not indicate who were government officials, particularly local justices of the peace and constables, who played vital roles in local government. To the assessor, these people were farmers, artisans, or merchants. Nevertheless, people who in 1796, served in state and local office have been removed from their initial categories and grouped together here.

These government officials may be further divided into two groups: petty officeholders, and the high government officials. Included among petty officeholders are justices of the peace, constables, two surveyors, an assessor,[3] a brigade inspector, a flour inspector, the sheriff, a county commissioner, and the federal revenue collector. High government officials include two state assemblymen, John Cunningham and John Smilie, State Senator Presley Carr Lane, Congressman Albert Gallatin, and associate county judges Edward Cook and Nathaniel Breading.[4]

The economic position of these government people was

TABLE 6.1

Occupational Structure, Total Population and Landed Population, by Township and Region, Fayette County, 1796

Region/Township	Professional		Mercantile		Yeoman		Dependent		Artisan		Speculator		Total	
	No.	%	No.	%	No.	%	No.	%	No.	%	No.	%	No.	%
River														
Washington	6	2.3	11	4.3	108	42.4	85	33.3	43	16.9	2	0.8	255	100.0
Landed	3	2.2	9	6.5	108	78.3	0	—	16	11.6	2	1.4	138	100.0
Luzerne	13	4.2	15	4.8	83	26.7	128	41.1	63	20.3	9	2.9	311	100.0
Landed	7	4.7	12	8.1	83	55.7	16	10.7	22	14.8	9	6.0	149	100.0
German	4	1.5	15	5.6	97	36.5	104	39.1	44	16.5	2	0.8	266	100.0
Landed	3	2.4	11	8.7	97	77.0	0	—	13	10.3	2	1.6	126	100.0
Springhill	4	1.1	16	4.4	91	25.2	197	54.4	49	13.5	5	1.4	362	100.0
Landed	3	2.2	12	8.8	91	66.9	7	5.2	18	13.2	5	3.7	136	100.0
Border														
Bullskin	8	2.2	12	3.3	110	30.6	150	41.7	31	8.6	49	13.6	360	100.0
Landed	7	3.3	11	5.2	110	52.2	15	7.1	19	9.0	49	23.2	211	100.0
Interior														
Tyrone	5	2.9	7	4.0	49	28.0	84	48.0	25	14.2	5	2.9	175	100.0
Landed	3	4.6	6	9.2	49	75.5	1	1.5	1	1.5	5	7.7	65	100.0
Franklin	20	4.3	22	4.8	121	26.1	162	35.0	134	28.9	4	0.9	463	100.0
Landed	9	4.6	17	8.7	121	61.7	3	1.5	42	21.4	4	2.1	196	100.0
Georges	4	1.4	6	2.1	103	36.7	144	51.2	10	3.6	14	5.0	281	100.0
Landed	4	2.9	6	4.4	103	75.2	4	2.9	6	4.4	14	10.2	137	100.0
GRAND TOTAL	64	2.6	104	4.2	762	30.8	1054	42.6	399	16.1	90	3.7	2473	100.0
Landed	39	3.4	84	7.2	762	65.8	46	4.0	137	11.8	90	7.8	1158	100.0

generally high. Only four of thirty-four—three constables and a surveyor—were landless. As Table 6.2 indicates, there was a tendency for the wealthier people to hold the more important offices. The high government officials were substantial landowners, and the justices of the peace, who held very important jobs in the local judicial system, were also economically well-off. The other local officeholders were a more diverse group economically, and constables were the poorest.

The local constable was selected by annual election. Sometimes landless tradesmen or dependents were chosen, but most often it was a landowner with moderate holdings. When a wealthy man was chosen, there was some tendency for him to obtain a deputy of lower economic status.[5] A number of the constable reports required at each court session were delivered by someone other than the regular constable. In 1796, two cordwainers, a landless dependent, a miller, and eight yeomen served as constables.

The other lesser officerholders, with the exception of one surveyor, were a group of fairly substantial landowners. The smallest landowner among them was Benjamin Wells, a local merchant and the collector of the whiskey excise. Although small in size, his holdings were important—seven lots in the town of Connellsville, where he had been the first merchant.[6] County Commissioner Nathaniel Ewing had only 100 acres, but he was also engaged in mercantile activities.[7] The other

TABLE 6.2
Landholdings of Government Officials,
Fayette County, 1796

| | | | Acreage | |
Office	Number	Landed	Range	Median
High government	6	6	190–600	300
Petty bureaucrat	8	7	0–1,200	250
Justice of the peace	8	8	160–450	275
Constable	12	9	0–700	138
TOTAL	34	30	0–1,200	200

petty officeholders held from 200 to 1,200 acres, with three having around 300 acres.

Justices of the peace were, as a group, more wealthy than constables; they were moderate to substantial landowners. They were appointed by the state executive "during good behavior," and many of them held office for several years. Most would have been classified as yeoman farmers except for their justice position, although one was a retailer, another had a sawmill, and a third was a blacksmith.

Among the high government officials, State Senator Presley Carr Lane had nearly the smallest holding, only 200 acres. Lane had come to Bullskin Township from Virginia and had taken an active role in county government. Although "quite wealthy" and one of the few men to be frequently styled a "gentleman," he was apparently satisfied with his moderate holdings.[8] Much of the same can be said for the two assemblymen. John Smilie, for all of his state and national prominence as a leading Pennsylvania Antifederalist, bought a 300-acre farm when he came into western Pennsylvania from Lancaster County in the 1780s and simply maintained it.[9] Less well known was John Cunningham, who had 190 acres of land. Coming west from Chester County after the Revolution, he and a fellow soldier, William Ramsey, entered the distilling business, trading whiskey downriver. Although he did not hold any other office, "Uncle John" Cunningham, as the bachelor legislator was called, served in the state assembly for thirteen successive years.[10] Individuals like these suggest that very large landholdings were not necessary to attain the highest political offices.

Three of the most prominent government officials, Congressman Gallatin and two associate judges, were obviously wealthy. Nathaniel Breading bought about 700 acres when he came to Luzerne Township from Maryland with a great deal of continental money. He had been in commissary work at Valley Forge in 1777 and had once run an academy. He owned mills, engaged in the flour and whiskey trade, and also entered the iron business just after 1796, purchasing a share of the failed Hayden and Nicholson venture in Georges Township. He still held 300 acres in Luzerne and perhaps more in Menallen. Edward Cook, of course, also came west with money, but before the war. He originally was a merchandiser, then kept a tavern. He still owned 600 acres of the 3,000 or more than he had bought and sold at various times. He, too, had mills, stills, and several slaves. Both he and Breading had military and local government experience.[11] Albert Gallatin had 350 acres in 1796, and the company he owned with his partners held another 550 acres. He was laying out his own town, had bought most of the lots (fifty-six) in the rival town across the river in Greene Township, was engaged in the glass business, and soon would be in the gun-manufacturing business. Considering Gallatin's national fame, he was undoubtedly western Pennsylvania's most prominent person.[12]

In summary, government officials were drawn from the upper classes. The simple fact that most of them were landowners placed them in the upper half of society, and the fact that more than 60 percent of them owned 200 acres or more placed most of them in the upper 14 percent of the total population. Over 25 percent of them were in the top decile of landowners.

Among the nongovernment professionals, the two town proprietors, Rees Cadwallader and Zachariah Connell, were quite wealthy. They shared the characteristics of high government officials more than any of the other nongoverment professionals.[13] The remaining professionals, as indicated in table 6.3, were usually landless or, at most, moderate landholders.

The clergy had more land than any remaining category of this group, but compared with the clergymen of Washington County, the Fayette clergy were of modest means. In 1793, the Rev. Matthew Henderson of Chartiers Township had 513 acres and a slave, while Rev. John McMillan of Strabane Township had 350 acres.[14] The single lawyer designated in the county was apparently a young man just beginning his career reading law or serving as a clerk. He does not appear ever to have been officially admitted to practice in the county courts. Fayette County, in fact, was just beginning to establish its own group of barristers. Of approximately thirty attorneys admitted to practice in the county courts, none were from Fayette

TABLE 6.3
Landholdings of Non-Governmental Professional Class,
Fayette County, 1796

			Acreage	
Class	*Number*	*Landed*	*Range*	*Median*
Proprietor	2	2	1L + 255–10L + 1,800	—
Schoolmaster	14	0	0	0
Student	5	0	0	0
Physician	5	3	1L–60	1L
Clergy	3	3	100–190	115
Lawyer	1	1	80	—
TOTAL	30	9	0–10L + 1,800	0

Note: L = town lot.

County prior to 1790, and by 1796, there were only a few.[15] Most of the legal talent in western Pennsylvania resided in the county-seat towns of Pittsburgh and Washington, while the other county-seat towns in the circuit—Bedford, Greensburg, and Uniontown—had fewer lawyers. The leading lawyers of Washington and Pittsburgh were sizeable landowners. Their activities appeared frequently on the tax assessments in their home township and they were listed as speculators elsewhere. The lone lawyer included in this occupational survey was certainly not typical.

Fayette County physicians had very little land; two were town lot owners, and two were landless, although the fifth did have sixty acres. None was as influential as Absolom Baird of Washington, who was a state senator in 1795–1796. Finally, no group given a specific designation on the assessments was as uniformly poor as the schoolmasters and students. Not even the lowly miller or the tailor was as frequently landless.[16]

The Mercantile Class

The mercantile category was somewhat larger than the professional category, a good 4 percent of the population. As a group, they were probably the wealthiest segment of the county's population (table 6.4). Millers, merchants, the new industrial companies, and the smaller shop and tavernkeepers comprised the bulk of this category—almost half were mill owners.

The wealthiest members of this mercantile group—the three companies excepted—were easily the ironmasters and gristmillers. Two of the ironmasters, Isaac Meason and John Hayden, were among the largest landowners—3,200 and 2,200 acres, respectively—and the wealthiest men in the county. Three others had above average holdings of between 200 and 426 acres, while two more had small holdings.[17] The gristmillers, as discussed in chapter 3, were probably as wealthy as any group in the county. Gristmillers clearly had more land than sawmill owners. Just under a third of them (eleven) had below 200 acres, and nearly half (sixteen of thirty-four) had 300 acres or more. Among sawmill owners, by comparison, only three of seventeen owned 300 or more acres, while 70 percent owned less than 200 acres. Most of the millers in the river townships probably were engaged in the flour trade down the river, and some of the millers in the interior townships

TABLE 6.4
Landholdings of the Mercantile Class,
Fayette County, 1796

| | | | Acreage | |
Class	Number	Landed	Range	Median
Gristmill owner	34	34	7½–600	285
Sawmill owner	17	15	0–500	140
Shopkeeper	16	8	0–300	½L
Retailer	5	1	0–L	0
Merchant	5	3	0–250	L
Tavernkeeper	10	8	0–600	4
Ironmaster	7	7	1L–3,200	242
Company	3	3	207–1,069	550
Clerk	3	1	0–100	0
Ferryman	4	4	¼–320	75
TOTAL	104	84	0–3,200	140

Note: L = town lot.

probably were also. Such men were conducting business on a scale as large as many merchants and probably larger than most shopkeepers.[18]

The various merchants and retail shopkeepers were generally not large landowners. Of all thirty-six shopkeepers, retailers, merchants, and tavernkeepers only seven had as much as 200 acres or more of land. Four of these were tavernkeepers who had 300 to 600 acres each. Eleven of them did own town lots, however. Insofar as wealth was expressed by land, these retail sellers were definitely less well-to-do than the millers and ironmasters. How much of their wealth was tied up in inventory cannot be said. In terms of total taxable wealth—which might give some indication of the value of a man's store, even if he had only a town lot—these retail people still were not wealthy. Only five—three shopkeepers and two tavernkeepers—were wealthy enough to be in the top decile of their township in terms of total taxable wealth, while sixteen were rated below the median taxable value for their township. The three clerks were of similar status. Two had taxable property and worked at Meason's ironworks, while the third had 100 acres and was rated above the median taxable value in his township.[19] Ferrymen also had moderate wealth. Two owned only a town lot each, while the third had 150 acres. The wealthiest ferryman was a 320-acre farmer-ferryman from Luzerne Township.

The Absentee Landowners

The final small category, absentees landowners, has been dealt with on a broad basis in chapter 4, and little more than a brief outline is needed here. A majority of absentee holdings were in mountainous Bullskin Township. The size of absentee-owned lands was smaller in Fayette County than elsewhere. In fact, considering all ninety absentee tracts, the median holding was 134 acres, almost exactly the median landholding for the county as a whole. Unseated tracts were naturally larger, with a median of 200 acres, while the landlords had a 160-acre median. So many town lots were apparently absentee owned that the median tract without livestock was two and a half town lots. The distribution of these absentee holdings is summarized in table 6.5. Ninety of the ninety-seven absentees and speculators discussed in chapter 4 remain in this category. The other seven county residents who were included as speculators of some type have been placed in their regular occupational category.[20]

In summary, these three small categories, consisting of only 10 percent of the total population, were a very diverse group. They did include many of the wealthiest people in the county, but they also included people with only moderate landholdings and several landless people. High government officials, millers, the ironmasters and companies, and the few large absentee landowners were among the wealthiest people in the county. Nongovernmental professionals and most clerks and shopkeepers were moderately situated, at best. Such economic diversity as was found in these three categories will not be matched in the three remaining categories. There were richer and poorer yeomen, but they were all landowners. A few dependents did have property, but they were overwhelmingly lower class. There were some wealthy artisans, but here, too, the general tendency was toward modest economic status. Great diversity was the exception. Nevertheless, in these smallest occupational groups—the professional and mercantile classes—were to be found the wealthiest individuals and the greatest diversity in economic status.

TABLE 6.5
Absentee Class,
Fayette County, 1796

Type of Absentee Land	Number of Tracts	Acreage	
		Range	Median
Unseated land	40	30–4,200	200
Lands without livestock	34	L–314	2½L
Landlords	16	50–400	160
TOTAL	90	L–4,200	134

Note: L = town lot.

The Yeomen

The sturdy yeoman has long been viewed in the Jefferson tradition as the backbone of early American society. A whole mythology developed around this central figure in the nation's march westward.[21] In light of this general adulation for the yeoman, it is perhaps surprising to discover that he constituted only about a third of the population of frontier western Pennsylvania, and in some townships, yeomen farmers were scarcely more than a quarter of the population. Yeomen, defined here as landowning farmers, were the principal landowners. They produced the surplus agricultural products that helped feed those without land and that entered the western trade. The yeomen of Fayette County, in fact, owned 65.8 percent of the land, even though they made up only 30.8 percent of the population. Obviously, a number of other landowners in other occupational categories, such as a farmer-miller in the mercantile group, or a farmer-justice in the professional group, contributed to production and could be classified as yeomen. Nevertheless, only 762 persons out of the 2,473 in this survey have been classified as landowning yeomen farmers.[22]

The primary factors to be considered regarding the yeomen are the amount of land they owned and their probable economic status. An examination of the various statistical measurements leaves little doubt that yeomen had adequate-sized farms. The mean acreage of their farms ranged from 143 acres in Luzerne Township to 220 in Tyrone Township. River townships had just slightly smaller mean acreages than interior townships, as might be expected, and both had collective means below the border township, Bullskin. The mean acreage for all yeomen was 175.7 acres, certainly sufficient for an adequate farm and above the 130-acre average for eastern Pennsylvania.[23]

More important than the size of a farm was whether sufficient land had been cleared by 1796. Fortunately, three township assessments included both cleared and total acreage to allow more detailed study (table 6.6). (It is interesting that they were townships with the most extreme mean acreage: Luzerne

TABLE 6.6
Size of Yeoman Farms, Mean and Median Acreages,
Luzerne, Washington, and Tyrone Townships, 1796

Township	Mean Farm Acreages			Median Farm Acreages		
	Township Mean	Yeoman Mean	Mean Acres Cleared by Yeomen	Township Median	Yeoman Median	Median Acres Cleared by Yeomen
Luzerne	114	143	52.7	107	107	50
Washington	158	158	36.3	125	134	30
Tyrone	239	220	51.9	200	175	40

and Washington, which had the lowest township and yeomen means, and Tyrone, which had the highest means.) Mean and median figures indicate that the average yeoman did have a viable farm, with thirty or more acres of cleared land. One can also observe the effect of growing economic complexity on land use. Luzerne Township was small in area, but it had one of the larger populations, large artisan and dependent classes, as well as early town development. The resulting pressures had forced Luzerne farms to be the smallest in the county, and at the same time, they were the most fully developed. These farms had over a third of the land cleared (nearly half by median figures), but in the other two townships, farms had median cleared acreages under 25 percent.[24]

From the distribution of cleared acreages in these three townships, it is evident that a majority of yeomen had enough cleared land to begin to produce an agricultural surplus regardless of the standard used. James Lemon estimated that seventy-five acres of cleared, usable land in eastern Pennsylvania would support "an average family of five comfortably" and leave a surplus for commercial markets. Charles Grant also estimated that in Kent, Connecticut, nine and a half acres, including two and a half arable, could support one person. A family of five, therefore, would need forty-seven and a half acres of cleared land, with twelve and a half acres in crops. Grant further divided Kent settlers into five economic classes, the first three of which produced an agricultural surplus. Class 4, which averaged about forty acres of cleared land (five plowed, another thirty-five in meadow, pasture, and nontimberlands), had enough land to "produce a subsistence but no more."[25] Subsequently, other studies have suggested roughly comparable acreage requirements, but the work of Bettye Hobbs Pruitt on self-sufficiency in Massachusetts convincingly argues that these acreage requirements are too high. She found in Massachusetts that twenty acres was the median cleared acreage, an amount too small for self-sufficient agriculture. However, she shows there was an extensive and complex network of local exchange, which allowed this small acreage to provide an adequate livelihood. Lucy Simler and Paul Clemens show similar local trading networks in eastern Pennsylvania that sustained smallholders and landless persons.[26]

As table 6.7 indicates, most western Pennsylvania yeomen

TABLE 6.7
Distribution of Cleared Land,
Luzerne, Washington, and Tyrone Townships, 1796

Cleared Acres	Luzerne	Washington	Tyrone	Total	Cumulative Percentage
0–19	10	28	7	45	19
					ᵃ
20–29	11	15	4	30	31
30–39	7	22	10	39	47
					ᵇ
40–49	11	16	6	33	61
50–74	23	18	15	56	84
					ᶜ
75–99	11	2	3	16	91
100–125	10	6	2	18	99
180–280	0	1	2	3	100
TOTAL	83	108	49	240	

Source: Bettye Hobbs Pruitt, "Self-Sufficiency and the Agricultural Economy of Eighteenth-Century Massachusetts," *William and Mary Quarterly* 41 (1984): 338–42; Charles E. Grant, *Democracy in the Connecticut Frontier Town of Kent* (New York, 1961), table 5; James T. Lemon, "Household Consumption . . . in Southeastern Pennsylvania," *Agricultural History* 41 (January 1967): 68, n. 51.

a. cutoff line for subsistence agriculture (20 acres) according to Pruitt.
b. cutoff line for subsistence agricultue (40 acres) according to Grant.
c. cutoff line for commercial agriculture (75 acres and above) according to Lemon.

were able to produce at a level sufficient to enter the local exchange networks and to make contributions to the down-river trade. For the 16 percent with seventy-five or more acres cleared, the situation had to be profitable. For the 19 percent with less than twenty acres cleared, life was still tenuous. The general picture, therefore, was favorable. With sizeable acreages still uncleared, more and more of these yeomen would be able to improve their general standard of living or to rise above the subsistence level, as the majority had already done. Western Pennsylvania yeomen had reason to view the future optimistically. They advertised their farms glowingly as situated in "good wheat country," and the growing river trade, especially following peace with the Indians and Pinckney's Treaty, promised future profits.[27]

There are additional considerations in evaluating the situation of western Pennsylvania yeomen. First, since this was new country, considerable woodlands remained. As late as 1809, Joshua Gilpin reported that about half the area remained in woodlands. To the extent that these larger western Pennsylvania farms could use any of this uncleared land for pasture, especially the forests for foraging hogs, cleared-acreage requirements could be reduced. This is balanced, however, by the recognition that the hilly nature of the region meant that some lands "were nearly useless for cultivation" and would yield little but timber.[28]

Second, western Pennsylvania farms had less livestock than farms in areas of longer settlement. Ninety percent of western Pennsylvania's taxable population owned three or fewer cattle, and roughly 80 percent owned two or less. These were adult "horned cattle," and one can confidently double the number to arrive at the total. Yet, Lemon found an average of three and a half adult cattle normal for eastern Pennsylvania, seven to ten cattle per farm, figures he found comparable to Massachusetts, Virginia, and North Carolina examples. Since Lemon allows thirteen acres to provide the necessary hay for seven cattle, clearly western Pennsylvania yeomen with fewer cattle had need for less cleared acreage. With regard to sheep, it appears that western Pennsylvania was more similar to eastern Pennsylvania. Only the assessments in the *Pennsylvania Archives* for the

1780s reported sheep, thus no comparisons over time are possible. Just over half of Washington County taxable individuals reported sheep in 1784, yet less than half the taxpayers in Lancaster and Chester had sheep. The average number of sheep per farm was just over five compared to about seven in eastern Pennsylvania. Several people in each township had flocks numbering in the teens, and a handful of western Pennsylvanians had more than twenty sheep, both amounts a little smaller than across the state. Lemon estimated sheep needed little acreage for grain and hay; an acre or so would meet the needs of sheep on most western Pennsylvania farms, according to his requirements.[29]

Finally, it should not be forgotten that this was a largely traditional society where hunting was still a significant activity for supplementing the family diet. Archeological evidence from Charles Foreman's tavern site at Hannastown, in use from 1785 to 1795, suggests that most meat came from pigs, then cattle, deer, chickens, squirrels, fish, and sheep. Wheat was the most abundant grain, followed by oats, rye, buckwheat, corn, and flax. The investigators noted that this is the "same sequence [of grain] that Lemon ascribed to southeast Pennsylvania between 1740 and 1790."[30] These results, therefore, appear reasonable, and they show that three of the seven kinds of meat were obtained by hunting and fishing. In addition, there are extensive comments by travelers regarding the amount of fish and game available in the region. Mary Dewers noted that the gentlemen in her party passed "their time in hunting deer, turkeys, ducks and every other kind of wild fowl, with which this country abounds." John May, staying in Pittsburgh, dined on "turtle, fish of various kinds, soup and fowl." During his stay, he spoke of quantities of fish just yards from his quarters, of lads bringing him fine fish, of "gunning" for squirrels. Joseph Doddridge described his family living six weeks on venison, turkey, and bear, and he noted how important hunting was to early subsistence.[31]

Thus, it would appear that the yeomen farmers of western Pennsylvania were doing well. They had large farms with sufficient cleared acreages for most of them to be producing various surplus commodities. These commodities entered the local networks of exchange and undoubtedly found their way to distant markets. The farmers still had additional lands to clear, and they could supplement their livelihood from the abundance of nature. One cannot get a true picture of the agricultural economy, however, without also including the tenant farmers and the farm laborers. They also added to the production of the region, but because they did not own land, they have not been classified as yeomen, but as dependents. As we turn to a discussion of dependents, it might be well to remember that this majority of Fayette County yeomen who produced at or above the twenty-acre subsistence level, constituted only 25 percent of the total taxable population.

The Dependent Class

Unlike the yeomen, no mythology hailed the dependent class. The status of these people did not make them candidates for emulation. Rather, dependent status was a cause for concern in the yeoman mythology. Lacking independence, these people could not fulfill the role of the virtuous citizen attributed to the yeoman. In fact, their status made them scarcely known at all. Yet, they comprised the largest group in Fayette County in 1796. Dependents have been defined as those persons without obvious means of self-support. Lacking both land and some trade or skill, they are the landless taxable individuals of most assessments. Some were the poor, the widows without land, the aged, and others in similar circumstances. A number were landless single freemen, young men over twenty-one years of age who had not yet become heads of their own households. They, too, were as dependent upon their father's lands as were the hired hands, and in fact, many of them had no family connections. Single freemen may have comprised about 15 percent of the dependent class and are spread throughout the various dependent categories in unknown proportions. (Single freemen, of course, were also artisans and are scattered throughout the other occupations discussed in this chapter.) A large number of the dependents were inmates, a category rarely found on the assessments, but a status widespread in the region, as will be demonstrated later. In combination, these various groups formed the dependent classes and comprised approximately 42 percent of the population of Fayette County in 1796.

Arriving at an aggregate total for the dependent class is considerably easier than determining the exact composition of this group. The problem is simply that no two assessments treated these people in the same way, and most simply left them as landless settlers with no specific notation. As a result, more than a half-dozen different categories that were inconsistently reported and had overlapping boundaries with each other had to be resolved into a few meaningful, self-contained categories.[32] To do this, six of the more explicit assessments for 1796—three from Washington County and three from Fayette County—have been used to build an estimated composite of the dependent classes. Information from the three most complete assessments is summarized in table 6.8. The composite indicates that approximately 25 percent of the dependent class were general laborers. Another 65 percent were farmers without land. The great majority of these—perhaps 50 percent of the whole dependent class—were probably tenant farmers. The rest were probably farm laborers. A final 10 percent were the old, the poor, and a few others not gainfully employed in any known way.

TABLE 6.8
Estimated Composition of Dependent Class (percent),
Three Townships, 1796

Dependent Groups	East Bethlehem	Greene	Franklin	Estimated Composition
Laborers	25.3	17.7	25.9	25.0
Poor	10.1	12.4	3.7	10.0
Landless farmers	64.6	64.6	63.6	65.0[a]
Unclassified	—	5.3	6.8	—
TOTAL	100.0	100.0	100.0	100.0

a. From other assessments, it is further estimated that this category includes 50 percent tenants and another 15 percent farm laborers.

The three townships with enough specific data to analyze—East Bethlehem and Greene in Washington County and Franklin in Fayette County—have surprisingly similar profiles of the dependent class. Their landless-farmer categories are almost identical. Their laboring-class figures are reasonably close. These labor figures are higher in the two more developed townships, Franklin with its ironworks, East Bethlehem with its small river town. The number of artisans in these townships reflects the same trend, higher in the developed townships, lower in Greene. The small percentage on two returns who are unclassifiable may add a percent or two to each of the other catagories.[33]

Three other township assessments include certain specific categories that are helpful in analyzing the dependent class. Luzerne Township, Fayette County, and Cecil Township, Washington County, specify renters and tenants. Tyrone Township, Fayette County, designates laborers. From Luzerne and Cecil, it is estimated that most landless farmers were actually tenants and that tenant farmers are 50 percent of the dependent class. In Luzerne, "renters" comprise 50.8 percent of the dependent group, and in Cecil, 73.6 percent of the dependent class are termed "tenants." The Cecil assessment is constructed completely around the landlord-tenant relationship, which obscures the differences between tenant farmers and inmates who rented lodgings while performing agricultural work or other kinds of labor. Thus, the Cecil figure seems too high to use for a general estimate even though it strongly emphasizes the reality and complexity of rental arrangements on the frontier.[34] Using an estimate that 50 percent of the dependent class are tenants correlates reasonably well with the 20 percent tenancy figures developed in chapter 4. Twenty percent of the total Fayette County taxable population of 2,473 would be 495 persons; fifty percent of the 1,054 dependent individuals would be 527. The landless farmer category, therefore, is estimated to contain two groups: farmers who rented their land and comprised perhaps 50 percent of the dependent class, and agricultural workers who comprised another 15 percent of the dependent class.

Tyrone Township was one of the few that identified laborers specifically. The township included the Turnbull iron-works, and undoubtedly, many of these laborers worked there. Compared with neighboring Franklin Township, which had its Meason ironworks, Tyrone had more laborers, but many fewer artisans. Perhaps some of the colliers and potters who worked with many laborers at Meason's were all called laborers by the Tyrone assessor. In any case, there is little other evidence to suggest that Tyrone's 32 percent general-labor figure is reasonable for the county as a whole. Thus, the 25-percent figure has been accepted as more realistic.[35]

In summary, the dependent classes include these basic groups: general laborers (25 percent), tenant farmers (50 per-cent), agricultural laborers (15 percent), and the poor (10 percent). Table 6.9 summarizes these categories in terms of the population as a whole.

Understanding the status of the dependent classes is equally as full of uncertainties as determining the composi-tion of the group. The small group of the poor and old were often cared for by their families, as a few assessment nota-tions made clear. The county courts certainly charged the family with responsibility where possible.[36] In addition, each township annually elected two persons to serve as overseers of the poor and to care for the needy. The overseers were also charged with collecting from men for desertion or main-taining bastard children, but the amounts were less than sons were charged for the maintenance of their fathers.[37] The

TABLE 6.9
Estimated Size of Dependent Class as Part of Total Population,
Fayette County, 1796

| | | Percentage | |
| | | Dependent | Total |
Dependent Class	Number	Class	Population
Common laborer	264	25.0	10.7
Tenant farmers	527	50.0	21.3
Agricultural laborer	158	15.0	6.4
Poor	105	10.0	4.2
TOTAL	1,054	100.0	42.6

poor could probably expect between 2s. and 7s. 6d. per week if they had no other means to support themselves. This would probably keep body and soul together, but it was considerably less than the common laboring man could expect to earn.

The wages earned by common laborers and hired farm hands in western Pennsylvania were probably quite adequate. The few wage rates found suggest that wages were high, and that all labor—skilled and unskilled—was in demand, as all the general accounts suggest.[38] Wages paid in the early 1790s to citizens hired by the army at Fort Pitt provide a public base for comparing wage rates. The lowest unskilled wage paid was $4 (£1.10) a month for a worker to care for the public boats. Various other workers and craftsmen were paid $10 to $30 per month, levels above those Jackson Main found nationally.[39] Certainly when one considers the growing economic maturity of the region, its new towns, the yearly flow of settlers numbering in the thousands moving west and buying provisions in the area, the growing river trade, and the many farms being carved out of forest land, one must conclude that there was need for skilled and unskilled labor.

The work done by historians in recent years throws much light on how these dependent classes survived. Particularly enlightening is the work by Lucy Simler and Paul Clemens on Chester County. By combining assessment records with a few extant farm account books, they have shown the complex interrelationships between landowners and those who rented from them. The renter or "cottager" was given a few acres of land to subsist on, use of woodlots, pasture, and farm equipment as needed in return for an annual rent and additional work. The cottager was obligated to supply seasonal help to the landowner in return for money wages. Yet, the cottager was also free to labor for others or to practice a trade. An artisan could rent space and supply the landlord family with shoes or cloth, for example, while practicing his trade in the neighborhood. While these were contractual relationships, "there was much left unstated."[40]

For example, in 1792, George Brinton of Chester County

took on two workers who rented cottages for £4 and were to be paid 2s. per day for common farm work, 2s. 6d. for mowing, and 5s. for cradling in the harvest season. Brinton also hired the wives of the cottagers at half that paid the men for peak harvest season and other work, and also hired for brief periods another male worker and another female worker that same year. Over the months and years, these relationships remained fluid; cottagers moved from landlord to landlord. They could expect to earn at least 2s. per day as male workers and maybe 18d. as female workers. One Brinton cottager earner £38.16.6 over a period of seventeen months.[41]

While one is hesitant to apply Chester County examples directly to the Monongahela Valley of western Pennsylvania, and account books to prove the relationships are lacking, nevertheless, there appear to be many similar relationships. In East Bethlehem, the only township to identify inmate relationships, lived Zephaniah Beall, a yeoman farmer with 209 acres, a frame farmhouse, two cabins, and two cabin barns. Living on Beall's land was son Thomas, a farmer-inmate according to the assessment, John Marker, a cordwainer-inmate, and Thomas Thompson and Alexander McKay, both laborer-inmates. On the land of Zephaniah Beall, Jr., a yeoman with 336 acres (once part of his father's larger holding), stood a log house and several cabins. Living here also were inmates Simon Simmons, a carpenter, and Samuel Scott and John Heaton, farmers. Scott owned one horse, and Heaton owned two horses and two cows.

As another example, William Heald was a yeoman farmer with eighty acres of land, two small houses, and a cabin barn. Living on his smaller holding was Jonathan Wilson, a single freeman tanner, who himself owned ten acres with a tan house and small shop, but who resided with Heald. Even a small landowner like cordwainer James Hartley, who owned only twenty acres with two cabins and a cabin barn, had a single freeman weaver, Samuel Smith, residing on his land. These examples can be expanded with many more: John Krebs, a farmer-ferryman with six inmates (two blacksmiths, a ferryman, and three laborers, including a free black man), or Joseph Townsend, a farmer-sawyer, with ten inmates on his

461 acres (three farmers, one cordwainer, one cooper, one weaver, one sawyer, one farmer-stiller, one mason, and one laborer). If both small and large landholders had inmates, it does not follow that all landowners had inamtes. Many landed yeomen did not; they operated farms up to 200 acres or more on their own, undoubtedly relying on family labor.

Although we have no account books to describe these relationships in detail, clearly something like Simler and Clemens's description of Chester County occurred in western Pennsylvania. Large landowners, both local and absentee—every absentee tract identified in East Bethlehem had inmates living on it—were using the labor of propertyless people for the tasks of clearing and working their farms. The landless often practiced their trade while living on the landlord's land and undoubtedly worked for the landlord and many others for money wages and produce exchanges. A Swiss traveler stated that "very many landowners lend their lands to people who are careful and hard-working in return for half the yield, and in addition furnish them with cattle and agricultural implements." Israel Shreve, after agreeing to rent a large farm in Fayette County, wrote his family that he intended to sublease portions to cover most of his rent.[42] What is certain from all of this is that the community relationships found in western Pennsylvania were much more complex than they would appear to be at first glance.

Even though the landless resident probably lived adequately, he did not accumulate property or stay long in the region. If East Bethlehem is any indication, the landless people in this river township were quite mobile. More than two-thirds of the inmates there in 1796 were new since 1793. Regarding laborers specifically, in Greene Township almost all laborers were new since 1793, and much turnover occurred in Luzerne.[43] The lack of property accumulation also suggests that laborers did not sink roots and that their wages, although adequate for living, were insufficient to purchase land in western Pennsylvania. In four townships that singled out laborers— Greene, East Bethlehem, Franklin, and Tyrone—only four laborers of 108 owned any land. One laborer in East Bethlehem had 100 acres, two laborers at Meason's ironworks had 73 and

100 acres, while a laborer in Tyrone had 119 acres—all modest holdings.

All of this suggests that agricultural labor and common labor was part of a complex system of maintenance and survival. As was concluded in chapter 4, tenancy was not the road to wealth. In point of fact, it is now clear that tenants and these laboring people are much the same people. They probably were able to provide an adequate living for themselves. Many accepted this labor system as normal and provided a continuing core of tenants and workers. Those who stayed in the region probably improved their comfort level even if they did not become property owners. A few apparently did well enough to become landowners.[44] As a group, however, their mobility was high. The gradually appreciating land values of western Pennsylvania probably meant that many decided to move west, hoping to purchase land on some distant frontier, rather than to remain in the laboring classes of western Pennsylvania.

Documenting these relationships is difficult. One of the more revealing descriptions of how the system worked and the mentality of the western settler is the letter written by Israel Shreve to his family explaining his situation in western Pennsylvania in 1789. He had come west with several other families and settled in Westmoreland County. Soon he obtained the George Washington mill tract tenanted by Gilbert Simpson, which he proceeded to sublet, and became a successful miller. The letter is quoted here in its entirety for its insight into the many relationships discussed in this chapter.[45] (Original spelling has been retained.)

Forks of the Yough
December 26th, 1789

Dear Brother:

Haveing an oppertunity to Philada. I embrace it and mention my situation an intended one. Since I have been here have wished to git Washington's Bottoms. I have at last obtained the whole tract on rent for five years. I wrote to the General by his agent in this country Colonel Canon who a few weeks ago returned from New York. The General was pleased to order Colonel Canon to let me have the whole of the Bottoms so called at my own offer. The old farm contains about

80 acres of improved upland and about 40 of the best kind of meadow, a bearing orchard of 120 apple and 100 peach trees. The buildings as good as most in this country. Pretty well situated and five other improved farms that at this time rents for £43-10. I am accountable for the whole rent, which altogether is £60, so that I shall rent the old place for £16-10, to be paid either in money or wheat at 3s per bushel. I considered that land at the Miami settlement was raiseing fast and that I had better pay this low rent for a well improved farm than Barter away my land at a lowe rate for land here. Land does not raise much in this place owning to the great immigration down the River. It seems as if people were mad to git afloat on the Ohio. Many leaves pretty good liveings here sets of for they know not where but too often find their mistake. I beleave this as good as any other settlement down the River for the present. The Mississippi trade is open at this time and all the wheat, whiskey, bacon, etc., buying up by those concerned in it. The highest price for wheat is 4s in trade or 3/9 cash, whisky 3/ cash and bacon 6d per 1 lb cash. On the farm where I am going is a good stream for a grist mill as any in the whole Forks and a mill that can be set going for I believe £50, and a number of years given for the repairs. I am in hopes of being able to set it going as it will produce more grain than all the 6 farms on the Tract. I am to have possession the first of April next and flatter myself I have as good a chance as any person in my present circumstance could expect. I shall have nothing to attend to but my own private conserns and think this way of life far preferable to any other. Richard Shreve is to have one of the small farms. They contain improved land as follows— one 40 acres of upland and 5 good meadows, one 35 acres upland and 7 good meadows, one about 35 acres upland and—meadows. The other too about 25 acres upland and 5 or 6 of good meadow each. The whole in good fence, they being the year before last rented for repairs only etc. Peggy Shreve has a daughter. She and her husband has been very sickly but recovered. I am grandfather to another son. John and his wife pretty well as is our family at present but expect measles as it is in the school where our boys goes. I hope you are all well also. I am with great respect and love

Your brother
Israel Shreve

The Artisan Class

The final category of occupations on the western Pennsylvania frontier was the artisan class. This class of skilled craftsmen was half as large as the yeomen class and made up 16 percent of the total population. This percentage is significant. It is above Jackson Main's general conclusion that artisans comprised only 10 percent of the northern population of revolutionary America. Pennsylvania figures tend to be higher than the average, Main notes, and the studies of James Lemon and others indicate this was true. Within a generation of settlement, therefore, western Pennsylvania achieved an occupational diversity equal to or exceeding that of many of the older sections of the nation.[46]

The composition of this artisan class in eight Fayette County townships includes 399 artisans, (table 6.10). Although 48 were simply checked as being "mechanics" in Springhill Township, the remaining 351 were spread among forty-one different trades. Nine trades included 75 percent of all the artisans. The weavers were easily the largest single group, followed by shoemakers, carpenters, blacksmith, coopers, tailors, millers, joiners, and potters. The greatest number of artisans appeared in Franklin Township. The Meason ironworks in that township employed at least forty-seven persons, representing thirteen different trades, as well as general laborers.[47] It seems most likely that Meason ran his ironworks much like a plantation, a common occurrence at that time. The appearance of a tailor and shoemaker among the artisans suggests as much, as does the fact that Meason also held some kind of fair on his property, either a trade fair, or perhaps just a holiday for his workers.[48]

No other township had even half as many artisans as Franklin. The river townships, collectively, had more artisans than the other regions. Luzerne, with its river town of Bridgeport, located just across the creek from Brownsville, led in both the number of artisans and in the number of different trades. The more agricultural township of Washington had the least. Although the distribution of trades in Springhill is unknown

TABLE 6.10
Artisans,
Fayette County, 1796

Trade	Number	Percentage
Weaver	66	18.8
Shoemaker[a]	41	11.7
Carpenter	35	10.0
Blacksmith	32	9.1
Cooper	27	7.7
Tailor	22	6.3
Miller	18	5.1
Joiner	13	3.7
Potter	11	3.1
Tanner	9	2.6
Mason	9	2.6
Wheelwright	7	2.0
Boat builder	6	1.7
Millwright	5	1.4
Collier	5	1.4
Fuller	4	1.1
Sadler	4	1.1
Wagon maker	4	1.1
Hammerman	3	0.9
Sawyer	3	0.9
Stiller	3	0.9
Six Trades[b], 2 in each	12	3.4
Twelve trades[c], 1 in each	12	3.4
TOTAL	351	100.0

a. Includes 32 shoemakers, 5 cordwainers, 2 cordwinders, and 2 cob-
blers.
b. Wagoner, jockey, packer, turner, tinker, and tradesman.
c. Hemp hackler, cheese maker, hatter, silversmith, gunsmith, nailer,
cutler, bricklayer, ferryman, clothier, founder, and keeper (at Isaac
Meason's works).

except for a fuller, the impression of this township suggests a
variety of trades and artisans equal to or exceeding those in
Luzerne. There was Albert Gallatin's glassworks, some nascent iron enterprises, plus the normal trades, like boat building, expected in a river township. The number of artisans in
the border township, Bullskin, was increased by the existence
of Connellsville. The remaining two interior townships, Ty-

rone and Georges, had fewer artisans. Some Tyrone artisans were probably included in the large listing of laborers given for that township. For example, there were no founders or potters listed for the Turnbull works as there were for the Meason works. The figures for Georges Township were simply too low because occupations were not given in 1795; using the extant assessment for that township and reading occupations back from 1798 and 1799 did not prove very successful because of artisan mobility. A truer accounting from this township would probably raise the total artisan percentage another point.

The figures on the distribution of artisans were apparently representative of western Pennsylvania as a whole (table 6.11). Comparison with fourteen selected Washington County townships in 1796 reveals similar results. In these townships, the percentage of the population who were artisans range from 7 to 33 percent, with a median of 17 percent. In actual numbers, the artisans range from nine to eighty-nine, with a me-

TABLE 6.11
Artisans and Trades by Township and Region
Fayette County, 1796

Region/Township	Number of Artisans	Percentage	Number of Trades
River			
Washington	43	10.8	9
Luzerne	63	15.8	21
German	44	11.0	18
Springhill	49	12.3	—
TOTAL	199	49.9	29
Interior			
Tyrone	25	6.3	9
Franklin	134	33.6	27
Georges	10	2.5	4
TOTAL	169	42.4	27
Border			
Bullskin	31	7.7	14
GRAND TOTAL	399	100.0	41

dian of thirty-three and a half while the number of different trades in a township ranges from seven to twenty-seven, with a median of twelve. These three median figures—thirty-three and a half artisans, representing twelve different trades and comprising 17 percent of the population—are quite comparable with the Fayette County figures.[49]

The artisan figures represent minimal estimates of the number in the actual population. They do not, for the most part, take into account the many trades in the towns. The artisan poulation of the larger towns like Washington and Pittsburgh was sizeable by the mid-1790s, and those of Brownsville and Uniontown (the two largest towns in Fayette County, for which, unfortunately, there are not extant assessments) may well have been as diverse. For example, the artisans in the town of Washington in 1792 represented nine additional trades not found among the forty-one in Fayette County.

The economic status of artisans in western Pennsylvania was probably favorable and noticeably above that of the common laborers. One standard for judgment was the prevailing wage rates paid in western Pennsylvania. The data on wage rates paid at Fort Pitt in 1794 is summarized in table 6.12. Jackson Main's work suggests that the wages of carpenters were typical of artisans nationally. They might earn 2s. 6d. or 3s. per day to as high as 6s. Weavers and tailors, paid by the piece, earned less, while masons and smiths earned more. Wages were about a third less where "found," that is, where room and board were provided.[50]

Wage rates paid at Fort Pitt were clearly at the highest end of the scale suggested by Main's study. Although there are some inconsistencies in equating the dollars paid with pounds, carpenters at Fort Pitt were paid $30 per month (6s. per day if £3 = $10; 7s. 6d. if £3 = $8). The carpenters' wage rate was typical for many other craftsmen. Masons, coopers, the armorer at the fort, packhorse masters, and boat masters earned similar wages. Common labors such as wagoners, boatmen and packmen, tasks nearly any able-bodied frontiersman could readily perform, were paid $10 per month. In some cases, rations were added to the wage as in the case of the blacksmith at the fort, and his apprentice was paid half his rate. Because of

TABLE 6.12
Selected Wage Rates Paid Civilian Workers at Fort Pitt,
January–March 1794

Name/Occupation	Monthly Rate (dollars[a])
Marcus Hurling, Sr., boat master	30
Marcus Hurling, Jr. boatman	12
Thomas Vaughn, boatman	10
John Wilson, boatman	10
Emanuel Conrad, care and feeding horses	10
Thomas Vickery, care of public boats	4
John McLeod, ships carpenter	20
Mordecai McLeod, ships carpenter	20
Lewis Thornell, driving public team	10
Several individuals, packmen	15
William Jemeson, pack horse master	30
James Baird, master blacksmith	16[b]
Apprentice blacksmith	8
Philip Francis, cooper	30[c]
Samuel Peoples, clerk, quarter master	30
Henry Wolf, armorer	30
James Clow, mason?	30[c]
James Blashford, carpenter	30[c]
Dennis Burns, public wagoner	10
William Burns, public wagoner	10
Thomas Love, weaver	—[d]
David Donley, weaver	—[d]

Source: Carnegie Library of Pittsburgh, Isaac Craig Collection, Microfilm 271, Reel 8, Account Book III-B, entries, 996, 997, 1001, 1003, 1004, 1006, 1010, 1011, 1017, 1028, 1039, 1043, 1079, 1094, 1133, 1145, 1146.

a. Dollars equated to pounds at £3 = $8 would be £11.5 = $30; at £3 = $10 would be £9 = $30.
b. Paid wage plus rations at 8¢ each.
c. Paid at the rate of $1 per day.
d. Paid for twilled bags at $1 each.

all the recruiting the army did for grain and horses, as well as for boatmen and packmen for the war effort in Ohio, these rates had to be well known. They provided a very public standard, but one that was probably high due to war demands. Nevertheless, one must conclude that wage rates in western Pennsylvania were quite attractive.[51]

Another standard for judging the status of artisans was the number who owned land. By this standard, a third of the artisans in Fayette County (34.3 percent) were property owners. Forty artisans (10.0 percent) owned town lots only, ninety-two artisans (23.6 percent) were landowners, and three artisans (0.7 percent) owned both lots and land. Of all artisans, the tanners were most likely to be landowners (77.8 percent); blacksmiths were second (62.5 percent), followed by mill-wrights (60 percent), and wheelwrights (57.1 percent). Carpenters were the typical group (34.3 percent owned land), while coopers (11.1 percent), millers (5.6 percent), colliers, and stillers (both landless) were on the bottom.[52]

Artisans normally owned only moderate-size tracts, however. The median artisan landowner, lot owners included, had only 50 acres, and with lot owners excluded, the median rose only to 80 acres. Both figures were below the county median of 131 acres. There were, to be sure, a few large landowners among the artisans. A Franklin Township wheelwright who owned 1,700 acres was the most spectacular, followed at some distance by a blacksmith, also in Franklin Township, who owned 500 acres. Eleven artisans owned 300 or more acres. A few landowning artisans were even landlords. Blacksmith James Colvan and fuller Matthew Atcheson of Cecil Township both had one tenant on their 100- and 150-acre farms. A number of artisans farmed as well as followed a trade, and one or two assessments listed artisans as following both occupations. Seven farmer-artisans lived in East Bethlehem Township: two tanners, two tailors, a cordwainer, a weaver, and a blacksmith. Whether such people earned more from their craft or from their farming is impossible to say. It is undoubtedly true, however, that in a society as agrarian as was western Pennsylvania, most artisans and other persons supplemented their income by some small-scale farming where possible. Undoubtedly even lot owners had their garden plots.[53]

The mobility of artisans, like other groups in western Pennsylvania, was conspicuous (table 6.13). There were twenty-nine landed artisans in East Bethlehem Township in 1796, and fourteen of them were new since 1793. A newcomer, like farmer-weaver James Carnihan, had acquired eighty-two acres; house

TABLE 6.13
Artisan Mobility,
East Bethlehem and Greene Townships, 1793–1796

| | | | | | Old Artisans | | |
| Township | Number of Artisans | New Artisans | | Improved | Same Landed | Same Landless | Lost |
		Landed	Landless				
East Bethlehem	62	14	24	7	8	6	3
Greene	42	8	15	3	5	6	5
TOTAL	104	22	39	10	13	12	8

carpenter William Hiller had ninety-one acres; and cordwainer Job Malin had three lots. Of the fifteen landed artisans who were in the township in 1793, seven improved their economic position, while the remaining eight held even. Typical of those who improved their positions was John Anderson, a boat builder, who was landless in 1793, but by 1796 had fifty acres of unimproved land. Gunsmith John Hormel had acquired a town lot, and hatter Edward Dowler had increased his holdings from one to nine town lots, most of them still unimproved, plus eight acres of land. Blacksmith David Townsend had made the greatest strides by increasing his one lot to ten lots plus twenty acres. The taxable wealth of every artisan increased three or four times over the three years, and some increased as much as ten times. Such increases were typical of the township as a whole and probably reflected both the growth of the township and a better assessment of market values.

Of the thirty-three artisans without land in East Bethlehem in 1796, twenty-four were new in the township since 1793, six were still landless, as they had been in 1793, but three others may have lost the land they had held in 1793, or more likely some change in inmate status had occurred and was inconsistently reported on the two assessments. A cordwainer who had a lot and two weavers who had 30 and 108 acres each were now landless inmates living with other property owners. The cordwainer's landowner, however, had a town lot as well as a farm, and there many have been no change of status at all. The other two may have just changed landlords, for they were now residing with owners of different-sized farms. If these three were losses, they were balanced by only two artisans (Anderson and Hormel) who had risen from a landless status.

Similarly, in Greene Township, of forty-two artisans noted in the township in 1796, twenty-three were new since 1793. Eight of these twenty-three had acquired land. Of the nineteen who were in the township in 1793, eleven still had the same status, three had improved their position, but five had lost ground. Blacksmith Samuel Baldwin made the greatest improvement, increasing his lands from 170 to 400 acres, and two others, a turner and a tailor, had each acquired 80 acres. The greatest loss was suffered by weaver Samuel Mills, who had 300 acres in 1793 but was landless in 1796. Boat builder Samuel Mannon lost 100 acres with a sawmill, and wheelwright Joseph Drake, who had no land but had a gristmill and sawmill in 1793, appeared in 1796 as landless. We have no specific indication of inmate relationships for this township (though they probably existed), so it is impossible to know whether these were indeed significant losses of land, or changes in inmate status, or some other situation. The wheelwright, for example, could easily be living and practicing his trade at a local mill. The other losses of whatever sort were less substantial; one artisan dropped from 40 to 24 acres, and the second dropped from 340 to 300 acres.

On balance, therefore, the mobility of the artisan class was positive; certainly better than that of the tenants and dependents. Skilled labor apparently made a difference. Almost 60 percent of the artisans in these two townships were new, and a third of these new artisans had acquired land. One-fourth of the original artisans had also increased their landholdings. Altogether, 30 percent of the artisans bought land within the three-year period; only 8 percent appear to have lost land, and some of those, at least, appear to have changed inmate situations.

It is clear from this summary of the occupational structure of Fayette County, assuming that it is indeed representative of the whole region, that western Pennsylvania had made giant strides toward economic maturity since the end of the Revolution. Already the proportion of artisans in the region equaled that of the nation as a whole. The groundwork had been laid for a number of industrial pursuits, particularly the iron industry in Fayette County. The yeomen of the region were producing agricultural surpluses that increasingly entered the western trade. The basis for the professions had been established on a small scale, and a mercantile network, whose roots stretched back into the prerevolutionary past, continued to supply the region adequately and looked forward to expanded commerce. Those characteristics that have come to be associated with emerging market economies—increasingly integrated regional markets and wage and price levels based on market rates—were already evident in western Pennsylvania. Stimulated by the constant flow of settlers through the region, the river trade, and the military activity in Ohio, the people of western Pennsylvania transformed the region into a surprisingly mature society within one generation.[54]

The emerging class structure also pointed toward maturity, but with a great deal of mobility. Settlers came and left frequently. The laboring classes lacked continuity; many moved on quickly. An important part of this fluid situation was the obvious economic opportunities the region presented. Many settlers entered the region and became landowners at once. The class structure of the region was not rigid or closed; there was room for the enterprising person to become a local leader. With initial wealth and ability, plus a measure of good fortune, a newcomer could enter the upper class as a government official, a merchant, or an industrialist. A number of common people could also look forward to moderate property holdings and quite adequate livings from farming, local mercantile pursuits, or skilled artisanry. For the less skilled and the landless, there were many opportunities to rent land for farming or to rent adequate habitations and to do general labor or practice a trade to make a living. It was also obvious, however, that the greatest opportunities were open only to those who had the wealth and resources to take advantage of them. Most of the population was lower or lower-middle class, and most of them would remain there. They had, at best, modest property holdings, and most of those without property would not acquire any. Those at the top were controlling more of the region's growing wealth; those at the lower levels were controlling less. Thus, by 1796, those natural processes that sort out and stratify people, that create a class structure in any society, had already left their imprint on the frontier society of western Pennsylvania. The frontier era was over; the transformation into a mature society was well under way.

7 *The Structure of Political Power*

IT CAN BE stated from the outset that western Pennsylvania in the late eighteenth century was governed by men drawn from the highest levels of the class structure. By the mid-1790s, a distinctive governing elite dominated the political life of the region. Each individual singled out to illustrate one of the transforming trends of the region—Gallatin, Ryerson, Cook, Meason, Canon—held high political office at some point in his career. Alexander Addison, whose description of the rapid growth and potential of the region provided the keynote and an organizing framework for this study, is also very typical of these political leaders.

Alexander Addison was born in 1759 in Ireland. He was educated at Edinburgh and was licensed to preach by the Presbytery of Aberlowe, Scotland. After emigrating to America, he was called by the Redstone Presbytery in December 1785 to the town of Washington. He soon, however, turned to the study of law, reading under David Redick in Washington, and he was admitted to the bar in March 1787. In 1791, Addison was selected to be president judge for the Western Pennsylvania Circuit. This was part of the judicial reform brought by the new 1790 state constitution that provided for persons learned in the law to preside over the courts, rather than prominent laymen like Edward Cook. Addison's Federalist political views placed him in good stead with both the new state and the national leadership. It was from this position that he made his famous charge to the grand jury during the Whiskey Rebellion.

Sometime shortly after 1795–1796, Addison moved to Pittsburgh, and there he continued his judicial career in an increasingly partisan and controversial manner. Addison's career ended abruptly in 1803. In the different political climate of Jeffersonian America, Addison was impeached by the Pennsylvania Senate on 27 January 1803 in what is still a famous and controversial event. He died some four years later on 24 November 1807. During his years of political and judicial influence, Addison was among the economic elite of his community. In 1793, the value of his property in Washington ranked in the top decile of the town. In addition, that year he owned unseated tracts of 120 acres and 500 acres in Donegal Township and another 500 unseated acres in Franklin Township. He also owned outlots surrounding the town of Washington. Unlike a number of the economic and political elite, Addison came rather late to the region, but like a number of others, he still found ample opportunity to use his ability to become a major influence in the region's development.[1]

The existence of a wealthy governing elite such as Addison represented may seem at odds with the traditional views of western Pennsylvania as a hotbed of democratic radicalism and opposition to propertied elites.[2] Yet this should be viewed in relationship to the social structure of the region. All the region's political elite, whether of Federalist persuasion like Addison and Pittsburgh's Hugh H. Brackenridge, or of Jeffersonian persuasion like Albert Gallatin, John Smiley, or William Findley, were drawn from the top levels of society. They all operated in a political climate that has often been called the most democratic in the new nation. The colonial voting requirement of fifty acres or £50 of personal property was dropped by the constitution of 1776. It specified that all freemen, aged twenty-one and older, who had resided in the state one year and had paid public taxes during that period, could vote. The constitution further provided that eligible sons of freeholders were not to be denied the vote even if they had not paid any tax. The colonial procedure, in use since at least 1766, of using tax lists as voting lists, continued under the new constitution. The test oath demanded by the supporters of the 1776 constitution, which disenfranchised many eastern residents, probably had only a limited effect in the west. The west generally supported both the test oath and the constitution, and furthermore, provision was made in 1785 that persons in the west who had taken the oath of loyalty to Virginia prior to the settlement of the boundary dispute were entitled to vote. The one property qualification that remained was that only freeholders could vote for justices of the peace.

Regardless of how much validity there may be in terming the constitution of 1790 "counterrevolutionary," the terms of the franchise as spelled out in that document continued the same liberal qualifications and, in fact, probably enlarged them. Now the sons of majority of any qualified freeman (not freeholder as in 1776) could vote even if they did not pay any tax. Furthermore, the test laws that disenfranchised many voters were dropped. However, voters no longer elected justices of the peace, who were now appointed by the governor.[3]

Considering these facts, it may be safely contended that during these years, Pennsylvania operated under a political system that very nearly approached universal male suffrage, and that tax assessment lists represented approximately 90 percent of the voting population. The election of men of property and position to political office by a population considered by some to be politically radical and opposed to property, cannot be attributed to a restricted franchise. Western Pennsylvanians could vote; the extent to which they exercised their vote may be another question. Very, very fragmentary evidence suggests many may not have voted. There is undoubtedly a tendency for those more involved in a society's affairs to be more involved politically. Thus, limited participation is not unexpected. The election of wealthy people does mean, however, that they governed at least with the tacit acceptance—if not outright approval—of the population as a whole. This raises questions about the adequacy of easy assumptions of the past that western Pennsylvanians were hostile to the propertied classes.

To study this relationship between political power and economic position, all the known officeholders on the national, state, and county levels, plus selected township officers, have been categorized and compared in two ways. First, officeholders above the township level have been separated into three groups, based upon their frequency of holding office. Group 1 officers, the primary political leadership group, are men who held office at least twice for a total of six years or more or held office three or more times regardless of the number of years. Group 2 officers are those who held two offices for five years or less, or one office more than three years. Because so many persons held the dual offices of justice of the peace and judge prior to 1790, and justices often served long terms, group 2 is almost exclusively judicial in character. Furthermore, because it is often difficult to determine precisely how many years these justices served, all persons holding only the appointment of justice or judge have been included in group 2, including Judge Addison. The exceptions are those justices found for the first time on a 1795 list for Fayette County and on a 1797 list for Washington County. They have been placed in group 3, which includes officers who held only one office for a duration of three years or less. The nine group 2 officers who were not members of the local judiciary are discussed in conjunction with this group of secondary leaders. A cutoff date of 1795–1796 (elected in the fall of 1795 and serving during 1796) has been used throughout, which means that some officers elected in the 1790s, who later went on to meet the criteria for inclusion in group 1, nevertheless appear in group 3.

The second way officeholders have been categorized is by the particular offices themselves. The profile of each office has been developed, including all the persons who held that particular office. From this profile, the characteristics of leaders elected to national, state, county, and township office can be determined and compared.

The officeholders in both of these categories have been compared on the basis of six major economic factors that were fundamental to the preceding discussions of the class structure. They have been compared with regard to (1) total taxable wealth, (2) land acreage, (3) whether their acreage increased or decreased, (4) speculative activities, (5) other forms of wealth such as slaves, businesses, or town proprietorships, and (6) above average livestock holdings. In addition, they have been compared on the basis of occupation and place of residence. Many other factors have been checked such as age, date of settlement, place of origin, and ethnic background. These latter factors have not been found in sufficient quantity to make their use valid except in the cases of group 1 officers, the primary political leaders. On this type of information the following discussion of the political structure of western Pennsylvania in the late eighteenth century is based.[4]

The Primary Political Leaders

Thirty-six men dominated the political life of Fayette and Washington counties. These men, ten from Fayette and twenty-six from Washington, held more than 120 major offices plus many minor posts, such as military commands, special appointments during the Revolution, township offices, select auditing committees, and the like. The number of years they spent in political life ranged from six years to full-time service throughout the period under study. Since twenty-nine of these men also held, at one time or another, judgeships and the office of justice of the peace, their political influence often carried beyond their terms in elected office. Because more information is known about this group than any other, it will be well to examine these men in some detail.

When they first settled in western Pennsylvania, these men were young; for the most part, they arrived before the end of the Revolution. The known ages of ten of them ranged from twenty to thirty-seven years of age when they arrived, with a median of twenty-nine years. Close approximate dates for another eight seem to fit the same pattern. The date of settlement for twenty-one of the men indicate that nine were in western Pennsylvania by 1773, that ten more came during the war years, 1776 to 1783, and that only two came later, in the years 1786 and 1788. The place of origin for nine of twenty-two was eastern Pennsylvania and three more came from New Jersey. Six were from Maryland and Virginia, while four were foreign-born. The ethnic background for most of them is not known, but like the region as a whole, Scottish and Irish backgrounds predominated. Ten of twelve had this background, and probably most or all of the four Irish were Protestant Irish. Thus, the personal profile of the typical leader made him a young man—probably Protestant Irish—who was in his late twenties when he came from eastern Pennsylvania during the Revolution to settle on the western frontier.

Once these men arrived in western Pennsylvania, they showed a marked tendency to settle in interior townships: twenty-six of the thirty-six (twenty in Washington and six in Fayette) lived in interior townships.[5] Three each lived in river and border townships of Washington County, while four in Fayette came from the river townships. Significantly, all twenty from the interior of Washington County came from the town of Washington or the four townships immediately surrounding it: Strabane, Amwell, Canton, and Chartiers. Except for John Smilie from Tyrone, all those from the interior in Fayette County came from Union or neighboring Franklin townships. As indicated earlier in the chapter on towns, the call of the county-seat town was strong for the political leaders. Unlike the population as a whole in which only 6 to 7 percent were town dwellers, thirteen men or 36 percent of the primary leadership group were town residents. Ten were from the town of Washington, two from Uniontown, and one from Canonsburg.[6]

To be sure, some officers came to reside in the county seat after they became officers, but their original residence was elsewhere. James Marshel retained his 1,400-acre holdings in Cross Creek township, although he lived most of the time in Washington while he performed his duties as sheriff and then as register of wills and recorder of deeds. Ephraim Douglas came to Uniontown as the result of his appointments as prothonotary and clerk of courts and county treasurer. Thomas Stokely, formerly of Westmoreland County, Andrew Swearingen from Chartiers Township, and Van Swearingen, who originally settled in Westmoreland County, also came to the town of Washington. However, others located in the towns for other than political reasons, and their political careers developed from their town residency. Like Alexander Addison, two lawyers, two merchants, a doctor, a tavernkeeper, and the town proprietor—all residents of Washington—developed political careers after they settled in town. Thus, the county-seat towns not only drew elected officials to them, but they also provided political opportunities to new political leaders.

The occupations of this primary leadership group are surprisingly diverse. A number of them tend to defy classification. In one sense, many could be called professional politicians (as some were classified in the occupational study in chapter 6), and in another sense, most could be called farmers. Nevertheless, the majority had some other calling prior to political life. These occupations were evenly spread over the professional, mercantile, and yeoman categories, with eleven in each, plus three others who might best be called land speculators. The artisan and dependent classes, not surprisingly, produced no major political figures. (William Findley is often referred to as a weaver in the discussions of the political life of this period, but since no tax assessments remain for Westmoreland during this period, he is excluded. Were he included, he may have been classified here as a professional politician.) It is significant that only two were lawyers, but only eight were simply yeoman farmers.

The mercantile group includes four millers, three merchants, two industrialists, a tavernkeeper, and a commissary officer. The professional group includes two lawyers, two town proprietors (John Canon could as easily be termed a miller), a doctor, and a surveyor. It also includes two men, Edward Cook and Henry Taylor, who were termed *judge*. Each was typical of a local potentate with large landholdings who dabbled in a variety of pursuits, sat for years on the bench, and performed numerous duties on local and state levels. The final three have been termed *professional politicians*. A case could be made for calling all of them farmers, or for calling one and perhaps two of them speculators, but their political activities tipped the balance in favor of calling them professional politicians. The yeomen category included three farmers, who were extensively engaged in the distilling business, and eight others, whose only apparent occupation was farming. Significantly, nine of the eleven yeomen had above average livestock holdings.

In addition to this background information, all of these political leaders came from the highest economic levels of the class structure (table 7.1). Probably no single factor is as important in illustrating the economic status of these leaders

TABLE 7.1
Taxable Wealth, Primary Leaders,
Fayette and Washington Counties, 1784–1796

Wealth Ranking by Half Decile	Primary Leaders	Percentage
First decile	26	72.2
Fifteen percent	3	8.3
Second decile	5	13.9
Twenty-five percent	2[a]	5.6

a. These two leaders rank in the top 10 percent in other townships because of large speculative holdings outside the township of residence.

as their ranking in terms of total taxable wealth. Every primary leader falls into the top 20 percent of the class structure in his respective township. The two leaders who rank below the second decile—merchant Matthew Ritchie and speculator Thomas Stokely—had only single lots in Washington, but each had over 1,200 acres of land scattered across the county. Ritchie's 874 acres in Hanover place him in the top 10 percent in both land size and tax value in that township. Stokely's lands in both Franklin and Greene townships were in the top 10 percent in size, and his holdings in Canton rank within the top 15 percent in total value.

Most significant, however, is the great majority of leaders who ranked within the top 10 percent of total taxable wealth. Twenty-six men fall within the top decile, and sixteen were among the five richest men in their township; seven *were* the richest men in their township. (The number would be eight if Andrew Swearingen's number-one ranking in Chartiers is counted rather than his number-four ranking in the town of Washington.) The fact that the majority of these thirty-six leaders had additional property outside their township of residence only made their economic leadership positions more pronounced.

In terms of landholdings, 50 percent of the primary leadership group who could be ranked (thirty-two of the thirty-six) had landholdings that placed among the largest 10 percent in their respective townships.[7] These sixteen holdings ranged from a lot and 10 acres in the town of Washington to 3,200 acres. The median fell between John McDowell's 400 acres and John Minor's 545 acres. None had less than 300 acres except for four Washington lot owners (all of whom had some additional land elsewhere, although for two of them this was only additional outlots). The other sixteen, who did not place in the top 10 percent of their respective townships, had holdings that ranged in size from one lot to 300 acres. Ten of these sixteen had additional lands elsewhere, such as Matthew Ritchie and Thomas Stokely, mentioned earlier, and David Redick, Andrew Swearingen, and Joseph Torrence.

Furthermore, 69 percent of these thirty-six leaders added to their landholdings during this period. This includes five who bought land for the first time, four of whom bought enough to enter the top decile of landowners. Only four had less acreage, including one leader who left the area entirely. Four others maintained the same acreage. Land speculation was also high among these political leaders. At least twenty-three of them, 64 percent, owned lands outside their home townships. For five, these other lands were only outlots, and for four more, it amounted to single tracts of less than 300 acres. For thirteen, however, these investments were very sizeable, often ranging to well over 1,000 acres. Furthermore, the size of these acreages do not indicate the amount of buying and selling that actually took place, but it must have been considerable.[8] Also, many of these leaders were undoubtedly landlords with various tenants and inmates maintaining their far-flung landholdings. How many were landlords cannot be determined, but most of those with extensive holdings probably were landlords. It is suggestive that in Franklin Township, Fayette County, where residence patterns can be traced, both officers from that township had tenants on their lands.

The conclusion is inescapable that, as a class, these leaders were among the largest and most active landowners in either county. To be sure, there were exceptions. No one served more faithfully in political life than James Edgar of Smith Township and John Smilie of Tyrone; each held six or more major offices. Yet Edgar simply maintained his 200-acre holding throughout, and Smilie maintained his of 300 acres. Ten of these leaders had 300 or fewer acres. As a class, however, they were representative of the major landowners. They actively speculated, many undoubtedly had tenants, and their lands were one of their primary sources of wealth.

These political leaders also had many other forms of wealth in addition to their land. Eight of them had mills, and three of them owned both a gristmill and a sawmill. Seven were also distillers. Fifteen were slave owners at one time or another during the period, and two had private servants. In addition, four were town proprietors, and two—Albert Gallatin and Isaac Meason—were major industrialists. Twenty-two of these thirty-six leaders had livestock herds larger than the common holdings of one or two horses and two or three cattle. Five owned a yoke of oxen. Collectively, thirty of these men held one or more of these other indicators of significant wealth. Of the six who did not, three engaged in extensive land speculation, and two had smaller land investments. James McCready, twice Washington County commissioner, was the only major leader who had no significant property beyond his 200-acre farm residence.

As a group, therefore, the thirty-six primary political leaders of Fayette and Washington counties came from the highest levels of the class structure. All ranked within the top two deciles in total wealth, and 72 percent were in the top 10 percent. Seven (or eight) were the richest men in their townships. A good majority had extensive landholdings and were deeply involved in land speculation. Eighty-three percent owned one or more specific items indicating above average wealth. The primary leadership class clearly dominated western Pennsylvania society in both economic wealth and political power.

The Secondary Leaders and the County Judiciary

The dominant status of the primary political leaders carried over into the secondary leaders and county judiciary, but to a somewhat lesser degree. Although judiciary officials tended to have greater wealth than secondary leaders, the difference was only a few percentage points. Their high economic status was the major characteristic of all officers.

The secondary officers include fifty-two classified in group 3 as those men holding one office three years or less. Also included with the secondary officers are nine from group 2a who held two offices, at least one nonjudicial, for five years or less. (The great majority of group 2 officers were judicial only and will be discussed later.) Together, these men constitute the sixty-one secondary officers. Another seven from group 3 served, but could not be identified adequately enough and so have been excluded. Those from group 2a tend to be a bit more wealthy than those from group 3. Over half of those from 2a are in the top decile in land size, but only a third of those in group 3 are. In total wealth, they are nearly identical—56 percent of group 2a and 57 percent of group 3 are in the top 10 percent.

By definition, secondary leaders held fewer offices, but they also tended to hold different offices (table 7.2). No secon-

TABLE 7.2
Offices Held by Primary and Secondary Leaders,
Fayette and Washington Counties, 1784–1796

Office	Offices Held by Primary Leaders		Offices Held by Secondary Leaders	
	Number	Percentage	Number	Percentage
National official	4	3.2	0	0
State official[a]	24	19.4	3	4.8
Assemblyman	18	14.5	11	17.8
Judicial official	47	37.9	22	35.5
County commissioner	11	8.9	18	29.0
Sheriff	5	4.0	4	6.5
County treasurer	4	3.2	0	0.0
Coroner	4	3.2	3	4.8
Prothonotary/clerk of courts	3	2.4	1	1.6
Register/recorder	4	3.2	0	0.0
TOTAL	124	99.9	62[b]	100.0

a. Includes state senate, council of censors, supreme executive council, and various state constitutional and ratifying convention delegates.
b. Two secondary leaders also held the post of clerk to the county commission.

dary leader held national office, and few held high state office. On the county level, secondary leaders rarely held the position of register and recorder or prothonotary and clerk. Secondary leaders did not serve as treasurer, but they served nearly as often as coroner. They also served fairly often in the assembly, in judicial offices, and clearly dominated the county commissioner post.

Not as much personal information was uncovered about the secondary officers. Too few ages were found to speculate on that matter, but the median date of settlement for nine of them was 1783, and that suggests that these secondary officers came a bit later to western Pennsylvania than did the primary leaders. Ethnic background and place of origin are known for only six or seven, but the information was too scarce and too diverse to be meaningful.

The geographical locations of the secondary leaders were more diverse than those of the primary group. Whereas 72 percent of the primary leaders came from the interior townships and were clustered around the county seats, only 41 percent of the secondary leaders came from the interior townships, and they were spread more evenly among most of the interior townships. Secondary leaders were also drawn more evenly from both river and border areas. Among secondary leaders, 31 percent came from river townships and 28 percent came from border townships, but among the primary leaders, the percentages were 20 and 8 percent, respectively. Only 16 percent of the secondary leaders came from towns—four each from Uniontown and Washington, and one each from Connellsville and Fredericktown. Secondary leaders were much more concentrated among the yeomen class than the primary leaders were. Seventy-one percent of the secondary leaders were yeomen, and very few engaged in distilling. Of the remaining officers, 21 percent were drawn from mercantile occupations—six merchants, three millers, three tavern-keepers, and a commissary merchant—and 8 percent came from professional occupations—two town proprietors, a lawyer, a teacher, and a minister. As a group, the secondary leaders probably came to western Pennsylvania later than primary leaders. They were much more representative of the various geographical regions, and most came from the yeomen class.

Although definitely concentrated in the upper levels of the class structure, the economic position of the secondary leaders ranged more widely than that of the primary leaders (table 7.3). In total taxable wealth, 56 percent of the secondary leaders rank in the highest decile of their respective townships, compared with 72 percent for the primary leaders. No primary leader falls below the top two deciles, but less than 80 percent of the secondary leaders rank in the top two deciles of the class structure. Three men were landless and rank in the bottom half of the class structure, while the position of two men from Union Township cannot be determined. Secondary leaders were, therefore, a cut below the primary leaders in total wealth, but they were still largely drawn from the top two deciles of the class structure. Other significant differences between these two leadership groups may be seen in a comparison of their lands and speculative activities.

The acreage owned by secondary leaders ranged more widely than that of the primary leaders—from zero to Thomas Ryerson's 40,000 speculative acres in Finley Township. Because fewer secondary leaders came from towns, their median landholding was a little larger than the primary group; it was 250 acres, compared to 230 acres for primary leaders. However, significantly fewer of the lesser leaders rank in the top

TABLE 7.3
Ranking of Secondary Leaders by Total Taxable Wealth,
Fayette and Washington Counties, 1784–1796

Wealth Ranking by Decile	Secondary Leaders	Percentage
First decile	34	55.7
Second decile	14	23.0
Third decile	3	4.9
Fourth decile	3	4.9
Fifth decile	2	3.3
Below fifth	3	4.9
Unknown	2	3.3

decile of landowners in their township of residence. Half of the primary leaders for whom land size is known rank in the top decile, but only 36 percent of the secondary leaders do. The secondary leaders were not the great speculators that the major political leaders were. Ryerson was an exception—most minor leaders did not speculate at all, let alone in such magnitude. Only 15 percent owned property outside of their township of residence. As landlords, however, secondary leaders may have been as deeply involved as the major leaders. Six men came from townships with known residence patterns. Two of four in Franklin Township had tenants, but neither man from East Bethlehem or Cecil did.

Important differences also occurred between the primary and secondary leaders in terms of what they did with their lands (table 7.4). Whereas 56 percent of the primary leaders increased their holdings between 1784 and 1796, only 18 percent of the secondary leaders did. However, twice as many secondary leaders had come during the decade and purchased new lands (26 percent compared with 14 percent) and twice as many maintained their original holdings (21 compared with 11 percent). The percentage of those whose acreages declined during the period was fairly similar, but changes were indeterminable more often among the secondary leaders.[9] A greater number of secondary leaders also disappeared from the tax lists.

TABLE 7.4
**Changes in Landholding, Primary and Secondary Leaders,
Fayette and Washington Counties, 1784–1796**

Type of Change	Primary Leaders		Secondary Leaders	
	Number	Percentage	Number	Percentage
Increased size	20	55.6	11	18.0
Purchased new	5	13.9	16	26.2
Remained same	4	11.1	13	21.3
Decreased size	3	8.3	7	11.5
Moved away	1	2.7	6	9.8
Unknown	3	8.3	8	13.1
TOTAL	36	99.9	61	99.9

Secondary political leaders must also take a back seat to the primary leaders regarding other forms of taxable wealth (table 7.5). Primary leaders had up to twice as many of these other forms of wealth. Only 11 percent of the secondary leaders had mills, compared with 22 percent among the primary group. (Three of the seven who had mills were among the nine men in group 2a.) Secondary leaders had proportionately fewer stills—13 percent, compared with 19 percent—and proportionately fewer were slaveowners—26 percent, compared with 47 percent (including 6 percent who had servants). Only 3 percent of the secondary leaders were town proprietors, compared with 11 percent of the primary leaders; no secondary leader was a major industrialist. Although secondary leaders were primarily yeomen, not quite as many of them owned large livestock herds. Sixty-one percent of the major leaders had three or more horses or four or more cattle, but only 57 percent of the secondary leaders did.

The picture of the secondary political leaders is thus complete, and it shows significant differences between them and the primary leaders. In capsule form, it can be said that almost all the political leaders came from the upper levels of the class structure, but that secondary political leaders were less

TABLE 7.5
Other Taxable Wealth Owned by Primary and Secondary Leaders, Fayette and Washington Counties, 1784–1796

Form of Wealth	Primary Leaders[a]		Secondary Leaders[b]	
	Number	*Percentage*	*Number*	*Percentage*
Mill	8	22.2	7	11.5
Still	7	19.4	8	13.1
Slave	17[c]	47.2	16	26.2
Town	4	11.1	2	3.3
Industry	2	5.6	0	0.0
Livestock	22	61.1	35	57.3

a. N = 36.
b. N = 61.
c. Includes 15 with slaves and 2 with personal servants.

likely to be the real economic leaders. Secondary leaders were substantial yeomen, and their interests were less diverse. Not as many of them came from the extreme top level of society. Few were active speculators. They were more likely to have come later and bought substantial lands, or maintained their original holding, but not to have increased what they had. Although initially overshadowed by the primary leaders, as time passed and population grew, these secondary leaders, yeomen of substance and stability in their respective communities, emerged as political leaders. They lacked the dynamic quality that marked the primary leaders.[10] Not concentrated in the towns or any one region, they were more broadly representative of the substantial yeomanry than were the primary leaders, even though their society was increasingly turning to other nonagrarian pursuits. Nevertheless, the primary fact is still that the political leaders of western Pennsylvania were overwhelmingly drawn from the top two deciles of the class structure. And while the secondary leaders may not have been the dominant class, they were certainly drawn from the upper-middle class.

The economic status of the county judiciary tended to return somewhat to the characteristics of the primary political leaders. There were, all told, 103 identifiable persons who held judicial appointments during the late eighteenth century in Fayette and Washington counties. These 103 appear in all three categories compiled for this study. Twenty-nine of the thirty-six men who were major political leaders held judicial office at some time, and twenty-one secondary leaders also held judicial appointment. For reasons peculiar to each group, these fifty men will be excluded from the following discussion: the major leaders, because the judiciary was only a passing office among many for them, and their extreme wealth was atypical in some categories; the secondary leaders, because they were almost all men who appeared as justices of the peace on lists found for Fayette County in 1795 and Washington County in 1797. They were, for the most part, new men coming to office, not the established ones who had served for some time during the 1780s and 1790s. Their exclusion scarcely affected the overall statistics on total taxable wealth and land size. Instead, attention will be focused upon the fifty-three men who make up group 2; those holding one office—justice of the peace—more than three years, or the joint office of justice and judge, regardless of the number of years.[11] Because the local judiciary performed so many important functions in local government, it will be good to briefly review their political role before discussing the specific economic details of the group 2 officials.

The Pennsylvania judicial system, under the constitution of 1776, provided, on the local level, for the freeholders of each township and county seat in the western counties to elect two (or more) men to the office of justice of the peace, one (or more) of whom was commissioned to serve by the president of the Supreme Executive Council of the state. The appointment was for seven years, and any three or more of these local justices constituted the county courts of Quarter Sessions, but only those justices especially commissioned made up the courts of Common Pleas. This created a judicial system—not unlike the one existing prior to the Revolution—that placed the choice of the judiciary in local hands and put no emphasis upon legal training as a qualification for judgeship. Under this system, most local justices received joint appointments as justice and as judge of the Court of Common Pleas. In their township districts, the justices served as courts of original jurisdiction for settling petty disputes and debts up to 40s., which was later raised in the mid-1780s to a £10 limit. Appeals or *writs of certiorari* could take these local decisions to the county court, where other justices (and presumably the original justice also) sat to decide the case. The constitution did provide that no justice could continue in office if elected to the state assembly.

Under the constitution of 1790, certain significant changes occurred. Justices of the peace were no longer elected but were appointed by the governor for life. Local justices no longer sat as the judges of the county courts. Instead, the state was divided into five judicial circuits, each presided over by an appointed president judge learned in the law. He was joined on the bench by three or four local men appointed by the governor to serve as associate justices. Thus was Alexander

Addison appointed to be president judge in western Pennsylvania. By the new system, the close link between township justices and the county courts was broken, and an emphasis was placed on legal training in the county courts. Local justices of the peace continued to serve as courts of original jurisdiction for petty disputes and debts under £10—under £20 after 1794.[12]

The effect of these changes was to materially alter the locus of power in the county judiciary, taking control of the judiciary out of the hands of local people and placing it in the hands of state officials. In terms of the actual economic position of the men involved, however, the effect was minimal. No striking difference occurred between the men elected in the 1780s and those appointed after 1790. The associate justices were, for the most part, men who had previously served on the court as justices of the peace, and Alexander Addison certainly fit the pattern of wealth associated with primary leaders. If anything, the justices of the peace appointed after 1790 had lower status than those chosen by the freeholders. Like secondary leaders, justices appointed during the 1790s tended to be substantial yeomen, not extremely wealthy persons, as the primary political leaders were. Here, too, declining land sizes and the growing diversity of economic pursuits undoubtedly allowed these substantial yeomen to stand out more clearly as propertied leaders. However, another factor also seems evident. With life appointments during good behavior, the petty judiciary was becoming a career in itself rather than a stepping-stone to higher office. The men appointed after 1790 were substantial property owners who represented position and stability in their local communities; they were not aspiring politicians.[13]

The status of the fifty-three men—thirty-eight from Washington and fifteen from Fayette—who served as the backbone of the local judiciary can be quickly summarized. As was the case of the secondary leaders, not too much personal information was discovered about them. From scattered information, however, they were probably more like primary leaders than like secondary ones. The median age of four of them at the time of settlement was twenty-nine and a half, and the median date of settlement of twelve of them was 1778. Six of nine were from eastern Pennsylvania, and four of six were Scottish or Irish. Because these men were township justices, their geographical distribution was naturally diverse. Nineteen came from the river townships (eleven from Washington, eight from Fayette); and seventeen were from border regions (fifteen from Washington, two from Fayette). (The great concentration of primary leaders in the interior townships cut down the number who served only as justices from these townships.) Towns were scarcely represented; only one lived in the town of Washington. They were mostly yeomen, but seven were in mercantile pursuits—four millers, a tavernkeeper, a storekeeper, and a ferry owner. Only one was a professional, lawyer Alexander Addison, the president judge, and he was the only town dweller. Two justices were artisans, the only ones among all the officers (both Hugh Scott of Nottingham and Abraham Stewart of German were blacksmiths). The remaining forty-three were yeoman farmers; eight of these were also distillers.

Most justices were substantial property owners (table 7.6). Ninety percent are within the top two deciles. The one man who ranks lower than the fourth decile was the son of a former justice of the peace who served briefly as a justice just prior to the adoption of the 1790 constitution. He was propertyless in 1796, but had just sold the site for the town of New Geneva to Albert Gallatin. Except for Addison's lot, the smallest holding was 80 acres, followed by two at 100 acres, and

TABLE 7.6
Ranking of Judiciary Officials by Total Taxable Wealth,
Fayette and Washington Counties, 1784–1796

Wealth Ranking by Decile	Judiciary Officials	Percentage
First decile	35	66.0
Second decile	13	24.5
Third decile	3	5.7
Fourth decile	1	1.9
Below fourth	1	1.9

others up to 800 acres. The median holding was 300 acres, higher than that of either the primary or secondary leaders.

Justices were not as likely as primary leaders to increase the size of their lands (23 percent, compared with 56 percent), but they were more likely to have entered the region later and to have bought lands for the first time (17 percent, compared with 14 percent) or to have held their original tract unchanged (26 percent, compared with 11 percent; see table 7.7). Fifteen percent lost land, nearly twice as many as the primary leaders, and 7.5 percent disappeared, while the status of 11 percent was undetermined. Justices definitely were not speculators. Only two had additional lands: Addison, clearly an exception, with lands in three townships, and the justice from Wharton Township, who had an additional 300 acres of mountain land. Justices were likely to be landlords, however. In the three test townships, Cecil, East Bethlehem, and Franklin, three of five justices had tenants.

The members of the petty judiciary also had less of the other forms of taxable wealth (table 7.8). Only five (9 percent) had mills, and eight (15 percent) owned slaves. Another had a ferry, and eleven (21 percent) had stills. However, 60.4 percent had above average livestock holdings, almost exactly the proportion held by the primary political leaders. Thus, these men, who performed the many functions of the petty judiciary, were primarily members of the substantial yeomanry.

TABLE 7.7
Changes in Landholding, Primary Leaders and Judiciary Officials, Fayette and Washington Counties, 1784–1796

Type of Change	Primary Leaders		Judiciary Officials	
	Number	Percentage	Number	Percentage
Increased size	20	55.6	12	22.6
Purchased new	5	13.9	9	17.0
Remained same	4	11.1	14	26.4
Decreased size	3	8.3	8	15.1
Moved away	1	2.7	4	7.5
Unknown	3	8.3	6	11.3
TOTAL	36	99.9	53	99.9

TABLE 7.8
Other Taxable Wealth Owned by Primary Leaders and Judiciary Officials,
Fayette and Washington Counties, 1784–1796

Form of Wealth	Primary Leaders[a]		Judiciary Officials[b]	
	Number	Percentage	Number	Percentage
Mill	8	22.2	5	9.4
Still	7	19.4	11	20.8
Slave	17[c]	47.2	8	15.1
Town	4	11.1	0	0.0
Industry	2	5.6	0	0.0
Livestock	22	61.1	32	60.4

a. N = 36.
b. N = 53.
c. Includes 15 with slaves and 2 with personal servants.

Ninety percent came from the top two deciles of the class structure. They were a little more well-to-do than the secondary leaders; but they definitely lacked the diversity of interests and the dynamic quality of the primary political leaders. The justices of the peace were men of property, status, and stability in their local communities.

Office Profiles

The men chosen for political office in western Pennsylvania were overwhelmingly upper class, as has been demonstrated, but was there any pattern regarding each particular office? Were members of the state senate more wealthy than county sheriffs? Were national representatives more wealthy than state representatives? Were township officials as wealthy as county officials? To answer these questions, officeholders have been reclassified by office, and the economic position of the holders of each office determined. From the comparison it is evident that a hierarchy of offices did exist, but this was not absolute. The men who held higher political offices tended to be more wealthy individuals than those who held lower offices, but several state and county offices were held by men of quite similar economic positions. Only the township office of constable was not consistently held by the well-to-do.

There were few residents of Fayette and Washington counties in national office during the period under study (table 7.9). Only three in this survey served in the national government after 1789: Albert Gallatin, Thomas Scott, and John Smilie. All three ranked within the top decile of their respective townships in total taxable wealth, but only Gallatin had extensive landholdings. Scott was a slave owner and Smilie had a servant. Both Gallatin and Smilie had herds of livestock that were above the average size, but only Gallatin had broad economic pursuits as indicated by his sawmill, glassworks, gun works, and his town proprietorship. All three served in the House of Representatives, and Gallatin also served briefly in the Senate. All were members of the primary leadership group and held from four to seven major offices.

The highest state offices held by western Pennsylvanians from Washington and Fayette counties were memberships in the Supreme Executive Council prior to 1790, the Council of Censors which met in 1783, the state senate after 1790, the two constitutional conventions, and the ratifying conventions. Collectively, nineteen different men held these offices, but some

TABLE 7.9
Ranking of State and National Officers by Total Taxable Wealth, Fayette and Washington Counties, 1784–1796

Wealth Ranking by Decile	National Official		State Official[a]		Assemblyman	
	Number	Percentage	Number	Percentage	Number	Percentage
First decile	3	100	14	74	20	69
Second decile	0		4	21	5	17
Third decile and lower	0		1	5	4	14
TOTAL	3	100	19	100	29	100

Note: Tables of officers cannot be directly compared with tables of offices. For example, the 3 national officers in this table held the 4 offices found on table 7.2.

a. Includes state senate, council of censors, supreme executive council, and the constitutional and ratifying conventions.

held more than one. (John Smilie held all five.) As a group, fourteen (74 percent) rank within the top decile in total wealth. None fall below the top quarter of the class structure. Nine of the seventeen whose landholdings can be determined rank among the top decile of landowners. Almost half of the group owned slaves; three had mills, and three were town proprietors. Some were very wealthy and prestigious, such as ironmaster Isaac Meason, Ohio Company speculator Dorsey Pentecost (who sold his vast holdings and returned to Maryland in the mid-1780s), and Col. John Neville (who became quite prominent in Allegheny County after its establishment, and had his estate set on fire by the whiskey rebels). These three were members of the executive council, had vast landholdings, were major slave owners, and had some of the largest livestock herds in the western part of the state. Others, like James Edgar and John Smilie, had less extreme wealth. Not more than three or four could legitimately be called farmers. Most had a variety of occupational pursuits and interests. All but three were members of the primary leadership group. Members from Fayette County were more wealthy than those from Washington County. Seven of eight men from Fayette County ranked in the top decile in total wealth, but only seven of eleven from Washington County did so. This difference between the two counties was evident throughout most of the office profiles.

The office of state assemblyman was filled from 1781 through 1796 by twenty-nine men, nine from Fayette County and twenty from Washington County. Their economic status was just a bit below that of the preceding officers. In total wealth, 69 percent rank in the top decile; only one man ranks below the top 25 percent. Fewer assemblymen were extensive landholders. Only 41 percent rank within the top decile in land size. Ten were slave owners; two had servants. One-fourth were millers; and two-thirds had above average livestock holdings. Three were town proprietors. Almost half of the assemblymen could be termed yeomen or farmer-stillers. A third were in mercantile pursuits. Most assemblymen came from the primary leadership group, but eleven others were secondary leaders, five from the small 2a group and the rest from group 3. As with the other state officials, eight of nine assemblymen from

Fayette County rank in the top decile in total wealth, but only twelve of twenty so ranked were from Washington.

Among the state and national officers, therefore, better than two of every three were men in the top 10 percent of their respective townships in total taxable wealth. Only one man out of fifty-one falls below the top quarter of the class structure. State and national offices were held only by men of substantial property or extreme wealth. In Fayette County, particularly, officers were almost certain to come from the top of the class structure.

The men who held office on the county level for the most part were at about the same economic level as state officers, although sheriffs, in particular, tended to be more wealthy and coroners less wealthy (table 7.10). The county sheriff was the chief enforcement officer and was charged with serving and executing the judgments of the county courts. He also conducted county elections, selected juries, and cared for the jail, among other duties. Sheriffs were elected to three-year terms under both constitutions. (It was actually an annual election for not more than three consecutive years, which invariably resulted in a three-year term.) Two men were elected (nominated) by the voters, and one was commissioned by the state executive, either the Supreme Executive Council or the governor.[14]

County sheriffs definitely came from the highest levels of the class structure. Eight of nine ranked within the top decile in total wealth; the position of the ninth was not determined. Only four had sufficient land to rank within the top 10 percent in land size, but six of nine were slave owners, and three had stills. At least five of the men had had military experience, the most famous of whom was David Williamson of Washington County, who led the Gnadenhutten massacre of Christian Indians in 1782. The sheriffs were generally yeomen, but one was a miller and another entered the mercantile business in Uniontown, probably after his term of office.

The office of county commissioner was filled by twenty-eight men over the years, sixteen in Washington County and twelve in Fayette County. A board of three county commissioners served as the executive body of the county, one being

TABLE 7.10

Ranking of County Officers by Total Taxable Wealth, Fayette and Washington Counties, 1784–1796

Wealth Ranking by Decile	Sheriff		Commissioner		Coroner		Treasurer		Prothonotary/ Clerk		Register/ Recorder	
	No.	%	No.	%	No.	%	No.	%	No.	%	No.	%
First decile	8	89	20	71	3	43	2	50	2	50	3	75
Second decile	0	0	4	14	4	57	2	50	1	25	0	0
Third decile and lower	0	0	3	11	0	0	0	0	1	25	1	25
Unknown	1	11	1	4	0	0	0	0	0	0	0	0
TOTAL	9	100	28	100	7	100	4	100	4	100	4	100

elected each year to a three-year term. Created in the early eighteenth century, county commissioners took over several executive functions previously performed by the courts of Quarter Sessions, but they were primarily in control of county taxation. They saw to it that the assessments were taken, tax rates set, and tax collections made. They also prepared voting lists, military lists, and were involved in selling delinquent property, caring for county buildings, and paying bounties.[15]

The twenty-eight county commissioners were about equal in economic status with the twenty-nine men who served in the assembly. Seventy-one percent are in the top decile; only two men rank below the top quarter of the class structure, plus one man whose position was not known. Twelve commissioners rank in the top decile in landholdings; twelve assemblymen are so ranked. Commissioners, however, had fewer forms of wealth. Only three were millers (compared with seven assemblymen who were), three had stills, and nine owned slaves. In both groups, however, nineteen had above average livestock holdings.

Sixteen men filled the four remaining county offices of importance, and three of them held two of these offices. Again, most were in Washington County, since the three men who held these four offices in Fayette County all held office throughout the period under study. The office of coroner was held by seven men, since it was the only elective office of the four. The chief duty of the coroner was to investigate mysterious deaths, but he was also charged with the duties of sheriff in case of a vacancy. Coroners were elected in the same manner as sheriffs and to the same three-year terms, with the exception that, in some unexplained way, Henry Beeson, town proprietor of Uniontown, continued to be reelected Fayette County coroner well into the nineteenth century. The two offices of prothonotary and clerk of courts were normally held by one man in this early period. His functions were to act as the clerk of both the Court of Common Pleas and the Court of Quarter Sessions respectively, and to record and issue the many official papers of these courts. One man also normally held the two offices of register of wills and recorder of deeds, whose duties were largely self-explanatory. Both of these dual offices were filled by state appointments. The final office, county treasurer, was selected by the county commissioners, and his duty was the care of county money.[16]

The economic position of these men was somewhat lower than the previous groups. Collectively only 50 percent are in the top decile in total wealth, and only three of the thirteen for whom land sizes are known are within the top decile in land size. All three from Fayette County are within the top decile in total wealth, but only five from Washington County are. The coroner's office contained the fewest wealthy men. Only three of seven occupants are in the top decile, but in the other three offices, half or three-fourths are so ranked. With regard to other forms of wealth—three had mills, one was a town proprietor, six had slaves, but only five had large herds of livestock. This lower economic status may be a bit deceptive, however, since twelve of these men were from the primary leadership group, and six, two of whom ranked below the top decile in their township of residence, had large speculative holdings. More important, most of these men were town dwellers. Ten of the sixteen were apparently residents of the county seats. These men—with the general exception of the coroners— were, therefore, the central core of county officials who kept county offices open and county government in operation.

At the bottom of the government hierarchy lay the township offices. These officers—supervisors of highways, overseers of the poor, constables, and other occasional officers like auditors and appraisers—performed their minor duties within the local township. Both supervisors and overseers could levy local rates, if necessary, to carry out their duties. Overseers could also bind out people in their charge, if desirable. That these duties were not always performed was evident from the several court indictments against various township officials for neglect of duty. Constables probably were the most important of these local officials. They served on the township level with much the same relationship to the justice of the peace as the county sheriff had with the county courts. The duties of constables included helping to conduct elections, suppressing disorder, and making a report at each court session on the various offenses that had occurred in their townships. The constable's report served as the formal presentment needed to initiate a trial. Some confusion exists over how these officials were chosen. Stevens and Kent state that justices appointed supervisors and overseers until 1802 and 1809, respectively. However, scattered election returns for the late eighteenth century for all of these officials have been found. Apparently, local people elected these township officials; justices may have confirmed the elected choice.[17]

Township officers varied more in economic position than any other group of officers. Some were the very wealthy, but there were also many modest landholders who held township office. When a landless young man was elected, it was not necessarily because he had a prominent family. Occasionally, a constable's deputy had more property than he did. The two men elected to serve as overseers or supervisors could differ significantly in the size of their property holdings. In other words, there was more representativeness with regard to the people serving as township officers than in any other group.[18]

The economic position of selected men who held these township offices has been summarized in the tables 7.11 and 7.12. The officers chosen for examination were those available for the years nearest the date of the assessments used in this study. In Fayette County, the years 1784, 1785, and 1795 have been used. (The constables changed at mid-year, so the 1795 constables included 1795 and 1796.) In Washington County, the lists for 1785, 1792, and 1793 have been selected. Not every officer could be found on the assessments, and, in the 1780s, values for some were available, but not land size. Because these officials did not appear among the major officeholders as have the men in the other office profiles, more information has been included in the tables on township officers than in the other tables.

Several things are quite evident. First, the lower economic status of the constables is obvious. Second, wealthier officers were chosen in Fayette County than in Washington County. Surprising consistency existed within each county among the freeholders who held the overseer and supervisor offices dur-

TABLE 7.11
Land and Other Wealth of Township Officers,
Fayette County, 1784, 1785, 1795

Office/Date	Percentage in Top Decile		Median Acreage	Percentage Owning Large Herds	Other Wealth[a]
	Total Wealth	*Land*			
Constable					
1784	12.5	12.5	100	37.5	1 st, 3 sl
1785	22.2	0	135	14.3	1 ml, 1 sl
1795	38.5	15.4	100	38.5	1 ml, 1 sl
Supervisor					
1784	61.1	42.6	350	85.2	5 sl
1785	58.8	30.8	300	61.6	1 ml, 2 st, 2 sl
1795	55.5	22.2	275	33.3	1 st, 1 sl
Overseer					
1784	55.0	43.8	235	66.8	2 ml, 3 sl
1785	57.9	46.6	300	40.0	2 ml, 2 st, 4 sl
1795	58.3	41.8	300	58.3	1 st
Appraiser[b]					
1785	63.9	70.0	305	90.0	1 ml, 5 st
1795	28.4	7.1	294	28.4	2 sl

a. ml = mill, st = still, sl = slave.
b. In 1795, includes auditors and appraisers; in 1785, appraisers only.

ing the decade. One could even say that there was consistent inconsistency among the appraisers of both counties.

The men who served as overseers and supervisors were drawn from approximately the same economic status as those in the other county offices. Some 50 to 60 percent of them in Fayette County came from the top decile in total taxable wealth, whereas some 20 to 30 percent were drawn from the top decile in Washington County. Those ranking within the top decile in land size were about 20 percent in Washington and about 40 percent in Fayette. Fayette officers tended to be 300-acre landowners, while those in Washington owned about 200 acres. Those with large herds of livestock varied more widely. Still, Fayette officers were about 20 percent more likely to be wealthy than those in Washington County. Thus, these township offices were a cut below the other offices in

TABLE 7.12
Land and Other Wealth of Township Officers,
Washington County, 1785, 1792, 1793

Office/Date	Percentage in Top Decile		Median Acreage	Percentage Owning Large Herds	Other Wealth[a]
	Total Wealth	Land			
Constable					
1785	7.7	8.3	255	33.3	
1792	24.0	20.0	122	16.0	1 st
1793	18.2	18.2	100	13.9	1 ml, 2 st
Supervisor					
1785	33.3	15.0	194	60.0	
1792	35.7	21.4	197	47.6	1 ml, 5 st, 6 sl
1793	26.2	21.4	200	42.8	5 st, 1 sl, 1 sv
Overseer					
1785	22.2	25.9	280	48.1	
1792	31.8	20.4	200	45.4	3 ml, 5 st, 1 sl
1793	30.2	25.7	203	39.5	2 ml, 5 st, 3 sl
Appraiser					
1785	47.6	33.3	300	71.4	
1792	20.4	17.5	184	32.0	2 st, 1 sl, 2 ty
1793	20.4	13.6	190	38.6	2 ml, 5 st, 1 sl

a. ml = mill, st = still, sl = slave, sv = servant, ty = tanyard.

consistently being filled by the wealthy, especially in Washington County. However, the offices of overseer of the poor and supervisor of highways were filled by men of property.

The office of constable, however, was a different matter. This office, more than any other office, was filled by people from the lower economic level. Perhaps it would be better to say that those holding the office of constable had a greater diversity of wealth than any other group. Several wealthy men held the office, but there were also men of modest means and men without land. Fewer constables were men of great wealth. Their lands were definitely smaller. Fewer of them had herds of livestock above average size or many other forms of taxable wealth. The extremes in wealth can be clearly seen. For example, in Fayette County in 1785, at the same time that the people of Menallen Township were electing as constable their wealthiest citizen, Thomas Brown, proprietor of Brownsville, the people of Georges Township elected John Chadwick, who owned twenty acres of land, and the people of Springhill elected James Holsclaw, who had thirty acres. Likewise in Washington County in 1793, when the people of Somerset Township elected Shasbazar Bentley, with his 1,000 acres, the people of six other townships elected men with less than 100 acres.

In summary, two things are clear concerning the types of people who held political office in western Pennsylvania. First, men of property completely dominated political office at every level. Second, the higher the political office, the more consistently it was filled by men of wealth and position. The situation in western Pennsylvania was similar to that which James Henretta found in colonial Boston. There was a nearly perfect "correlation between town office and social and economic position."[19] The correlation may not have been as exact on the western Pennsylvania frontier as in Boston after a century and a half, but the trend was definitely the same. As in Boston, where "all the important offices of the town . . . were lodged firmly in the hands of a broad elite," so, too, in western Pennsylvania a broad propertied leadership class dominated political life. The requirements for this dominant status differed. In Boston it was "commercial achievement and family background."[20] In western Pennsylvania, family background still played a minor role, and economic success was broader than commercial achievement.[21] Nevertheless, the end result was the same: a structured society with political leadership coming predominately from the highest levels.

8 Conclusion

WHEN, IN 1794, Alexander Addison stated that "the progress of this country to wealth has been exceedingly rapid," he was correct. The first generation of settlers transformed western Pennsylvania from a wilderness to a structured, well-developed society. Any number of developments illustrate how quickly social ordering and class division happened. Within the first generation, a very large and important landless class developed. It constituted at least a third of the population, and in some townships it was over half. Also, a significant amount of tenancy existed. It was not a tenancy of economic bondage so much as it was one of mutual benefit to the landless and the landed in this early period. The landowners needed labor to clear forests and plant fields, and the landless needed places to live and opportunities for work.

The region developed a strong degree of occupational diversity. The beginnings of industry upon which so much of the region's future economic development would rest were laid. A number of small towns, founded by wealthy proprietors, quickly provided small scale economic, social, political, and intellectual networks typical of urban areas. Artisan populations were highly visible, especially in these new towns and nascent industrial centers. Many of the yeoman farmers, who constituted approximately one-third of the population, had cleared enough land to participate in the growing river trade of the region. Continuing land speculation, the remnants of slavery, and the distribution of gristmills throughout the region, all added to the diversity within the maturing social structure.

Within this increasingly ordered society, mobility was quite evident. Many people entered the region and immediately purchased enough land for viable farms. A number of artisans also quickly acquired land. Members of the lower classes came and left the region very rapidly. Nevertheless, a definite ordering of society along economic lines existed very early, and it was becoming more pronounced. A wealthy elite increased its influence over the region.

It can be argued that such social ordering was fundamental to the development of the region. The new society needed men of wealth and ability to supply the capital and entrepreneurship for development. For example, this was an agrarian society where many people did not own land. It was the wealthy who supplied it. Speculators sold it; landlords rented it; fathers divided it among their sons; families with excess acreages took in inmates. Sawmills and gristmills, necessary services in an agrarian society, were largely supplied by the wealthy. It was also the enterprising wealthy who laid the basis for industry and that platted the new towns of the region.[1]

Political leadership was simply the capstone. The same type of people who supplied the social and economic leadership that transformed the region also supplied the political leadership. The major political leaders almost always were these same dynamic individuals who had taken leading roles in the economic life of the region. In fact, it could be argued that economic leadership was the prerequisite for nearly all political leadership.

One need not fit the transformation of western Pennsylvania into either a mold of developing capitalism or a mold of communal *mentalité*.[2] Both are clearly evident. The entrepreneurial activity of an Isaac Meason, the merchandising of the shopkeepers and artisans in the county seat of Washington, the river traders of Pittsburgh and around Fort Pitt clearly testify to the capitalistic endeavor. On the other hand, the widespread evidence of inmate relationships between the landed and the landless, and the number of tenant relationships, bespeak an earlier social ordering with roots in a dim feudal past. Rather, it is the speed and the diversity of the transformation taking place in western Pennsylvania in the late eighteenth century that is remarkable.

From the beginnings of effective, organized government, a high degree of social ordering can be found on the very first tax assessments taken for the region. The landless, the tenants, the wealthy were all there. The mythology of a classless society on the frontier where everyone had his own land was precisely that—mythology. It never occurred in western Pennsylvania.[3] These trends accelerated over the next two decades. By the dawn of the nineteenth century, western Pennsylvania no longer was a frontier region. The population growth approximated the growth of the state as a whole. The artisan population came to equal or exceed the proportions of the older areas of eastern Pennsylvania and the northern states. Within the lives of the founding generation the transformation was essentially completed.

The diversity of the region in these years is also remarkable. One can easily point to the premier leaders, to the industrialists like Albert Gallatin or Isaac Meason, and to enterprising individuals like Edward Cook or John Canon. Such people provided both the economic and political leadership of the region. Yet, there were many others in a wide variety of circumstances, each with his own role to play in the transformation of the region. A black laborer named Bob resided and worked at a major ferry crossing. A tenant named Henry Harlan gave up his artisan trade and became the resident tenant for a wealthy Philadelphia landlord. An extended family like that of Jacob Gard and his relatives worked as agricultural laborers during the period with little indication of any social mobility. A well-to-do farmer and sawyer named Joseph Townsend, the owner of 461 acres of land, provided residences and work opportunities for ten inmates who practiced a diversity of skilled trades as well as common labor. An enterprising yeoman, Israel Shreve, financed the purchase of a large farm by simultaneously subletting several portions of it to tenants. Individuals like these, multiplied many times over, formed the social fabric of western Pennsylvania. Together, the elite and the common brought about the rapid transformation of western Pennsylvania.

Appendixes
Notes
Index

Appendix A

TABLE A.1
Border Region Taxable Population and Landowners,
by County and Township, 1783–1785

County/Township	Taxable Population	Landed Population	
		Number	Percentage
Westmoreland County, 1783			
Armstrong	177	177	100.0
Fairfield	80	75	94.8
Donegal	61	48	78.7
TOTAL	318	300	94.3
Washington County, 1784			
Robinson	211	173	82.0
Smith	210	188	89.5
Hopewell	235	170	72.3
Donegal	171	131	76.6
Greene	182	136	74.7
TOTAL	1,009	798	79.1
Fayette County, 1785			
Bullskin	128	76	59.4
Wharton	83	69	83.1
TOTAL	211	145	68.7
REGIONAL TOTAL	1,538	1,243	80.8

TABLE A.2
Interior Region Taxable Population and Landowners,
by County and Township, 1783–1785

County/Township	Taxable Population	Landed Population	
		Number	Percentage
Westmoreland County, 1783			
Hempfield	256	164	64.1
Derry	155	143	92.3
Huntington	462	241	52.2
Mt. Pleasant	373	193	51.7
TOTAL	1,246	741	59.5
Washington County, 1784			
Cecil	341	205	60.1
Strabane	191	136	71.2
Somerset	148	106	71.6
Amwell	211	158	74.9
Morgan	135	95	70.4
TOTAL	1,026	700	68.2
Fayette County, 1785			
Tyrone	136	56	41.2
Franklin	261	142	54.4
Georges	232	109	47.0
TOTAL	629	307	48.8
REGIONAL TOTAL	2,901	1748	60.3

TABLE A.3
River Region Taxable Population and Landowners,
by County and Township, 1783–1785

County/Township	Taxable Population	Landed Population Number	Landed Population Percentage
Westmoreland County, 1783			
Pitt	188	97	51.6
Rostraver	504	238	47.2
TOTAL	692	335	48.4
Washington County, 1784			
Peters	401	260	65.0
Nottingham	219	124	56.6
Fallowfield	262	149	56.9
Bethlehem	287	176	61.3
Cumberland	214	116	54.2
TOTAL	1,383	825	59.6
Fayette County, 1785			
Washington	177	93	52.5
Luzerne	149	68	45.6
German	200	98	49.0
Springhill	236	104	44.1
TOTAL	762	363	47.6
REGIONAL TOTAL	2,837	1,523	53.7

Note: The percentage of landowners for the whole region in the 1780s (tables A.1, A.2, A.3) is 62.0: 4,514 landowners of 7,276 taxable persons.

TABLE A.4
Border Region Landholdings,
by County and Township, 1783–1785

County/Township	Acreage			
	Range	Mean	Median	Mode
Westmoreland County, 1783				
Armstrong	300–1,500	378	300	300
Fairfield	100–1,200	313	300	300
Donegal	20–600	153	100	100
TOTAL	20–1,500	326	300	300
Washington County, 1784				
Robinson	50–2,800	403	300	300
Smith	40–4,700	344	300	300
Hopewell	30–1,300	231	200	(a)
Donegal	20–1,425	287	250	300
Greene	50–3,900	298	300	300
TOTAL	20–4,700	315	300	300
Fayette County, 1785				
Bullskin	20–1,200	224	150	100
Wharton	40–950	261	300	300
TOTAL	20–1,200	242	200	300
REGIONAL TOTAL	20–4,700	309	300	300

a. Both 200 and 300 acres.

TABLE A.5
Interior Region Landholdings,
by County and Township, 1783–1785

County/Township	Acreage			
	Range	*Mean*	*Median*	*Mode*
Westmoreland County, 1783				
Hempfield	20–600[a]	211	200	300
Derry	30–900	196	200	100
Huntington	15–1,300	234	200	300
Mt. Pleasant	5–700	175	150	100
TOTAL	5–1,300	206	200	300
Washington County, 1784				
Cecil	15–1,358	241	200	100
Strabane	2–660	221	200	300
Somerset	35–800	188	150	100
Amwell	20–1,000	190	150	100
Morgan	40–1,600	161	100	100
TOTAL	2–1,600	207	150	100
Fayette County, 1785				
Tyrone	15–2,100	232	235	300
Franklin	16–2,200	207	200	300
Georges	L–600	183	150	300
TOTAL	L–2,200	203	200	300
REGIONAL TOTAL	L–2,200	206	200	300

Note: L = town lot.

a. Joint ownership of 1,200 acres.

TABLE A.6
River Region Landholdings,
by County and Township, 1783–1785

County/Township	Range	Acreage Mean	Median	Mode
Westmoreland County, 1783				
Pitt	4–1,400	275	230	300
Rostraver	20–1,500	223	200	300
TOTAL	4–1,500	238	200	300
Washington County, 1784				
Peters	20–1,200	208	181	300
Nottingham	9–2,000	223	150	100
Fallowfield	10–1,430	217	180	200
Bethlehem	15–500	158	125	100
Cumberland	15–1,100	188	150	100
TOTAL	4–2,000	199	150	100
Fayette County, 1785				
Washington	13–900	211	200	(a)
Luzerne	30–1,200	224	200	300
German	10–1,400	203	200	200
Springhill	12–500	173	150	100
TOTAL	10–1,400	200	160	300
REGIONAL TOTAL	4–2,000	208	180	300

Note: The statistics for the entire region (tables A.4, A.5, A.6) are: range, L–4,700; mean, 234.9; median, 200; mode, 300.

a. Both 150 and 200 acres.

TABLE A.7
Distribution of Landholdings
by Ten-Acre Intervals, 1783–1785

Acres	Westmoreland	Washington	Fayette	Total Landholdings
1–9	3	2	2[a]	7
10–19	6	5	8	19
20–29	10	11	14	35
30–39	9	16	16	41
40–49	14	41	11	66
50–59	49	104	50	203
60–69	13	39	13	65
70–79	6	30	9	45
80–89	9	46	12	67
90–99	5	13	6	24
100–09	203	390	115	708
110–19	9	3	5	17
120–29	2	27	16	45
130–39	6	17	9	32
140–49	4	19	7	30
150–59	135	194	85	414
160–69	10	9	10	29
170–79	3	6	6	15
180–89	1	20	5	26
190–99	3	8	5	16
200–09	208	316	96	620
210–19	2	2	3	7
220–29	5	2	3	10
230–39	2	6	9	17
240–49	2	9	3	14
250–59	42	75	28	145
260–69	4	9	8	21
270–79	6	6	10	22
280–89	9	11	2	17
290–99	0	3	2	5
300–09	493	491	160	1,144
310–19	0	11	3	14
320–29	1	3	5	9
330–39	1	4	3	8
340–49	0	6	4	10
350–59	6	15	3	24
360–69	0	6	0	6
370–79	1	4	3	8
380–89	1	3	1	5

Acres	Westmoreland	Washington	Fayette	Total Landholdings
390–99	0	2	0	2
400–09	10	171	24	205
410–19	0	1	0	1
420–29	0	1	0	1
430–39	1	1	2	4
440–49	0	2	2	4
450–59	3	6	4	13
460–69	0	1	0	1
470–79	0	0	0	0
480–89	2	1	0	3
490–99	0	0	0	0
500–09	9	30	7	46
510–19	0	0	2	2
530–39	0	0	1	1
540–49	0	2	0	2
550–59	3	3	0	6
560–69	1	2	2	5
570–79	0	1	0	1
590–99	0	1	0	1
600–09	37	45	11	93
610–19	1	0	0	1
630–39	0	1	0	1
640–49	0	1	0	1
650–59	0	1	1	2
660–69	0	1	0	1
700–09	4	5	0	9
730–39	0	1	0	1
750–59	1	2	0	3
760–69	0	1	0	1
800–09	3	20	2	25
900–09	10	8	1	19
930–39	1	0	0	1
950–59	0	0	1	1
990–99	0	2	0	2
1,000	0	11	0	11
1,100	1	1	0	2
1,160	1	0	0	1
1,200	2	3	2	7
1,202	0	1	0	1
1,218	1	0	0	1
1,300	1	2	0	3
1,358	0	1	0	1
1,400	1	0	1	2

Acres	Westmoreland	Washington	Fayette	Total Landholdings
1,425	0	1	0	1
1,430	0	1	0	1
1,500	5	0	0	5
1,600	0	1	0	1
2,000	0	3	0	3
2,100	0	0	1	1
2,200	0	0	1	1
2,800	0	1	0	1
3,900	0	1	0	1
4,700	0	1	0	1
TOTAL	1,376	2,323	815	4,514

Note: Above 500 acres, intervals are given only when there is a landholding; above 1,000 acres, the few holdings are identified by exact acreage.

a. Both were town lots.

TABLE A.8
**Landholdings and Livestock of Median Taxpayers by County
and Township, Fayette and Washington Counties, 1784–1785**

Township/Taxpayers	Acreage	Horses	Cattle	Sheep[a]	Total Value
			Livestock		
Fayette County, 1785					
Bullskin					
James McDowell	100	2	2	0	£34.15
George Trump	100	3	3	0	35.5
Wharton					
Daniel Davis	200	1	0	0	18.0
Tyrone					
Thomas Bell	0	2	1	0	6.10
Edmund Rice[b]	0	3	2	0	56.10
Franklin					
Henry Gillian	50	2	3	0	32.10
Georges					
Jesse Worthington	0	2	1	0	9.0
Zachariah Wheat	0	1	0	0	5.0
Washington					
John Peck	35	1	1	0	18.0
Luzerne					
William Brooks	0	2	1	0	12.0
German					
Henry Weaver	0	2	3	0	17.0
Benjamin Wright	0	1	1	0	7.0
Springhill					
Hector Hardin	0	1	0	0	5.0
Nestor Hardin	0	1	0	0	5.0
Washington County, 1784					
Robinson					
Joshua Carmen	300[c]				45.0
Smith					
John McCarty	300	3	4	3	112.0
George McCaslin	300	1	1	1	40.0
Hopewell					
Matthew Fowler	150	2	2	7	78.0
Donegal					
William Humphrey	200	0	0	0	82.0
Greene					
George Sebzer	200	3	3	3	63.0
William Thomas	200	2	2	0	56.0
Cecil					
Ambrose Quillin	100	1	0	0	56.0

| Township/Taxpayers | Acreage | Livestock | | | Total Value |
		Horses	Cattle	Sheep[a]	
Strabane					
William Bushears	150	1	2	3	92.0
Somerset					
Phillip Hooper	100	2	3	6	59.0
William Hamilton	100	3	2	0	62.0
Amwell					
Isaac McVeigh	100	1	1	0	46.0
Morgan					
Joseph Case	100	1	2	4	29.0
Peters					
John Morrow	100	2	2	1	103.0
Nottingham					
Nicholas Devore	80	3	4	3	96.0
Fallowfield					
Silas Hopkins	60	2	0	0	54.0
James Young	60	2	2	4	91.0
Bethlehem					
Henry Alspigh	55	0	1	0	17.0
Cumberland					
John Eaton	50	1	1	0	43.0
Robert Gorral	50	1	1	0	52.0

a. Sheep are not included in any Fayette County assessment.
b. Also owned one slave.
c. Unseated.

TABLE A.9
Border Region Taxable Population and Landowners,
by County and Township, 1793–1796

County/Township	Taxable Population	Landed Population	
		Number	Percentage
Washington County, 1793			
Robinson	94	71	75.5
Smith	220	156	70.9
Hanover	178	153	86.0
Hopewell	234	157	67.1
Cross Creek	217	145	66.8
Donegal	205	158	77.1
Finley	139	127	91.4
Greene	341	227	66.6
TOTAL	1,628	1,194	73.3
Fayette County, 1796			
Bullskin	360	211	58.6
REGIONAL TOTAL	1,988	1,405	70.7

TABLE A.10
Interior Region Taxable Population and Landowners,
by County and Township, 1793–1796

County/Township	Taxable Population	Landed Population	
		Number	Percentage
Washington County, 1793			
Cecil	137	89	65.0
Chartiers	241	147	61.0
Strabane	256	138	54.9
Washington	111	80	72.1
Canton	156	84	53.8
Somerset	207	128	61.8
Amwell	197	132	67.0
Morris	218	157	72.0
Morgan	222	160	72.1
Franklin	98	77	78.6
TOTAL	1,843	1,192	64.7
Fayette County, 1796			
Tyrone	175	65	37.1
Franklin	463	196	42.3
Georges	281	137	48.8
TOTAL	919	398	43.3
REGIONAL TOTAL	2,762	1,590	57.6

TABLE A.11
River Region Taxable Population and Landowners,
by County and Township, 1793–1796

County/Township	Taxable Population	Landed Population	
		Number	Percentage
Washington County, 1793			
Peters	137	85	62.0
Nottingham	249	132	53.0
Fallowfield	206	128	62.1
Pike Run	205	109	53.2
East Bethlehem	173	108	62.4
West Bethlehem	213	120	56.3
Cumberland	315	164	52.1
Total	1,498	846	56.5
Fayette County, 1796			
Washington	255	138	54.1
Luzerne	311	149	47.9
German	266	126	47.4
Springhill	362	136	37.6
Total	1,194	549	46.0
Regional Total	2,692	1,395	51.8

Note: The percentage of landowners for the whole region in the 1790s (tables A.9, A.10, A.11) is 59.0: 4,390 landowners of 7,442 taxable persons.

TABLE A.12
Border Region Landholdings,
by County and Township, 1793–1796

| County/Township | Acreage | | | |
	Range	Mean	Median	Mode
Washington County, 1793				
Robinson	10–800	194	163	200
Smith	8–775	181	100	100
Hanover	40–1,900	255	200	200
Hopewell	11–400	131	100	100
Cross Creek	40–2,400	223	180	100
Donegal	20–1,000	192	150	100
Finley	26–40,000	716	200	200
Greene	L–3,400	235	161	100
TOTAL	L–40,000	258	160	100
Fayette County, 1796				
Bullskin	L–4,200	212	150	L
REGIONAL TOTAL	L–40,000	251	150	100

Note: L = town lot.

TABLE A.13
Interior Region Landholdings,
by County and Township, 1793–1796

	Acreage			
County/Township	*Range*	*Mean*	*Median*	*Mode*
Washington County, 1793				
Cecil	3–600	173	150	100
Chartiers	L–1,416	150	110	100
Strabane	L–900	161	128	100
Washington	L–204	5	L	L
Canton	L–800	192	150	200
Somerset	23–1,000	160	128	100
Amwell	2–800	164	136	200
Morris	5–800	150	100	100
Morgan	4–800	131	100	100
Franklin	30–1,000	205	200	200
TOTAL	L–1,416	150	100	100
Fayette County, 1796				
Tyrone	1–631	239	200	300
Franklin	L–3,200	186	130	100
Georges	L–2,148	171	130	50
TOTAL	L–3,200	190	140	100
REGIONAL TOTAL	L–3,200	160	118	100

Note: L = town lot or outlot.

TABLE A.14
River Region Landholdings,
by County and Township, 1793–1796

County/Township	Range	Acreage Mean	Median	Mode
Washington County, 1793				
Peters	20–700	160	100	100
Nottingham	6–700	144	100	100
Fallowfield	18–656	165	130	100
Pike Run	10–540	162	130	100
East Bethlehem	L–1,169	138	100	100
West Bethlehem	12–600	179	162	100
Cumberland	L–1,600	177	145	100
TOTAL	L–1,600	162	126	100
Fayette County, 1796				
Washington	10–600	158	125	100
Luzerne	L–450	114	107	50
German	¼–500	185	167	200
Springhill	L–1,069	166	150	100
TOTAL	L–1,069	154	123	100
REGIONAL TOTAL	L–1,600	159	123	100

Note: The statistics for the entire region (tables A.12, A.13, A.14) are: range,
L–40,000; mean, 189; median, 140; mode, 100. L = town lot.

TABLE A.15
Distribution of Landholdings
by Ten-Acre Intervals, 1793–1796

Acres	Washington	Fayette	Total Landholdings
Lot only	121	109	230
1–9	22	16	38
10–19	25	12	37
20–29	27	11	38
30–39	49	28	77
40–49	84	21	105
50–59	204	52	256
60–69	84	38	122
70–79	96	37	133
80–89	111	40	151
90–99	96	22	118
100–09	526	134	660
110–19	33	18	51
120–29	68	23	91
130–39	54	32	86
140–49	63	21	84
150–59	216	56	272
160–69	52	23	75
170–79	49	17	66
180–89	58	16	74
190–99	22	17	39
200–09	378	96	474
210–19	11	8	19
220–29	21	14	35
230–39	29	10	39
240–49	21	14	35
250–59	81	35	116
260–69	25	7	32
270–79	16	6	22
280–89	29	9	38
290–99	12	10	22
300–09	191	72	263
310–19	4	6	10
320–29	4	9	13
330–39	9	10	19
340–49	16	3	19
350–59	25	8	33
360–69	13	2	15
370–79	16	4	20

Acres	Washington	Fayette	Total Landholdings
380–89	10	1	11
390–99	5	1	6
400–09	130	27	157
410–19	3	3	6
420–29	1	0	1
430–39	2	5	7
440–49	3	3	6
450–59	9	5	14
460–69	0	1	1
470–79	2	1	3
480–89	2	2	4
490–99	1	1	2
500–09	15	10	25
510–19	2	0	2
520–29	1	0	1
530–39	1	0	1
540–49	4	0	4
550–59	4	4	8
580–89	1	1	2
590–99	0	1	1
600–09	21	7	28
620–29	0	2	2
630–39	0	1	1
650–59	3	1	4
660–69	1	0	1
700–09	9	1	10
750–59	2	0	2
770–79	1	1	2
800–09	13	1	14
830–39	1	0	1
870–79	1	0	1
900–09	1	2	3
1,000	7	0	7
1,040	0	1	1
1,069	0	1	1
1,169	1	0	1
1,200	1	2	3
1,300	1	0	1
1,400	1	0	1
1,416	1	0	1
1,600	1	0	1
1,700	0	1	1
1,800	0	2	2

Acres	Washington	Fayette	Total Landholdings
1,900	1	0	1
2,148	0	1	1
2,400	1	0	1
2,800	1	0	1
3,100	1	0	1
3,200	0	1	1
3,400	1	0	1
4,000	1	0	1
4,200	0	1	1
7,000	1	0	1
12,000	1	0	1
40,000	1	0	1
TOTAL	3,232	1,158	4,390

Note: Above 500 acres, intervals are given only when there is a landholding; above 1,000 acres, the few holdings are identified by exact acreage.

TABLE A.16
Landholdings and Livestock of Median Taxpayers,
Washington County, 1793

Township/Taxpayer	Acreage	Horses	Cattle	Value
Robinson				
William Ryan	100	1	1	£34.0
John Robb Jr.	100	1	2	30.15
Smith				
Alex McMillan	100	1	2	63.10
John Marques	100	0	0	50.0
Hanover				
David Drennen[a]	200	2	2	71.0
Robert Duke[b]	200	2	2	55.0
Hopewell				
D. Charles Wells	70	1	2	53.0
Joseph Wells[c]	70	1	2	100.10
Cross Creek				
James Smith, Jr.	100	0	0	30.0
Donegal				
Joseph Paxton	100	2	3	21.0
Finley				
Samuel Davis	200	2	3	28.0
Greene				
William Jameson	100	1	3	16.0
Cecil				
Nathaniel Coughy	100	2	1	52.10
Chartiers				
William Johnston, Sr.	50	2	2	58.5
Strabane				
John Hoge	10-acre outlot	1	1	17.0
Hugh Wilson	9-acre outlot	0	0	9.0
Washington				
William Marshal	1 lot	0	2	46.0
Canton				
Alexander Addison	15-acre outlot	0	0	7.10
Absolom Baird	13-acre outlot	0	0	9.15
Somerset				
Henry McDonough[c]	70	2	2	62.0
Amwell				
David Morris	90	1	1	20.0
Morris				
John Clark	83	0	1	10.0
John Doty	85	1	1	16.0

Township/Taxpayer	*Acreage*	*Horses*	*Cattle*	*Value*
Morgan				
Robert Fulton	80	1	2	24.0
William Heaton	80	2	2	22.0
Franklin				
Robert Bradford	150	2	5	35.0
Daniel Devall, Sr.	150	2	3	30.0
Peters				
John McMillan	79	3	2	47.14
Nottingham				
John Madden	34	0	2	23.0
Fallowfield				
Robert George	56	2	2	27.0
John W. Riddle	58	0	0	17.0
Pike Run				
Thomas Crow	50	1	1	22.0
E. Bethlehem				
Henry Smith	46	2	3	35.0
W. Bethlehem				
John Beaty	60	1	1	20.0
Cumberland				
James Miller, single freeman	1 lot	0	0	5.0

a. Also owned one still.
b. Also had one servant.
c. Also owned one slave.

TABLE A.17
Offices Held by Primary Political Leaders,
Washington and Fayette Counties, 1784–1796

Name	Offices Held
James Allison	judge, county commissioner, assemblyman
Absolom Baird	judge, justice of the peace, state senator
Nathaniel Breading	judge, justice of the peace, supreme executive councilman, ratifying convention
John Canon	judge, justice of the peace, assemblyman
Samuel Clark	county commissioner, coroner, register/recorder
Edward Cook	judge, justice of the peace, convention delegate
Ephraim Douglas	judge, justice of the peace, treasurer, prothonotary/clerk
James Edgar	judge, justice of the peace, treasurer, assemblyman, supreme executive councilman, council of censors member
James Finley	judge, justice of the peace, county commissioner, assemblyman, state senator
Albert Gallatin	assemblyman, convention delegate, U.S. representative, U.S. senator
James Hammond	county commissioner, sheriff
John Hoge	judge, justice of the peace, state senator, convention delegate
Daniel Leet	judge, justice of the peace, assemblyman
Alexander McClean	judge, justice of the peace, assemblyman, register/recorder
James McCready	county commissioner (twice)
John McDowell	justice of the peace, county commissioner, assemblyman, council of censors member
William McFarland	judge, justice of the peace, coroner
John Marshall	justice of the peace, coroner
James Marshel	justice of the peace, register/recorder, sheriff, assemblyman, ratifying convention
Isaac Meason	judge, assemblyman, supreme executive councilman
William Meetkirk	justice of the peace, county commissioner
John Minor	judge, justice of the peace, assemblyman
Dorsey Pentecost	judge, justice of the peace, county commissioner, supreme executive councilman
David Redick	treasurer, prothonotary/clerk, supreme executive councilman, convention delegate
Craig Richie	justice of the peace, assemblyman
Matthew Richie	judge, assemblyman

Name	Offices Held
Thomas Scott	judge, justice of the peace, prothonotary/clerk, assemblyman, ratifying convention, U.S. representative
John Smilie	assemblyman, supreme executive councilman, council of censors member, convention delegate, ratifying convention, state senator, U.S. representative
Thomas Stokely	judge, justice of the peace, register/recorder, assemblyman, state senator
Andrew Swearingen	justice of the peace, treasurer
Van Swearingen	justice of the peace, sheriff
Henry Taylor	judge, justice of the peace, supreme executive councilman
Joseph Torrence	county commissioner, sheriff, assemblyman
Henry Van Meter	judge, justice of the peace, county commissioner
William Wallace	judge, justice of the peace, sheriff, assemblyman
Joseph Wherry	justice of the peace, coroner

Note: This group of primary political leaders is composed of men holding at least two offices for at least six years, or men holding three or more offices regardless of the number of years.

TABLE A.18
Residence and Occupation of Primary Political Leaders, Fayette and Washington Counties, 1784–1796

Name	Residence[a]	Occupation	Land Speculator[b]
James Allison	Chartiers	farmer	
Absolom Baird	Washington (town)	doctor	X
Nathaniel Breading	Luzerne	farmer/stiller	X
John Canon	Chartiers	proprietor/miller	X
Samuel Clark	Washington (town)	merchant	X
Edward Cook	Washington	judge	X
Ephraim Douglas	Uniontown (town)	military commissary merchant	X
James Edgar	Smith	farmer	
James Finley	Union	farmer	
Albert Gallatin	Springhill	industrialist	X
James Hammond	Luzerne	farmer/stiller	
John Hoge	Washington (town)	proprietor	X
Daniel Leet	Canton	farmer/stiller	
Alexander McClean	Uniontown (town)	surveyor	
James McCready	Strabane	farmer	
John McDowell	Strabane	farmer	
William McFarland	Amwell	farmer	
John Marshall	Cross Creek	miller	
James Marshel	Washington (town)	politician	X
Isaac Meason	Franklin	ironmaster	X
William Meetkirk	Washington (town)	tavernkeeper	X
John Minor	Greene	miller	
Dorsey Pentecost	Nottingham	speculator	X
David Redick	Washington (town)	lawyer	X
Craig Richie	Canonsburg (town)	merchant	X
Matthew Richie	Washington (town)	merchant	X
Thomas Scott	Washington (town)	lawyer	X
John Smilie	Tyrone	politician	
Thomas Stokely	Washington (town)	speculator	X
Andrew Swearingen	Washington (town)	speculator/politician	X
Van Swearingen	Strabane	speculator	X
Henry Taylor	Strabane	judge	X
Joseph Torrence	Franklin	farmer	X
Henry Van Meter	Cumberland	farmer	
William Wallace	West Bethlehem	miller	X
Joseph Wherry	Chartiers	miller	X

a. Unless otherwise specified, all residences are in townships.
b. Engaging in any speculative activity or holding lands outside the place of residence is indicated by an X.

TABLE A.19

Land and Other Forms of Wealth Held by Primary Political Leaders, Fayette and Washington Counties, 1784–1796

Name	Landholding in Lots/Acres[a]	Land Changes Over Period	In Top Decile[b] Total Value	In Top Decile[b] Land Size	Livestock[c] Horses	Livestock[c] Cattle	Other Wealth
Allison	600	increase	X4	X	3	7	
Baird	5L	new					
Breading	300	same	X		3	8P	1 still, 2 slaves
Canon	700	increase	X2	X	8	6P	2 mills, town
Clark	1L/10	new	X	X			1 slave
Cook	600	decrease	X1	X	3	10	2 mills, 1 still, 3 slaves
Douglas	N/A	N/A	X5				3 slaves
Edgar	200	same	X		3	4	
Finley	N/A	N/A					2 slaves
Gallatin	900	new	X4	X	4		1 mill, glassworks, town
Hammond	318	increase	X5	X	5	9P	1 still, 2 slaves
Hoge	3L/56	increase	X1	X			town
Leet	800	increase	X1	X	3		2 stills
McClean	N/A	N/A	X4				3 slaves
McCready	200	increase					
McDowell	400	increase	X4	X	3	8	
McFarland	180	increase			3	4	

Name	Acreage	Change						Property
Marshall	200	same				4		1 mill
Marshel	3L/10	increase	X1				X	1 still
Meason	3,200	increase	X1		17		X	1 mill, 3 slaves, town, ironworks
Meetkirk	4.5L/20	increase					X	
Minor	545	increase	X3		3	5	X	2 mills, 1 still, 1 slave
Pentecost	2,000	gone	X1		5	10	X	15 slaves
Redick	2L	increase						
Richie, C.	1L/150	increase			3			1 still, 1 servant
Richie, M.	1L	decrease						
Scott	4L	increase	X	X				
Smilie	300	same	X	X	3	6		2 slaves
Stokely	2L	increase						1 servant
Swearingen, A.	1L	increase	X4 (speculative)			6P		2 slaves
Swearingen, V.	N/A	new	X1 (speculative)					9 slaves
Taylor	800	increase	X1	X	4	4		
Torrence	300	increase	X		5	5		2 slaves
Van Meter	230	increase	X		7	12		
Wallace	100	decrease	X		4	5		1 mill, 1 slave
Wherry	300	new	X	X		P		1 mill

Note: Acreage sizes not available for three from Union Township or for Van Swearingen, although a taxable wealth ranking is available for Union. Also, Albert Gallatin's acreage is a combination of his and his company's.

a. L = town lots.

b. An X indicates the man ranked among the top 10 percent of his township in total taxable value and in land size. Those who ranked among the five richest people in their township are indicated by the numbers 1 through 5.

c. A P beside the number of cattle indicates a pair of oxen; Breading had 3 oxen.

Appendix B

THE FOLLOWING MAPS are based upon that of Reading Howell, 1792, reprinted in Solon J. and Elizabeth H. Buck, *The Planting of Civilization in Western Pennsylvania* (Pittsburgh, 1939), pp. 562–63. Original township boundary lines of Washington County are unknown, but according to Boyd Crumrine, they probably "followed the courses of the larger streams or the dividing ridges between the smaller ones"; *History of Washington County* (Philadelphia, 1882), p. 228.

Based upon this information and the two maps especially drawn for the Crumrine history, one for 1781–1788 and one for 1880, plus an official "Road Map of Washington County, Pennsylvania, 1966," approximate township boundaries have been reconstructed for Washington County and imposed upon the basic Reading Howell outline. Thus, boundary lines are close approximations, but not necessarily exact.

The maps were drawn by Wendell Hoover of Buchart-Horn Consulting Engineers and Planners.

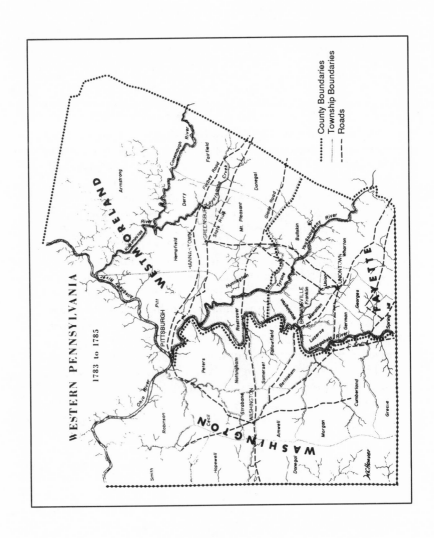

WESTERN PENNSYLVANIA
1783 to 1785

County Boundaries
Township Boundaries
Roads

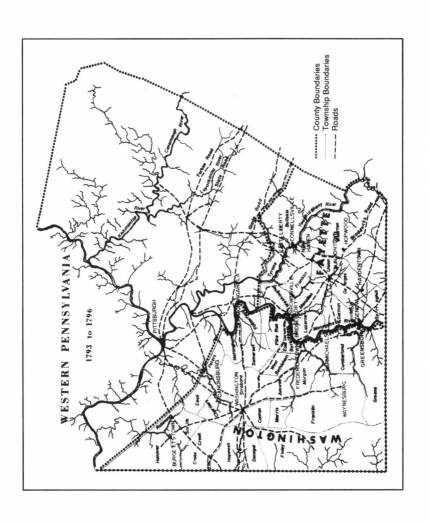

WESTERN PENNSYLVANIA

1793 to 1796

County Boundaries
Township Boundaries
Roads

Notes

Preface

1. *Pennsylvania Archives*, 2d series, vol. 4 (Harrisburg, 1852–1935), pp. 242–43.

2. Robert E. Brown's *Middle Class Democracy and the Revolution in Massachusetts, 1691–1780* (Ithaca, N.Y., 1955) was followed by a study of Virginia that sought to prove the democracy thesis was also true for a planter-dominated society: Robert E. Brown and B. Katherine Brown, *Virginia, 1705–1786: Democracy or Aristocracy?* (East Lansing, Mich., 1964). Merle E. Curti looked at the democratic process in a western frontier county less stridently in *The Making of an American Community: A Case Study of Democracy in a Frontier County* (Stanford, Calif., 1959); and Charles Grant examined the social context of democracy in *Democracy in the Connecticut Frontier Town of Kent* (New York, 1961).

3. Jesse Lemish's "Jack Tar in the Streets: Merchant Seamen in the Politics of Revolutionary America," *William and Mary Quarterly* 15 (1968): 371–407, paved the way for other studies. A fascinating study of an artisan is Robert F. Young's "George Robert Twelves Hewes (1742–1840): A Boston Shoemaker and the Memory of the American Revolution," *William and Mary Quarterly* 38 (1981): 561–623. Among many studies of working people in early America are Gary B. Nash's "Up from the Bottom in Franklin's Philadelphia," *Past and Present* 77 (1977): 57–83; Billy G. Smith's "The Material Lives of Laboring Philadelphians, 1750 to 1800," *William and Mary Quarterly* 38 (1981): 163–202; and Raymond A. Mohl's "Poverty in Early America, a Reappraisal: The Case of Eighteenth-Century New York City," *New York History* 50 (1969): 5–27. A good summary of recent scholarship in labor history is Stephen Innes, ed., *Work and Labor in Early America* (Chapel Hill, N.C., 1988).

4. Sumner Powell, *Puritan Village: The Formation of a New England Town* (Middletown, Conn., 1963); Darrett B. Rutman, *Winthrop's Bos-*

ton: Portrait of a Puritan Town (Chapel Hill, N.C., 1965), and *Husbandmen of Plymouth: Farms and Villages in the Old Colony, 1620–1692* (Boston, 1967) provided important early studies; Philip Greven, *Four Generations: Population, Land and Family in Colonial Andover, Massachusetts* (Ithaca, N.Y., 1970); Kenneth Lockridge, *A New England Town: The First Hundred Years* (New York, 1970); John Demos, *A Little Commonwealth: Family Life in Colonial Plymouth* (New York, 1970); Richard L. Bushman, *From Puritan to Yankee: Character and the Social Order in Connecticut, 1690–1765* (New York, 1970); Michael Zuckerman, *Peaceable Kingdoms: New England Towns in the Eighteenth Century* (New York, 1970). See also James A. Henretta, "The Morphology of New England Society in the Colonial Period," *Journal of Interdisciplinary History* 2 (1971): 379–98, for a review article on the Demos, Greven, Lockridge, and Zuckerman books.

5. Robert Zemsky, *Merchants, Farmers, and River Gods: An Essay on Eighteenth Century Politics* (Boston, 1971); Robert A. Gross, *The Minute Men and Their World* (New York, 1976); Paul Boyer and Stephen Nissenbaum, *Salem Possessed: The Social Origins of Witchcraft* (Cambridge, Mass., 1974).

6. Aubrey Land, "Economic Base and Social Structure: The Northern Chesapeake in the Eighteenth Century," *Journal of Economic History* 25 (1965): 639–54, and "Economic Behavior in a Planting Society: The Eighteenth Century Chesapeake," *Journal of Southern History* 33 (1967): 469–85; Paul G. E. Clemens, *The Atlantic Economy and Maryland's Eastern Shore: From Tobacco to Grain* (Ithaca, N.Y., 1980); Russell R. Menard, P. M. G. Harris, and Lois Green Carr, "Opportunity and Inequality: The Distribution of Wealth on the Lower Western Shore of Maryland, 1638–1705," *Maryland Historical Magazine* 69 (1974): 169–84; Russell R. Menard, Lois Green Carr, and Lorena S. Walsh, "A Small Planter's Profits: Estate and Growth in the Early Chesapeake Economy," *William and Mary Quarterly* 40 (1983): 171–96. Lois Green Carr and Lorena S. Walsh have written numerous articles detailing life in Maryland. See their article "Economic Diversification and Labor Organization in the Chesapeake, 1650–1820," in Innes, *Work and Labor,* for their latest work and references to earlier work.

7. Richard Beeman, *Evolution of the Southern Backcountry: A Case Study of Lunenburg County, Virginia, 1746–1838* (Philadelphia, 1984); Darrett B. Rutman and Anita H. Rutman, *A Place in Time: Middlesex County, Virginia, 1650–1750* (New York, 1984); Allan Kulikoff, *Tobacco and Slaves: The Development of Southern Cultures in the Chesapeake, 1680–1800* (Chapel Hill, N.C., 1986); Rhys Isaac, *The Transformation of Virginia, 1740–1790* (Chapel Hill, N.C., 1982).

8. James A. Henretta, "Economic Development and Social Structure in Colonial Boston," *William and Mary Quarterly* 22 (1965): 75–92; Gary B. Nash, "Urban Wealth and Poverty in Pre-Revolutionary America," *Journal of Interdisciplinary History* 6 (1976): 545–84; Billy G. Smith, "Vicissitudes of Fortune: The Careers of Laboring Men in Philadelphia, 1750–1800," in Innes, *Work and Labor;* Allan Kulikoff, "The Progress of Inequality in Revolutionary Boston," *William and Mary Quarterly* 28 (1971): 375–412; G. B. Warden, "Inequality and Instability in Eighteenth Century Boston: A Reappraisal," *Journal of Interdisciplinary History* 6 (1976): 585–620.

9. Jackson T. Main, *The Social Structure of Revolutionary America* (Princeton, N.J., 1965).

10. James T. Lemon, *The Best Poor Man's Country: A Geographical Study of Early Southeastern Pennsylvania* (Baltimore, Md., 1976); Stephanie G. Wolf, *Urban Village: Population, Community, and Family Structure in Germantown, Pennsylvania, 1683–1800* (Princeton, N.J., 1976); Jerome H. Wood, Jr., *Conestoga Crossroads: Lancaster, Pennsylvania, 1730–1790* (Harrisburg, Pa., 1979).

11. Sung Bok Kim, *Landlord and Tenant in Colonial New York: Manorial Society, 1644–1775* (Chapel Hill, N.C., 1978); Stephen Innes, "Land Tenancy and Social Order in Springfield, Massachusetts, 1652–1702," *William and Mary Quarterly* 35 (1978): 33–56; Lorena S. Walsh, "Land, Landlord, and Leaseholder: Estate Management and Tenant Fortunes in Southern Maryland, 1642–1820," *Agricultural History* 59 (1985): 373–96; Lucy Simler, "Tenancy in Colonial Pennsylvania: The Case of Chester County," *William and Mary Quarterly* 43 (1986): 542–69. See also a brief discussion in Carole Shammas, "The Rise of the Colonial Tenant," *Reviews in American History* 6 (1978): 490–95.

12. Carole Shammas, "How Self-Sufficient Was Early America?" *Journal of Interdisciplinary History* 13 (1982): 247–72; Winifred B. Rothenberg, "The Emergence of a Capital Market in Rural Massachusetts, 1730–1838," *Journal of Economic History* 45 (1985): 781–808; Bettye Hobbs Pruitt, "Self-Sufficiency and the Agricultural Economy of Eighteenth-Century Massachusetts," *William and Mary Quarterly* 41 (1984): 333–64. See also the forum discussion: Carole Shammas, "Food Expenditures and Economic Well-Being in Early Modern England," Gloria L. Main, "The Standard of Living in Colonial Massachusetts," Lorena S. Walsh, "Urban Amenities and Rural Sufficiency: Living Standards and Consumer Behavior in the Colonial Chesapeake, 1643–1777," Paul G. E. Clemens, "Discussion," *Journal of Economic History* 43 (1983): 89–119. Allan Kulikoff has

summarized the self-sufficiency question and provided a theoretical framework in "The Transition to Capitalism in Rural America," *William and Mary Quarterly* 46 (1989): 120–44. See also Paul G. E. Clemens and Lucy Simler, "Rural Labor and the Farm Household in Chester County, Pennsylvania, 1750–1820," in Innes, *Work and Labor.*

13. Dorothy E. Fennell, "From Rebelliousness to Insurrection: A Social History of the Whiskey Rebellion, 1765–1802" (Ph.D. diss., University of Pittsburgh, 1981); Thomas P. Slaughter, *The Whiskey Rebellion: Frontier Epilogue to the American Revolution* (New York, 1986).

14. Jackson T. Main has called probate records "the most valuable and almost untouched source materials for the socio-economic history of early America." *Social Structure*, p. 288.

15. See "A Communication" from Kenneth A. Lockridge that indicates that New England "probate records account for a surprisingly small and perhaps quite biased segment of the population," *William and Mary Quarterly* 25 (July, 1968): 516. Probate records and inventories can be very valuable sources for showing social and economic trends, but care is necessary in their use. See Gloria L. Main, "Probate Records as a Source for Early American History," and Daniel Scott Smith, "Underregistration and Bias in Probate Records: An Analysis of Data from Eighteenth-Century Hingham, Massachusetts," *William and Mary Quarterly* 32 (1975): 89–99 and 100–10.

16. Ella Chalfant, *A Goodly Heritage: Earliest Wills on an American Frontier* (Pittsburgh, 1955), app. C. Will Book 1 included 320 names. The first three books, going well into the nineteenth century, contained only 900 names.

17. Single freemen were designated on nearly every assessment. See James T. Mitchell and Henry Flanders, eds., *The Statutes at Large of Pennsylvania from 1682 to 1801* (Harrisburg, 1896–1915), 10, ch. 944 (21 June 1781), pp. 328, 330–31; 11, ch. 1137 (16 March 1785), p. 470, for statuatory authority for taxing single freemen and the amounts of that tax. The tax was singularly unequal. Many young sons taxed at 10s. paid more than their landed fathers. One example: In Franklin Township, Fayette County, 1785, William Carson, who had no taxable property, paid 10s. John Carson, who had 200 acres and seven head of livestock, paid 8s. 5d.

18. Ibid., 15, ch. 1852 (17 April 1795), pp. 322–30. Actually, the 1781 law authorized the taxation of "all professions, trades, and occupations" except ministers and schoolmasters, but "at the discretion of" the local assessors. Ibid., 10, ch. 944, pp. 330–31. The act of 1785 kept the same provisions but added mechanics and manufactur-

ers to the list of excepted occupations. Ibid., 11, ch. 1137, p. 470. However, the net effect in western Pennsylvania was that no occupations were taxed until 1796.

19. The method used to arrive at the number and percentage of males aged twenty-one and above was simply to take half of the males in the age sixteen to twenty-six category and subtract that figure from the combined total of all males aged sixteen and above. It should be noted that these figures are for free white males only. The category of other free persons (1.1 percent of the free population in 1800 and 0.2 percent in 1790) was not divided by sex and was omitted.

20. This was computed as follows: 13,850 − 8,602 = 5,248 ÷ 7 years = 750 per year increase × 4 years to 1790 = 3,000 taxable persons added to the 8,602 in 1786, or 11,602 taxable persons in 1790. U.S. Bureau of the Census, *Heads of Families at the First Census of the United States Taken in the Year 1790* (Washington, D.C.: Government Printing Office, 1907–08).

21. This estimate was obtained from three Westmoreland County townships that, in 1783, included a census with the assessment. This resulted in a ratio of 4.65 persons to 1 taxable person. By using this ratio and the tax assessment for Westmoreland County in 1783 and Washington County in 1784, it has been estimated that there were 15,900 persons in Washington County and 17,600 in Westmoreland County. Since for these dates these two counties included the whole region, the total free population of western Pennsylvania has been estimated as 33,500 persons. See a more complete discussion in chapter 1.

22. The percentage of white males in the free population of 1800 was 51.3; females, 47.5. The percentage of white males in the free population of 1790 was 52.9; females, 46.9. Assuming a still larger proportion of males in the earlier years of settlement, the percentage of white males in the free population of 1783–1784 was estimated at 54.0. Thus, the calculations were: free population of 33,500 × 54% = 18,090 males × 40% = 7,236 taxable persons.

Chapter 1: Early Settlement

1. *Pennsylvania Archives*, 2d series, vol. 4 (Harrisburg, 1852–1935), p. 714. A large section at the end of this volume deals with the question of frontier defense in the 1790s. See passim.

2. Ibid., pp. 700, 660, 724–25.

3. Ibid., p. 715.

4. Solon J. and Elizabeth H. Buck, *The Planting of Civilization in Western Pennsylvania* (Pittsburgh, 1939), pp. 140–43.

5. The standard estimate of the ethnic composition of western Pennsylvania may be found in ibid., pp. 152–55. The method of distinctive surnames was developed by Howard F. Barker in the *American Historical Association, Annual Report, 1931* (Washington, 1932), pp. 126–359. Applying Barker's method, Buck found the following percentages for each ethnic group in 1790:

County	English	Welsh	Scottish	Irish	German	Other
Allegheny	43	8	25	16	4	4
Fayette	47	7	11	19	11	5
Washington	43	9	20	16	5	7
Westmoreland	32	3	15	31	10	9

6. Ibid., p. 307. The Protestant Irish included the Scotch-Irish, English-Irish, and Ulster Celts. Also included in the Irish group are the Catholic southern Irish, who comprise 6 percent of the Irish group in Allegheny and Fayette counties and about 4 percent in the other two counties; Buck and Buck, *Civilization*, p. 153. The immigration of German population has been summarized, though not in any systematic fashion, by Homer T. Rosenberger, "Migration of the Pennsylvania Germans into Western Pennsylvania," *Western Pennsylvania Historical Magazine* 53 (October 1970): 319–36. He found concentrations of German settlement along the Forbes Road route through Bedford and Westmoreland counties, and concentrations in Fayette County, near the Westmoreland border, and in German Township.

7. The first article to question the adequacy of the standard figures for the Celtic population was Forrest McDonald and Ellen Shapiro McDonald's "The Ethnic Origins of the American People, 1790," *William and Mary Quarterly* 37 (1980): 179–99. Subsequently, the whole question was debated in "The Population of the United States, 1790: A Symposium," *William and Mary Quarterly* 41 (1984): 85–135, with articles by Thomas L. Purvis, "The European Ancestry of the United States Population, 1790," pp. 85–101; Donald H. Akenson, "Why the Accepted Estimates of the Ethnicity of the American People, 1790, Are Unacceptable," pp. 102–19; and "Commentary" by Thomas L. Purvis, Donald H. Akenson, Forrest McDonald, and Ellen Shapiro McDonald, pp. 119–35. The percentages developed for Pennsylvania by Purvis, "European Ancestry," p. 98, and the McDonalds, "Ethnic Origins," p. 198, are:

	Purvis	*McDonald*		*Purvis*	*McDonald*
English	25.8	19.5	German	38.0	33.3
Welsh	3.6	5.9	Dutch	1.3	1.8
Scotch-Irish	15.1	—	French	0.9	1.8
Scottish	7.6	26.7	Swedish	0.6	0.8
Irish	7.1	10.2	TOTAL	100	100

It should be noted that the McDonalds did not identify a separate Scotch-Irish category from the Scottish and Irish groups, although they believed that "possibly the vast majority" of Scottish and Irish came "by way of Ulster" (p. 195). The McDonalds combine the Welsh, Scottish, and Irish numbers into a 42.8 percent Celtic subtotal in their table.

8. In the "Commentary" of the "Symposium," the McDonalds accepted the changes made by Purvis for the German and other continental groups which they had not challenged (p. 129), but they refused to accept the lower Welsh figure (p. 130), and they suggested revisions that approximately split the difference on the Celtic groups (p. 131). Following that prescription, the statewide percentages for Pennsylvania would be about 40 percent German and other continentals, another 40 percent Celtic, leaving 20 percent English. A similar statewide consensus figure for Virginia would be approximately 8 percent German and other continentals, 38 percent Celtic, and 54 percent English. How these consensus figures would merge in western Pennsylvania cannot be determined until someone reworks the whole process. The McDonalds's estimate that Washington County was more than 75 percent Celtic can be found in "Ethnic Origins," p. 199.

9. Buck and Buck, *Civilization,* pp. 145, 162–63, 196; Boyd Crumrine, ed., *History of Washington County* (Philadelphia, 1882), pp. 126–33; James Veech, *Monongahela of Old* (Pittsburgh, 1858, 1892), pp. 99–100; Robert L. Brunhouse, *The Counter-Revolution in Pennsylvania, 1776–1790* (Harrisburg, 1942), pp. 127–28, 133. Brief general accounts of the full boundary controversy may be found in Buck and Buck, *Civilization,* pp. 156–74; Crumrine, *Washington County,* pp. 158–96; Veech, *Monongahela,* pp. 249–59. Crumrine has also discussed the controversy and edited the minutes of the Virginia courts that sat in Pennsylvania; Carnegie Museum of Pittsburgh, *Annals* 1 (Pittsburgh, 1902), pp. 505–68; 2 (Pittsburgh, 1903), pp. 71–140, 205–429. The boundary dispute may be seen in its proper national perspective in Merrill Jensen, *The Articles of Confederation* (Madison, Wis., 1963), pp. 185–238; Jack M. Sosin, *The Revolutionary Frontier,*

1763–1783 (New York, 1967), pp. 39–60, especially pp. 57–60; and Peter S. Onuf, *The Origins of the Federal Republic: Jurisdictional Controversies in the United States, 1775–1787* (Philadelphia, 1983), ch. 3, especially pp. 55–56, 59–61, and 66–69.

10. Thomas P. Abernethy, *Western Lands in the Revolution* (New York, 1959), pp. 218–28, especially p. 224; Crumrine, *Washington County*, pp. 188–90, 192; Buck and Buck, *Civilization*, p. 144.

11. Thomas Sergeant, *A View of the Land Laws of Pennsylvania* (Philadelphia, 1838), pp. 55–76, 81–92; Veech, *Monongahela*, pp. 96–98.

12. See chapter 2 for a full discussion of the patterns of landownership.

13. George Dallas Albert, *History of the County of Westmoreland* (Philadelphia, 1882), p. 50.

14. Veech, *Monongahela*, p. 256; Crumrine, *Washington County*, p. 199; Continuance Docket, Court of Common Pleas, Westmoreland County; Continuance Docket, Court of Common Pleas, Fayette County; Appearance Docket, Court of Common Pleas, Washington County.

15. Buck and Buck, *Civilization*, pp. 175–203. Accounts of the Revolution and Indian problems fill all the county histories, but see particularly Crumrine, *Washington County*, pp. 74–137; and John N. Boucher, *History of Westmoreland County* (New York, 1906), vol. 1, pp. 145–85. The standard account of Indian conflict is Randolph C. Downes's *Council Fires on the Upper Ohio* (Pittsburgh, 1940); see pp. 273–76, 290–95, 301–03, 332–36 regarding events discussed here. See also Consul W. Butterfield, ed., *Washington-Irving Correspondence* (Madison, Wis., 1882), passim, for military and supply problems in western Pennsylvania, and pp. 77, 176–77, 250–54 for the specific impact of raids upon the settlers.

16. Indicative of the manpower drain was the 1784 militia roll of Washington County (Crumrine, *Washington County*, pp. 136–37), which indicates that slightly more than 1,700 men were in the county militia. Based upon population estimates and the age and sex proportions of the 1790 census, there were approximately 8,400 males aged sixteen and above in all of western Pennsylvania in the early 1780s. If Washington County had half of them—a generous estimate on the basis of tax data—then better than 40 percent of the total manpower of Washington County aged sixteen and above was in the militia.

17. Buck and Buck, *Civilization*, pp. 186, 188, 195. In the 1770s and 1780s, western Pennsylvania probably produced little surplus agriculture. See production estimates for tenant farmers in chapter 4 and for yeomen in chapter 6.

18. *Pennsylvania Archives*, 3d series, vol. 13, pp. 701–82, 369–453. Gary B. Nash and Billy G. Smith, "The Population of Eighteenth-Century Philadelphia," *Pennsylvania Magazine of History and Biography* 99 (July 1975): 363, found that using the number of taxable persons is "a more reliable method of calculating population."

19. Three of the eighteen townships in the Westmoreland County return contain census lists (*Pennsylvania Archives*, 3d series, vol. 13, pp. 369–94). In them, 4,807 white persons were represented by only 1,033 taxable persons, a ratio of 4.65 to 1. The ratio in each township was Rostraver, 4.61 to 1; Franklin, 4.8 to 1; and Tyrone, 4.46 to 1. The 3,418 taxable persons in Washington and 3,789 taxable persons in Westmoreland were then multiplied by 4.65 for a total population of 33,513. These three township censuses divided the population between whites and blacks; all the blacks appear to have lived with whites and, therefore, were presumably slaves. They numbered a little more than 3 percent of the whites, but considering the Virginia origin of many settlers, especially in Washington County, a 4 percent plus estimate has been used in estimating a total population of 35,000. By comparison, the slaves and "other free" persons in the 1790 census numbered 945, a reduction of perhaps 500, which is not unlikely considering the number of slave owners who probably moved to Kentucky because of the gradual abolition laws.

20. U.S. Bureau of the Census, *Heads of Families at the First Census of the United States Taken in the Year 1790* (Washington, D.C.: Government Printing Office, 1907–08); U. S. Census Office, *Second Census, 1800* (Washington, D.C., 1801; facsimile rpt., Brooklyn, N.Y.: Central Book Co., n.d.).

21. Samuel Hazard, ed., *Hazard's Register of Pennsylvania* (Philadelphia, 1828–1836), 4 (July 1829), pp. 12–13. *Hazard's Register* contains the lists of taxable persons used for this comparison.

22. An explanation is needed for what constituted western Pennsylvania for each of these years. The attempt has been made to compare population within the same geographical areas regardless of the new counties erected. Thus, in 1770, Cumberland County was the only western county and in 1779 Cumberland, Bedford, and Westmoreland counties constituted a similar area. To compare 1779 with 1786, Cumberland has been eliminated and the more western counties of Bedford and Westmoreland have been compared with Bedford, Westmoreland, and Fayette in 1786. When comparing 1786 with 1793, Bedford has been dropped, and Westmoreland, Fayette and Washington counties in 1786 have been compared with these three, plus Allegheny County, in 1793. (Wash-

ington County, erected in 1781, was not included until this 1786
comparison because, prior to settling the boundary dispute, this
area was essentially Virginia territory.) The final comparison includes Westmoreland, Fayette, Washington, and Allegheny counties
in 1793 and the same four counties, plus Greene County, in 1800.
The Pennsylvania figures are simply the total of all counties at the
given dates.

Chapter 2: The Pattern of Land Ownership

1. Franklin Ellis, ed., *History of Fayette County* (Philadelphia,
1882), pp. 807–08, 781–82, 152; Solon J. and Elizabeth H. Buck, *The
Planting of Civilization in Western Pennsylvania* (Pittsburgh, 1939), pp.
280, 455, 369; *Pennsylvania Archives*, 2d series, vol. 4 (Harrisburg,
1852–1935), p. 191.

2. John W. Harpster, ed., *Pen Pictures of Early Western Pennsylvania* (Pittsburgh, 1938) gives many such descriptions. Johann David
Schoepf in 1784 called it a "desolate and wild mountain . . . exhaust-
ing for horse and man" (p. 133). Sally Hastings in 1800 described
people weeping, "totally exhausted" (p. 235). See also pp. 141,
144, 178.

3. Joseph E. Walker, ed., *Pleasure and Business in Western Pennsylvania: The Journal of Joshua Gilpin, 1809* (Harrisburg, 1975), pp. 43–44.

4. John W. Jordan, ed., "Notes of Travel of William Henry, John
Heckewelder, John Rothrock, and Christian Clewell, to Gnaden-
hutten on the Muskingum, in the Early Summer of 1797," *Pennsylvania Magazine of History and Biography* 10 (1886): 155.

5. Ibid.; Walker, *Journal of Joshua Gilpin*, p. 44.

6. Department of Agriculture, Soil Conservation Service, *Soil
Survey of Fayette County, Pennsylvania, 1971*, pp. 2–4, 13–14; and *Soil
Survey of Greene and Washington Counties, Pennsylvania, 1983*, pp. 3–5,
60–61; Harpster, *Pen Pictures*, p. 144.

7. Because this geographic pattern of settlement and landownership is so basic to the analysis that follows, and because there will be
thirty-three townships in three counties in the 1780s and thirty-three
townships in two counties in the 1790s, the following list of townships—given north to south by region for each county—has been
included to aid the reader. Attention is also called to the maps in
appendix B and to the fact that township spellings are present-day
spellings. Fayette County, 1780s: border—Bullskin, Wharton; interior—Tyrone, Franklin, Georges; river—Washington, Luzerne, Ger-

man, Springhill. There are no extant records for Union and Menallen townships, nor for Wharton Township in the 1790s.

Washington County, 1780s: border—Robinson, Smith, Hopewell, Donegal, Greene; interior—Cecil, Strabane, Somerset, Amwell, Morgan; river—Peters, Nottingham, Fallowfield, Bethlehem, Cumberland. 1790s: border—Robinson, Smith, Hanover, Hopewell, Cross Creek, Donegal, Finley, Greene; interior—Cecil, Chartiers, Strabane, Washington, Canton, Somerset, Amwell, Morris, Morgan, Franklin; river—Peters, Nottingham, Fallowfield, Pike Run, East Bethlehem, West Bethlehem, Cumberland.

Westmoreland County, 1780s: border—Armstrong, Fairfield, Donegal; interior—Derry, Hempfield, Mt. Pleasant, Huntington; river—Pitt, Rostraver. No returns exist for the 1790s.

8. James Veech, *Monongahela of Old* (Pittsburgh, 1858, 1892), pp. 21, 76, 83; Buck and Buck, *Civilization*, pp. 138–41. Several matters regarding the data used in compiling the statistics should be discussed. The data for Fayette County are in the first extant assessment for each township found in the Fayette County Courthouse. The county was erected in 1783 from Westmoreland County, and the first extant assessments are generally those for 1785, with the exception of 1786 for three townships and 1787 for one. Unfortunately, no data could be located for two townships, Union and Menallen, until the nineteenth century. Fayette County assessments in the *Pennsylvania Archives*, 3d series, vol. 22, pp. 544–641 are unsatisfactory since they list only taxes due, but no property. From the *Archives*, however, it can be determined that there were 213 taxable persons in Menallen and 204 taxable persons in Union. Thus, the total of taxable persons was 2,019, a figure comparable to Westmoreland. In all probability, the inclusion of these two missing townships would only further accentuate the county's more mature land pattern. These were perhaps the two most important townships in the county. They included the two major towns, Brownsville, on the river, and Uniontown, the county seat. Thus, it should be remembered that Fayette County data represent only 80 percent of the county, and that the missing areas were probably well-advanced communities.

The data for Westmoreland came solely from the *Pennsylvania Archives*, 3d series, vol. 22, pp. 369–453. Although Westmoreland was the oldest county, erected in 1773, no original tax data survive until that from the first decade of the nineteenth century. The *Archives* data are for 1783, just before Fayette County was separated from Westmoreland. All the statistics, however, have excluded the four townships that became Fayette County, and thus reduced dupli-

cation to a negligible level. The whole county in 1783 had 1,881
landowners out of 3,277 taxable persons—a percentage of 57.4, two
points below the percentage with Fayette removed. However, one
excluded Fayette County region returned only a list of 512 names
without property, making an exact comparison impossible.

The Washington County data are also from the *Pennsylvania Archives*, 3d series, vol. 22, pp. 701–82. Although they are printed for
the year 1781, the year the county was erected, the names are identical to the first extant tax data found in the Washington County
Courthouse for the year 1784. Furthermore, the *Archives* assessments
contain two townships which were not created until after 1781. Unfortunately, the extant originals are tax duplicates containing the
amount of tax due, but no property. Property returns earlier than
the late 1780s and 1790s are not available; therefore, the *Archives*
material has been used for the early 1780s.

Does the use of some data from different years cause any of the
differences between the counties? The answer is yes, but only to a
very limited extent. Comparisons between areas that were in Westmoreland County in 1783 and then in Fayette County in 1785 indicated only small changes. Tyrone Township in 1785 had a percentage of landownership of 41.2 compared with 41.8 for a larger
Westmoreland township. Franklin, in 1785, had a percentage of
54.4, compared with a somewhat larger Franklin in 1783, which had
a percentage of 55.0. Washington Township in 1785 had a percentage of 52.5, compared with Rostraver's 47.2 and Franklin's 55.0, the
two townships from which it was formed.

9. Not every township fit the pattern perfectly. Derry Township,
Westmoreland County, was the leading exception. Although it was an
interior township and also an area of early settlement, it had a
landowning percentage of 92.3 in 1783. This was probably because of
the Indian wars of the preceeding summer. Derry was north of both
Forbes Road and Hannastown, the county seat destroyed by the Indians. Probably most of the population fled the region, and the assessment rolls for 1783 reflect primarily the landowners who would continue to be assessed for their land even if they temporarily fled with
most of the nonlanded population. See George Dallas Albert, *History
of the County of Westmoreland* (Philadelphia, 1882), p. 463; John N.
Boucher, *History of Westmoreland County* (New York, 1906), vol. 1, p.
157. There were also a few interior townships with lower percentages
than might have been expected. Tyrone Township in Fayette County
had the lowest percentage of all, 41.2 percent. Georges Township,
Fayette County, and Cecil Township, Washington County, also had

low percentages of landownership. The most reasonable explanation for this is that these were more important areas of early settlement. See the full list of township percentages in appendix A.

10. See the full distribution in appendix A. Two factors need to be mentioned that influenced the data for Washington and Westmoreland counties. In Washington, the 400-acre holding was much more prominent than elsewhere, reflecting the Virginia land system under which many Washington settlers first acquired land. There were 171 such holdings in Washington, but only 10 in Westmoreland, the center of Pennsylvania loyalties. The second problem concerns Westmoreland's two northern border townships where officials simply listed 234 holdings as "1 tract," or "2 tracts," but not in acres. How to calculate these tracts is the problem; the solution—to count them all as 300-acre holdings—is not wholly satisfactory. There is little doubt that most of these tracts in 1783 represented land claims, not actual settlements. For example, the names of several prominent men living elsewhere can be found here.

Other border townships—Robinson, Smith, Greene in Washington, and Wharton in Fayette—had similar speculative activity. The median and modal figures in them were 300 acres, and that gives some justification for the arbitrary 300-acre figure. Yet obviously not every claimant had 300 acres; no township was without diversity. Projecting the land pattern for the remainder of Westmoreland into these areas would not be satisfactory, and considering the earlier settlement of Fayette County, and Washington's initially different land system, projecting figures from other border areas would not be any better. In terms of total acreages involved, the 300-acre figure is probably not far wrong, but it does overemphasize the 300-acre level in the full distribution. The arbitrary 300-acre figure has been used as the simplest and easiest—if perhaps not best—solution to an insolvable problem, and the reader is so advised.

11. In illustrating the median taxable persons—or any other median—in a township with an even-numbered population, rather than select the fictitious median between the two middle persons, both middle persons have been included as typical. Also, median taxable persons were selected by adding the landless population to the bottom end of the land distribution and selecting the middle case according to the normal alphabetical listing of each township. Full tax information has been listed for each median taxable. No valuation figures appear on the Westmoreland returns, but where a census appears on the return, this has been included. It should also be noted that this is the only time when the full 1783 Westmoreland

return has been used without first excluding the future Fayette County areas to avoid duplication. The four townships normally excluded are marked as such in the table. See the table of median taxable persons for the other two counties in appendix A.

12. The Springhill assessment included 238 tracts of land ranging in size from 1 to 150 acres. Only ten persons had more than 50 acres, and only five had more than 75 acres, but fifty-two had from 1 to 10 acres. The median was 20 acres; the mean, 24.5; the mode, 30 acres. The median taxable person was landless, since only 48.4 percent of the population owned land. Three years later, Springhill, as a smaller Fayette County township, had a median landholding of 150 acres, a mean of 173, and a mode of 100 acres. Such changes within three years are incomprehensible, and the 1783 Springhill return makes no sense unless the assessor accidently listed only cleared land instead of total land.

13. James T. Lemon, "Household Consumption in Eighteenth Century America and Its Relation to Production and Trade: The Situation Among Farmers in Southeastern Pennsylvania," *Agricultural History* 41 (January 1967): 68–69, is responsible for the seventy-five acre figure, and Charles S. Grant, *Democracy in the Connecticut Frontier Town of Kent* (New York, 1961), pp. 32–35, is responsible for the forty-acre figure. For a discussion of criticisms of these standards and the acreage needs for self-sufficiency versus commercial farming, see the discussion of acreage requirements in chapters 4 and 6.

14. It should be recalled that Springhill occupied the southernmost part of Fayette County and fronted on the Monongahela River. According to the general land pattern, it may have been a little more developed than interior and border regions. Springhill's cleared-acreage figures, therefore, may have been among the largest in the whole region. Having 100 or 150 acres cleared, however, seems unusual unless it was the combined clearings from tenants on a large tract or from a multiple holding. Such appears to be the case, for three years later one of these is listed as a 415-acre tract of a prominant individual, another is a 311-acre tract whose owner has two slaves, and a third is a 250-acre tract. The fourth name is missing after three years.

15. No original assessment data remain for Allegheny or Westmoreland counties in the 1790s, and the published records in the *Pennsylvania Archives* stop with 1790. Therefore, discussion of the 1790s will be limited to Washington and Fayette, the two southern counties. They occupied about half of the geographical area involved in the discussion of the 1780s, and they had the most dissimi-

lar statistical patterns for that period. A composite of the two, therefore, should still be representative of the whole region. Even though the geographical area has been halved, the statistical population remains nearly the same due to population growth. The data used for Washington County are a nearly full run of original assessments for the year 1793. Only three townships out of twenty-four then in the county are missing, and they have been included by taking the nearest extant assessment: 1792 in one case and 1794 in two others. The county-seat town of Washington County, also bearing the name Washington, now had its own separate jurisdiction. In addition, a number of Washington County assessments for 1796 have been used, but a full run is lacking. In Fayette County, the assessments used were for the year 1796, except in one case, the year was 1795. Unlike Washington County, no new townships were created in Fayette until 1798. Direct township comparisons are, therefore, possible in Fayette, but somewhat hazardous in Washington due to the many boundary changes. Unfortunately, during the course of this research, the tax book for Wharton Township disappeared, and although early notes suggest its information was skimpy, nevertheless, three townships— Wharton, Union, and Menallen—are missing from the Fayette County statistics. The statistics for the county would probably be about 25 percent larger than they are if these three townships could be included.

16. See the complete township figures for the 1790s in appendix A.

17. The inclusion of lots in the land distribution accounted for approximately one-sixth of the total decline in acreages during the decade. The following median and mean figures for the 1790s, compiled with lots excluded from the taxable and landed populations, were only 10 acres larger than those in table 2.3. These medians and means, respectively, were: Fayette—150, 195; Washington—150, 201; river—130, 167; interior—130, 172; border—160, 261; western Pennsylvania total—150, 199.

18. Again, acreage figures included in each decile were about 10 acres larger with town lots excluded from consideration. The range of acreages—lots excluded—in each decile were: 1st, 1–50; 2d, 50–80; 3d, 80–100; 4th, 100; 5th, 100–50; 6th, 150–80; 7th, 180–200; 8th, 200–70; 9th, 270–350; 10th, 350–40,000.

19. See the full distribution for the 1790s in appendix A.

20. Merle E. Curti, *The Making of an American Community: A Case Study of Democracy in a Frontier County* (Stanford, Calif., 1959), p. 78.

21. If the figures for Greene and Cecil townships in 1796 are

indicative, Washington County may have had less cleared land. Greene, the large, southern border township, had only 13.5 percent of its land cleared, and Cecil, a northern interior township, had 21.0 percent cleared.

22. Porter did not lack for livestock; the 300 acres he held in 1785 had been divided and given to Charles, Jr., and perhaps others of the nine landed Porters in the township, all of whom had livestock.

23. Samuel Burns was another case of subdivision. He and Thomas Burns each had 125 acres in 1796, while a second Samuel Burns had no acreage. In the 1780s, only one Samuel Burns, presumably the father, was taxed for 250 acres. Thomas had 30 acres cleared, compared with Samuel's 15 acres.

24. The list of median taxable persons for Washington County may be found in appendix A. In general, they were small farmers. All owned land, but some were lot owners. Those lots in Strabane and Canton townships were outlots of the town of Washington and were, for the most part, owned by important county personages as speculative holdings. They were, therefore, atypical of lot owners in Washington County.

Chapter 3: The Concentration of Wealth

1. Franklin Ellis, ed., *History of Fayette County* (Philadelphia, 1882), pp. 502–03, 152; Solon J. and Elizabeth H. Buck, *The Planting of Civilization in Western Pennsylvania* (Pittsburgh, 1939), p. 304.

2. It should be emphasized that these are mean percentages. Since each township had its own rate structure for assessing property, and since no two used the same rates, absolute figures would be misleading. Thus, regional or total percentages are simply the averages of the individual township means.

It is no longer surprising to find significant social stratification in early American society. James T. Lemon, *The Best Poor Man's Country: A Geographical Study of Early Southeastern Pennsylvania* (Baltimore, Md., 1972), pp. 10–11, found the wealthy (top decile) of southeastern Pennsylvania increased their share of wealth from 24 to 38 percent during the eighteenth century. Jerome H. Wood, Jr., found that the top decile in Lancaster Borough increased its share of taxable wealth from 33 to 49 percent between 1751 and 1788. The bottom decile declined from 2.9 to 0.5 percent; *Conestoga Crossroads: Lancaster, Pennsylvania, 1730–1790* (Harrisburg, 1979), table 8-2, p. 168. Likewise, Stephanie G. Wolf found that in Germantown from 1773 to 1791 wealth increased from 36.5 to 40 percent for the top decile and fell from 4.5 to 1.0 percent for the bottom decile; *Urban Village: Population, Community, and Family Structure in Germantown, Pennsylvania, 1683–1800* (Princeton, N.J., 1976), pp. 123–24. More extreme differences occurred in the larger urban areas during the eighteenth century. See James H. Henretta, "Economic Development and Social Structure in Colonial Boston," *William and Mary Quarterly* 22 (1965): 75–92. Henretta was one of the first to call attention to the matter. See also Gary B. Nash, "Urban Wealth and Poverty in Pre-Revolutionary America," *Journal of Interdisciplinary History* 6 (1976): 545–84.

3. Such procedures naturally involve difficulties. Tracing names was the most consistent problem. Often the same surname appeared, but with a different personal name. On occasion, county histories helped identify them, but many tracts with questionable names remained and have been labeled *probable* in the tables. Also, early assessments tended to list land in round numbers, but later, with official surveys completed, more specific numbers appeared. Because of this, any tract within twenty-five acres of its original size has been considered unchanged, and perhaps even this was not enough leeway. Then, changing township and county boundaries caused problems. Sometimes a person in one township appeared in another one a decade later. As much as possible, these changes have been taken into consideration.

The erection of Allegheny County in 1788, which incorporated a large section of northern Washington County into its borders, was of greater consequence. Three townships—Robinson, Cecil, and Peters—lost much or most of their land and population. This resulted in a great number of disappearing tracts, which distorts the statistics. For example, the inclusion of Robinson increases the percentage of tracts that disappeared in the border townships from 33 to 49 percent. A number of these vanished tracts can be found on a 1791 tax list for Allegheny County, but since this is a list of taxes due only, with no property listing, it is of little comparative use; *Pennsylvania Archives*, 3d series, vol. 22, (Harrisburg, 1852–1935), pp. 645–97. Therefore, these three townships are excluded from the tabulations. This eliminated 113 large tracts out of 397 from consideration.

Finally, it should be noted that no direct comparison can be made between the two surveys. The total number of landowners in the 1780s who increased or maintained their holdings will not exactly equal the old landowners on the 1790s survey. Several things cause this. For example, a person with 1,000 acres in the 1780s and 600 in the 1790s had a smaller tract, but still maintained his leading status. A person whose 400-acre tract became 377 acres in the 1790s was credited with maintaining his status in the 1780s, but his 377 acres excluded him from the 1790s survey. Also a person from township A in the 1780s, who increased his holdings but ended up in township B in the 1790s, was given credit for that increase in township A, but was listed with the old landowners of township B in the 1790s.

4. Ellis, *Fayette County*, pp. 235–36, 465–66; Papers, Court of Quarter Sessions, Fayette County.

5. Ellis, *Fayette County*, pp. 767–69, 807–08.

6. Buck and Buck, *Civilization*, p. 304; Ellis, *Fayette County*, pp. 233, 502–03; William A. Hunter, "John Badollet's 'Journal of the time I spent in Stony creek glades,' 1793–1794," *Pennsylvania Magazine of History and Biography* 104 (April 1980): 170.

7. Only Fayette County millers can be compared, because the 1784 Washington County return in the *Pennsylvania Archives* did not indicate any other taxable property except livestock. The new tax system begun in 1796 made comparison difficult even in Fayette, for these other taxable items were not always listed separately. Nevertheless, a fairly accurate ranking is possible to construct. It should also be noted that the top decile of landowners was a smaller group of people than the top decile of all taxable persons.

8. Victor S. Clark, *History of Manufactures in the United States* (New York, 1929), vol. 1, pp. 177–81; Carl Bridenbaugh, *The Colonial Craftsman* (New York, 1950), p. 19; Continuance Docket, Court of Common Pleas, Fayette County, passim. For an example of patronizing a local mill, see Rev. Robert Ayres, Journal, passim, and especially the entry of 19 January 1796 in which he tried Andrew Lynn's new mill, by having two and a half bushels of corn ground, instead of using one of Robert Jackson's three mills. Box 33, Western Pennsylvania Historical Society.

9. Mitchell and Flanders, eds., *The Statutes at Large of Pennsylvania from 1682 to 1801* (Harrisburg, 1896–1915), vol. 10, ch. 871 (1 March 1780), p. 67, ch. 972 (13 April 1782), p. 463. The abolition law and settling the boundary dispute in favor of Pennsylvania are generally believed to have induced many slave owners to move to Kentucky. See James Veech, *Monongahela of Old* (Pittsburgh, 1858, 1892), pp. 99–100.

10. George Dallas Albert, *History of the County of Westmoreland* (Philadelphia, 1882), p. 60; Boyd Crumrine, ed., *History of Washington County* (Philadelphia 1882), p. 256; U.S. Bureau of the Census, *Heads of Families at the First Census of the United States Taken in the Year 1790*

(Washington, D.C.: Government Printing Office, 1907–08); U.S.
Census Office, *Second Census, 1800* (Washington, D.C.: 1801; facsimile rpt., Brooklyn, N.Y.: Central Book Co., n.d.). Some residents of
the area that would be Washington County registered their slaves in
Westmoreland County following the passage of the law, until Washington County was erected in 1781, thus accounting for the large
difference in the number of slaves registered in the two counties.
Also, the total of 106 slaves in Washington in 1800 is actually the total
of Washington county (84) and Green County (22), which was
erected out of Washington in 1796.

11. The Fayette figure does not include the two townships of
Union and Menallen. They contained a quarter of the 282 slaves
reported on the 1790 census, and undoubtedly they had a similar
proportion five years earlier. Even so, the number of slaves appears to
have increased temporarily in Fayette County in spite of the abolition
law. The increase from 1785 to 1790 was greatest in the three river
townships of Washington, Luzerne, and Springhill. Part of the difference undoubtedly stemmed from the tax laws that taxed only for
slaves above twelve years of age. Children were thus not on the assessments, but were on the census. Still, there were also absolute increases.
For example, Margaret Hutton was taxed for seven slaves in 1785, but
had twenty-four in 1790. The difference here was not untaxed children, for she had registered only nine slaves in accordance with the
abolition law. Mitchell and Flanders, eds., *Statutes at Large*, vol. 10, ch.
944 (21 June 1781), p. 330; Veech, *Monongahela*, p. 99.

12. The distribution of slaves by county on these assessments is as
follows:

Number of Slaves	Number Taxed for Slaves in Fayette County, 1785	Number Taxed for Slaves in Washington County, 1793
1	45	77
2	18	25
3	11	6
4	6	1
5	2	1
6	0	0
7	1	0
8	1	0

Comparison of slaves over time cannot be done because of limitations in the 1784 Washington assessments and the 1796 Fayette assessments.

Chapter 4: Tenancy and Absenteeism

1. Hugh Cleland, *George Washington in the Ohio Valley* (Pittsburgh, 1955), p. 296.
2. For example, Solon J. and Elizabeth H. Buck, *The Planting of Civilization in Western Pennsylvania* (Pittsburgh, 1939), pp. 273, 281, in their discussion of labor in western Pennsylvania, make no mention of tenancy at all. Stevenson Whitcomb Fletcher, *Pennsylvania Agriculture and Country Life, 1640–1840* (Harrisburg, 1950), pp. 107–22, makes no mention of tenancy in the chapter on labor, although an occasional reference to tenancy does appear in the work; for example, pp. 305, 315. Likewise, Wayland F. Dunaway, *A History of Pennsylvania*, 2d ed. (New York, 1949), pp. 205–10, makes no mention of tenancy in his discussion of labor. Richard B. Morris's *Government and Labor in Early America* (New York, 1965) does not even have the word *tenant* in the index.

Even Jackson T. Main concludes there were only "occasionally tenants" on the northern frontier in *The Social Structure of Revolutionary America* (Princeton, N.J., 1965), p. 17, although he does suggest that some of the landless persons found on western Pennsylvania assessments "may have been tenants" (p. 16). Part of Main's difficulty is that he relied only on the published *Pennsylvania Archives*, and he tabulated only the first third of the townships in Washington County, not the whole county. Nevertheless, Main's detailed work blazed a path many have followed. For example, tenancy along the Hudson River has long been known and now has received definitive treatment in Sung Bok Kim's *Landlord and Tenant in Colonial New York: Manorial Society 1664–1775* (Chapel Hill, N.C., 1978). Stephen Innes has called attention to the role of the Pynchon family in western Massachusetts in "Land Tenancy and Social Order in Springfield, Massachusetts, 1652–1702," *William and Mary Quarterly* 35 (January 1978): 33–56, and in his book *Labor in a New Land: Economy and Society in Seventeenth-Century Springfield* (Princeton, N.J., 1983).

Much work has been done on colonial Maryland, including Lorena S. Walsh's "Land, Landlord and Leasehold: Estate Management and Tenant Fortunes in Southern Maryland, 1642–1820," *Agricultural History* 59 (July 1985): 373–96. James T. Lemon first elaborated tenancy in Pennsylvania in his highly regarded study of agricultural society in southeastern Pennsylvania, *Best Poor Man's Country: A Geographical Study of Early Southeastern Pennsylvania* (Baltimore, Md., 1972), pp. 92–93. Stephanie G. Wolf, in *Urban Village: Population, Community, and Family Structure in Germantown* (Princeton, N.J., 1976), pp. 83–86, and

Jerome H. Wood, Jr., in *Conestoga Crossroads: Lancaster, Pennsylvania, 1730–1790* (Harrisburg, 1979), pp. 171–72, discuss the role of tenancy in these two urban areas. Lucy Simler most clearly defines the various elements of the tenant class in Pennsylvania in her enlightening work "Tenancy in Colonial Pennsylvania: The Case of Chester County," *William and Mary Quarterly* 43 (October 1986): 542–69.

3. Fragmentary evidence proves that tenancy existed in both of these counties in the 1780s, even though the published returns in the *Archives* do not indicate it. The manuscript tax duplicate for Cecil Township, Washington County, 1784, indicates that about 7 percent of the landowners there were landlords. A 1783 manuscript assessment for Mt. Pleasant Township, Westmoreland County, now lost, but reprinted by George Dallas Albert in *History of the County of Westmoreland* (Philadelphia, 1882), pp. 534–36, mentions persons "who had land rented in the township."

4. There were other indications that the use of the term *estate* referred to landlords and not to the surviving property of some deceased person. In East Bethlehem, two persons with estate designations in 1793 appeared in 1796 as landless inmates living on the land of absentees. In Somerset Township, Edward Dehaven, with a fifty-acre estate, was marked "gone," an unlikely notation for an established landowner, but a likely one for a temporary tenant. Also, of the fourteen people with estates listed in Donegal in 1793, four were there in 1784, and three of these persons had no land, while the fourth was assessed for the same acreage that he was renting in 1793.

5. See Simler, "Tenancy in Colonial Pennsylvania," for a discussion of the complexity she found in Chester County regarding inmates, single freemen, tenant farmers, and smallholders. Chapter 6 in this book will provide an additional discussion of the status of landless dependent persons.

6. Mitchell and Flanders, eds., *Statutes at Large of Pennsylvania from 1682 to 1801* (Harrisburg, 1896–1915), vol. 10, ch. 900 (18 March 1780), p. 141, ch. 921 (19 December 1780), p. 240, ch. 944 (21 June 1781), p. 331; vol. 11, ch. 1137 (16 March 1785), p. 475; vol. 15, ch. 1852 (17 April 1795), p. 327.

7. Cleland, *Washington,* pp. 276, 287–90.

8. The scope of tenancy in Pennsylvania is beginning to take shape. Lemon, *Best Poor Man's Country,* table 19, p. 94, states a tenancy rate for Chester County in 1760 and 1782 as 27 percent for both years and a rate for Lancaster County as 36 and 32 percent in the same years. For urban areas, Wood, *Conestoga Crossroads,* p. 171, lists rates for Lancaster of 26 to 39 percent for 1755 to 1775 that

declined to 28 percent by 1788. Wolf, *Urban Village*, p. 93, found 56 percent of Germantown residents were nonlandowners in 1767 and 1780, with the number specified as renting increasing from 26 to 39 percent during that period.

Lucy Simler's work makes it clear why arriving at a tenancy figure is so difficult. She found it necessary to distinguish between tenant farmers who worked a normal-sized farm and smallholders who leased a few acres (under twenty) from a landowner to provide a part of their subsistence needs while pursuing a trade, performing common labor, and supplementing the labor of the local landowner. The matter is further complicated by the role of single freemen and inmates who were not landowners but laborers of various kinds. She found rates for tenancy increased in the mid-eighteenth century to 25 percent of householders (17 percent of taxable persons), then declined to 20 percent (13 percent of taxable persons) by 1774. Simler estimates that tax lists missed approximately 5 percent of the tenants, about 1 percent of the population of her tax lists; "Tenancy in Colonial Pennsylvania," pp. 546–52.

The problem of sorting out the exact status of the landless is evident in Lemon's work on southeastern Pennsylvania. He states that "in 1760 and 1782 about 30 percent of Lancaster's and Chester's married taxpayers were landless . . . , and about the same number of farmers fell into the tenant category, possibly half of them sharecroppers." He goes on to note that tenancy occurred most around the ironworks and in the best farming areas. But he never resolves the differences between the combined 60 percent who are landless and who are tenants with the tenancy rates in table 19, pp. 94–95. An increasing percentage of farm laborers is expected according to frontier theory. See Merle Curti, *The Making of an American Community: A Case Study of Democracy in a Frontier County* (Stanford, Calif., 1959), p. 154.

9. Cleland, *Washington*, pp. 284, 289–90, 296; Cecil E. Goode, "Gilbert Simpson: Washington's Partner in Settling His Western Pennsylvania Land," *Western Pennsylvania Historical Magazine* 62 (1979): pp. 151–52; Joseph E. Walker, ed., *Pleasure and Business in Western Pennsylvania: The Journal of Joshua Gilpin, 1809* (Harrisburg, 1975), pp. 52–53, 59; G. D. Skull, "General Sir Frederick Haldimand in Pennsylvania," *Pennsylvania Magazine of History and Biography* 8 (1884): 303.

10. In compiling a complete survey of all civil and criminal cases in four counties, and in examining a few hundred court papers, the author discovered only one case that seemed to deal with a landlord-tenant contract. Some forcible entry and ejectment cases did on occa-

sion mention a tenant—this is in addition to the normal use of fictitious tenants in certain pleas such as ejectment proceedings used to
clarify rival land claims—but these were not contractual matters.
Merchant contracts certainly appeared in abundance, and chance
surely would have revealed more than one case if the landlord-
tenant relationship was a formal, rigidly enforceable one.

11. Walker, *Journal of Joshua Gilpin*, p. 53; Goode, "Gilbert Simpson," pp. 160–62, 164. The people on Washington's land in Cecil
Township had apparently bought their land from George Croghan
and were assessed for their lands by the county. Unwilling to lose
their titles, they refused to become Washington's tenants and, as the
introductory quotation indicates, they decided to stand suit for their
land. Washington won the suit in the Pennsylvania state courts in
1786, but he was thereafter too busy to take advantage of the ruling.
By the mid-1790s, his land had passed to local owners. It is ironic
that one of the landlords of Cecil Township in 1796 was one of those
who had agreed to stand suit against Washington ten years earlier.
Cleland, *Washington*, pp. 285–89, 297 n. 80, 298 n. 84. Colonel Israel
Shreve, "Journal From Jersey to the Monongahela, August 11,
1788," *Pennsylvania Magazine of History and Biography* 52 (1928): 203.

12. John W. Harpster, ed., *Pen Pictures of Early Western Pennsylvania* (Pittsburgh, 1938), p. 249.

13. Goode, "Gilbert Simpson," p. 156. Rents in the Bedford example were £10 and £12; Skull, "General Haldimand," p. 303. A few
rents were noted in Morris Township in 1796 ranging from £8 to two
tenants paying £39. In Franklin Township, Fayette County, in 1796,
rents paid ranged from £6 to £18, with most paying between £10 and
£12. In 1784, Washington offered the squatters on his land a rate of
£10 per 100 acres, and he offered similar rates to prospective tenants
in Maryland—£10 the first year, £15 the second year, £25 the third
year. He also was able to rent Gilbert Simpson's land for 500 bushels
of wheat, a seemingly high rent, but this was a gristmill site, and the
£100 equivalent rent was probably reasonable; Cleland, *Washington*,
pp. 296, 284, 289.

Concerning the value of tenant property, the median tenant in
Cecil Township in 1796 had taxable property of £13 (one horse, £10,
and one cow, £3), and the taxable property of all tenants in the
township ranged from £0 to £49. The property of tenants in
Luzerne, given in dollars (£3 = $8) was comparable. By 1809, when
Joshua Gilpin visited his tenements, his annual rates were $100 to
Henry Harlan for a tract of over 300 acres, with 80 acres cleared, but
$16 on a lease to Isaac Fordyce for a small 12-acre tract. John Hay-

cock leased some 350 to 400 acres, of which approximately 80 of the 200 acres of prime farmland was cleared. The leasehold also included a sawmill, and Haycock also paid $100 for the whole tract; Walker, *Journal of Joshua Gilpin,* pp. 52–53, 58–59. The holdings of Fordyce and Harlan are examples of what Lucy Simler differentiated as smallholders, who generally held 20 acres or less, and tenant farmers, who were the larger leaseholders; "Tenancy in Colonial Pennsylvania," pp. 545, 557, 562.

14. The tenants of Cecil Township in 1796 had a median acreage of twenty, a modal acreage of fifteen. This was computed by dividing the amount of cleared land charged to a landlord by the number of tenants plus the landlord, or by the tenants only if the landlord did not have livestock—and presumably, did not use the land himself. By the standards established by James T. Lemon for southeastern Pennsylvania of forty acres of cleared land needed for subsistance farming and seventy-five acres cleared for commercial farming, these tenants were short of the land needed; "Household Consumption . . . in Southeastern Pennsylvania," *Agricultural History* 41 (January 1967), pp. 69, 68, n. 50. By the standards established by Charles Grant in his study of Kent, Connecticut (which may fit frontier western Pennsylvania better than they do the Germans and other farmers of Lancaster County), they probably managed to get by. Grant maintained that nine and a half acres, two and a half arable, would support one person; *Democracy in the Connecticut Frontier Town of Kent* (New York, 1961), pp. 32–35. A cleared acreage of fifteen to twenty acres, therefore, should have supported a family of five, and with two and a half to seven and a half acres left for a cash crop of wheat to pay the rent.

Bettye Hobbs Pruitt found in her study of Massachusetts in 1771 that twenty acres of cleared land was the median holding for the whole province. She questioned Lemon's acreage requirements, as well as other similar estimates, as too large, and Lemon has conceded that he may have been overly generous; Pruitt, "Self-Sufficiency and the Agricultural Economy of Eighteenth-Century Massachusetts," *William and Mary Quarterly* 41 (July 1984): 338, 340–43. See also the communication between Pruitt, Lemon, and Daniel Vickers in *William and Mary Quarterly* 42 (October 1985): 553–62.

It would take the two and a half to seven and a half acres to produce sufficient wheat in western Pennsylvania to pay a £10 rent. If, as Lemon suggests, one acre produced ten bushels of wheat and wheat sold for 10s. a bushel, two acres would pay the rent. Fletcher, *Pennsylvania Agriculture,* p. 145, agrees with the ten bushels per acre wheat yields, as does Pruitt for Massachusetts agriculture (p. 361).

However, evidence for western Pennsylvania indicates that wheat brought only 4s. per bushel in the mid-1790s. If so, it would take five acres of wheat to pay the rent. See Ella Chalfant, *A Goodly Heritage: Earliest Wills on an American Frontier* (Pittsburgh, 1955), p. 18; *Pittsburgh Gazette,* 29 March, 19 April 1794; 12 March, 4 April, 11 April 1795. All of this assumes considerable use of woodland pasture, and perhaps even harvesting hay from uncleared meadows. Any considerable use of cleared acreage for maintenance of livestock, as in eastern Pennsylvania, would make a tenant's livelihood very tenuous indeed. Pruitt frankly states that farms of this size could not have been self-sufficient, but she goes on in her article to establish that exchanges of grain and labor existed widely in rural communities, allowing for community self-sufficiency, if not individual self-sufficiency. Pruitt's study of local exchange relationships suggests a tenancy situation much like that described by Simler for Chester County and also seems to fit the situation found in western Pennsylvania.

This tenuous situation for tenants is also suggested by the work of Carole Shammas. Using data largely developed by Lemon, *Best Poor Man's Country,* table 27, Shammas has looked in detail at self-sufficiency needs in Massachusetts and has concluded that "the costs of self-sufficiency would have excluded the resources available to many households;" Carole Shammas, "How Self-Sufficient Was Early America?" *Journal of Interdisciplinary History* 8 (Autumn 1982): 252.

15. One tenant remained in Cecil Township in 1784; the other was found in Chartiers, which was erected out of Cecil. By 1796, the one in Cecil did have seventy acres of his own and was not a tenant. The search for wills located only one tenant, who died in 1799.

16. The years of the extant returns for Georges are 1787, 1788, 1791, 1793, 1795, 1798, 1799. The following is a summary of when the names of these thirteen tenants of 1795 disappeared from the preceding and succeeding tax lists. The first five, for example, were not in the township in 1793, and were gone by 1798. Thus they could not have been in the township for more than four years. Coming after 1793 and gone by 1798 were five people; coming after 1791 and gone by 1798, three people; coming after 1788 and gone by 1799, two people; coming after 1791 and gone by 1800, one person; coming after 1793 and gone by 1808, one person; coming before 1783 and gone by 1804, one person.

Simler argues that smallholding was a way to social advancement for some, allowing them more security than common labor or a trade, and providing the opportunity to accumulate tools and capital for possible land purchases. The western Pennsylvania situation does not contradict this suggestion, even though not much advancement took place overall; Simler, "Tenancy in Colonial Pennsylvania," pp. 563ff. One example, Gilpin's tenant Henry Harlan, was not simply a landless weaver in Luzerne; he may have planned to move across the river to Fredericktown in East Bethlehem, where he was the absentee owner of two lots. Apparently before he could do so, the opportunity to tenant Gilpin's Luzerne lands came open and he stayed. Harlan was a Chester County Quaker and he may have known Gilpin or may have been recommended by Gilpin's local agent because of his origin. Walker, *Journal of Joshua Gilpin*, pp. 52–53.

17. All 69 absentee landlords were in Fayette County in 1785, while 88 of the 104 were in Washington County in 1793 and the other 16 were in Fayette County in 1796.

18. The most complete report of unseated lands in the 1780s came from three border townships in Washington County, which reported all 158 tracts. No unseated lands, as such, appeared on the Westmoreland returns, but those lands in Fairfield and Armstrong townships that were listed simply as tracts have been treated as unseated. These tracts comprised 76 percent of the landed population of Fairfield, and this same proportion has been used to determine the probable number of unseated lands in Armstrong, which was listed completely as tracts on the assessments. Thus, 57 tracts in Fairfield and 135 of 177 tracts in Armstrong have been included as representing unseated lands. In Fayette County, the only tracts reported were 12 in Wharton Township, separately listed as "to one improvement." None were reported in Bullskin Township, which reported most of those in 1796. By the 1790s, unseated lands were reported much more widely; eleven of twenty-five townships in Washington and 5 of 8 in Fayette reported them. This is representative enough—compared with the 1789 tax list for unseated lands in Washington County—that it can be taken as a fairly accurate indication of the extent of unseated lands in the 1790s without further refinement. The 1780s figures are probably low.

19. The "no livestock" figures for Westmoreland County in the 1780s (table 4.1) need a word of explanation because they are higher than the other counties and because the acreage percentage is lower than the landed percentage. This situation was largely caused by Indian depredations in northern Westmoreland County in the summer of 1782. Derry Township, an early center of settlement lying north of the burned county seat, Hannastown, reported seventy-seven tracts without livestock, half of the taxable listings for the township. No other township had as many as thirty. Settlers driven from their farms probably account for this increase. Also,

since these were small settled farms, not large original tracts, the acreage percentage is lower. However, the lower acreage percentages in the 1790s are directly attributable to the appearance of smaller town lots.

20. The complete breakdown of these categories is as follows: Bullskin: outside—Philadelphia, 8; Lancaster and Kentucky, 2 each; New Jersey, 1; and a company of unknown location for whom town proprietor Zachariah Connel served as agent; neighboring county—Westmoreland, 6; Somerset, 3; Washington and Allegheny, 1 each; neighboring townships—Tyrone, 6; Franklin, 3; Union, 4; Wharton, 1; same township—5 persons with sizable unseated holdings in addition to their normal residence or trade, plus 2 young sons of resident farmers who had unseated lands. The 8 unknowns could be outsiders or local people whose trade is obscure since 2 had small tracts without livestock, 3 had unseated tracts only, and 3 had town lots only. Greene: outside—Philadelphia, 5; Cumberland, Lancaster, and Elk, 1 each; and 4, residence unknown, for whom local resident Stephen Gapen acted as agent; three from neighboring Fayette County; 4 from within the county—1 each from Washington (town), Canonsburg, Cumberland Township, and 1 unknown. From the same township was Stephen Gapen with 2,100 unseated acres, in addition to his improved 1,900 acres. East Bethlehem: outside—Maryland, 3; Philadelphia, 2; Virginia, 1; neighboring county—Fayette, 3; neighboring townships—Cumberland, Pike Run, and West Bethlehem, 1 each; Washington (town), 2; five of these 14 East Bethlehem absentees held town lots in Fredericktown.

21. Thomas Sergeant, *A View of the Land Laws of Pennsylvania* (Philadelphia, 1838), pp. 74–75.

22. Continuance docket, Court of Common Pleas, Fayette County, 29 April 1789, 26 October 1790, 26 April 1791; Appearance docket, Court of Common Pleas, Washington County, 4 November 1789, 29 September 1791, 27 June 1793.

23. Ellis Paxson Oberholtzer, *Robert Morris: Patriot and Financier* (New York, 1903), pp. 314–44; Charles Page Smith, *James Wilson: Founding Father, 1742–1798* (Chapel Hill, N.C., 1956), pp. 383–88.

24. Compiled from the Continuance Docket, Court of Common Pleas, Westmoreland County; Continuance Docket, Court of Common Pleas, Fayette County; Appearance Docket, Court of Common Pleas, Washington County.

25. Cleland, *Washington*, p. 290; Walker, *Journal of Joshua Gilpin*, pp. 52, 60.

26. Mitchell and Flanders, eds., *Statutes at Large*, vol. 11, ch. 1137 (16 March 1785), p. 478, ch. 1140 (25 March 1785), p. 503; vol. 12,

ch. 1237 (11 September 1786), pp. 264–65, ch. 1255 (27 November 1786), p. 338; vol. 13, ch. 1374 (4 October 1788), p. 145, ch. 1397 (18 March 1789), p. 224, ch. 1442 (26 September 1789), p. 336, ch. 1519 (6 April 1790), pp. 530–31; vol. 14, ch. 1538 (24 March 1791), pp. 27–28, ch. 1622 (3 April 1792), p. 231; vol. 15, ch. 1852 (17 April 1795), p. 328.

27. Ibid., ch. 1895 (1 April 1796), pp. 431–32.

28. *Pittsburgh Gazette*, 31 May 1794; Buck and Buck, *Planting of Civilization*, pp. 205–06.

Chapter 5: Town Development

An earlier version of this chapter has appeared as "Town Development in Early Western Pennsylvania," *Western Pennsylvania Historical Magazine* 71 (January 1988): 3–26.

1. The standard statement of the role of towns in western development is by Richard C. Wade, *The Urban Frontier: The Rise of Western Cities, 1790–1830* (Cambridge, Mass., 1959). Although Wade is concerned with larger towns such as Pittsburgh, Cincinnati, and Louisville, the same patterns he describes hold for the smaller towns of western Pennsylvania. A theoretical explanation of the roles of frontier towns may be found in Joseph A. Ernst and H. Roy Merrens's " 'Camden's Turrets Pierce the Skies!': The Urban Process in the Southern Colonies during the Eighteenth Century," *William and Mary Quarterly* 30 (October 1973): 549–74.

2. Boyd Crumrine, ed., *History of Washington County* (Philadelphia, 1882), pp. 601–07, 468–72, 869.

3. An additional town, West Alexander in Donegal Township, Washington County, was technically platted in 1796, but settlement was delayed—partially due to a court suit—until the turn of the century; ibid., p. 747. Towns like Hopewell and Middletown were founded in 1797, a year after the cutoff date for this study; ibid., pp. 816, 819. No evidence of them appears on the 1796 assessments. Some doubt exists concerning the founding dates of some towns. The Fayette County history states that Haydentown was not laid out until just after 1790; Franklin Ellis, ed., *History of Fayette County* (Philadelphia, 1882), p. 567. However, two town lots appeared on the Georges Township assessment in 1787, and no other town is known to have existed in the township. The town may have begun on a small scale at the earlier date.

Bridgeport was reported as founded in 1794; ibid., pp. 465–66.

But a deed from the proprietor to Jacob Beeson for lots numbered one and thirty-one was dated 1793; Fayette County Deed Book A, p. 450. In Washington County, the date for the founding of Greensboro was given as 1781 by Greene County historian Samuel P. Bates; *Greene County* (Chicago, 1888), p. 521. But a collection of newspaper columns by Andrew J. Waychoff, *Local History* (Waynesburg, Pa., n.d.), articles 34 and 139, gives the date as 1791, as does Solon J. and Elizabeth H. Buck's *The Planting of Civilization in Western Pennsylvania* (Pittsburgh, 1939), pp. 149, 218. The latter must be correct, since only six lot owners were assessed in 1796. One of the lot owners in 1796 was Albert Gallatin, who was assessed for fifty-four lots, while no other person had more than six. Henry Adams, *The Life of Albert Gallatin* (1879: reprint, New York, 1943), pp. 152–53, recorded that, in 1795, Gallatin bought all the remaining lots in, and 20 acres of bottomland around, Greensboro, which lay directly across the river from the town site he was developing at the same time. Gallatin's town, New Geneva, was not officially platted until 1797, but he acquired the site in 1794, and a small settlement including a mill and boat yards had already begun there before he purchased and formalized its development.

No founding date has been found for Carmichaels in Bates, *Greene County,* and Washington County historians did not include Greene County areas when they discussed local subdivisions. Since no other towns were apparently founded earlier, the few town lots found on the Cumberland Township assessment of 1793 have been assumed to be in Carmichaels, and its founding date was probably a year or two before. One final town, Finleyville in Nottingham Township, was supposedly founded in 1788, according to Joseph F. McFarland, *Washington and Washington County* (Chicago, 1910), p. 436. Boyd Crumrine, however, gives no founding date, but indicates that founder James Barclay was only licensed to operate a tavern in that year, *Washington County*, p. 965. Since no town lots appeared in Nottingham in 1793, since there was no Finley for whom the town was supposedly named, and since Barclay was assessed for only 100 acres (and that in neighboring Peters Township), it appears doubtful that any formal town was laid out during the period under study.

4. Adams, *Gallatin*, p. 152.

5. Information on town location has been gleaned from several sources and from personal experience. County histories have information on each town. See the appropriate discussions in Ellis (*Fayette County*) and Crumrine (*Washington County*), passim. The Bucks also have a brief description of towns (*Civilization*, pp. 218–19).

6. Ellis, *Fayette County,* pp. 281, 424; Crumrine, *Washington County,* pp. 819.

7. Bates, *Greene County,* p. 521; Crumrine, *Washington County,* pp. 476–77.

8. James Hadden, *A History of Uniontown* (Uniontown, Pa., 1913), p. 12; Crumrine, *Washington County,* p. 917; Fayette County Deed Book B, p. 150, C-2, p. 631, C-3, p. 1131; Ellis, *Fayette County,* pp. 426, 567.

9. Fayette County Deed Book A, p. 450, B, p. 336, C-1, p. 451, C-2, p. 631.

10. Fayette County Deed Book C-3, p. 1362, B, p. 356.

11. John Reps, *Town Planning in Frontier America* (Princeton, N.J., 1969), pp. 3–6; Ellis, *Fayette County,* p. 424; Fayette County Deed Book C-3, p. 1364; *Atlas of the County of Fayette and the State of Pennsylvania* (Philadelphia, 1872: reprint, Knightstown, Ind., 1972), pp. 15, 23, 25, 29, 43, 46–47, 55; Crumrine, *Washington County,* pp. 916–17, 607; Bates, *Greene County,* p. 279. Reps does not include any of these towns in his text, but his words on the expansion of Pittsburgh could be readily applied to most of these towns: "urban growth proceeded with little attention to sound planning and orderly development. The drabness of its endless gridiron extensions stamped on the rugged terrain of the site was matched by the conditions of the atmosphere produced by coal-powered industry" pp. 265–66.

12. Hadden, *Uniontown,* pp. 12, 14; Fayette County Deed Book A, p. 450, C-1, p. 451, C-2, p. 631; Crumrine, *Washington County,* p. 607; Westmoreland County Deed Book B, p. 287; *Pittsburgh Gazette,* 4 April 1795.

13. Hadden, *Uniontown,* pp. 12, 14; Crumrine, *Washington County,* pp. 477, 607; Ellis, *Fayette County,* pp. 424, 686; Fayette County Deed Book C-1, p. 451.

14. Ellis, *Fayette County,* p. 686; Appearance Docket, Court of Common Pleas, Washington County, 1793; Crumrine, *Washington County,* p. 477, 607; Fayette County Deed Book A, p. 450.

15. Appearance Docket, Court of Common Pleas, Washington County, 1793; Fayette County Deed Book C-3, p. 1362.

16. Hadden, *Uniontown,* p. 12; Ellis, *Fayette County,* p. 686; Crumrine, *Washington County,* p. 607; Waychoff, *Local History,* no. 139; Fayette County Deed Book C-3, p. 1362; Appearance Docket, Court of Common Pleas, Washington County, 1793.

17. Two situations are exceptions. One case involves John and William Hoge, the Washington proprietors. Their father laid out the town of Washington in 1781 as a speculative venture when he

learned the county would be erected that year. He never left his Carlisle home, but the sons did and became the official proprietors in 1785. Only the older son, John, has been singled out for discussion, but William was only slightly less prominent; Crumrine, *Washington County*, pp. 476–79.

The second case involves considerable uncertainty regarding the proprietorship of Haydentown. The town grew up around a mill and a forge and was known initially as George Town. Who platted the town and when is unclear. Robert Peoples sold lots along Mill Street and its intersection with Forge Street in the mid-1790s. The town is named, however, for John Hayden, whose considerable activity in and around the town in the 1780s and 1790s included farming and distilling; he also became an ironmaster. Robert Peoples bought the tract from which he sold lots in March 1792, and the chain of title includes Philip Jenkins and Jonathan Rees, two prominent farmer-millers. In 1793, Peoples sold fifty-one acres, including the ironworks, to Hayden and his partner, John Nicholson of Philadelphia, a comptroller of Pennsylvania. (Nicholson may have been Hayden's brother-in-law.) The partnership failed to build the furnace it had intended and went bankrupt. Hayden sold the forge site to his son Jonathan in 1797. Nicholson's biographer claims fraud on the part of Hayden. Peoples might have been the proprietor except that he did not acquire the site until five years after the first lots appear on the assessment, and the assessors never seem to have recognized him as such. He was not on the 1787 assessment; in 1795, he was landless, with stills and livestock, probably renting land. In 1798, he was listed with a single lot and no livestock. He is supposed to have run the mill for a number of years, however.

A few houses may have been built around the mill early on. Peoples apparently formalized the plat, and Hayden's considerable activities, including ownership of lands in and adjacent to the site, became the focal point of the settlement. Both Peoples and Hayden are credited with the proprietorship in this study. Ellis, *Fayette County*, p. 567; Fayette County Deed Book A, p. 392, B, pp. 301, 352, C, pp. 49, 132, 183, 270, 366, C-2, p. 711; Robert D. Arbuckle, *Pennsylvania Speculator and Patriot: The Entrepreneurial John Nicholson, 1757–1800* (University Park, Pa., 1974), pp. 150–51.

18. Even the exceptions proved the rule. Frederick Wise and George Burgett were second-generation settlers whose fathers' large landholdings had been subdivided by 1793. The older Wise originally had 400 acres, and Sebastian Burgett had 650 acres before his accidental death. Both were major holdings, and by 1796, Wise's heirs had

moved back into the top decile in taxable wealth. Joseph Parkinson did own less land than other proprietors, but he was a merchant and ferryman where the important Glade Road crossed the Monongahela. He owned two slaves, and his settlement was one of the real hotbeds of opposition during the Whiskey Rebellion. He did not lack influence. Robert Peoples from Haydentown was a miller and stiller at times, and the county historian referred to him and miller Jonathan Rees as "two of the most energetic businessmen of the frontier country." Howard L. Lecky, *The Ten Mile Country and its Pioneer Families* (Waynesburg, Pa., 1950), vol. 2, pp. 41–42; Crumrine, *Washington County*, pp. 917–18, 565–67; Ellis, *Fayette County*, pp. 567, 569.

19. Ellis, *Fayette County*, pp. 365–66, 465–66, 502–03, 512, 567, 766–68; Crumrine, *Washington County*, pp. 476–79, 565–67, 601–03, 679, 917–18; Bates, *Greene County*, p. 521; Waychoff, *Local History*, nos. 95, 139; Lecky, *Ten Mile Country*, vol. 2, pp. 41–42. Those proprietors not included here, because assessment data were lacking for them, fit the same picture. Thomas Hopwood had 400 acres; Henry Beeson (Uniontown) had multiple landholdings, a mill, and held local office; Thomas Brown had multiple landholdings; Ellis, *Fayette County*, pp. 279–81, 421–24, 686; Hadden, *Uniontown*, pp. 10–11. Only Waynesburg lacked a proprietor. Five trustees were appointed by the state assembly to select a site for the county seat when Greene County was erected; James T. Mitchell and Henry Flanders, eds., *The Statutes at Large of Pennsylvania from 1682 to 1801* (Harrisburg, 1896–1915), vol. 15, ch. 1870, p. 383.

20. Ellis, *Fayette County*, pp. 282–86.

21. Ibid., pp. 425–27; Wade, *Urban Frontier*, p. 41.

22. Buck and Buck, *Civilization*, p. 306; Daniel R. Kovar, "Social Life in Early Fayette County as Seen Especially in Church and Court Records" (Master's thesis, University of Pittsburgh, 1929), pp. 14–15, 10.

23. Joseph E. Walker, ed., *Pleasure and Business in Western Pennsylvania: The Journal of Joshua Gilpin, 1809* (Harrisburg, 1975), pp. 48, 47.

24. Hugh Cleland, *George Washington in the Ohio Valley* (Pittsburgh, 1955), p. 245; John W. Harpster, ed., *Pen Pictures of Early Western Pennsylvania* (Pittsburgh, 1938), pp. 136, 157; Wade, *Urban Frontier*, pp. 7–13, 43–49.

25. Crumrine, *Washington County*, pp. 484–92; Harpster, *Pen Pictures*, p. 171; "John Heckewelder's Journey to the Wabash, 1792," *Pennsylvania Magazine of History and Biography* 11 (1887), p. 469; and John W. Jordan, ed., "Notes of Travel of William Henry, John

Heckewelder, John Rothrock, and Christian Clewell, to Gnaden-hutten on the Muskingum, in the Early Summer of 1797," *Pennsylvania Magazine of History and Biography* 10 (1886), p. 154.

26. Crumrine, *Washington County*, pp. 607, 769; Fayette County Deed Book B, pp. 301, 352, C, p. 183; Appearance Docket, Court of Common Pleas, Washington County, 1793; Ellis, *Fayette County*, p. 772; Buck and Buck, *Civilization*, p. 218.

27. Towns functioned as a center for artisans throughout Pennsylvania. Stephanie G. Wolf, *Urban Village: Population, Community, and Family Structure in Germantown, Pennsylvania, 1683–1800* (Princeton, N.J., 1976), emphasizes the importance of crafts and processing facilities in Germantown (pp. 102–07). Jerome H. Wood, Jr., *Conestoga Crossroads: Lancaster, Pennsylvania, 1730–1790* (Harrisburg, 1979), found a fairly constant 80 percent of the Lancaster population were artisans and laborers from 1759 through 1788 (p. 160). Similarly, in Reading, a wide range of craftsmen gathered in the town in the first couple of decades, according to Laura L. Becker, "The People and the System: Legal Activities in a Colonial Pennsylvania Town," *Pennsylvania Magazine of History and Biography* 105 (April 1981): 136. Also, in opening northwestern Pennsylvania in the early nineteenth century, the town of Meadville was where the artisans of Crawford County gathered, according to Robert D. Ilisevich, "Class Structure and Politics in Crawford County, 1800–1840," *Western Pennsylvania Historical Magazine* 63 (April 1980): 106–08.

28. Acheson's death necessitated a court order to issue the deed to Acklin. Appearance Docket, Court of Common Pleas, Washington County, March 1794.

29. Washington County paid £648.2.8 and £464.6.8 in wolf and squirrel bounties, respectively, from 1783 through 1788. Treasurer's Account, Docket, Court of Quarter Session, December 1789. Several brands were registered with the courts. See the Docket, Court of Quarter Sessions, Washington County, September 1786, January 1793, March 1794.

30. Rev. Robert Ayers, "Journal," 28–29 March 1796, Box 33, Western Pennsylvania Historical Society.

31. In the 1780s, especially, many people were apparently "willing to run in debt and go to law" (letter of Ephraim Douglas to Gen. James Irvine, February 1784, quoted in Ellis, *Fayette County*, pp. 283–84). However, a full tabulation of all debt cases in the courts revealed no untoward amount of debt in the 1780s. When Westmoreland and Washington counties were established, the whole county did vote in the county seat, and only later were election districts provided; Mitch-

ell and Flanders, eds., *Statutes at Large,* vol. 8, ch. 678 (26 February 1773), p. 315; vol. 10, ch. 931 (28 March 1781), p. 273.

32. Mitchell and Flanders, eds., *Statutes at Large,* vol. 13, ch. 1359 (24 September 1788), pp. 84–87; John N. Boucher, *History of Westmoreland County,* vol. 1 (New York, 1906), pp. 49, 191; Claude M. Newlin, *The Life and Writings of Hugh Henry Brackenridge* (Princeton, N.J., 1932), pp. 73, 76, 78–80, 85.

33. Mitchell and Flanders, eds., *Statutes at Large,* vol. 11, ch. 1016 (22 September 1783), p. 196; Ellis, *Fayette County,* pp. 279–80.

34. Mitchell and Flanders, eds., *Statutes at Large,* vol. 8, ch. 678 (26 February 1773), pp. 314–17; Boucher, *Westmoreland County,* pp. 45–51, 186–92; George Dallas Albert, *History of the County of Westmoreland* (Philadelphia, 1882), p. 489; Roland M. Baumann, "The Removal of the Westmoreland County Seat to Newtown (Greensburg), 1784–1786," *Western Pennsylvania Historical Magazine* 60 (July 1977), pp. 278–81; Articles of Agreement, Deed Book B, Westmoreland County, p. 287. See the series of statutes changing the trustees: Mitchell and Flanders, eds., *Statutes at Large,* vol. 11, ch. 1080 (22 March 1784), pp. 273–74; vol. 12, ch. 1176 (13 September 1785), pp. 52–53; vol. 12, ch. 1257 (27 December 1786), p. 344.

35. Mitchell and Flanders, eds., *Statutes at Large,* 10, ch. 931 (28 March 1781), pp. 272–75; Crumrine, *Washington County,* pp. 463–64, 476–79; Russell J. Ferguson, *Early Western Pennsylvania Politics* (Pittsburgh, 1938), p. 47; Owen S. Ireland, "The Ratification of the Federal Constitution in Pennsylvania" (Ph.D. diss., University of Pittsburgh, 1966), pp. 246–52.

36. Mitchell and Flanders, eds., *Statutes at Large,* vol. 15, ch. 1870 (9 February 1796), pp. 380–83; Bates, *Greene County,* pp. 277–78; Waychoff, *Local History,* no. 95.

37. Ephraim Douglas to General Irvine, quoted in Ellis, *Fayette County,* pp. 283–84.

38. Ayers, "Journal," 29 March 1796; Crumrine, *Washington County,* p. 769; Ellis, *Fayette County,* p. 786; Buck and Buck, *Civilization,* p. 378.

39. Ayers, "Journal," 13 May, 21 May, 4 July, 28 April 1796. Buck and Buck, *Civilization,* p. 306. Bookstores are discussed by Buck and Buck (pp. 386–87), but they believe the first one was not established until 1798 in Pittsburgh.

40. *Pittsburgh Gazette,* 14 September 1793.

41. Buck and Buck, *Civilization,* pp. 468–69; typed copy of the society's formation taken from the *Pittsburgh Gazette,* 14 February 1789, CA File, Western Pennsylvania Historical Society.

42. Mitchell and Flanders, eds., *Statutes at Large*, vol. 12, ch. 1264 (28 February 1787), p. 357, ch. 1314 (24 September 1787), p. 528, ch. 1302 (10 September 1787), p. 489; vol. 15, ch. 1674 (8 April 1793), p. 392; Docket, Court of Quarter Sessions, Washington County, December 1788; Buck and Buck, *Civilization*, pp. 392–93.

43. Buck and Buck, *Civilization*, pp. 393–94, 396–97; *Pittsburgh Gazette*, 12 October 1793.

44. Buck and Buck, *Civilization*, pp. 389–90; James Veech, *Monongahela of Old* (Pittsburgh, 1858, 1892), pp. 104–05. At least fourteen schoolmasters were teaching in Fayette County in 1796.

45. Buck and Buck, *Civilization*, p. 413.

46. Boucher, *Westmoreland County*, p. 304; Ellis, *Fayette County*, p. 444; Buck and Buck, *Civilization*, have a full chapter on religious life (pp. 401–29) that details the beginnings of each denomination. The discussion of intellectual life in general (pp. 372–400) is also much broader than the brief discussion presented here. Most of it, however, concerns the period between 1796 and 1815, when cultural developments were greater.

47. Buck and Buck, *Civilization*, pp. 365–67; Crumrine, *Washington County*, p. 988; Kovar, "Social Life," p. 60; Wade, *Urban Frontier*, pp. 143–48, 206–08.

48. See the class descriptions in Wade, *Urban Frontier*, pp. 106ff; Jackson T. Main, *The Social Structure of Revolutionary America* (Princeton, N.J., 1965), pp. 34–41. James A. Henretta's "Economic Development and Social Structure in Colonial Boston," *William and Mary Quarterly* 22 (January 1965): 75–92, was the groundbreaking statement about the increasing class polarization in colonial cities. Gary B. Nash's "Urban Wealth and Poverty in Pre-Revolutionary America," *Journal of Interdisciplinary History* 6 (Spring 1976), pp. 545–84, is one of a growing number of such studies, discussing the increasing concentration of wealth in New York, Philadelphia, and Boston. See also Wolf, *Urban Village*, pp. 123–25, for a similar trend in a smaller town.

49. It should be noted that the 1793 assessment did not list specific occupations. Occupations used here have been read back into the 1793 assessment from the court records and from Crumrine's *Washington County*, pp. 489–92. The artisan figures, in particular, are too small. Not all of the artisan trades listed in the *American Museum or Universal Magazine* of 1792 could be identified. Furthermore, some artisans are known, but are not on the magazine's list. One result is that at least thirteen of those without specific trades who are listed as dependents in the table were probably those unidentified artisans.

With occupations coming from such diverse sources and for years ranging from 1792 to 1798, the Washington figures must be read as suggestive rather than as precise.

50. Chapter 7 will focus on the full range of county and township officials.

51. Docket, Court of Quarter Sessions, Washington County, 1793; Minute Book B, Court of Quarter Sessions, Westmoreland County, March 1795.

Chapter 6: The Occupational Structure

1. It should be remembered that Fayette County figures do not include Union or Menallen, the two most urban townships, nor Wharton, the large mountain township. The records for all three are lost. The figures for Georges are from 1795, supplemented by 1798 and 1799. The 1796 return for that township is missing, and its occupational structure will be inadequately represented in the following discussion. In Washington County, a number of townships lack 1796 assessments, therefore, a composite picture for that county has not been made. However, several individual township returns contain very valuable information, which has been used to supplement the Fayette material.

2. These categories generally follow those used by Merle Curti in his study of Trempealeau County, with certain modifications necessitated by the character of this study and the data; *The Making of An American Community: A Case Study of Democracy in a Frontier County* (Stanford, Calif., 1959), appendix 2. There are, naturally, a number of questions of judgment in any such categorization; the elements comprising each category will be explained in the notes, and the reader may make the mental adjustments necessary.

3. This man was not one of the regular township assessors who compiled the property lists, but he apparently worked in some other capacity. Each township normally had three landowners compile the annual assessments. Since this was not a regular job, but required only a week or two to complete, usually in January, the regular assessors have been left in their basic occupational category. They always signed each assessment, but never indicated assessor as their normal occupation.

4. There were two other associate judges: James Finley, who apparently lived in Union Township, the records for which are missing, and Isaac Meason, who could be included in this list, but because

he made his greatest impact on the county as an ironmaster, has been left in the mercantile category.

5. See, for example, the court order allowing the German Township constable "to employ another fit person to do his duty, he being responsible for his conduct." Minute Book, Court of Quarter Sessions, Fayette County, March 1784.

6. Franklin Ellis, ed., *History of Fayette County* (Philadelphia, 1882), p. 366.

7. Ewing was apparently in the commissary business and was perhaps a brother-in-law of Judge Breading; ibid., p. 650–51. He was sued in the county court because he allegedly had not delivered certain goods to Vincennes, Indiana, in 1793; Continuance Docket, Court of Common Pleas, Fayette County, March 1795. Three commissioners served at one time, but the other two for 1796 were from Union and Menallen townships, and their status cannot be determined.

8. Ellis, *Fayette County*, p. 488.

9. Edward George Everett, "John Smilie in Pennsylvania Politics," (Master's thesis, University of Pittsburgh, 1948), pp. 60–64.

10. Ellis, *Fayette County*, p. 639.

11. Ibid., pp. 641, 650, 807–08.

12. Ibid., pp. 768, 770, 772.

13. The inclusion of only two proprietors is admittedly arbitrary. Generally, they have been placed where they seemed to have made the most impact: Meason and Hayden as ironmasters, Dickerson as a miller, and so on. Some could not be included for lack of data for Union and Menallen townships. Connell and Cadwallader were the proprietors of the small Fayette County towns discussed in chapter 5, and their proprietary activity was important, especially for Connell. One could justifiably place Cadwallader as a miller.

14. The established clergy of Fayette County may have been better-off than the table suggests. Again, with both Union and Menallen townships missing, clergymen like the Rev. Robert Ayres of Brownsville and the Rev. Benjamin Stone of Uniontown were excluded. Furthermore, one of the three men in the table was only a "preacher at times," and a second was a Georges Township single freeman with no occupation listed in 1795 but who was listed as a minister in 1798. Therefore, Fayette County ministers may have had more property than the table indicates; even so, they were moderate landowners. A significant amount of property owned by ministers would correlate well with the findings of Jackson T. Main, *The Social Structure of Revolutionary America* (Princeton, N.J., 1965), pp. 96–98.

15. Ellis, *Fayette County*, pp. 140, 286. The court dockets noted each new lawyer admitted to practice before the court.

16. The inclusion of physicians, schoolmasters, and especially students in this category may be questioned by some. Indeed, these occupations were looked upon as no better than any other trade in the late eighteenth century, and they did lower the economic level of the professional class. The case for physicians and schoolmasters as professionals is the obvious one, but the case for students needs justification. Merle Curti, with good reason, places them with the dependent classes, and perhaps they should be so included here (*American Community*, p. 59). Nevertheless, because these students were so few in number and over twenty-one years of age (otherwise they would not be on the tax list), because education then was so infrequent that these men must have been preparing for some kind of professional career (one was called a "colleger"), and because they did not fit into the other categories very well, they have been included here as professional people. Jackson T. Main also found that the status of teachers was quite low, and that physicians may have been better-off elsewhere than in western Pennsylvania; See *Social Structure*, pp. 91–95, 99.

17. One of the iron producers with a smallholding had only a single lot, but on it he had a $3,000 forge. He probably had begun as a blacksmith and expanded his operation, but he was not in the same category as Isaac Meason or the Turnbull Company. The second small iron manufacturer had eighty-two acres of land, but his operations did not appear in the county histories. He may very well have been a blacksmith with a forge who later became a tavernkeeper; Ellis, *Fayette County*, p. 502. The other five iron men appeared in the county histories. It should be added that one of the companies, Turnbull and Company, was in the iron business, and a second one, Oliphant and Company, probably was also. The county history does not indicate that Oliphant engaged in the iron business until 1798, but the company was assessed in 1796 and was presumably in the iron business. Oliphant is included among the seven ironmasters, but Turnbull, because he spent most of his time in Philadelphia and let his partners run the business, has been classified as an absentee landowner with no livestock; ibid., pp. 233–37.

18. There were a number of court cases that involved debts or broken covenants. For example, Samuel Jackson, Washington Township miller, brought suit in March 1786 against Richard Stevens for £353.12.9, because Stevens had not paid for 200 barrels of flour weighing 41,080 pounds. In the 1790s, a number of covenant cases

involved flour or other grains not delivered or not paid for. Sometimes suits involved unspecified merchandise, such as in the suit in
September 1792 against Israel Shreve, who took over the mill tenement of George Washington; or they involved whiskey, as in the
fraud case brought by Jacob Beeson against William Finley in June
1791 over 215 gallons; Papers, Court of Common Pleas, Fayette
County, passim.

19. The shopkeepers, merchants, and retailers were probably all
shopkeepers. All five merchants came from one township. *Merchant*
apparently was the term used by that assessor for shopkeepers. None
were wealthy wholesale or importing merchants, which the term
might suggest. A number of the shopkeepers, particularly the landless, may have been simply clerks, keeping the shop for the owner;
there were occasional indications that such was the case. Retailers
also were just small shopkeepers, not large merchants. Two sold
cider, another had a butcher shop, a fourth was a tobacco seller
("tobaconist"), and the fifth was a retail shopkeeper.

20. Two of the absentees in Luzerne in chapter 4 were millers
whose actual residence was Menallen Township but who owned mills
in Luzerne. Both of them appear in the mercantile class of Luzerne
Township. Five persons in Bullskin Township also appear as absentees in chapter 4, but now appear in other categories. Two were
professionals—town proprietor Connell, who had 1,600 acres of unseated land, and surveyor Ausman, who had 1,200 acres of unseated
land. Two others were yeomen farmers owning small farms plus
unseated tracts of 150 and 188 acres. The fifth was a blacksmith who
held 200 acres of unseated land in addition to his town lot. All five
probably had mountain land.

21. Henry Nash Smith has examined the origins and influence of
the yeoman mythology in his excellent book *Virgin Land* (Cambridge,
Mass., 1950). See particularly pp. 121–44, and especially the "free-
hold concept," p. 126.

22. Yeomen are defined as landowning farmers. On the assessments, often no occupation was given for these people. A few assessments did label farmers, and while they confirmed that most landowners were farmers, they also revealed a number of landless "farmers."
No landless farmer appears in this yeoman category; they appear in
the dependent category. Yeomen do include those many farmers who
had stills, but farmers with mills or taverns or some artisan skill have
been placed in those categories. The same is true for those farmers
who held government office. Thus, a number of other persons made
at least part of their living from farming but do not appear in that

category. An attempt has been made to limit the category to those whose primary occupation was farming. Ownership of a still was not felt to be sufficient cause to place still owners in the mercantile class, but ownership of a mill was considered sufficient cause. This definition is reasonably similar to that of Allan Kulikoff: "petty producers who owned their own means of production . . . and participated in commodity markets in order to sustain family autonomy and local exchange"; "The Transition to Capitalism in Rural America," *William and Mary Quarterly* 46 (1989): 141.

23. James T. Lemon, "Household Consumption . . . in Southeastern Pennsylvania," *Agricultural History* 41 (January 1967): 68. Township mean acreages in Fayette County were: Washington— 158, Luzerne—143, German—190, Springhill—188, Tyrone—220, Franklin—170, Georges—167, Bullskin—190. By geographical regions, the mean acreages were: river—170, interior—178, border—190.

24. The Luzerne farmer who had the median cleared acreage was Samuel Miller, who had 50 of 200 acres cleared, two horses, two cows, a house, and three cabins, all valued at $1,172. (Abraham Merritt, who had 53 of 107 acres cleared, fit the Luzerne statistical median almost perfectly.) The Washington medians were John Lynch, who had 30 of 136 acres cleared, one cabin, one horse, and one cow, valued at $872, and Archibald McKee, who had 30 of 223 acres cleared, one house, one barn, one out building, two horses, and two cattle, valued at $1,485.50. The median cleared acreage in Tyrone belonged to James Gonie, who had 40 of 144 acres cleared, one horse, and one cow, valued at $170.

25. Lemon, "Household Consumption," p. 68, n. 51. Charles S. Grant, *Democracy in the Connecticut Frontier Town of Kent* (New York, 1961), table 5, pp. 32–33, and the explanations on following pages, especially p. 37.

26. Bettye Hobbs Pruitt, "Self-sufficiency and the Agricultural Economy of Eighteenth-Century Massachusetts," *William and Mary Quarterly* 41 (July 1984): 38–48, table 2; Paul G. E. Clemens and Lucy Simler, "Rural Labor and the Farm Household in Chester County Pennsylvania, 1750–1820," in Stephen Innes, ed., *Work and Labor in Early America* (Chapel Hill, N.C., 1988), pp. 106–43.

27. See the advertisements for land near Devore's ferry and for Alexander Well's land; *Pittsburgh Gazette*, 7 and 14 December 1793. See also Alexander Fowler's advertisement for a partner for his mill "in the heart of the wheat country" of Washington County; *Pittsburgh Gazette*, 14 September 1793. Leland D. Baldwin discusses the grow-

ing importance of the western trade through 1800 in chapter 1 of *The Keelboat Age on Western Waters* (Pittsburgh, 1941), pp. 1–38, especially pp. 29–30, 32. The advantages of Pinckney's Treaty were well known in the region. Rev. Robert Ayers noted in his journal that lawyer Hugh H. Brackenridge and Judge Alexander Addison discussed the treaty at the meeting of the county courts; 29 March 1796; Box 33, Western Pennsylvania Historical Society.

28. Joseph E. Walker, ed., *Pleasure and Business in Western Pennsylvania: The Journal of Joshua Gilpin 1809* (Harrisburg, 1975), p. 44, quotation, p. 58.

29. James T. Lemon, *The Best Poorman's Country: A Geographical Study of Early Southeastern Pennsylvania* (Baltimore, Md., 1972), pp. 161, 152–53, 166–67.

30. James B. Richardson III and Kirk C. Wilson, "Hannas Town and Charles Foreman: The Historical and Archeological Record, 1770–1806," *Western Pennsylvania Historical Magazine* 59 (April 1976): 181–83.

31. John W. Harpster, ed., *Pen Pictures of Early Western Pennsylvania* (Pittsburgh, 1938), p. 183; see also pp. 186–87, 191, and 203 for other examples. *Journal and Letters of Col. John May, of Boston, Relative to Two Journeys to the Ohio Country in 1788 and 1789* (Cincinnati, Oh., 1873), pp. 32–36, 41, 49, 52–53; Joseph Doddridge, *Notes on the Settlement and Indian Wars . . . 1763 to 1783, inclusive . . .* (Pittsburgh, 1912), pp. 98–101. At a different level, John Badollet describes a wretched family in the mountains of Fayette County, "the most compleat human wretchedness I had ever any idea of," residing "under a bark shelter," and "living on hunting and fishing" for two years; William A. Hunter, "John Badollet's 'Journal of the time I spent in Stoney creek Glades,' 1793–1794," *Pennsylvania Magazine of History and Biography* 104 (April 1980): 189.

32. For example, one assessment simply listed these people without any notation, trade, or land, while others indicated only single freemen. Some labeled these landless people *farmers* or *laborers*. Occasionally, these people appeared as town lot owners, but without any indication as to how they were making a living. Thus, an individual assessment may have had as few as one or as many as six different groupings that finally appeared in this dependent category.

33. The six unclassified in Greene Township, for example, included one man probably belonging in the poor category, who was listed as with "no trade or property." A second single man probably lived with a relative of the same surname who was a landless farmer, and therefore, was probably an agricultural worker. A third man had

sufficient cattle to also suggest that he was an agricultural laborer. Three others had neither relatives nor property and were perhaps general laborers. A list of similar estimates could be given for the eleven unclassified persons of Franklin Township.

34. Certain Cecil artisans, for example, were listed as tenants; they appear in the artisan class. Where more than one person of the same name was listed beneath a landlord, it is unclear whether both had rental obligations or were family members sharing the same cabin and acreage. In other townships, all would probably appear as landless farmers. Since the Cecil return did not specify laborers, some of these tenants may have followed that general occupation. The return apparently tried to include all of those renting and, thus, if taken at face value, would overemphasize farm tenancy. The Luzerne return listing renters may have had some of the same problem in reverse, but its more specific categories and its structure seem to mitigate this.

35. As a check upon these consensus figures, it might be worthwhile to apply them to a township where supplemental information allowed a tentative categorization by educated guessing. The dependent classes of Luzerne Township totaled 128, including 65 renters (the 50.8 percent figure); 27 persons, landless with no trade; 24 single freemen, also landless with no trade; 10 adults who owned a town lot, but had no indication of occupation; 1 single man with a lot; and 1 landless farmer. The renters overwhelmingly owned a horse or a cow, suggesting the tenant farmer and inmate agricultural worker statuses.

Of the twenty-seven landless with no trade, three men and two widows can be removed and placed with one lot-owning widow, making a poor category of six persons. Four more of these twenty-seven were free blacks, living near Crawford's ferry, an important river crossing point. Living in this river location, they probably were common laborers, not agricultural workers. Of the remaining eighteen, five have been classified as farm laborers on the basis of farm-owning relatives or their own livestock holdings. The remaining thirteen were classified as common laborers. Most were not in the township two years, while a few had laboring or town-dwelling relatives.

The twenty-four single freemen, however, have been assigned in reverse, fourteen to agricultural labor, ten to general labor. Most still lived on the family farm or had tenant relatives. The remaining lot owners—nine adults, one single man—have all been assigned to general labor on the presumption that their lots indicate some sort of town or river occupation. The one landless farmer naturally was assigned to agricultural labor. These estimates resulted in thirty-seven common laborers (28.9 percent), eighty-five agricultural laborers (66.4 percent), which includes the sixty-five (50.8 percent) renters, and six (4.7 percent) poor—results reasonably close to the consensus figures. If more information were known about all the persons without land or trade, maybe a few more poor persons would be found, making that figure somewhat closer to the consensus figure.

36. On two occasions, sons were charged by the court with the maintenance of their old fathers at a rate of 7s. 6d. per week. Docket, Court of Quarter Sessions, Washington County, April 1788 and June 1790.

37. In one desertion case, the overseers were simply directed to sell the man's property for the maintenance of his wife and two children, and the man had very little property. In each of two bastardy cases, the man involved was assessed a basic £5–7 for the mother's lying-in expenses, plus 2s. per week or 10s. per month maintenance for the first years of the child's life. In these two cases, one and four years were the time periods mentioned, but two years was probably the more normal figure. The phrasing of such orders, to the effect that payments were to be made for two years if the child lived so long, was grim testimony to the realities of infant mortality; Docket, Court of Quarter Sessions, Washington County, June 1794, March and June 1791.

38. See Richard B. Morris, *Government and Labor in Early America* (New York, 1965), pp. 44–47; Carl Bridenbaugh, *The Colonial Craftsman* (New York, 1950), pp. 134–35; Solon J. and Elizabeth H. Buck, *The Planting of Civilization in Western Pennsylvania* (Pittsburgh, 1939), pp. 312–13. Stephen Innes summarizes the recent status of labor studies in early America in "Fulfilling John Smith's Vision," in Innes, *Work and Labor,* pp. 3–48, especially the demand for labor (p. 8) as well as the hardships endured by early labor (pp. 10–17).

39. Account Book III-B, entry 1003, Carnegie Library of Pittsburgh, Isaac Craig Collection, microfilm 271, reel 8. Jackson T. Main suggests that unskilled laborers could earn approximately 2s. per day, but that a carpenter typically earned 2s. 6d. to 3s. per day (£4.10 per month). Main, *Social Structure,* pp. 71, 78; Stevenson Whitcomb Fletcher, *Pennsylvania Agriculture and Country Life, 1640–1840* (Harrisburg, 1950), p. 307, supports Main's figures. Unskilled workers at Fort Pitt earning $10 (£4.5) per month had a wage similar to the typical skilled carpenter elsewhere. See a further discussion of wage rates and the problems involved in equating pounds and dollars in the discussion of artisans that follows.

40. Clemens and Simler, "Rural Labor . . . in Chester County," in Innes, ed., *Work and Labor,* p. 108.

41. Ibid., pp. 129–30, 134.

42. Harpster, ed., *Pen Pictures,* p. 249; Colonel Israel Shreve, "Journal From Jersey to the Monongahela, August 11, 1788," *Pennsylvania Magazine of History and Biography* 52 (1928): 203.

43. In the estimates made for Luzerne Township in note 35, four of ten lot owners, four of five free blacks, including a single man, and ten of eighteen men with no trade or occupation were gone within one year. Thus eighteen of these thirty-three common laborers came and left between 1795 and 1797.

44. Other studies have noted that persons who stayed in a region had a reasonable chance to improve their status. See Jerome H. Wood, Jr., *Conestoga Crossroads: Lancaster, Pennsylvania, 1730–1790* (Harrisburg, 1979), p. 172; Stephanie G. Wolf, *Urban Village: Population, Community, and Family Structure in Germantown, Pennsylvania, 1683–1800* (Princeton, N.J., 1976), p. 81.

45. Israel Shreve, "Journal," p. 203.

46. Main, *Social Structure,* p. 43. James T. Lemon found "from 30–40 percent of the rural taxable persons were non-farmers." Totaling western Pennsylvania's professional (2.6 percent), mercantile (4.3 percent), artisan (16.0 percent), and common laboring classes (10.7 percent), but excluding all agricultural workers and tenants, results in a comparable 33.6 percent; "Urbanization and the Development of Eighteenth Century Southeastern Pennsylvania and Adjacent Delaware," *William and Mary Quarterly* 24 (October 1967): 527. Lee Soltow and Kenneth W. Keller, "Rural Pennsylvania in 1800: A Portrait from the Septennial Census," *Pennsylvania History* 49 (January 1982): 35–36, found the following state occupational categories: agricultural—42 percent, manufacturing/mechanical—32 percent, domestic—10 percent, trade/transport—5 percent, professional—2 percent, other—9 percent.

47. The assessment used such phrases as "Meason's works," "Meason's land," "Meason's furnace," and "at Meason's" under the residence column for these artisans.

48. See Bridenbaugh, *Colonial Craftsman,* pp. 16–18, and Morris, *Government and Labor,* pp. 138–40, on the adaptability of iron manufacturing to a plantation-type operation. Reference to Meason's fair comes from a chance notation in a court case which states that "On the Day that the pole was Raiz'd at Mr. Meason's Fair . . . " Paper no. 1103, Court of Quarter Sessions, Fayette County.

49. The Washington townships included: river—Nottingham,

East Bethlehem, West Bethlehem, Cumberland; interior—Cecil, Canton, Strabane, Amwell, Morris, Morgan, Franklin; border— Smith, Hopewell, Greene. The listings of artisans were made at the time the original records were examined. They have not been subjected to the complete categorization as have the Fayette County occupations. Some minor changing of categories, such as removing constables from their original category, has not been done. Such changes would not, however, make more than a percentage point of difference.

50. Main, *Social Structure,* pp. 77–78.

51. Carnegie Library of Pittsburgh, Isaac Craig Collection, Account Book III-B, entries 996 through 1146. During this period, the army switched from using pounds to dollars, but the equivalency was not always the same. In two 1794 examples, workers taking care of the public boats were paid at £9 for 6 months (£1.10 per month) and at $4 per month. This is the equivalent of the £3 = $8 conversion frequently found in the assessments. Boatmen in 1792 were paid £3 per month, but in 1794 $10 per month. Other comparisons were tested: rations paid per day and the purchase of oats resulted in conversions of £2.10 = $8 and £2.13.6 = $8. Ibid., Account Book III-A, pp. 4, 29, 78, 88, 91, Account Book III-B, pp. 6–8. The army requested extensive price lists from county officials in November 1794. Officers from Fayette and Washington counties reported oats at 2s. per bushel, but officers from Allegheny County reported 2s. and 2s. 6d. suggesting some inflation around Pittsburgh. These rates, when equated with the 25¢ per bushel paid at the fort, give an equivalency of £3.4 to $8 and £4 to $8. *Pennsylvania Archives,* 2d series, vol. 4 (Harrisburg, 1852–1935), pp. 434, 442–43. Because of all this variation, exact equivalencies between pounds and dollars are very difficult to determine. Using £3 = $8 or even £3 = $10 are reasonable.

52. There were, of course, millers and stillers who owned land. In the process of categorization, however, those millers with indications of mill ownership were placed in the mercantile category. The artisans were merely the mill tenders. Many farmers were also stillers, but they were left in the yeoman category as still owners, not still tenders. The very process of categorization, therefore, dictates that these artisans would not likely be landowners, and it may have biased their true position somewhat if more precise information were known.

53. See the problems the loss of these early garden plots caused city people in the nineteenth century; Richard C. Wade, *The Urban*

Frontier: The Rise of Western Cities, 1790–1830 (Cambridge, Mass., 1959), p. 112.

54. See Allan Kulikoff, "The Transition to Capitalism in Rural America," pp. 120–44 for a conceptualization of the transformation to market economies; especially p. 130 for the indicators of this transition. Winifred B. Rothenberg, beginning with "The Market and Massachusetts Farmers, 1750–1855," *Journal of Economic History* 41 (1981): 283–314, has pioneered the investigation of market transformation in rural areas. Her work and that of many others are summarized in the Kulikoff article.

Chapter 7: The Structure of Political Power

1. Boyd Crumrine, ed., *History of Washington County* (Philadelphia, 1882), pp. 243–44, 485. Further elaboration of Addison's political views may be found in G. S. Rowe's "Alexander Addison: The Disillusionment of a Republican Schoolmaster," *Western Pennsylvania Historical Magazine* 62 (July 1979): 221–50; and in Norman Rosenberg's "Alexander Addison and the Pennsylvania Origins of Federalist First Amendment Thought," *The Pennsylvania Magazine of History and Biography* 108 (October 1984): 399–418.

2. Interpreting Pennsylvania politics during the revolutionary period in terms of some class conflict between the democratic west, which produced and governed under the constitution of 1776, and the propertied east, which regained control through the constitution of 1790, became the standard interpretation in the 1930s; Paul J. Selsam, *The Pennsylvania Constitution of 1776* (Philadelphia, 1936); Robert L. Brunhouse, *The Counter-Revolution in Pennsylvania, 1776–1790* (Harrisburg, 1942); Harry M. Tinkcom, *The Republicans and Federalists in Pennsylvania, 1790–1801* (Harrisburg, 1950), especially section 1, in which Tinkcom reviews the political climate around 1790. He argues against a strict east-west split, but without complete success. The statement of a contrary view of the political life of revolutionary Pennsylvania cast primarily in terms of ethnic and religious differences can be found in Owen S. Ireland's "The Ratification of the Federal Constitution in Pennsylvania," (Ph.D. diss., University of Pittsburgh, 1966).

3. Pennsylvania Constitution of 1776, ch. 2, sec. 6, in *Pennsylvania Archives*, 4th series, vol. 3 (Harrisburg, 1852–1935), p. 633; Pennsylvania Constitution of 1790, art. 3, sec. 1, art. 5, sec. 10; *Pennsylvania*

Archives, 4th series, vol. 4, pp. 122, 125; James T. Mitchell and Henry Flanders, eds., *The Statutes at Large of Pennsylvania from 1682 to 1801* (Harrisburg, 1896–1915), vol. 2, ch. 28, p. 24, ch. 137, pp. 212–13; vol. 7, ch. 539, pp. 32, 37; vol. 12, ch. 1175, pp. 25, 42; Brunhouse, *Counter-Revolution*, pp. 7–8; Sylvester K. Stevens and Donald H. Kent, eds., *County Government and the Archives in Pennsylvania* (Harrisburg, 1947), p. 32.

4. The data for this discussion have been drawn from many sources. Lists of officers may be found in the *Pennsylvania Archives*, 2d series, vol. 3, pp. 679–88, and vol. 9, pp. 817–18. Election returns for the 1780s—normally without the actual number of votes cast— can be found in the 6th series, vol. 11, pp. 193–96, 393–400, and 403–11. Officer lists may also be found in Crumrine, *Washington County*, pp. 468–72, and in Franklin Ellis, ed., *History of Fayette County* (Philadelphia, 1882), pp. 149–155. The series *Inventory of the County Archives of Pennsylvania*, published by the Historical Records Survey, also has officer lists in each county volume, but they appear to have been taken from the above sources. See, for example, Eugene Marr Braderman, ed., *Fayette County* no. 26 (Philadelphia, 1940), pp. 251– 60. Additional lists of local officers have been found randomly in the minute books and dockets of the courts of Quarter Sessions in the various counties. The dockets sometimes list the current officers, particularly when a new book was begun. Occasional lists of all active justices of the peace appear, and at times, the swearing in ceremonies of newly elected officers are noted. Numerous results of township elections also are recorded, normally without voting statistics, how- ever. Scatttered information on wealth and occupations also appears in the dockets of the courts of Quarter Session, such as lists of tav- ernkeepers, and in the dockets of the courts of Common Pleas, such as the information that Nathaniel Ewing was in the military commis- sary business. Book A, County Treasurer's Account Book, helped clarify some (but not all) of the obscurities in the Fayette County officer lists. Also, Miller Myers graciously shared his relevant lists of state officers for the 1790s, which he compiled for his graduate research in "Pennsylvania Politics, 1790–1805."

Information about these officers has been drawn largely from the assessment records. In addition, occasional information appears in the dockets. The 1790 census was helpful in rounding out slave holdings. Personal information on many officers has been found in the county histories by Crumrine and Ellis. Occasional material can also be found in James Veech's *Monongahela of Old* (Pittsburgh, 1858,

1892), and in Solon J. and Elizabeth H. Buck's *The Planting of Civilization in Western Pennsylvania* (Pittsburgh, 1939). Material on Westmoreland County gathered for this study has not been used because the assessment data—listing only land and livestock for the 1780s—were too incomplete for meaningful comparison. Since some Fayette and Washington county officials held prior offices in Westmoreland, the works of John N. Boucher, *History of Westmoreland County,* 2 vols. (New York, 1906), and George Dallas Albert, *History of the County of Westmoreland* (Philadelphia, 1882), have pertinent information. A conscientious effort has been made to avoid omissions or errors, and where real doubt occurred, some officials have been omitted from consideration. Undoubtedly a few errors still remain, but they would not alter in any significant way the broad pattern of political leadership developed in this chapter.

5. Residence was based on the 1793 and 1796 assessments, except for a few cases when the 1780s assessments provided the only information. See appendix A for a summary of the activities of these thirty-six political leaders.

6. The turnover of county officers, especially court clerks, treasurer, and coroner, was much greater in Washington County than in Fayette County. Fifteen different men held these jobs in Washington, but only three men in Fayette held them for the duration of the period under study. This explains why the county seat of Uniontown had so few in comparison with Washington.

7. Four men cannot be ranked. Three—Ephraim Douglas, Alexander McClean, and James Finley—were all from Union Township, for which the only available assessments were those listing only taxes due; *Pennsylvania Archives,* 3d series, vol. 22, pp. 549–54. The fourth was Van Swearingen. He has been counted as living in Strabane Township since he lived in Washington County as the first sheriff of the county. His holdings in Strabane were not included for some reason on the published assessments in ibid., pp. 778–82, but his tax listed on the original 1784 records in Washington County was the largest in the township. He also had 400 acres in Donegal Township in 1784. However, in 1783, he was still assessed for more than 700 acres in Westmoreland, where he had served as justice of the peace, and he was one of the absentee landlords indicated in Fayette County in 1785. He soon left Washington for neighboring Ohio County, Virginia, but in 1793, the year of his death, he still had 550 acres in the border regions of Washington County (Crumrine, *Washington County,* pp. 710–11).

8. For example, Judge Edward Cook sold, during his lifetime,

49 different tracts of land, but the assessments only revealed that he had 900 acres in 1785 and 600 acres in 1796. The greatest land magnate in Fayette County, Isaac Meason, who had increased his holdings from 2,100 acres in 1786 to 3,200 acres in 1796 and would have 6,400 acres by 1799 (Ellis, *Fayette County*, pp. 502–03), actually bought 67 different tracts during his lifetime and sold 124; Grantee and Grantor Indexes, Fayette County.

9. Five from Union Township and three with no land were indeterminable. All three without acreage were new names in the 1790s. Two were the sons of officers. Isaac Leet, Jr., was a county commissioner, but his father was a group 2 justice of the peace and deputy sheriff. Both Isaac, Sr., and Daniel Leet ranked in the top decile in taxable wealth. Alexander Scott briefly held the joint office of prothonotary and clerk of courts. He was the son of Thomas, a group 1 leader, who turned the office over to his son when he went off to Congress. Thomas Scott, a lawyer, also served as a judge, justice of the peace, and assemblyman, and ranked in the top decile in taxable wealth. The third landless secondary officer held the minor post of clerk to the county commissioners for several years.

10. A similar difference in attitude appeared among the large landholders in chapter 3. Those owning above 400 acres were more dynamic, more speculative, and their holdings changed frequently. Those owning just their original 400-acre tract were less dynamic and tended to maintain and farm their lands. The former were like the primary leaders; the latter were more like those who emerged as secondary leaders.

11. Comparisons between the 53 men in group 2 and all 103 judicial officials reveals them to be almost identical in total wealth and landownership. For example, 65 percent of all 103 judicial officers are in the top decile of total wealth, and 65 percent of the 53 in group 2 are so ranked. Forty-one percent of the 103 and 42 percent of the group 2 officials are in the top decile in landholding.

12. Constitution of 1776, sec. 30, *Pennsylvania Archives*, 4th series, vol. 3, pp. 641–42; Constitution of 1790, art. 5, secs. 4, 5, 10; *Pennsylvania Archives*, 4th series, vol. 4, pp. 124–25; Mitchell and Flanders, eds., *Statutes at Large*, vol. 11, ch. 1093, p. 306, ch. 1160, p. 573; vol. 15, ch. 1754, pp. 98–99; Stevens and Kent, *County Government*, pp. 32–33; William H. Lloyd, *The Early Law Courts of Pennsylvania* (Boston, 1910), pp. 105–06, 124–25, 132–34.

13. The fifty-three judiciary officials in group 2 were evenly divided between twenty-six who were elected for the first time in the 1780s and twenty-seven who were appointed for the first time in the

1790s. Their economic position was very similar. Of those first chosen in the 1780s, 65 percent ranked in the top decile, another 27 percent in the second decile, and 8 percent below the second decile. Those appointed in the 1790s ranked 70 percent in the top decile, 19 percent in the second decile, and 11 percent below the second decile. In land size, the judiciary officials elected in the 1780s had more land. Half of them ranked in the top decile, 35 percent below, and 15 percent were indeterminable; for those appointed in the 1790s, 37 percent were in the top decile, and 63 percent below. Those judicial officials in wealthy group 1 served primarily during the 1780s by a twenty-two-to-seven ratio. The seven appointed in the 1790s kept the group 1 high economic ranking—five were in the top decile in both wealth and land. Those in group 3 appointed in the mid-1790s, however, were definitely less wealthy: 53 percent ranked in the second decile, but 26 percent ranked below the second decile. Only 32 percent ranked in the top decile in land size. Thus, if any significant trend is observable, it is that western voters, all landowners, elected more wealthy individuals than the state appointed. This apparently was the result of both the changed status of the office of justice of the peace to a local office and away from membership on the county courts, and to some extent to the changing economic patterns of the region rather than by any design of the state executive.

14. For a more complete discussion of the duties and evolution of the office of sheriff in Pennsylvania, see Stevens and Kent, *County Government,* pp. 289–97.

15. Ibid., pp. 96–110, 124.

16. Ibid., pp. 8–10, 306, 184, 231–32, 166–68, 258–63, 360–67.

17. Ibid., pp. 43–44, 80, 408–09, 415–16; Mitchell and Flanders, eds., *Statutes at Large,* vol. 8, ch. 653, p. 185–86; vol. 15, ch. 1754, p. 102; Papers, Court of Quarter Sessions, Fayette County.

18. This representativeness was also evident among those who voted. In Georges Township in March 1795, fifty-six persons voted in the township election. The votes for constable were spread among five candidates as follows: forty-five, twenty-three, nineteen, eleven, and two. The votes for overseers were fifty-five, fifty-three, two; and for supervisors of highways, fifty-five each. Two men were to be elected to each post; the two overseers and two supervisors both served together, but the county court selected just one constable from the two elected. The 56 people who voted may be divided as follows: twenty-three were landowners whose lands ranged in size from 30 to 589 acres, with a median of 100 acres. Twenty-two were landless taxpayers, including at least four tenants and three single

freemen. Another four were not on the assessment but were apparently, based upon their names, the sons of eligible freemen and thus were eligible themselves to vote even though they did not pay taxes. Beyond this, there were seven more names, including two sets of brothers, not on the assessment at all.

Based upon the tax list, 56 voters out of 281 eligible to vote was almost a 20 percent voter turnout, but 12 percent of the voters could not be identified by the tax list. (One perhaps turned up in 1798 as landless tailor.) The tax list in this one case was only 80 to 90 percent effective in disclosing the voting population. Since only 23 of the 56 voters were known to be landed, it is obvious that the majority were landless. Did they then vote for people of less property, particularly in the constable race, where the candidates did not have to be freeholders? The answer is no. The man with the highest vote (45 votes) was a gristmill owner with 100 acres of land and a tax value in the top 10 percent. The second highest vote (23 votes) for constable went to a man with 449 acres and a tax value in the top 15 percent. However, the third man had no land and the fourth man had 30 acres. A majority of the voters were landless, but the candidates of similar economic status lost the race for constable. In the overseers race, the highest vote went to a man with 116 acres, the second to a man with 193 acres, and the final two votes went to the second man's brother who had 405 acres. (It is possible that two voters made a mistake and wrote Jacob when they meant James.) In the supervisors race, a man with 200 acres and a tax value in the top decile and a man who owned a tanyard situated on unspecified acreage were elected. (In 1798, the latter had 106 acres.) One example does not make a rule, but it does seem that popular participation in elections involved people from a broad economic spectrum. It also appears that, even on the township level, voters tended to elect persons of status, rather than persons of their own social rank.

19. James Henretta, "Economic Development and Social Structure in Colonial Boston," *William and Mary Quarterly* 22 (January 1965): 90.

20. Ibid.

21. Family background apparently had little effect in western Pennsylvania. There was some intermarriage, naturally, among leading families, but the region was basically too new for family background and connections to yet dominate the political structure. The Hoge proprietors of Washington and David Redick were related and all were prominent. Lawyer David Bradford (a group 2a officer) had two brothers-in-law who were group 1 leaders. Three of the five sheriffs in Fayette County were closely connected by marriage and

friendship (two were not related but left together for Kentucky). The John Neville family connections in Allegheny County are well-known. These and other occasional family connections were discovered, but the most important fact was the relative lack of family connections among the leadership group.

Chapter 8: Conclusion

1. Much the same kind of argument is made by Aubrey Land on behalf of the great planters of the Chesapeake region. Because of their "bolder vision and broader talents," a few great planters—he finds "entrepreneur" the best term to describe them—reaped great economic reward. "In a nutshell," he concluded, "they provided services for an agrarian society as merchants, moneylenders, and land dealers. And as manufacturers and processers they supplied some consumer goods. Clearly, they saw in the community needs an economic opportunity, and their estates show the consequences of their perception." "Economic Behavior in a Planting Society: The Eighteenth Century Chesapeake," *Journal of Southern History* 32 (1966): 475–76, 485.

2. Such an analytical typology is developed by Allan Kulikoff in his summary article, "The Transition to Capitalism in Rural America," *William and Mary Quarterly* 46 (1989): 122–26. The concept of a pre-capitalistic *mentalité* was first forcefully argued by James Henretta, "Families and Farms: *Mentalité* in Pre-Industrial America," *William and Mary Quarterly* 35 (1978): 3–32.

3. Ray Allen Billington, the leading disciple of Frederick Jackson Turner and a defender of the frontier thesis, has confirmed this mythology. "Of the many myths associated with the frontier," he stated, "none has been more persistent than the belief that class divisions vanished there." *America's Frontier Heritage* (New York, 1966), p. 97.

Index

Absentee landlords: an early indication of tenancy, 62; extent of, 63, 69–71; and tenancy relationships, 64

Absentee ownership: extent of, 69–71; defined, 69; proportional decline but increased acreage, 71; summary description of, 74; speculative profits from, 75–77; appreciated value of improved holdings, 77; failed investments from, 77–78; agents for, 78–79, 80; in towns, 94; economic status of owners, 115–16; tracts of have inmates in East Bethlehem, 128; mentioned, xviii, 58, 107

Achesan, David, 103

Achesan, John, 94

Acklin, Samuel, 94

Acreage requirements, 120–21. *See also* Cleared acreage; Subsistence requirements

Addison, Judge Alexander: charge to grand jury of (1794), x–xi; progress in WP was "amazingly rapid," xi, 172; as outlot owner, 77; brief biographical sketch of, 141–42; mentioned, 16, 94, 102, 144, 146, 157–58, 159, 160

Allegheny County: population on tax lists, xvii; early population, xvii–xviii; settlement into, 5; ethnic composition of, 6–7, 214; early settlement location, 7; ratio of population to taxables in, 14–

15; established (1788), 29; delinquent taxes in, 79–80; Pittsburgh selected as county seat of, 95; mentioned, xv, xvi, 163

Allegheny Front, 18

Allegheny Plateau, 18–19

Allegheny River, 80

The American Museum or Universal Magazine, 90

Amwell township, 146

Anderson, John, 137, 138

Appalachian Mountains, 5

Appraisers, 167–69

Armstrong township, 26–28

Artisan class: drawn to towns, 89–93; in towns, 102–04, 105, 116; size and composition of, 131–34; economic status of, 134–38; wage rates high for, 134–35; land ownership by, 136; economic mobility of, 136–38; part of emerging market economy, 139; no primary leaders from, 147; two justices from, 159; visibility of, 172; size of, 174; mentioned, 37, 61, 62, 65, 67, 89, 94, 100

Asbury, Bishop Francis, 99

Assemblyman, 108, 111, 152, 163–64

Atchesan, Matthew, 136

Augusta County, Virginia, 82

Ayers, Rev. Robert, 98

Badollet, John, 51

Baird, Dr. Absolom, 77, 113

261